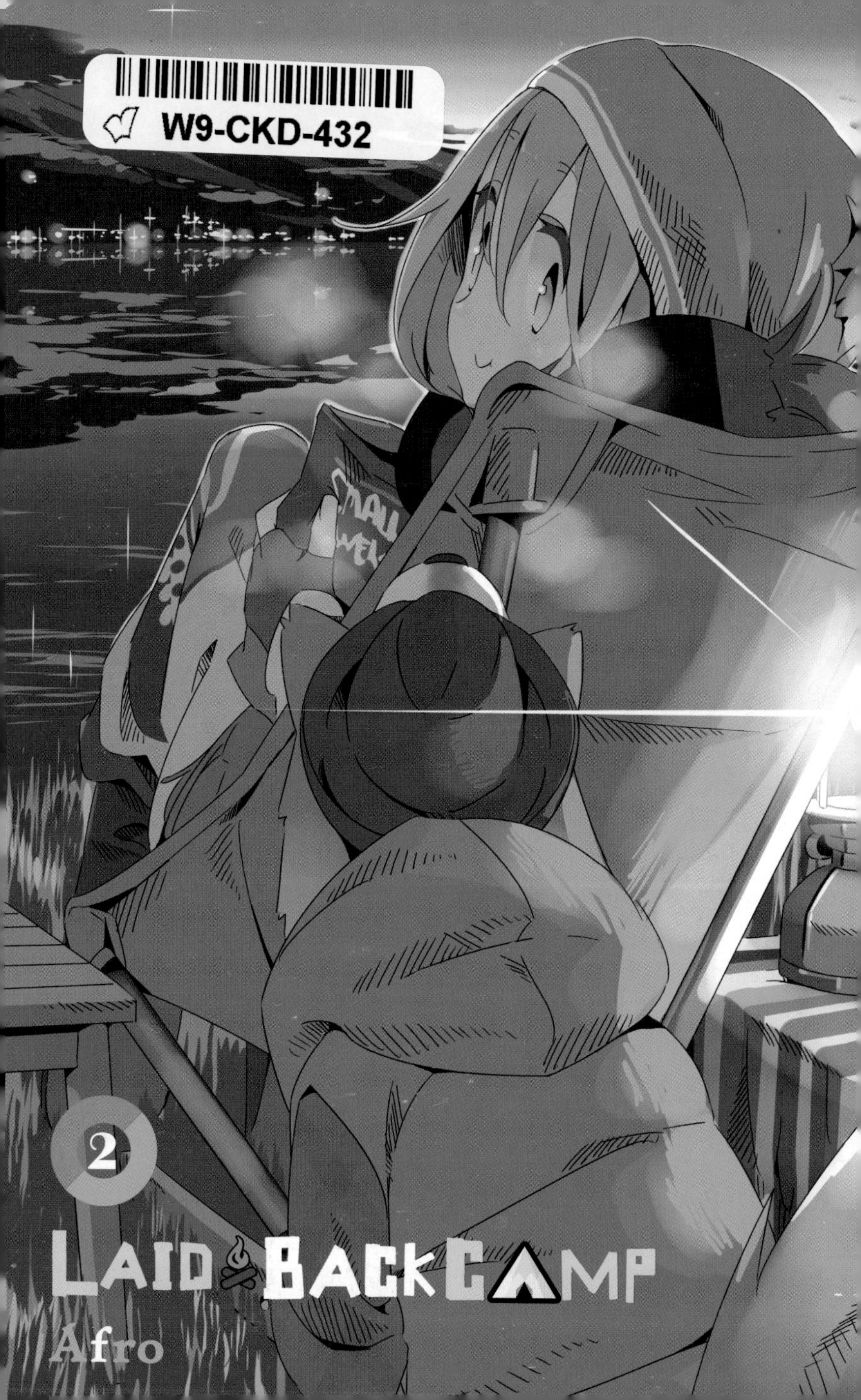
2
LAID BACK CAMP
Afro

2

LAID-BACK CAMP

contents

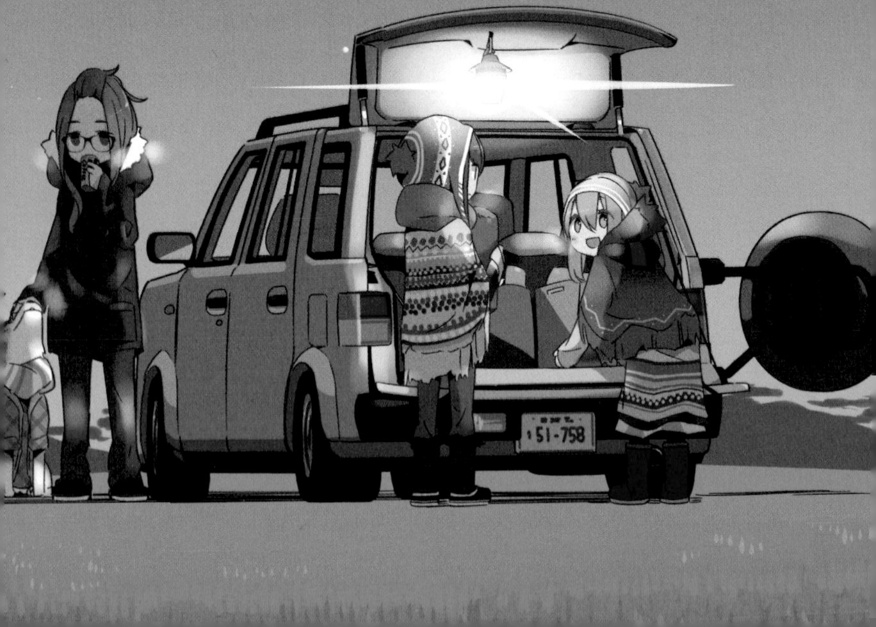

51-758

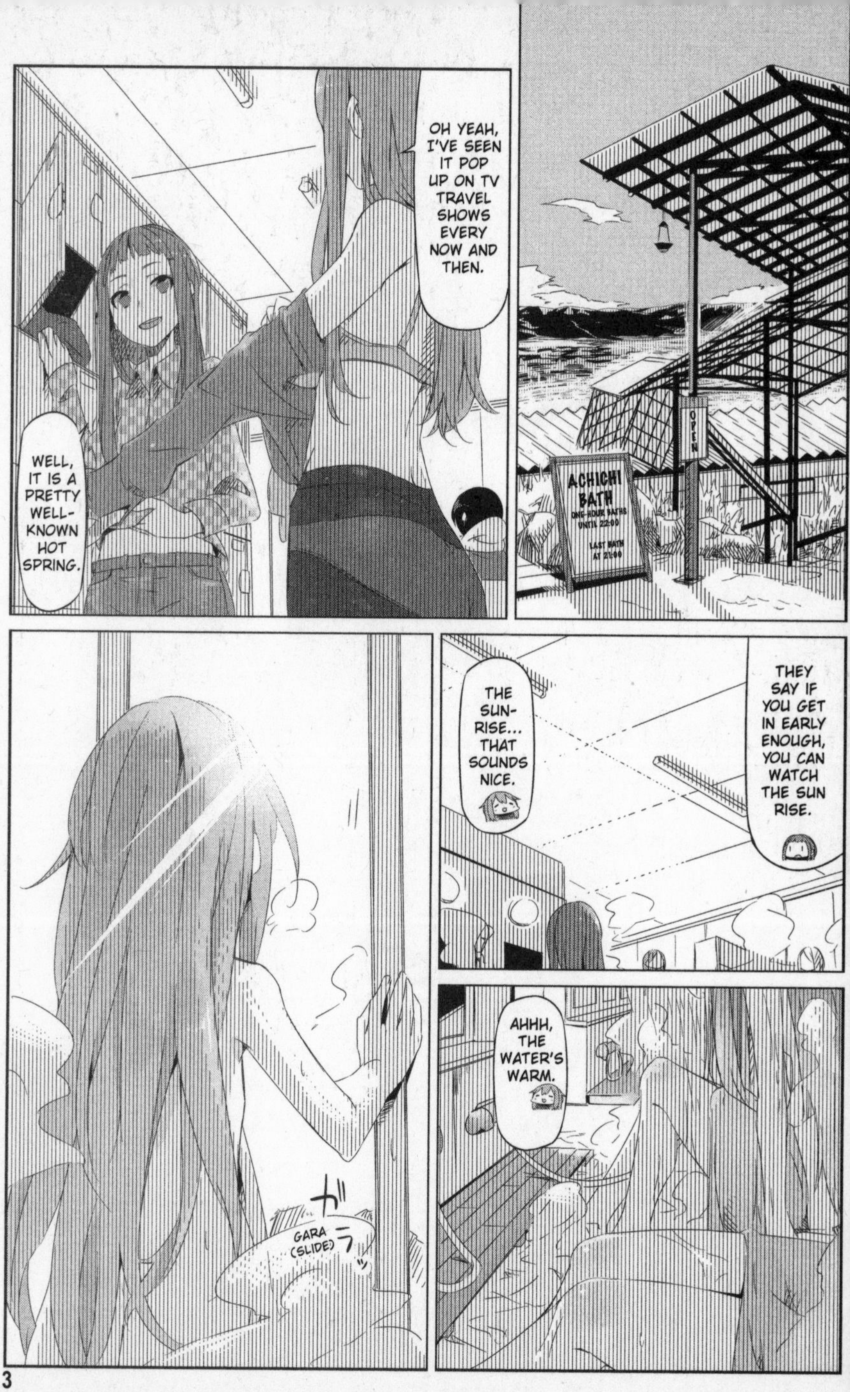
OPEN
ACHICHI BATH
ONE-HOUR BATHS UNTIL 22:00
LAST BATH AT 21:00
OH YEAH, I'VE SEEN IT POP UP ON TV TRAVEL SHOWS EVERY NOW AND THEN.
WELL, IT IS A PRETTY WELL-KNOWN HOT SPRING.
THEY SAY IF YOU GET IN EARLY ENOUGH, YOU CAN WATCH THE SUN RISE.
THE SUN-RISE... THAT SOUNDS NICE.
AHHH, THE WATER'S WARM.
ガラッ
GARA (SLIDE)

CHAPTER 7 HOT SPRINGS, 'BOCCHI, AND MOUNTAIN COOKING

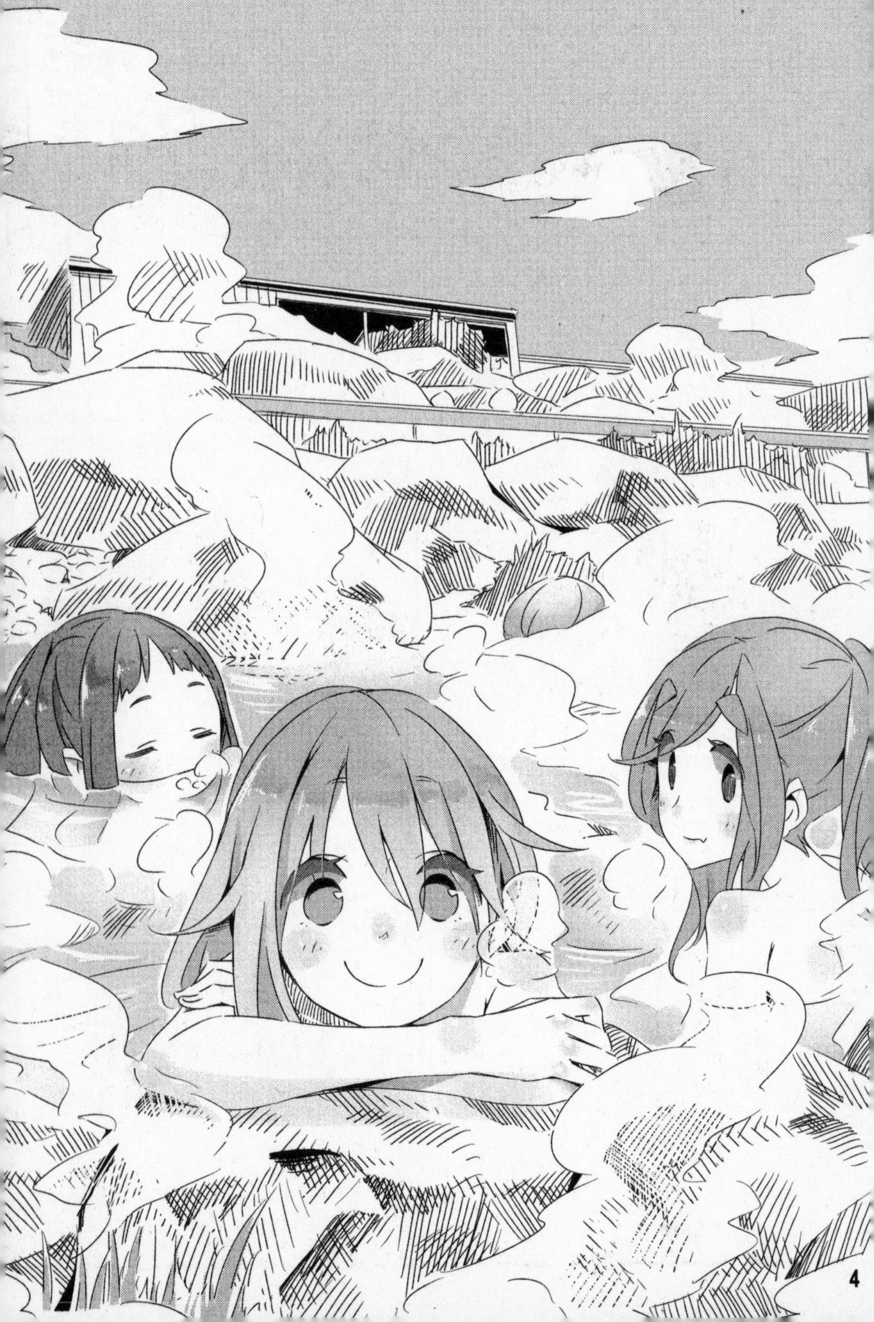

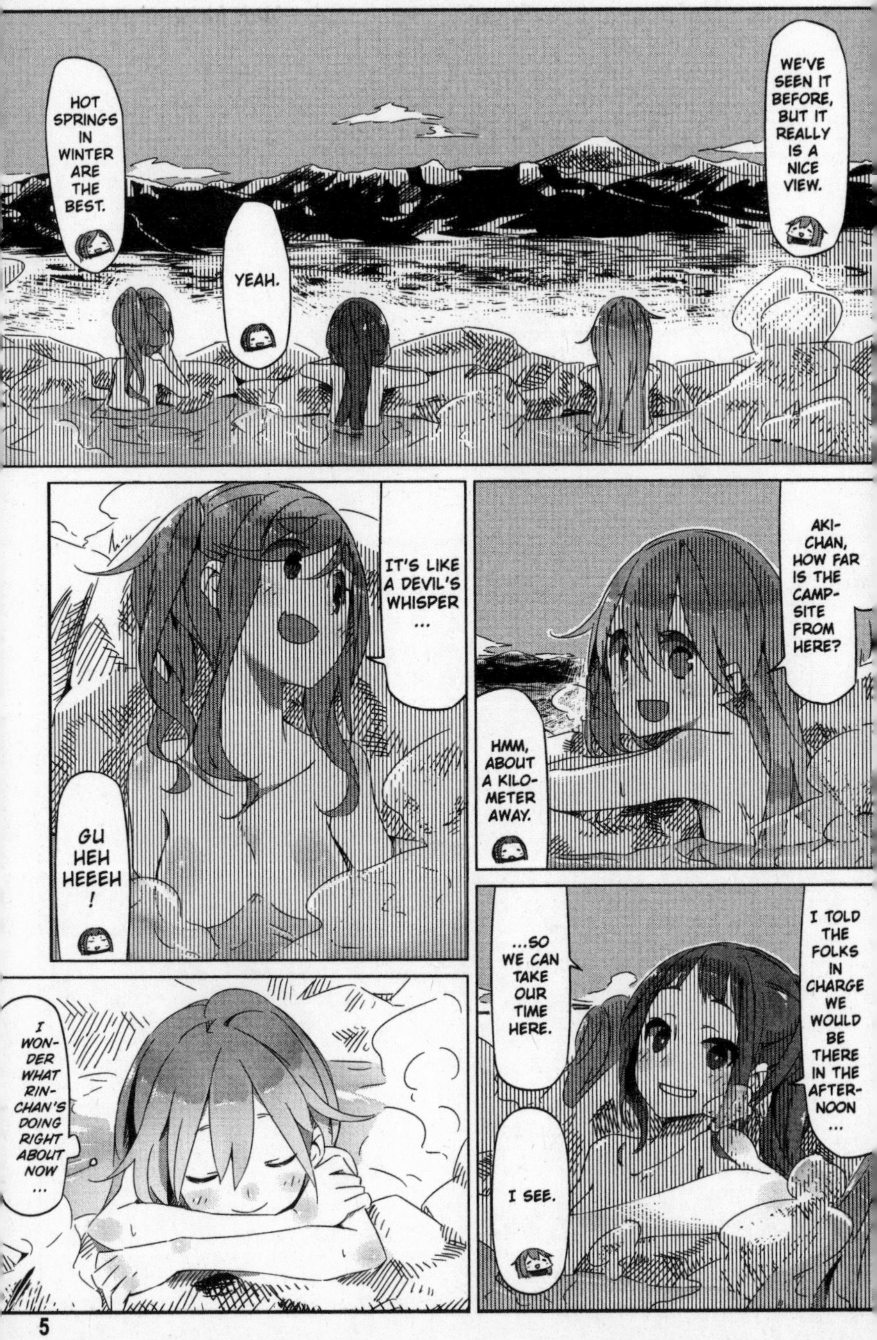

WE'VE SEEN IT BEFORE, BUT IT REALLY IS A NICE VIEW.
YEAH.
HOT SPRINGS IN WINTER ARE THE BEST.
AKI-CHAN, HOW FAR IS THE CAMPSITE FROM HERE?
HMM, ABOUT A KILOMETER AWAY.
IT'S LIKE A DEVIL'S WHISPER...
GU HEH HEEEH!
I TOLD THE FOLKS IN CHARGE WE WOULD BE THERE IN THE AFTERNOON...
...SO WE CAN TAKE OUR TIME HERE.
I SEE.
I WONDER WHAT RIN-CHAN'S DOING RIGHT ABOUT NOW...

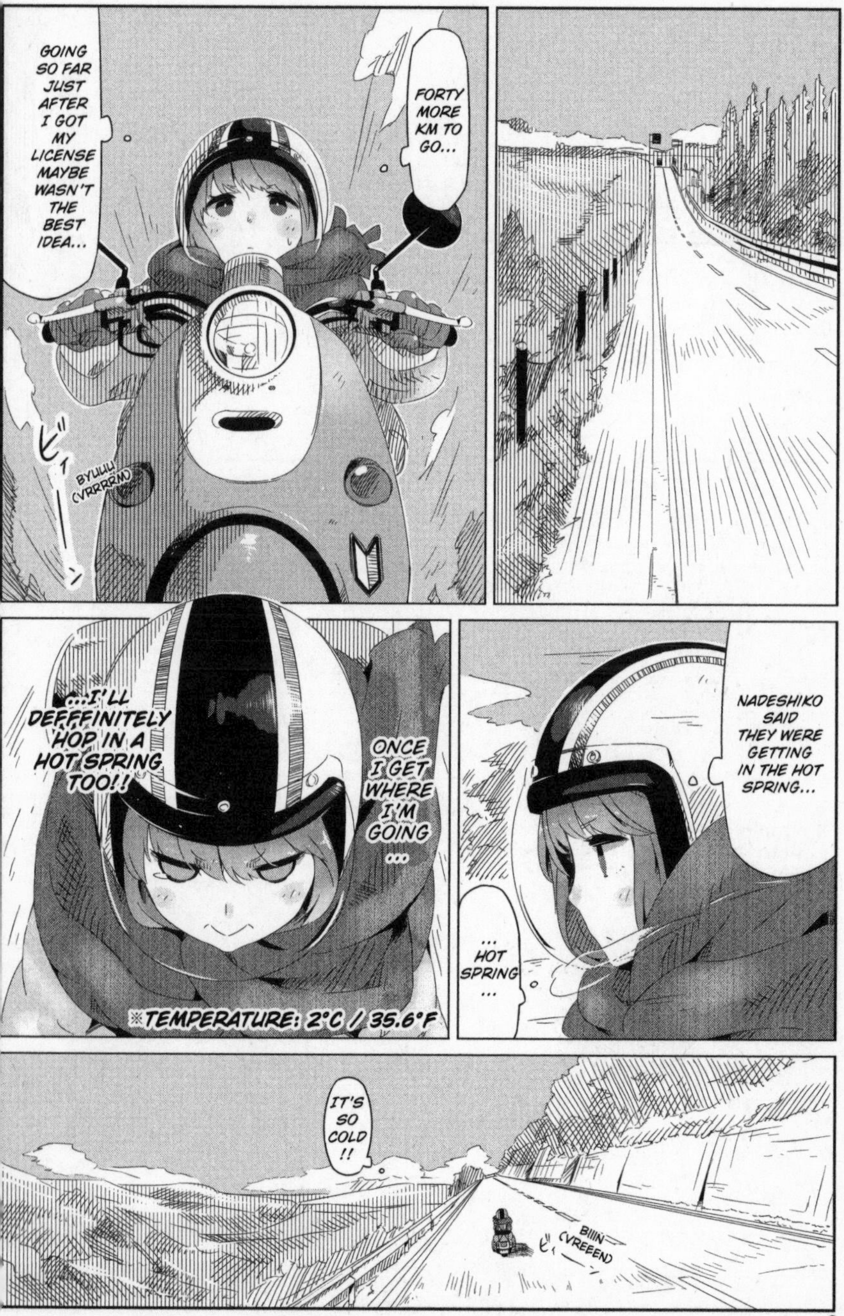
FORTY MORE KM TO GO...
GOING SO FAR JUST AFTER I GOT MY LICENSE MAYBE WASN'T THE BEST IDEA...
ビィー
BYUUU (VRRRRM)
NADESHIKO SAID THEY WERE GETTING IN THE HOT SPRING...
... HOT SPRING ...
ONCE I GET WHERE I'M GOING ...
...I'LL DEFFFINITELY HOP IN A HOT SPRING TOO!!
※TEMPERATURE: 2°C / 35.6°F
IT'S SO COLD !!
ビィー
BIIIN (VREEEN)

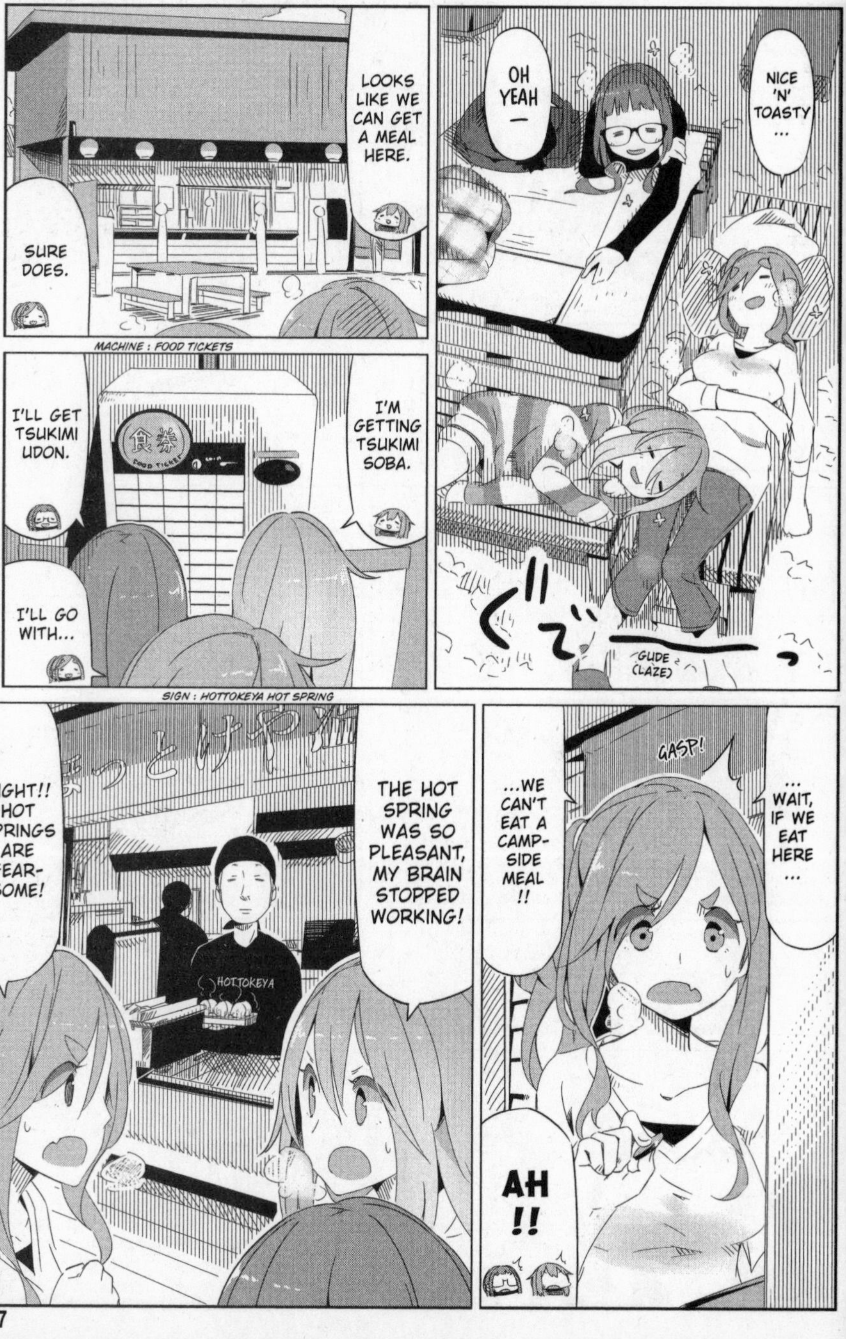
NICE 'N' TOASTY ...
OH YEAH —
GUDE (LAZE)
LOOKS LIKE WE CAN GET A MEAL HERE.
SURE DOES.
MACHINE : FOOD TICKETS
I'M GETTING TSUKIMI SOBA.
I'LL GET TSUKIMI UDON.
I'LL GO WITH...
GASP!
... WAIT, IF WE EAT HERE ...
...WE CAN'T EAT A CAMP-SIDE MEAL !!
AH !!
SIGN : HOTTOKEYA HOT SPRING
THE HOT SPRING WAS SO PLEASANT, MY BRAIN STOPPED WORKING!
HOTTOKEYA
RIGHT!! HOT SPRINGS ARE FEAR-SOME!

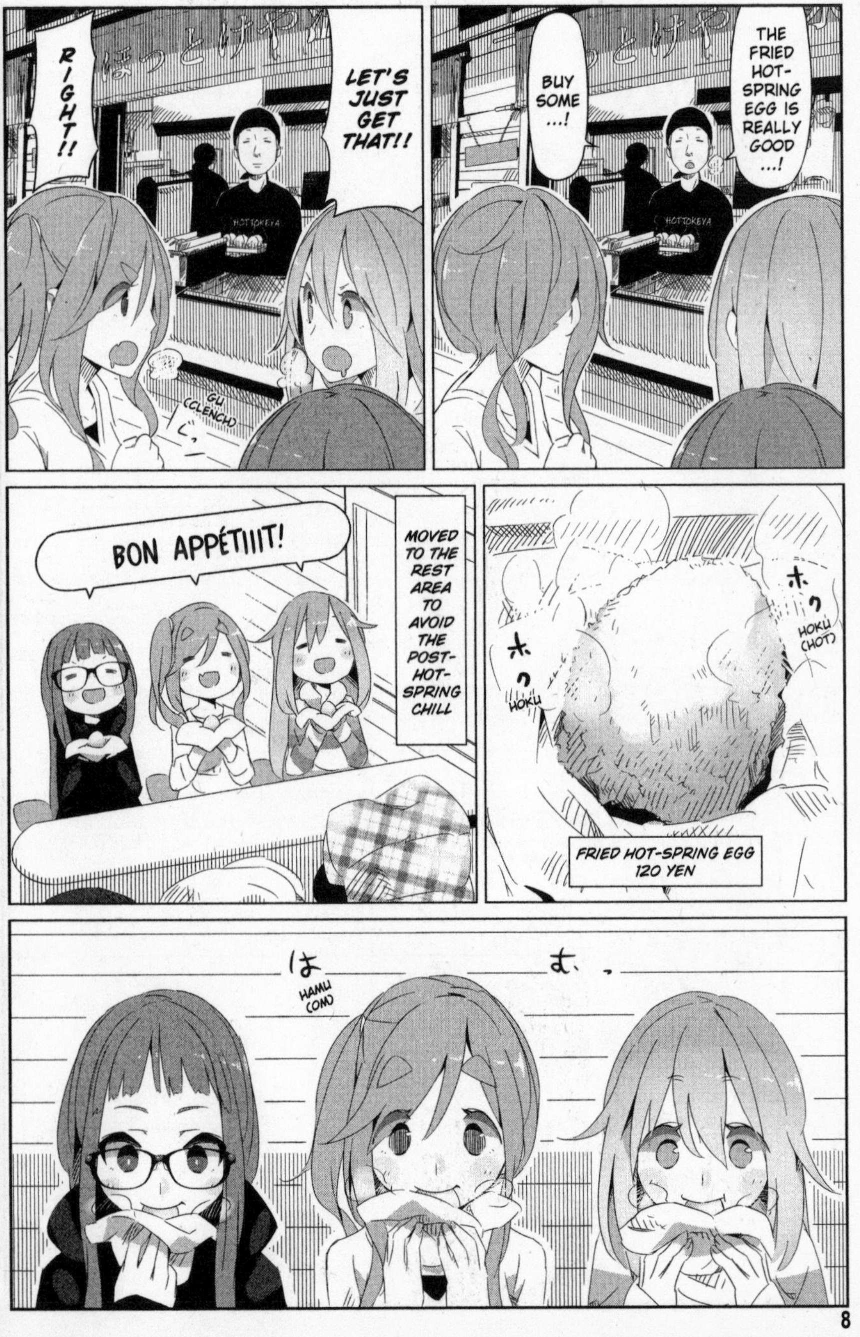
THE FRIED HOT-SPRING EGG IS REALLY GOOD ...!
BUY SOME ...!
LET'S JUST GET THAT!!
RIGHT!!
ぐっ
GU (CLENCH)
ホク
HOKU (HOT)
ホク
HOKU
FRIED HOT-SPRING EGG 120 YEN
MOVED TO THE REST AREA TO AVOID THE POST-HOT-SPRING CHILL
BON APPÉTIIIT!
はむっ
HAMU (OM)

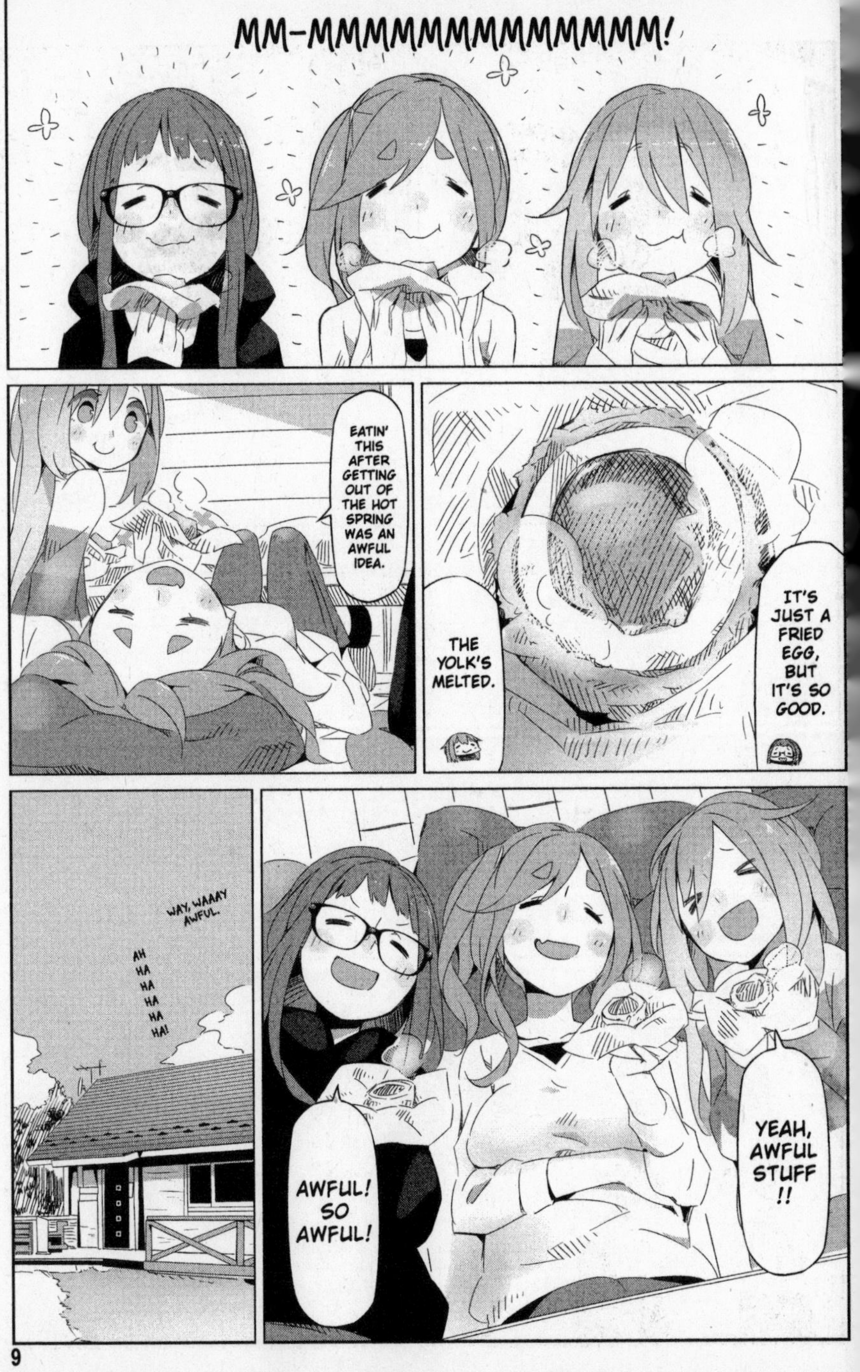
MM-MMMMMMMMMMMMMM!
IT'S JUST A FRIED EGG, BUT IT'S SO GOOD.
THE YOLK'S MELTED.
EATIN' THIS AFTER GETTING OUT OF THE HOT SPRING WAS AN AWFUL IDEA.
YEAH, AWFUL STUFF!!
AWFUL! SO AWFUL!
WAY, WAAAY AWFUL.
AH HA HA HA HA HA!

SIGN: YATSUGATAKE-CHUUSHIN KOUGEN QUASI-NATIONAL PARK, TAKABOCCHI PLATEAU

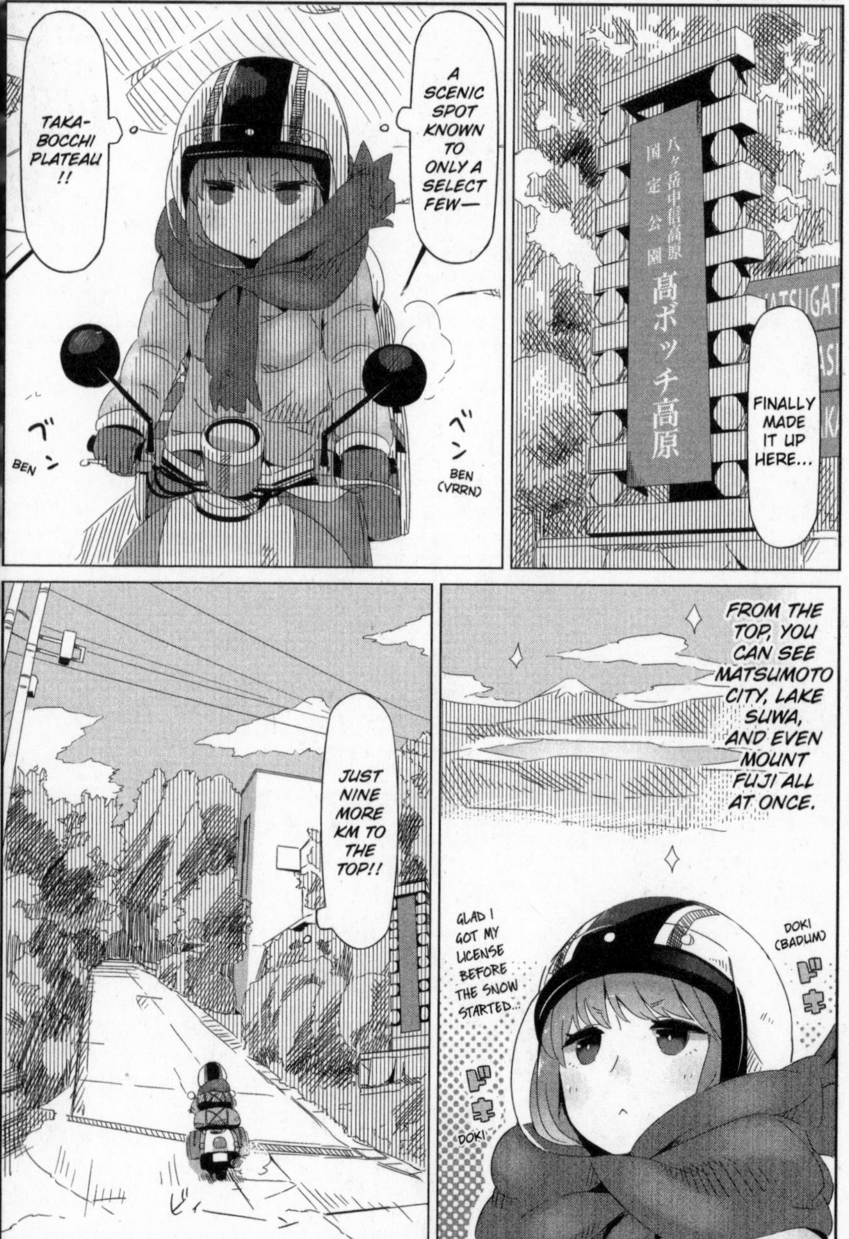
八ヶ岳中信高原
国定公園
高ボッチ高原
FINALLY MADE IT UP HERE...
A SCENIC SPOT KNOWN TO ONLY A SELECT FEW—
TAKA-BOCCHI PLATEAU!!
ベン BEN (VRRN)
ベン BEN
FROM THE TOP, YOU CAN SEE MATSUMOTO CITY, LAKE SUWA, AND EVEN MOUNT FUJI ALL AT ONCE.
ド キ DOKI (BADUM)
GLAD I GOT MY LICENSE BEFORE THE SNOW STARTED...
ド キ DOKI
JUST NINE MORE KM TO THE TOP!!
ビィーン

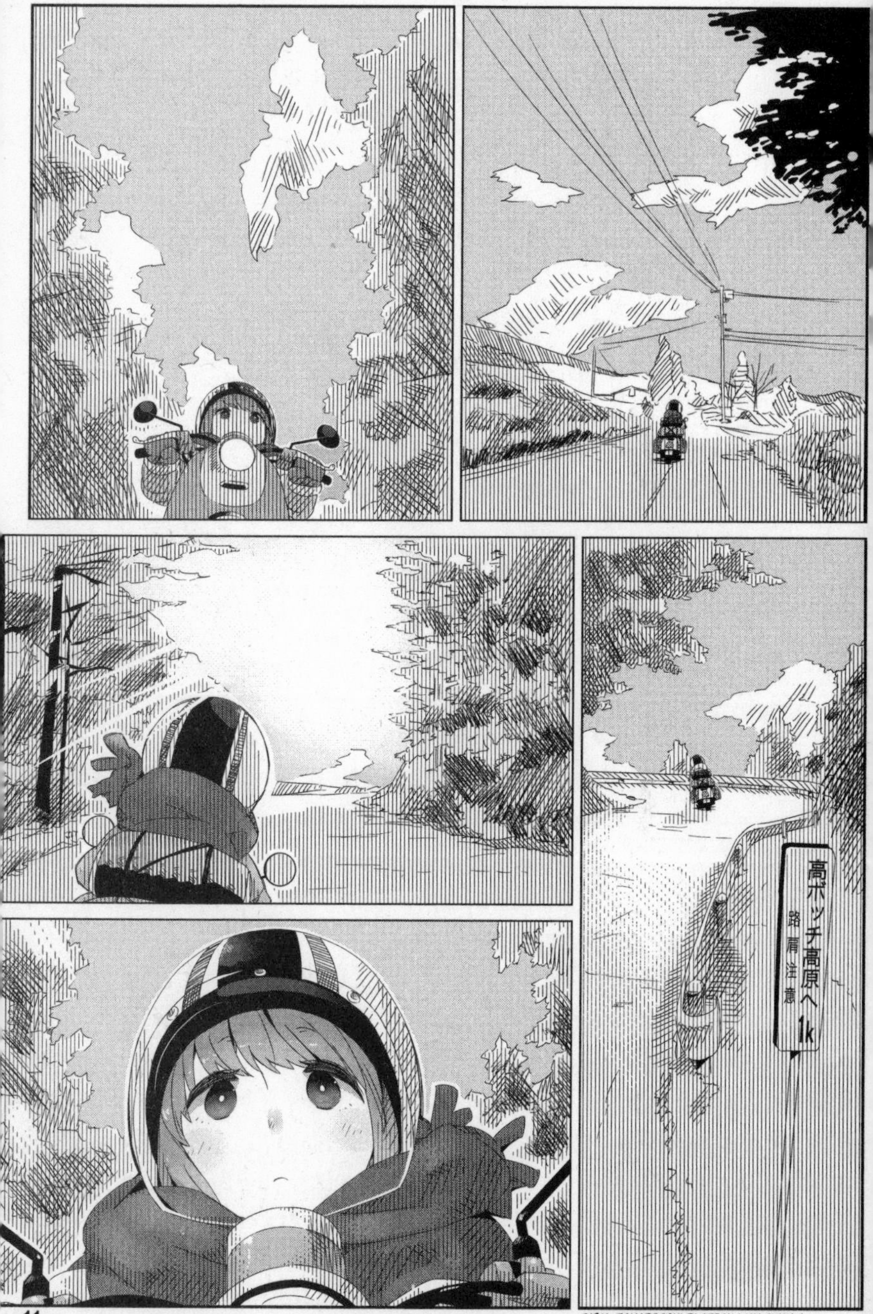
高ボッチ高原へ
1k
路肩注意

SIGN: TAKABOCCHI PLATEAU 1 KM AWAY / MIND THE SHOULDER

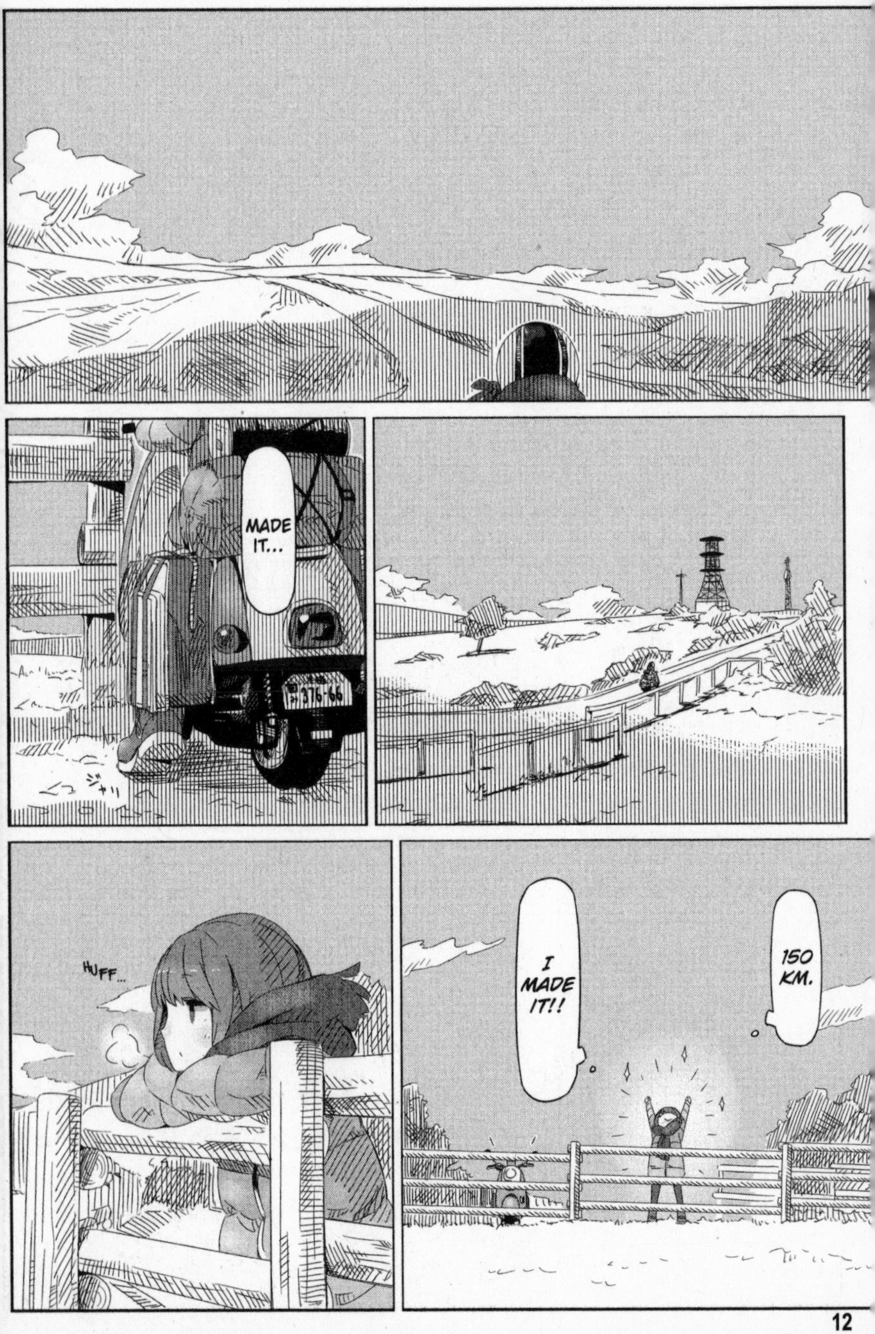
MADE IT...
150 KM.
I MADE IT!!
HUFF...

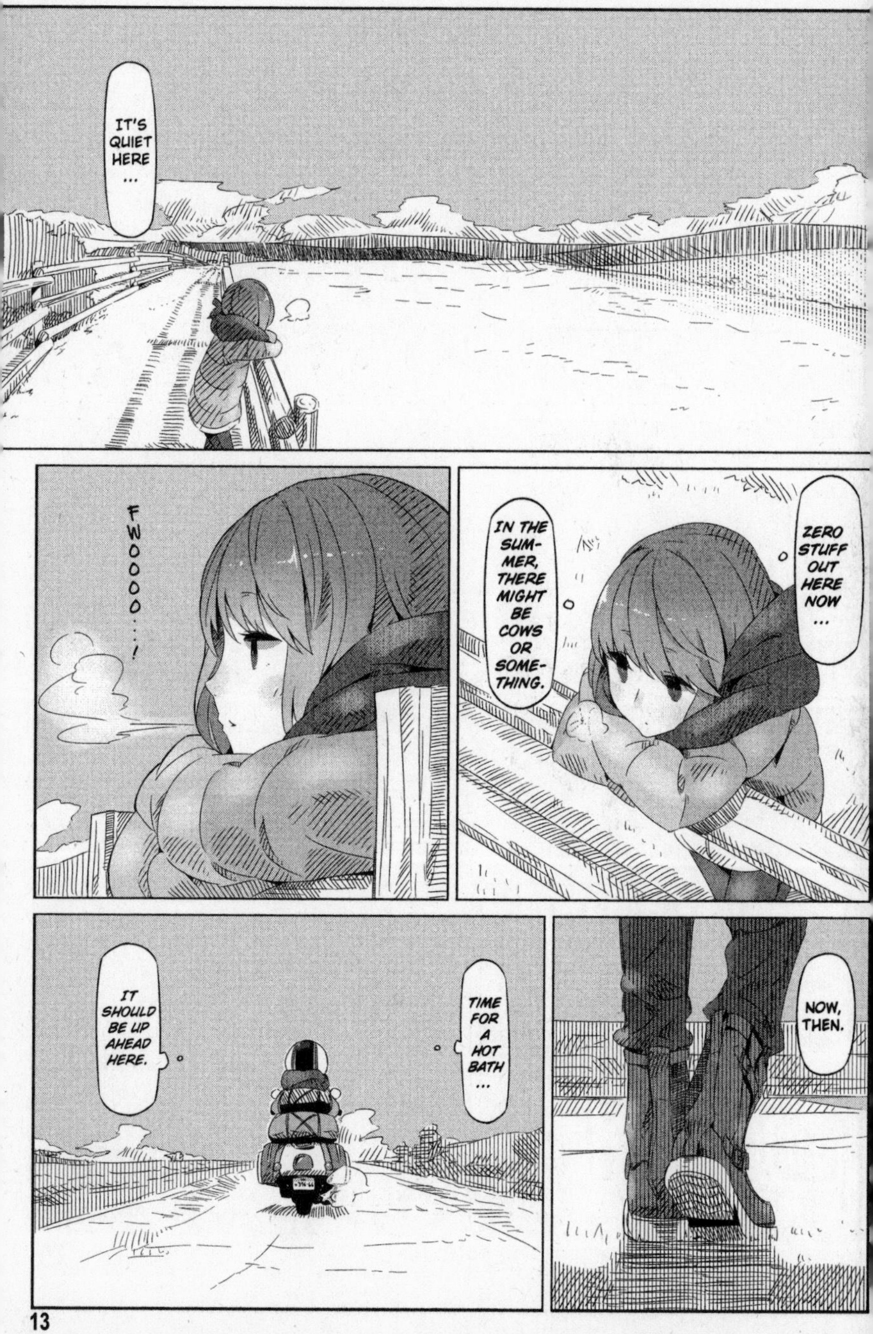
IT'S QUIET HERE ...
ZERO STUFF OUT HERE NOW ...
IN THE SUMMER, THERE MIGHT BE COWS OR SOMETHING.
FWOOOO...!
NOW, THEN.
TIME FOR A HOT BATH ...
IT SHOULD BE UP AHEAD HERE.

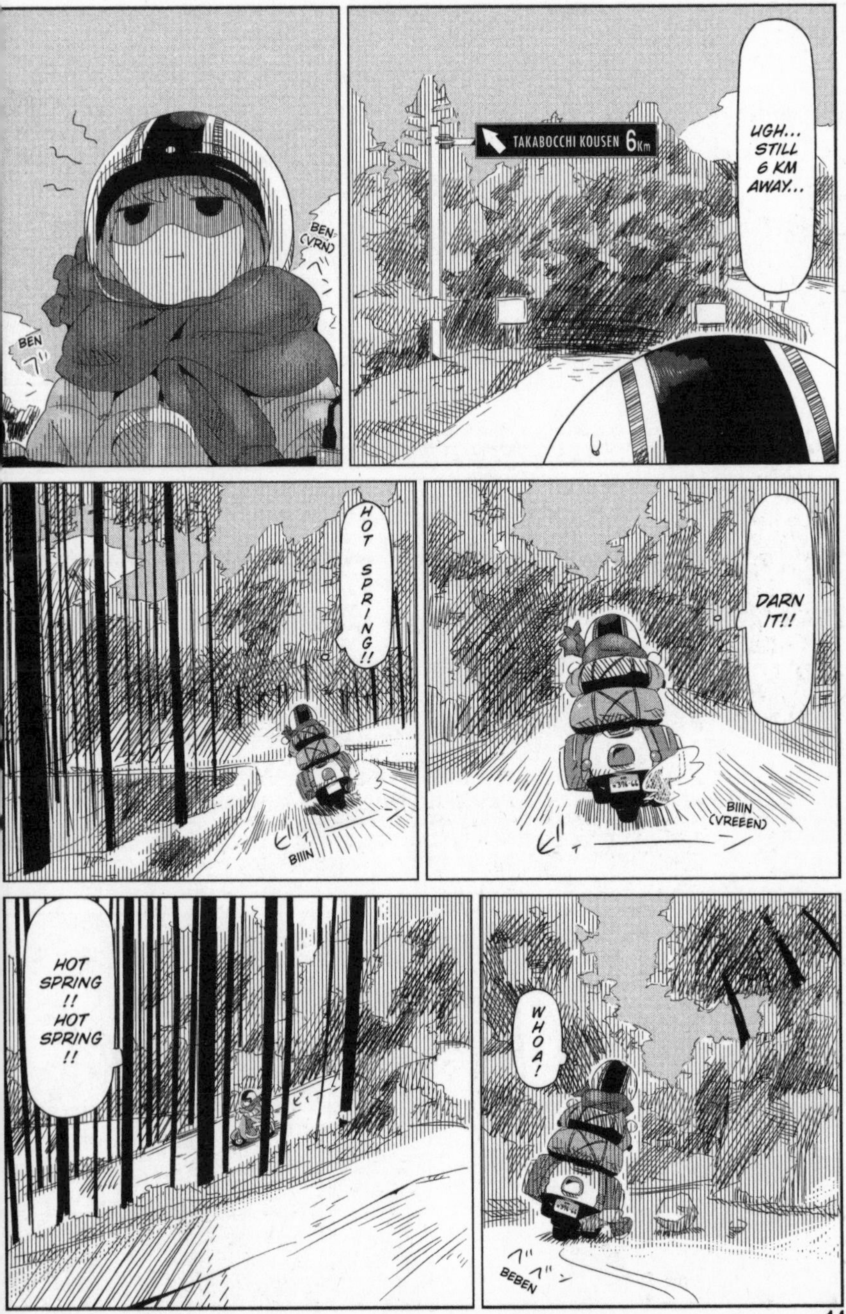
TAKABOCCHI KOUSEN 6Km
UGH... STILL 6 KM AWAY...
BEN (VRN)
BEN
DARN IT!!
BIIIN (VREEEN)
HOT SPRING!!
BIIIN
WHOA!
BEBEN
HOT SPRING!! HOT SPRING!!

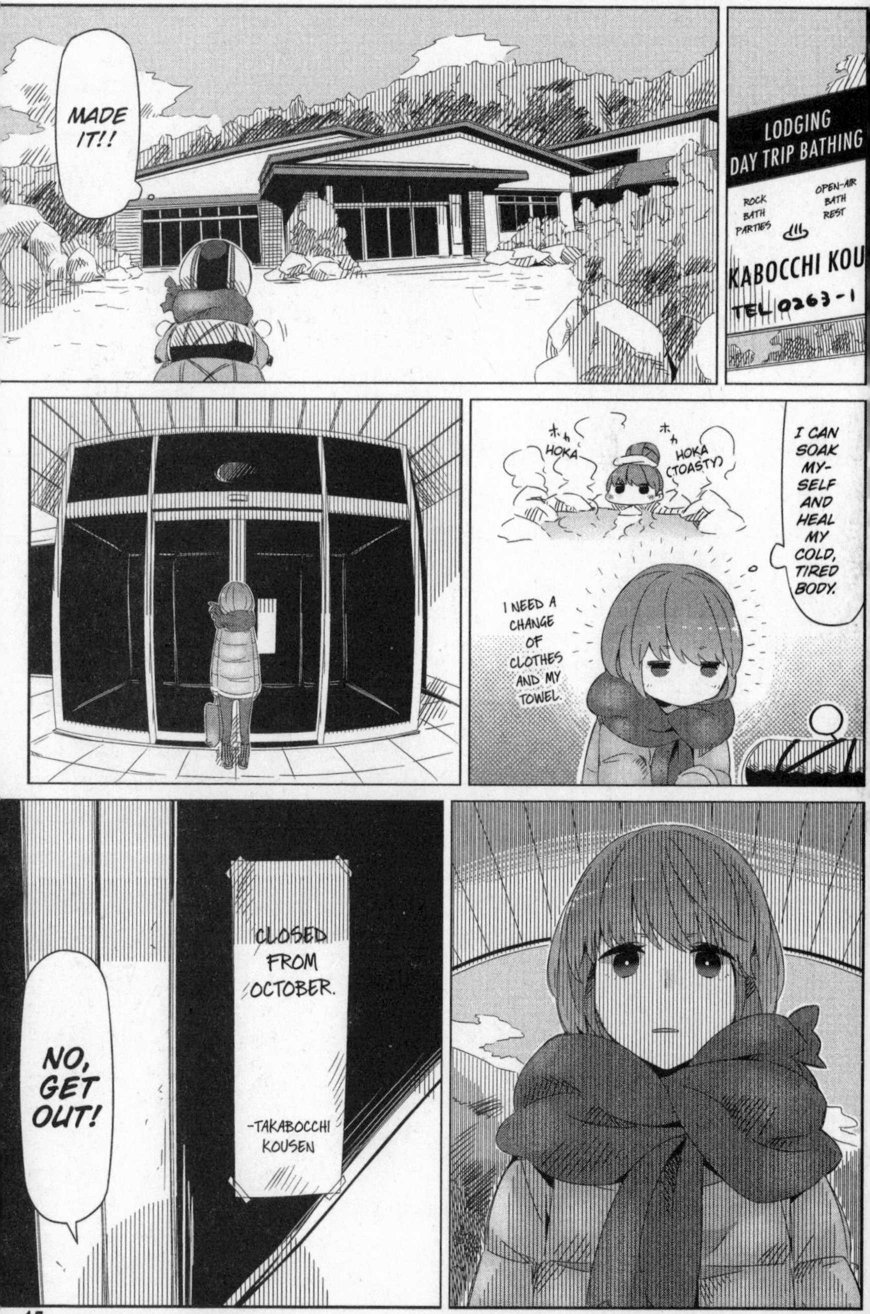
LODGING
DAY TRIP BATHING
OPEN-AIR BATH REST
ROCK BATH PARTIES
KABOCCHI KOU
TEL 0263-1
MADE IT!!
I CAN SOAK MYSELF AND HEAL MY COLD, TIRED BODY.
ホカ HOKA (TOASTY)
ホカ HOKA
I NEED A CHANGE OF CLOTHES AND MY TOWEL.
CLOSED FROM OCTOBER.
-TAKABOCCHI KOUSEN
NO, GET OUT!

LEFT: ALPS MOUNTAIN RANGE / PANORAMIC / OBSERVATION DECK / 1,643 METERS ABOVE SEA LEVEL

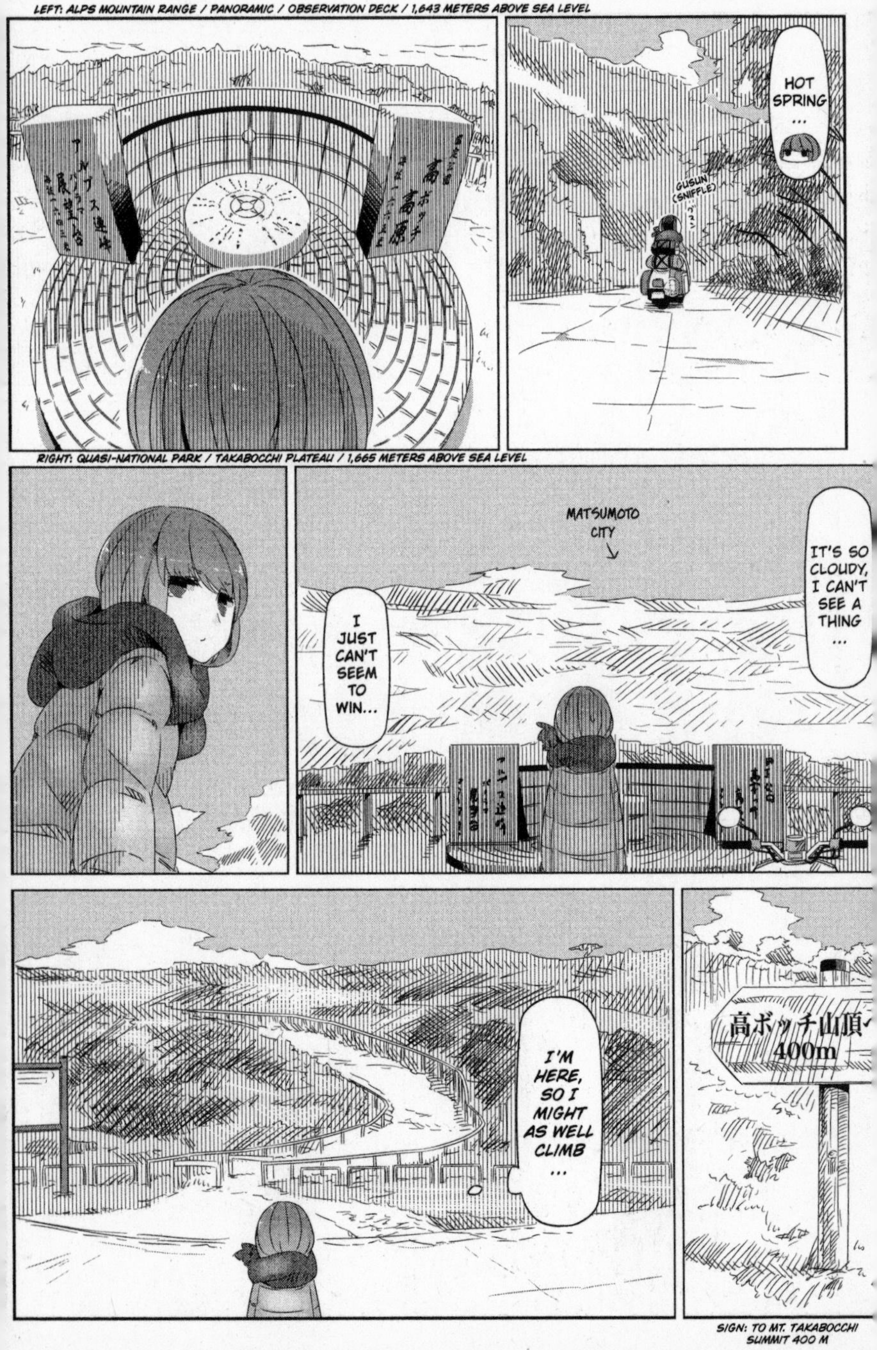
HOT SPRING...
GUSUN (SNIFFLE)
RIGHT: QUASI-NATIONAL PARK / TAKABOCCHI PLATEAU / 1,665 METERS ABOVE SEA LEVEL
IT'S SO CLOUDY, I CAN'T SEE A THING...
MATSUMOTO CITY
I JUST CAN'T SEEM TO WIN...
高ボッチ山頂
400m
I'M HERE, SO I MIGHT AS WELL CLIMB...

SIGN: TO MT. TAKABOCCHI SUMMIT 400 M

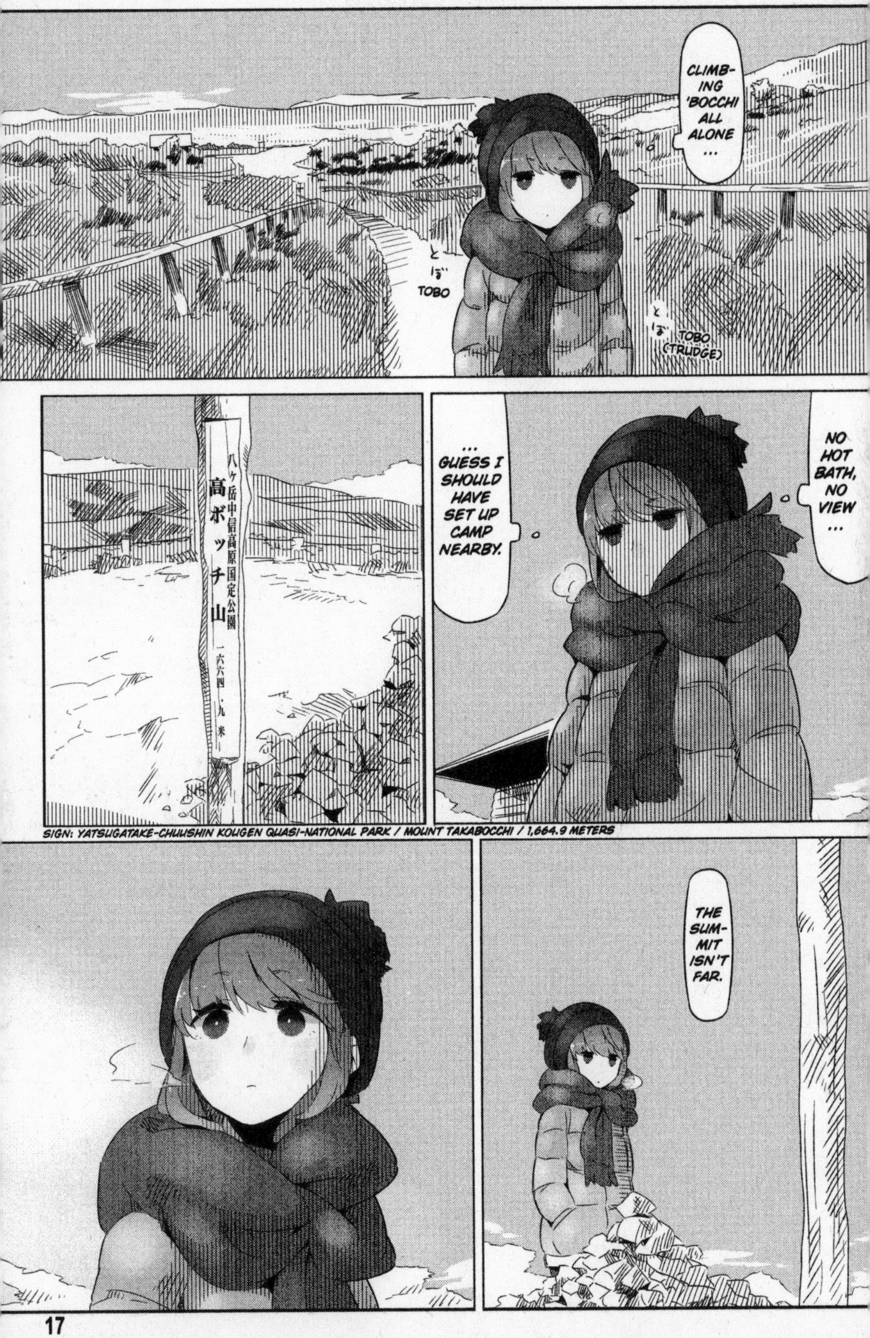
CLIMBING 'BOCCHI ALL ALONE...
とぼ TOBO
とぼ TOBO (TRUDGE)
NO HOT BATH, NO VIEW...
...GUESS I SHOULD HAVE SET UP CAMP NEARBY.
八ヶ岳中信高原国定公園
高ボッチ山
一六六四・九米
SIGN: YATSUGATAKE-CHUUSHIN KOUGEN QUASI-NATIONAL PARK / MOUNT TAKABOCCHI / 1,664.9 METERS
THE SUMMIT ISN'T FAR.

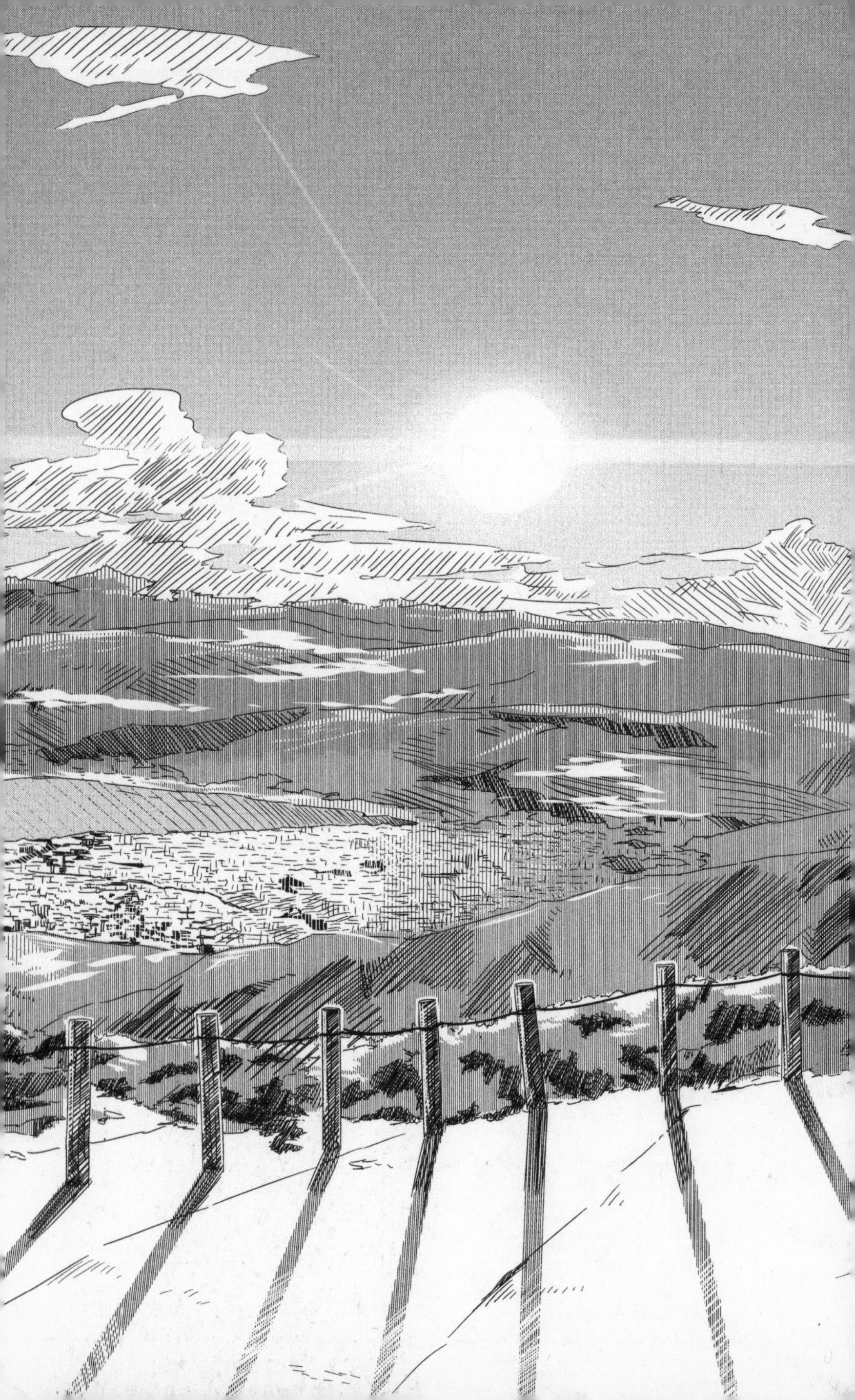

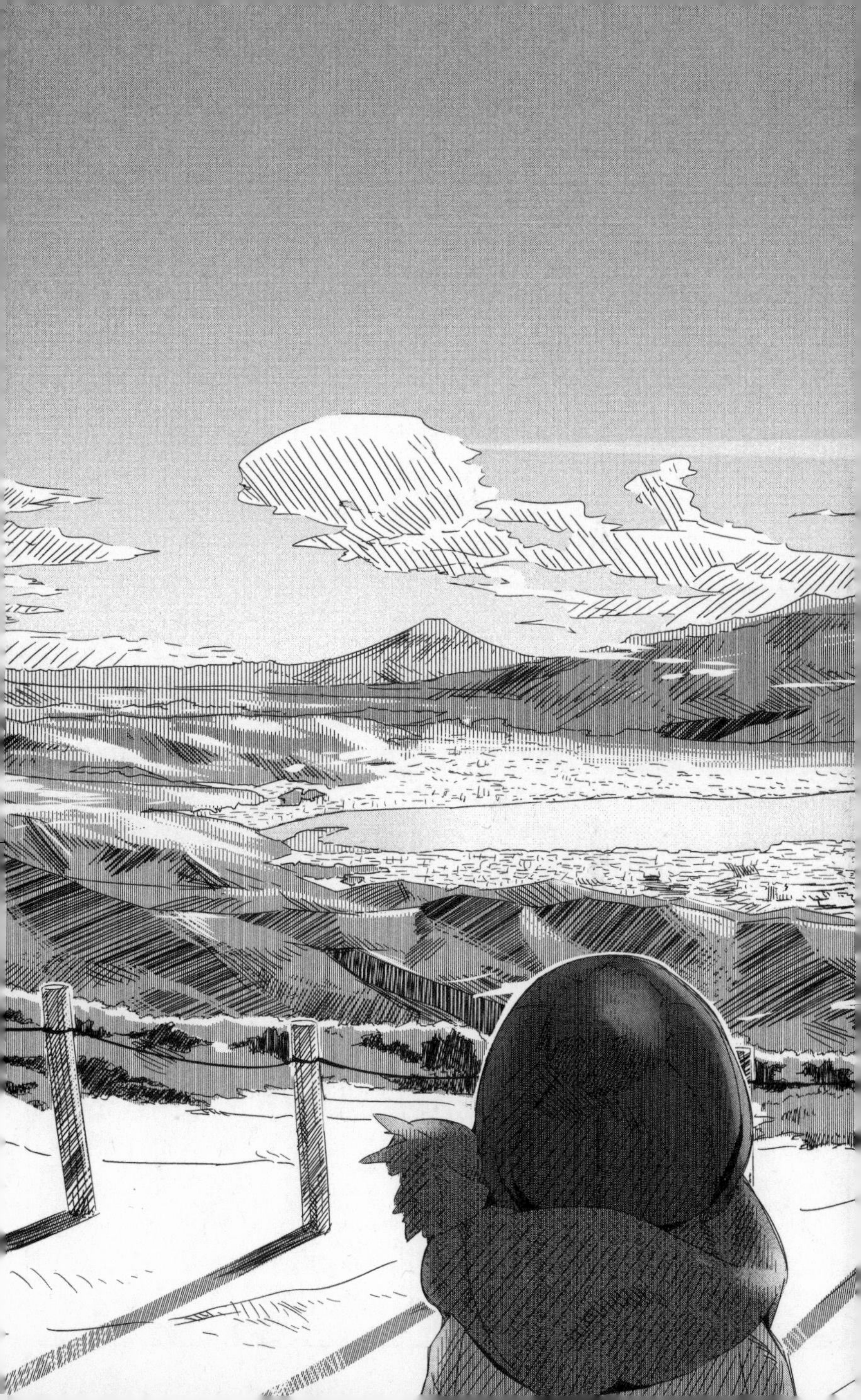

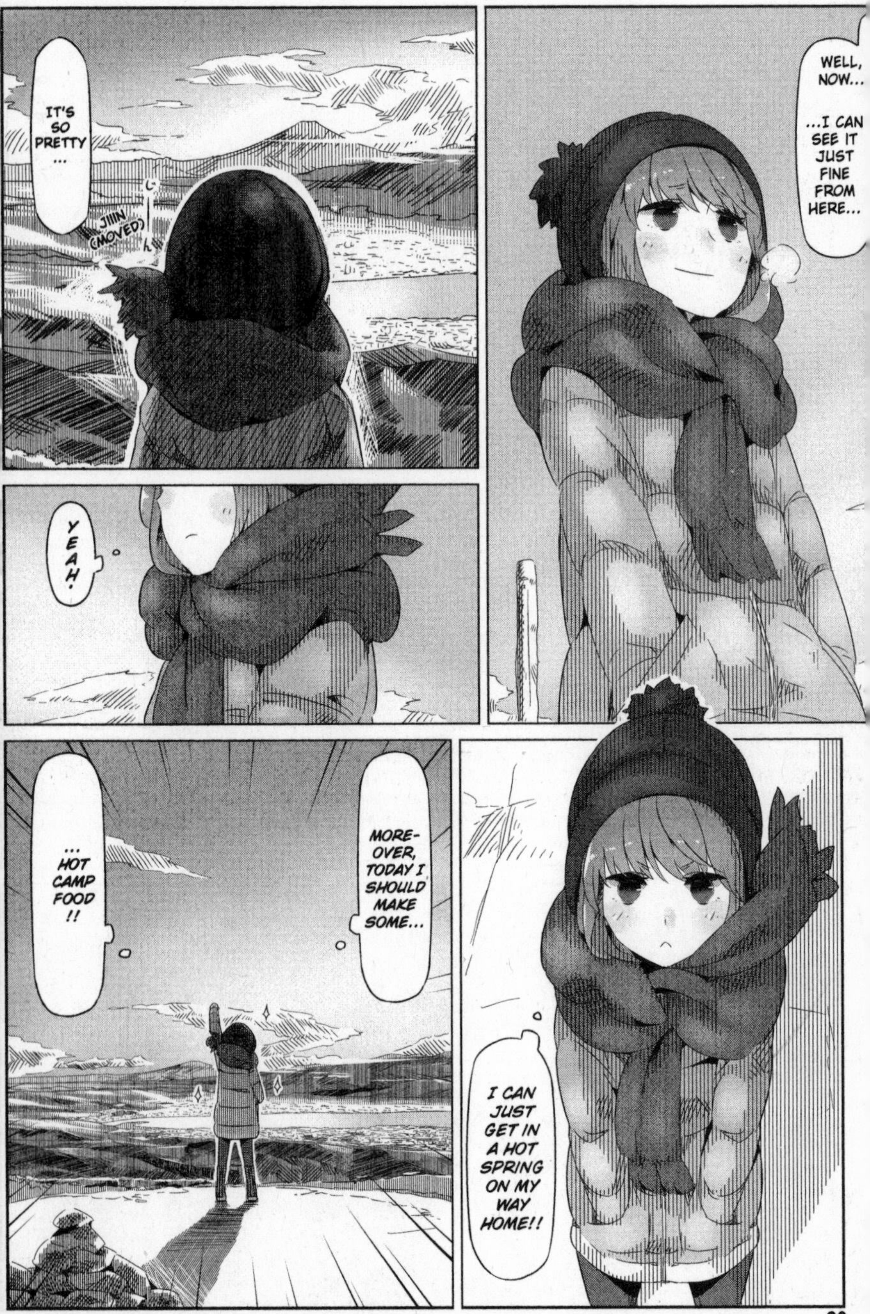
WELL, NOW...
...I CAN SEE IT JUST FINE FROM HERE...
IT'S SO PRETTY...
JIIN (MOVED)
YEAH!
I CAN JUST GET IN A HOT SPRING ON MY WAY HOME!!
MORE-OVER, TODAY I SHOULD MAKE SOME...
...HOT CAMP FOOD!!

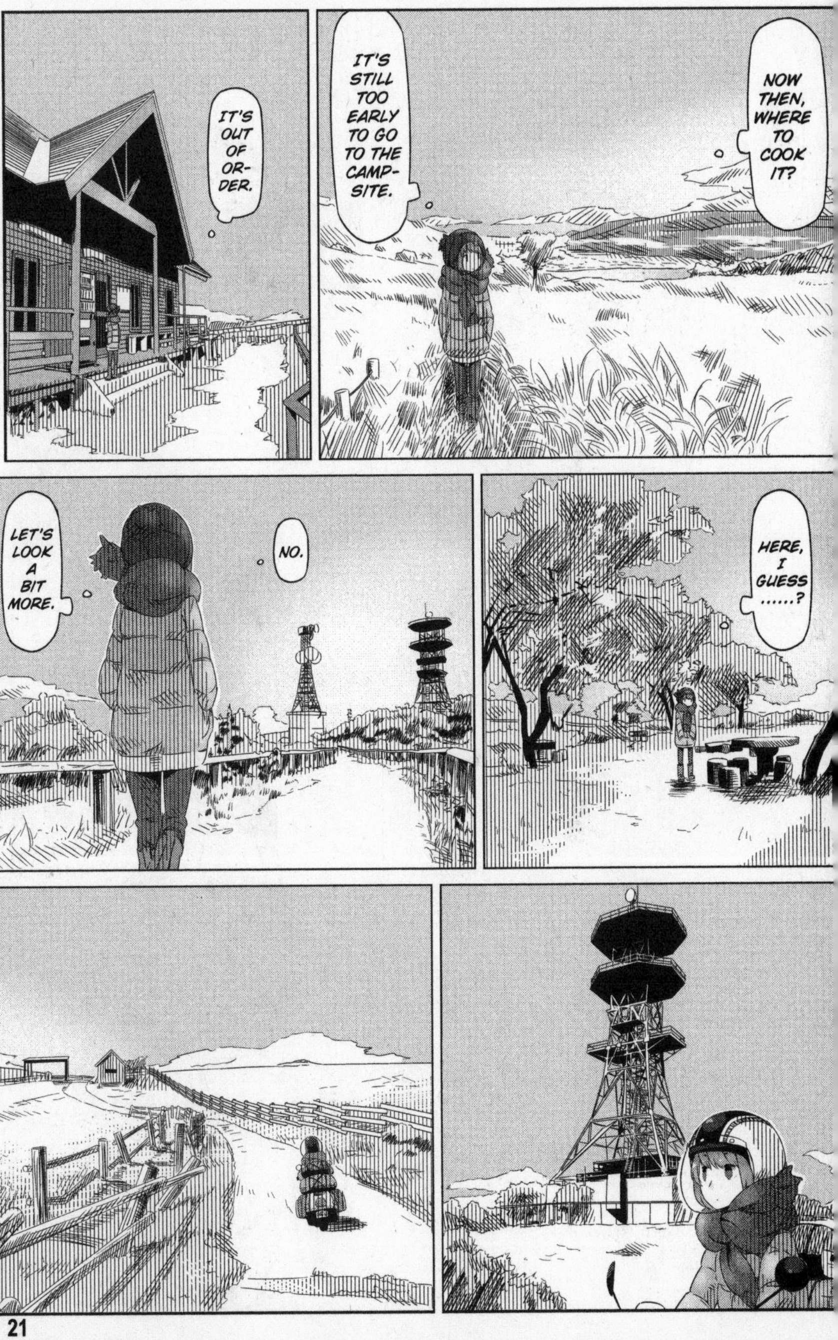
NOW THEN, WHERE TO COOK IT?
IT'S STILL TOO EARLY TO GO TO THE CAMP-SITE.
IT'S OUT OF OR-DER.
HERE, I GUESS ......?
NO.
LET'S LOOK A BIT MORE.

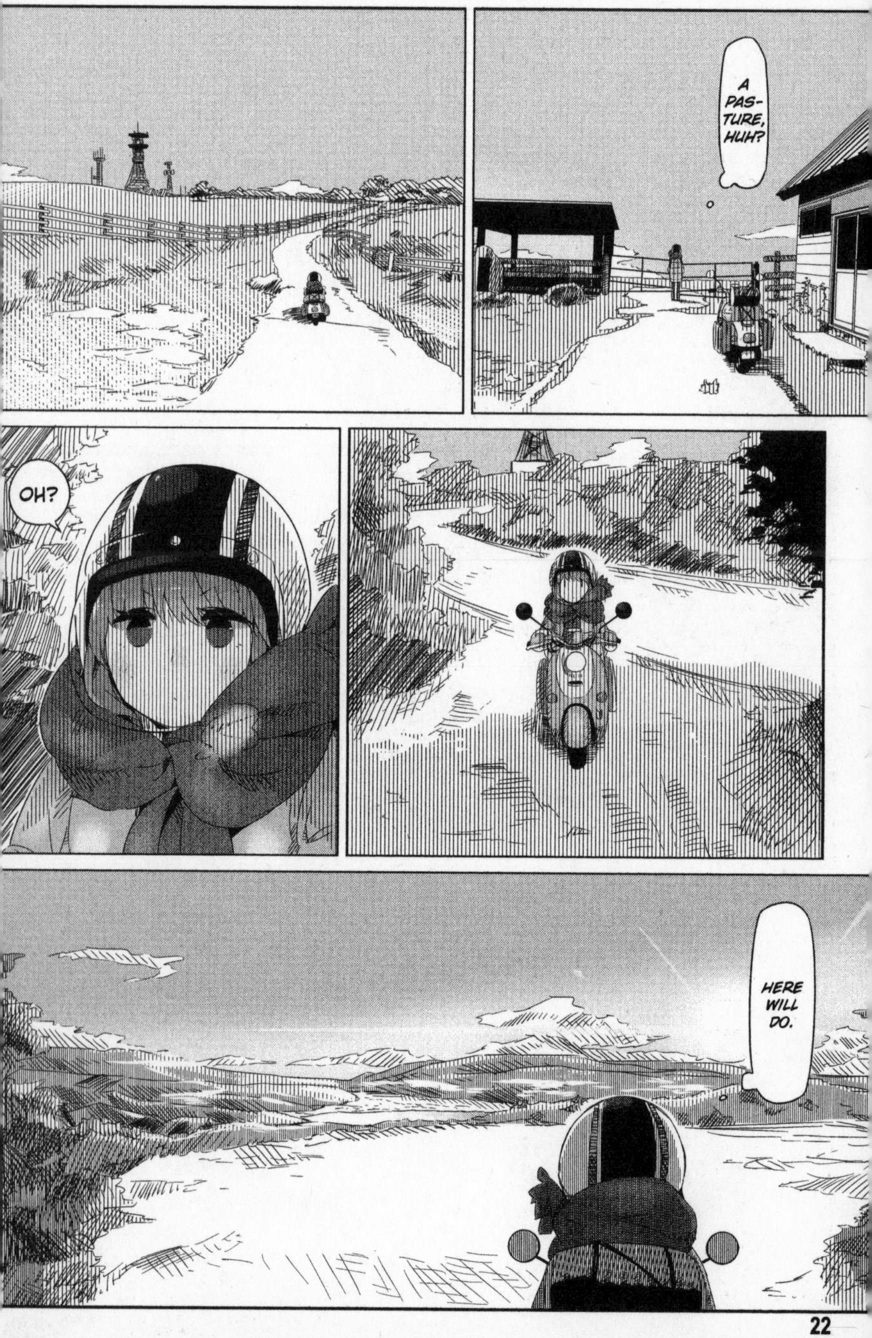
A PASTURE, HUH?
OH?
HERE WILL DO.

CARTON : SERIOUSLY TASTY MILK / TUBE: GARLIC

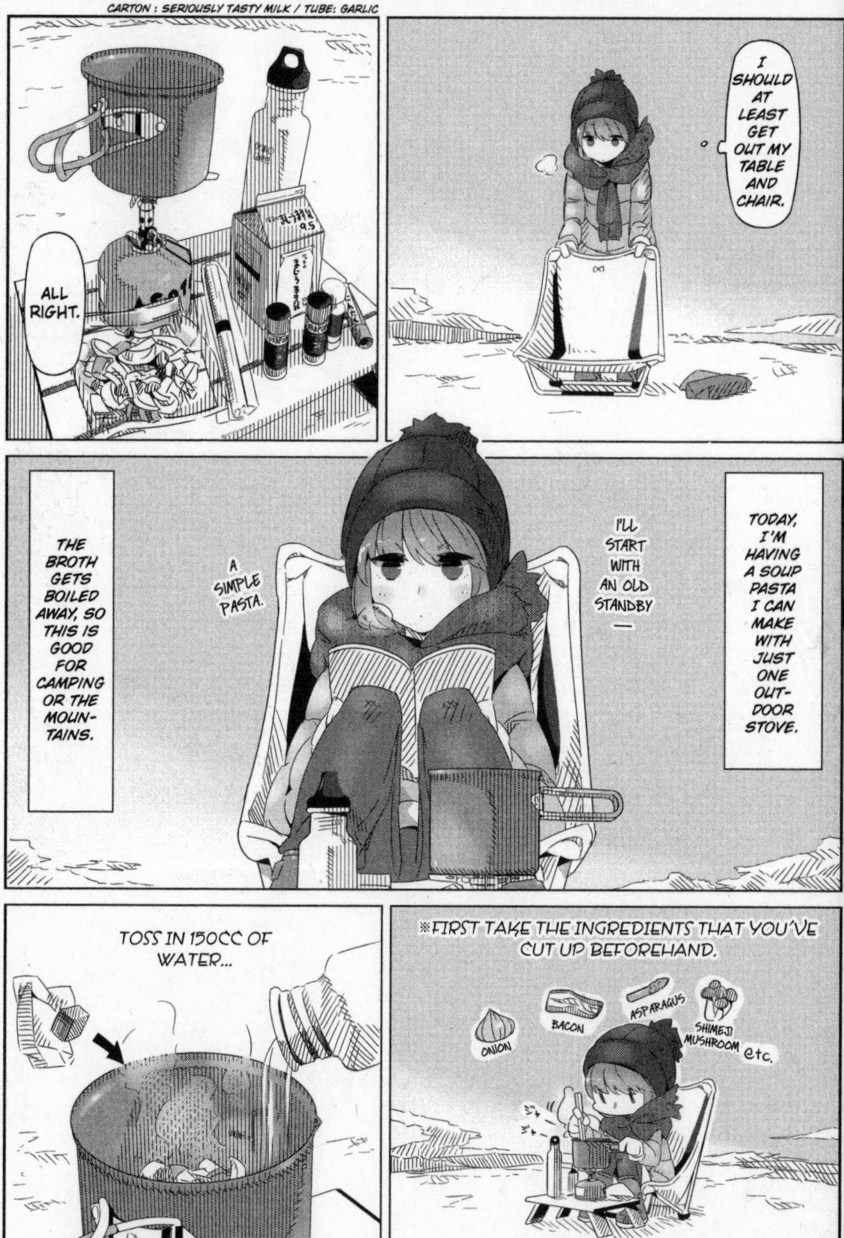

I SHOULD AT LEAST GET OUT MY TABLE AND CHAIR.
ALL RIGHT.
TODAY, I'M HAVING A SOUP PASTA I CAN MAKE WITH JUST ONE OUT-DOOR STOVE.
I'LL START WITH AN OLD STANDBY—
A SIMPLE PASTA.
THE BROTH GETS BOILED AWAY, SO THIS IS GOOD FOR CAMPING OR THE MOUN-TAINS.
※FIRST TAKE THE INGREDIENTS THAT YOU'VE CUT UP BEFOREHAND.
ONION
BACON
ASPARAGUS
SHIMEJI MUSHROOM
etc.
STIR-FRY THEM IN A LARGE AMOUNT OF OLIVE OIL WITH A SMALL GRATED ONION.
TOSS IN 150CC OF WATER...
...AND ONE PACK OF CONSOMMÉ, THEN BRING TO A BOIL.

※SINCE INGREDIENTS QUICKLY GO BAD IN THE SUMMER, IT'S BEST NOT TO MAKE THIS THEN.

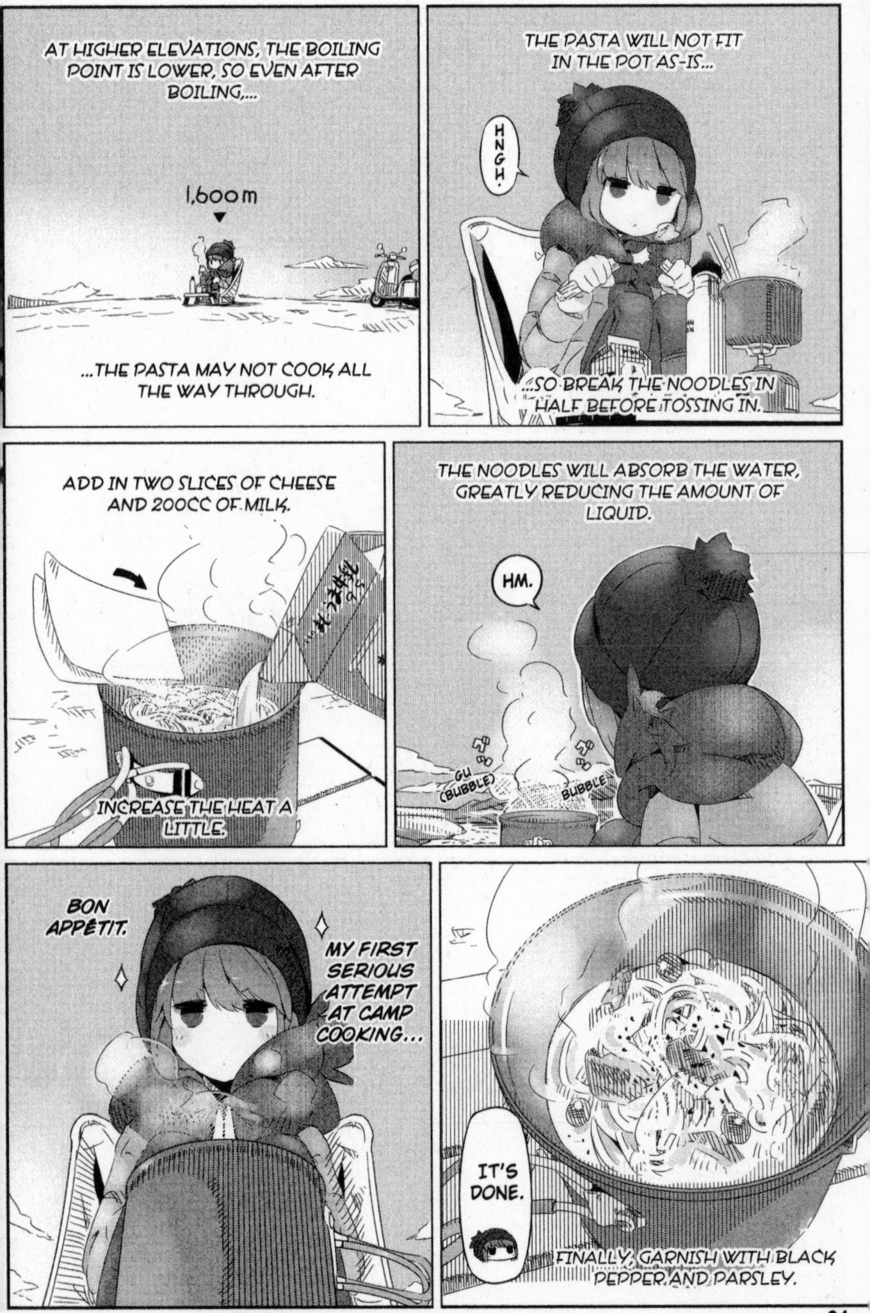
THE PASTA WILL NOT FIT IN THE POT AS-IS...
HNGH.
...SO BREAK THE NOODLES IN HALF BEFORE TOSSING IN.
AT HIGHER ELEVATIONS, THE BOILING POINT IS LOWER, SO EVEN AFTER BOILING,...
1,600m
...THE PASTA MAY NOT COOK ALL THE WAY THROUGH.
THE NOODLES WILL ABSORB THE WATER, GREATLY REDUCING THE AMOUNT OF LIQUID.
HM.
BUBBLE
GU (BUBBLE)
ADD IN TWO SLICES OF CHEESE AND 200CC OF MILK.
INCREASE THE HEAT A LITTLE.
IT'S DONE.
FINALLY, GARNISH WITH BLACK PEPPER AND PARSLEY.
MY FIRST SERIOUS ATTEMPT AT CAMP COOKING...
BON APPÉTIT.

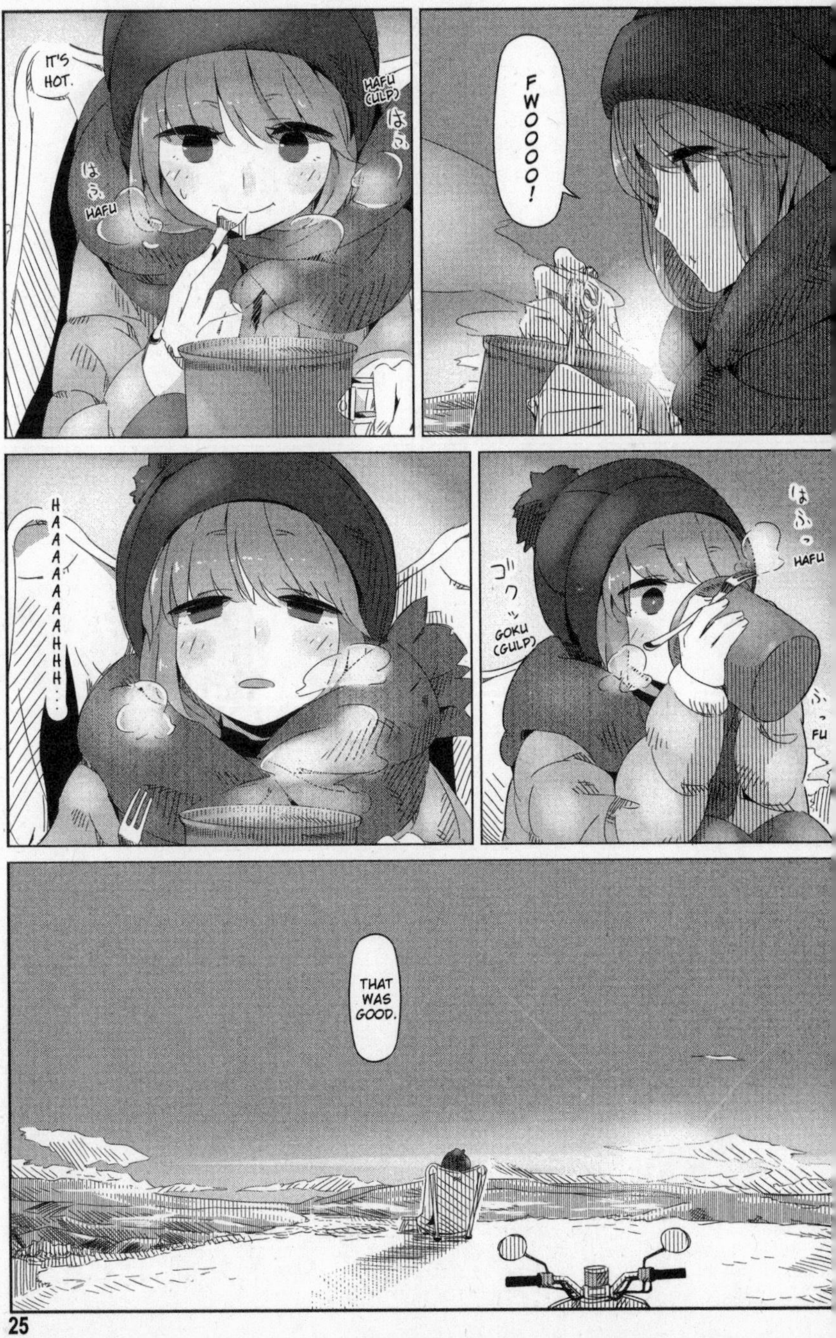
FWOOOOO!
IT'S HOT.
HAFU (GULP)
はふ
はふ
HAFU
はふっ
HAFU
ゴクッ
GOKU (GULP)
ふっ
FU
HAAAAAAAAHHH...
THAT WAS GOOD.

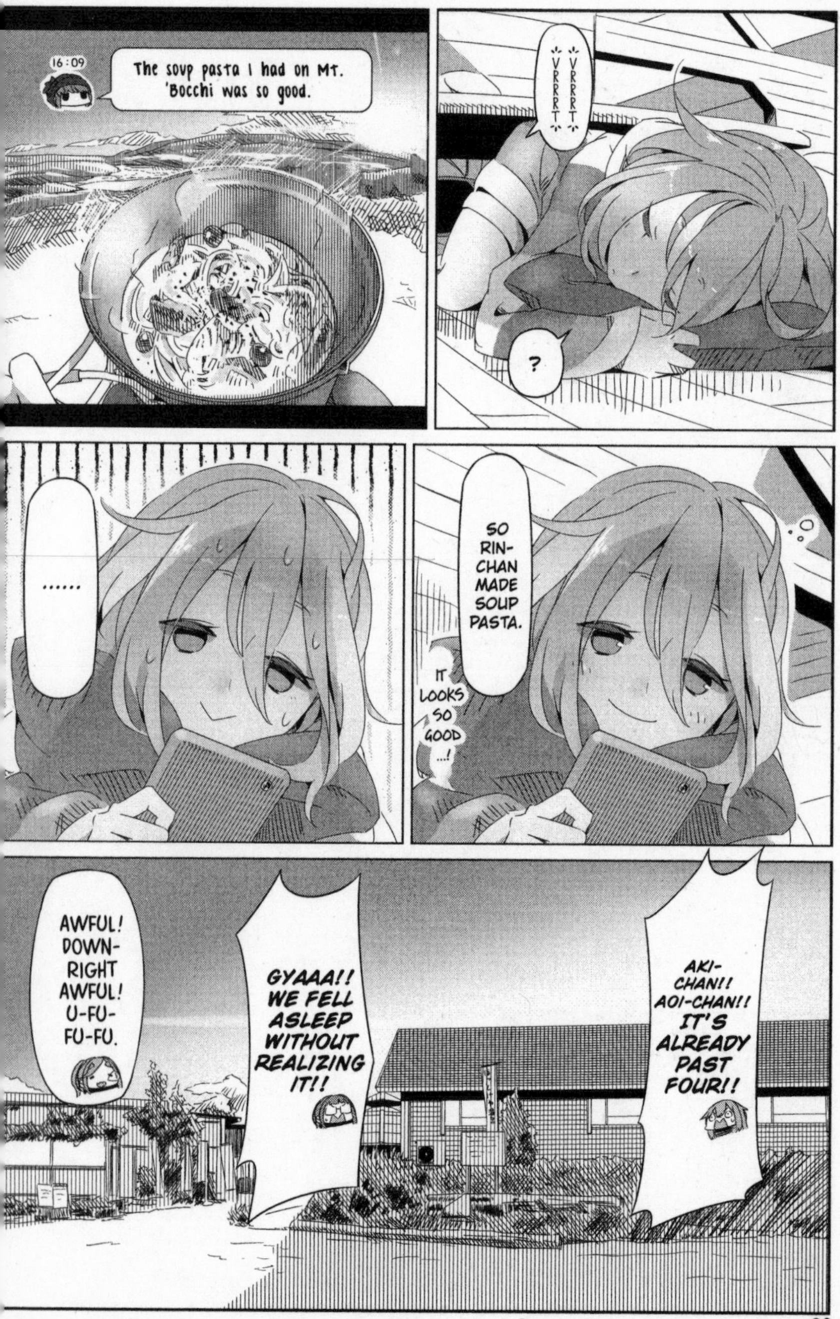
VRRRT VRRRT
?
16:09
The soup pasta I had on Mt. 'Bocchi was so good.
SO RIN-CHAN MADE SOUP PASTA.
IT LOOKS SO GOOD ...!
......
AKI-CHAN!! AOI-CHAN!! IT'S ALREADY PAST FOUR!!
GYAAA!! WE FELL ASLEEP WITHOUT REALIZING IT!!
AWFUL! DOWN-RIGHT AWFUL! U-FU-FU-FU.

THE SUN'S ALREADY GOING DOWN!!
IT'S ONE MORE KM TO THE CAMP-SITE!!
HURRY UP, YOU GUYS!
A FRESH BATCH OF FRIED HOT-SPRING EGGS!
COME AND GET IT...!
THANK YOU, COME AGAIN.

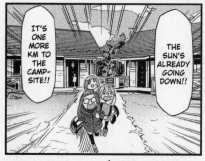

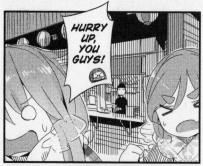

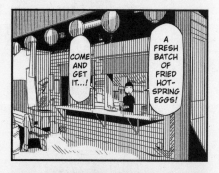

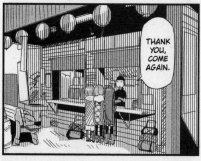

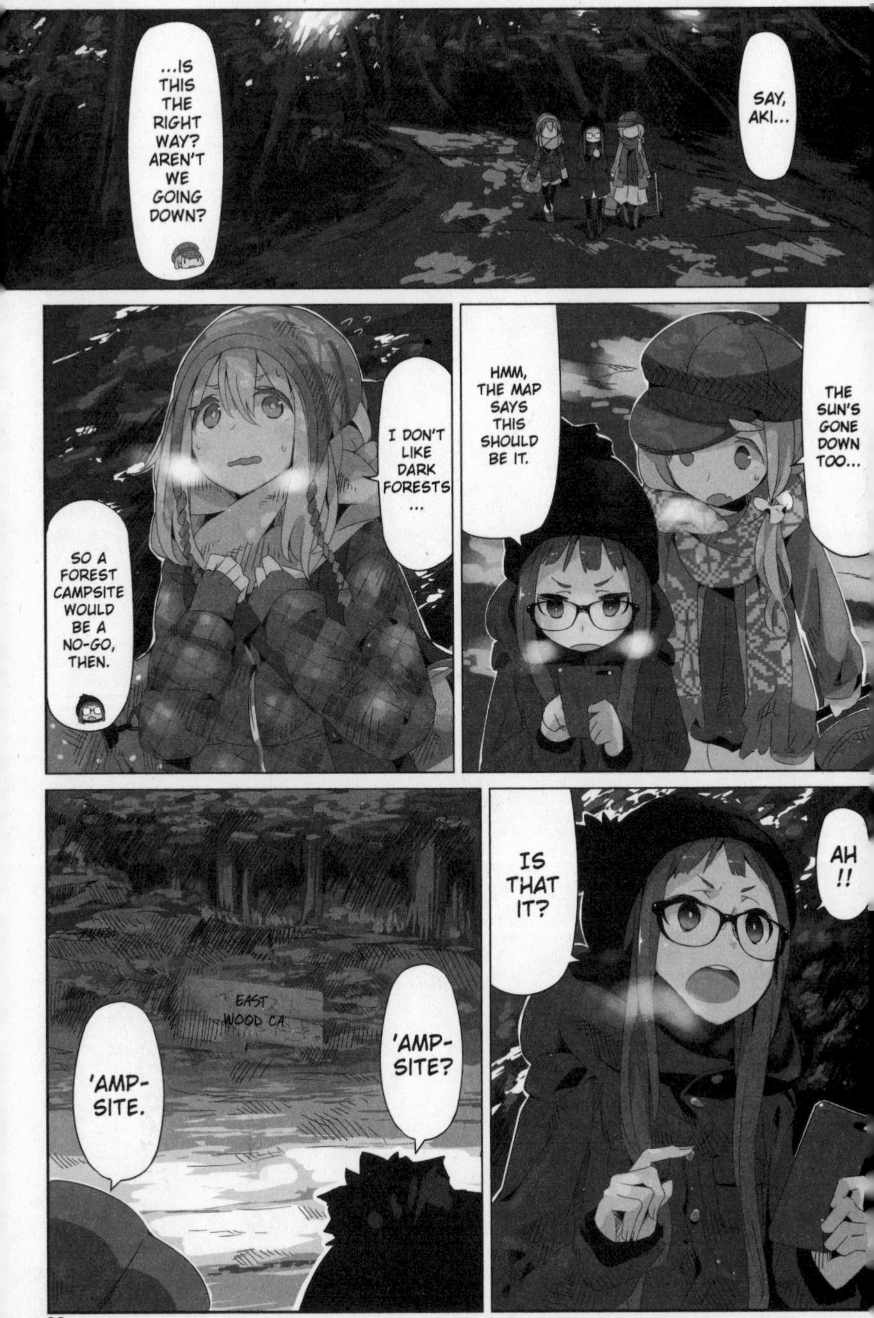
SAY, AKI...
...IS THIS THE RIGHT WAY? AREN'T WE GOING DOWN?
THE SUN'S GONE DOWN TOO...
HMM, THE MAP SAYS THIS SHOULD BE IT.
I DON'T LIKE DARK FORESTS...
SO A FOREST CAMPSITE WOULD BE A NO-GO, THEN.
AH!!
IS THAT IT?
EAST WOOD CA
'AMP-SITE?
'AMP-SITE.

CHAPTER 8 TWO DIFFERENT CAMPSITES, ONE SCENIC VIEW

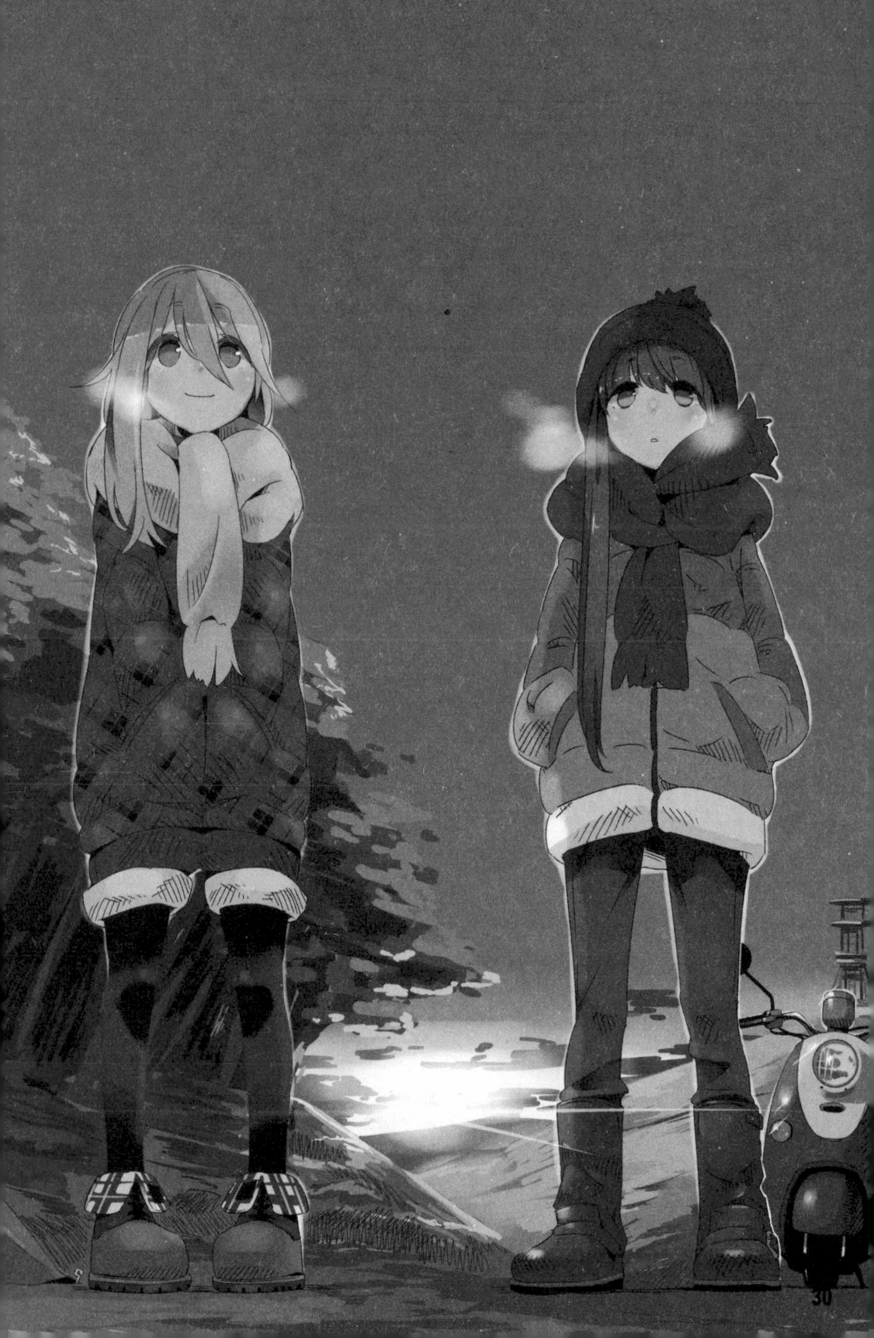

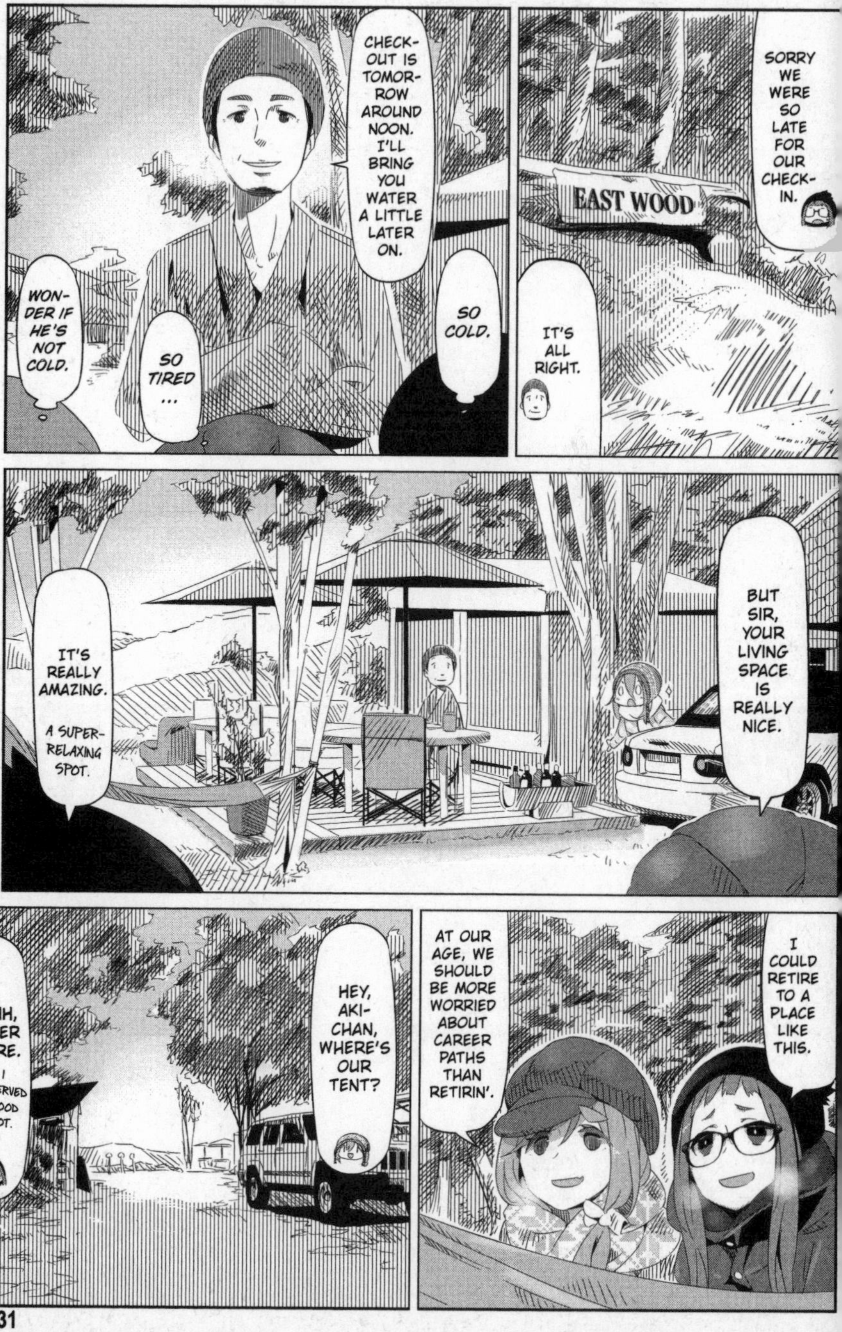
SORRY WE WERE SO LATE FOR OUR CHECK-IN.
EAST WOOD
IT'S ALL RIGHT.
CHECK-OUT IS TOMORROW AROUND NOON. I'LL BRING YOU WATER A LITTLE LATER ON.
SO COLD.
SO TIRED ...
WONDER IF HE'S NOT COLD.
BUT SIR, YOUR LIVING SPACE IS REALLY NICE.
IT'S REALLY AMAZING.
A SUPER-RELAXING SPOT.
I COULD RETIRE TO A PLACE LIKE THIS.
AT OUR AGE, WE SHOULD BE MORE WORRIED ABOUT CAREER PATHS THAN RETIRIN'.
HEY, AKI-CHAN, WHERE'S OUR TENT?
OHH, OVER HERE.
I RESERVED A GOOD SPOT.

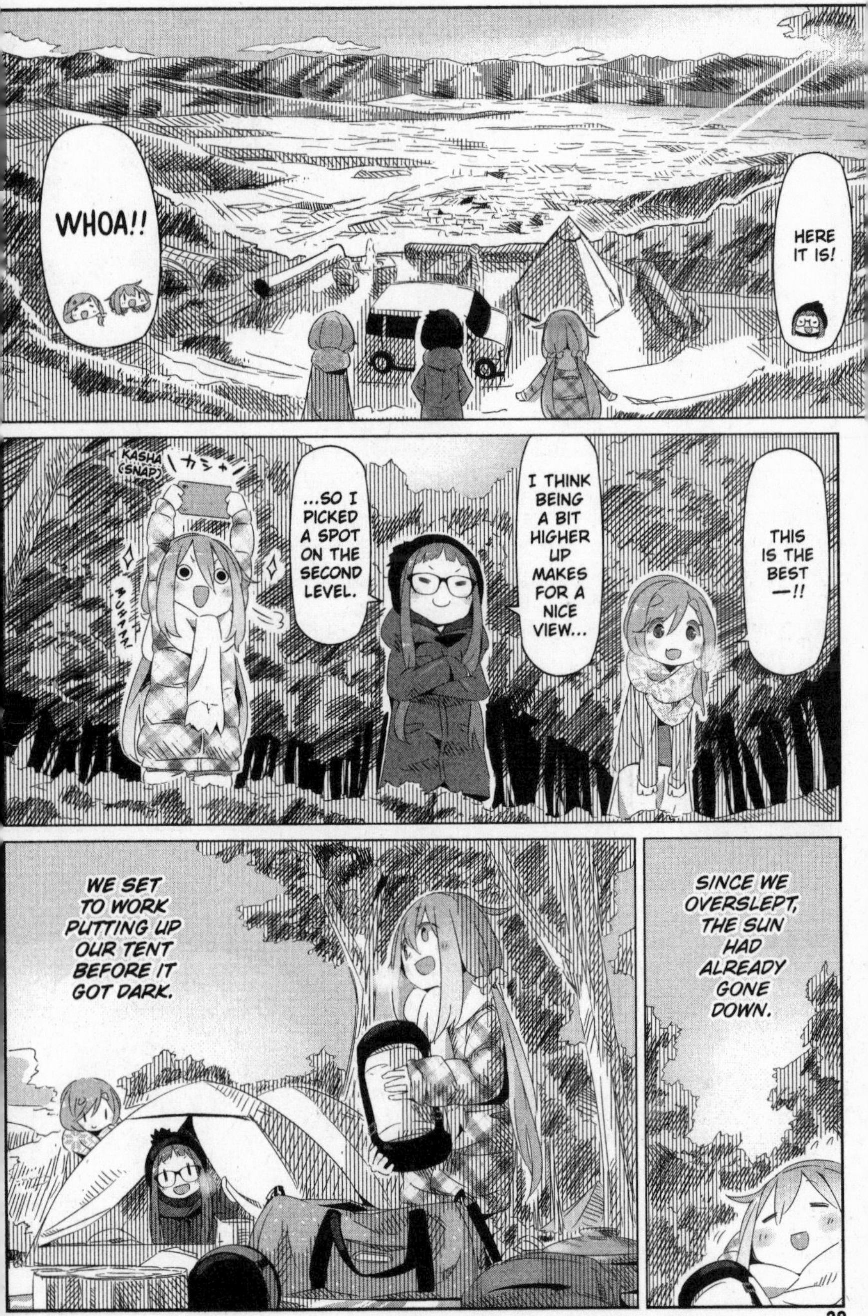
HERE IT IS!
WHOA!!
THIS IS THE BEST—!!
I THINK BEING A BIT HIGHER UP MAKES FOR A NICE VIEW...
...SO I PICKED A SPOT ON THE SECOND LEVEL.
KASHA (SNAP)
SINCE WE OVERSLEPT, THE SUN HAD ALREADY GONE DOWN.
WE SET TO WORK PUTTING UP OUR TENT BEFORE IT GOT DARK.

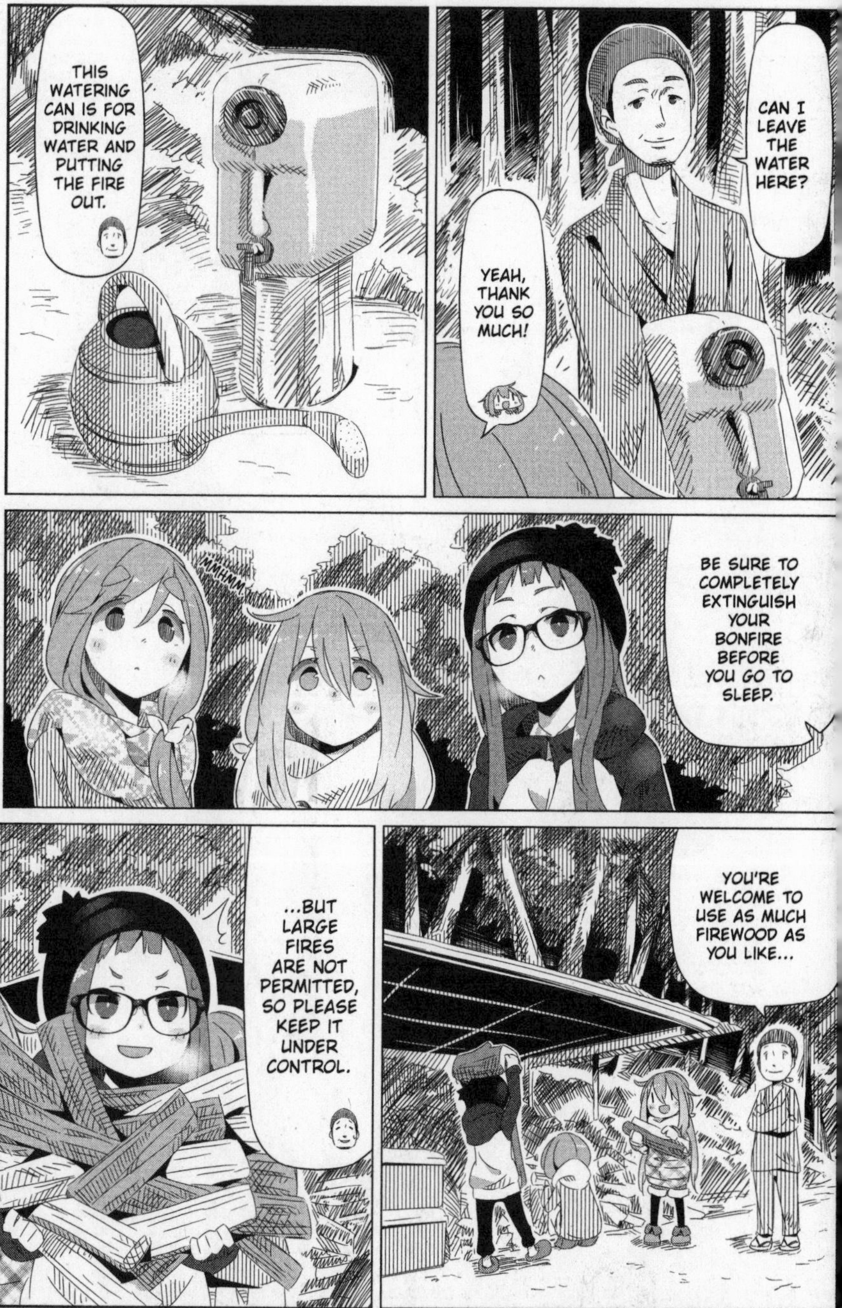
CAN I LEAVE THE WATER HERE?
YEAH, THANK YOU SO MUCH!
THIS WATERING CAN IS FOR DRINKING WATER AND PUTTING THE FIRE OUT.
BE SURE TO COMPLETELY EXTINGUISH YOUR BONFIRE BEFORE YOU GO TO SLEEP.
MMHMM
YOU'RE WELCOME TO USE AS MUCH FIREWOOD AS YOU LIKE...
...BUT LARGE FIRES ARE NOT PERMITTED, SO PLEASE KEEP IT UNDER CONTROL.

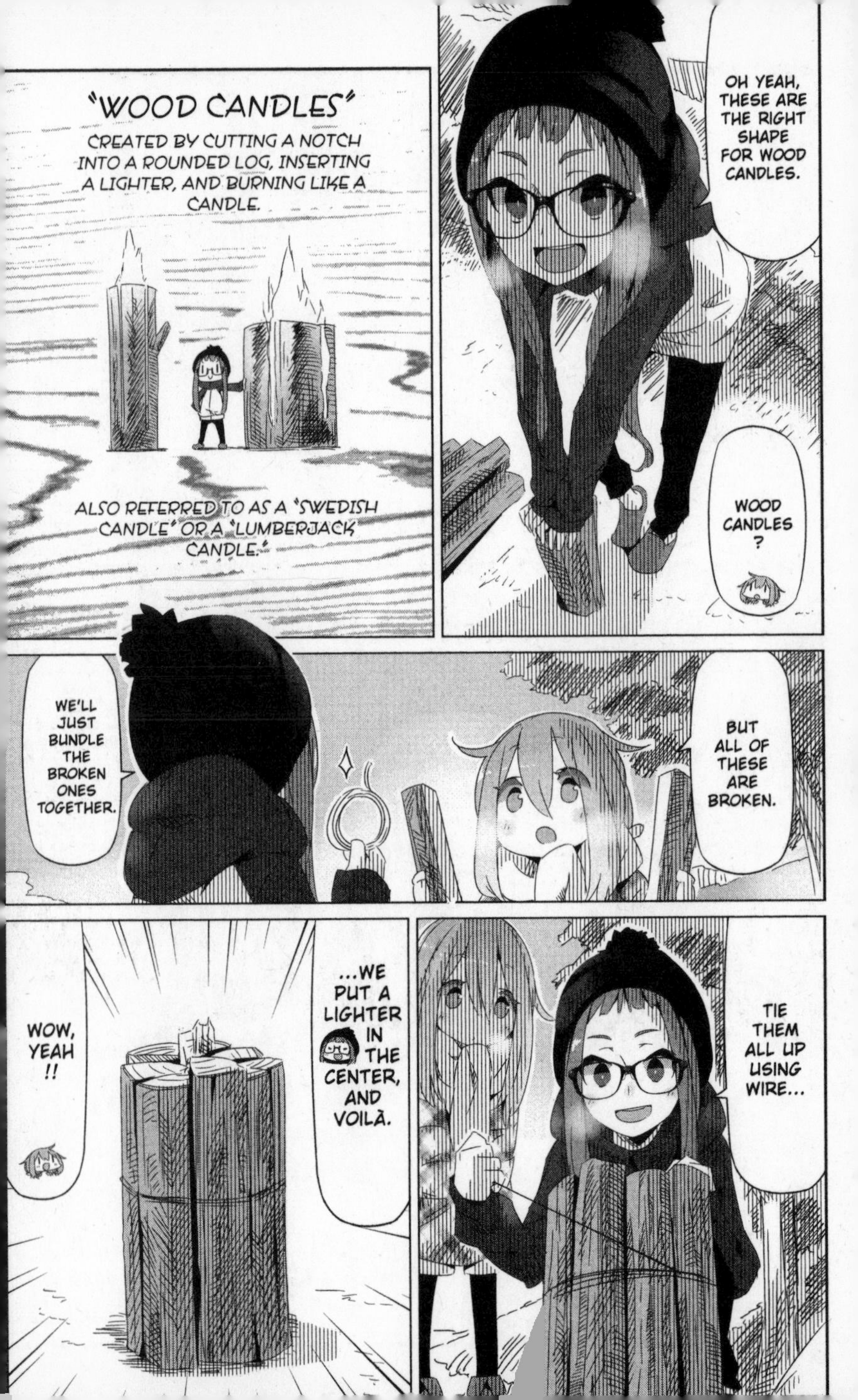
OH YEAH, THESE ARE THE RIGHT SHAPE FOR WOOD CANDLES.
WOOD CANDLES ?
"WOOD CANDLES"
CREATED BY CUTTING A NOTCH INTO A ROUNDED LOG, INSERTING A LIGHTER, AND BURNING LIKE A CANDLE.
ALSO REFERRED TO AS A "SWEDISH CANDLE" OR A "LUMBERJACK CANDLE."
BUT ALL OF THESE ARE BROKEN.
WE'LL JUST BUNDLE THE BROKEN ONES TOGETHER.
TIE THEM ALL UP USING WIRE...
...WE PUT A LIGHTER IN THE CENTER, AND VOILÀ.
WOW, YEAH !!

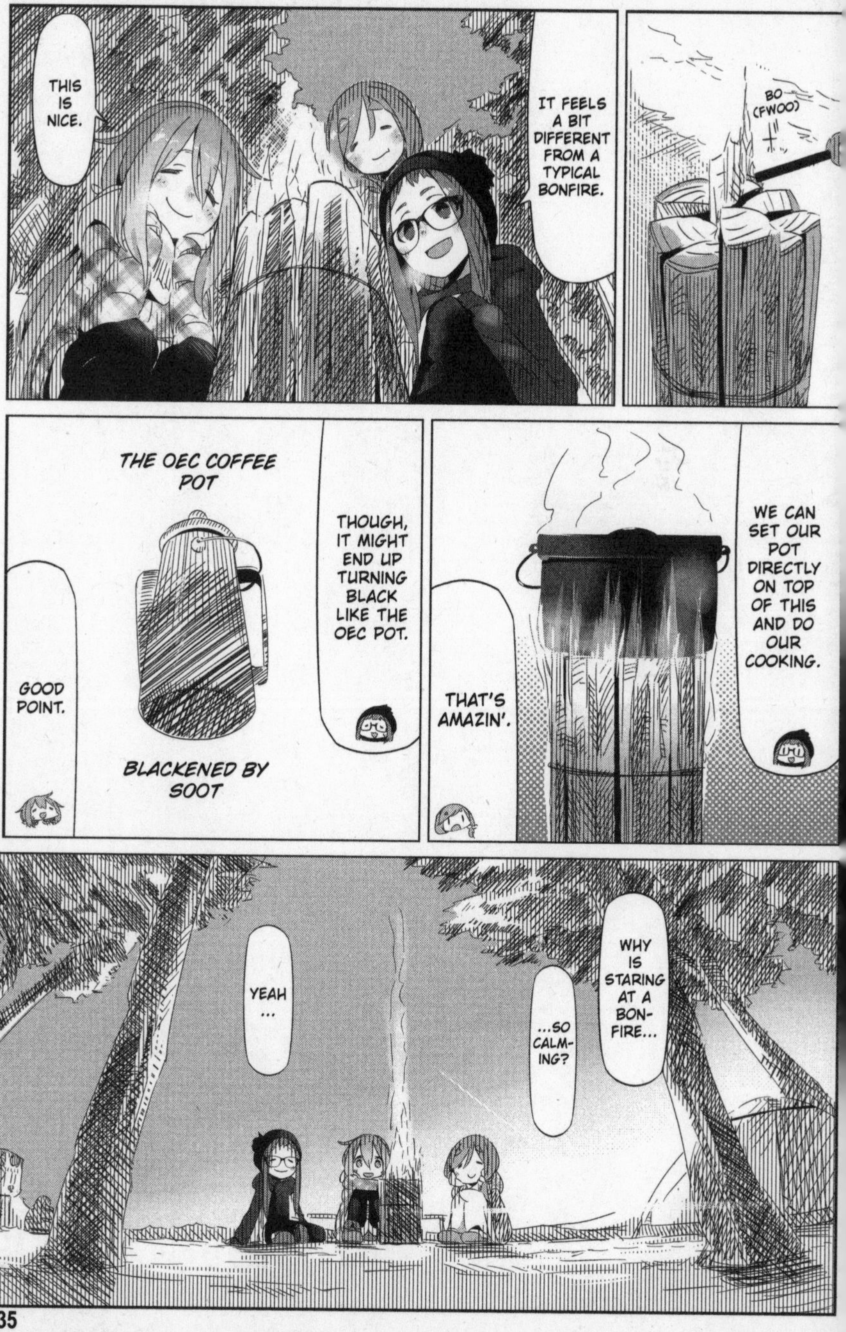
BO (FWOO)
IT FEELS A BIT DIFFERENT FROM A TYPICAL BONFIRE.
THIS IS NICE.
WE CAN SET OUR POT DIRECTLY ON TOP OF THIS AND DO OUR COOKING.
THAT'S AMAZIN'.
THOUGH, IT MIGHT END UP TURNING BLACK LIKE THE OEC POT.
THE OEC COFFEE POT
BLACKENED BY SOOT
GOOD POINT.
WHY IS STARING AT A BON-FIRE...
...SO CALMING?
YEAH ...

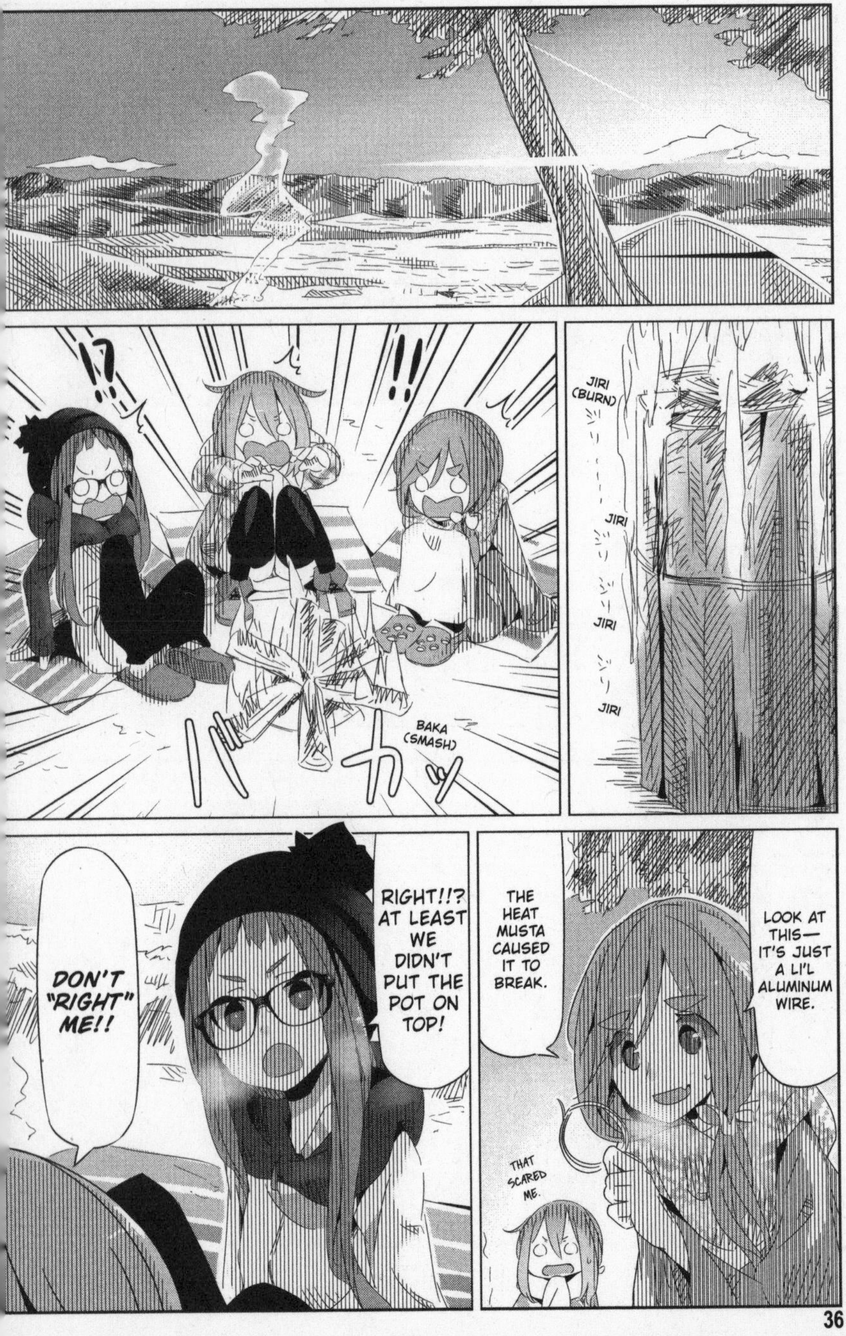
JIRI (BURN)
JIRI
JIRI
JIRI
!?
!!
BAKA (SMASH)
LOOK AT THIS— IT'S JUST A LI'L ALUMINUM WIRE.
THE HEAT MUSTA CAUSED IT TO BREAK.
THAT SCARED ME.
RIGHT!!? AT LEAST WE DIDN'T PUT THE POT ON TOP!
DON'T "RIGHT" ME!!

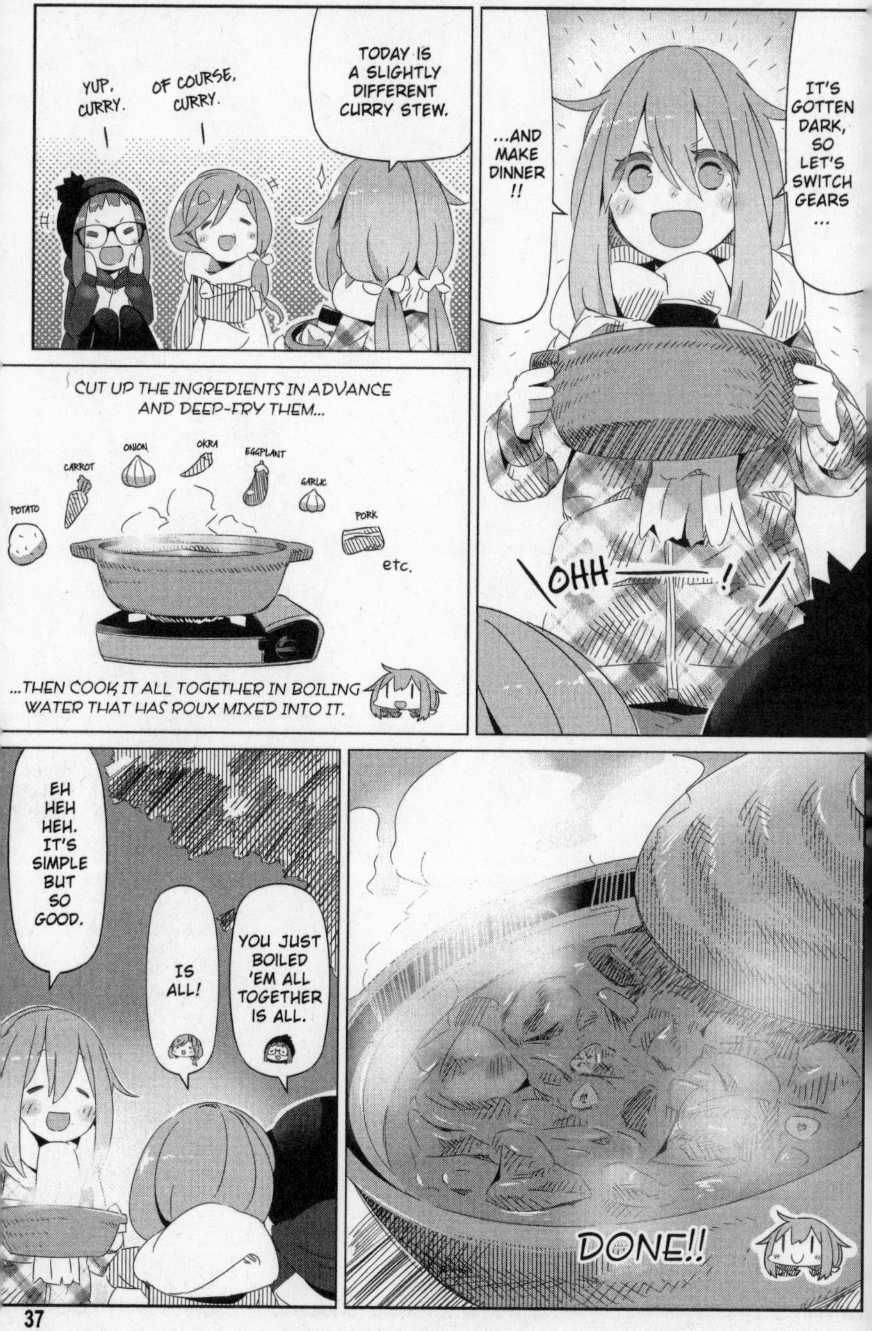
IT'S GOTTEN DARK, SO LET'S SWITCH GEARS...
...AND MAKE DINNER!!
OHH—!
TODAY IS A SLIGHTLY DIFFERENT CURRY STEW.
OF COURSE, CURRY.
YUP, CURRY.
CUT UP THE INGREDIENTS IN ADVANCE AND DEEP-FRY THEM...
EGGPLANT
OKRA
ONION
CARROT
GARLIC
POTATO
PORK
etc.
...THEN COOK IT ALL TOGETHER IN BOILING WATER THAT HAS ROUX MIXED INTO IT.
DONE!!
EH HEH HEH. IT'S SIMPLE BUT SO GOOD.
YOU JUST BOILED 'EM ALL TOGETHER IS ALL.
IS ALL!

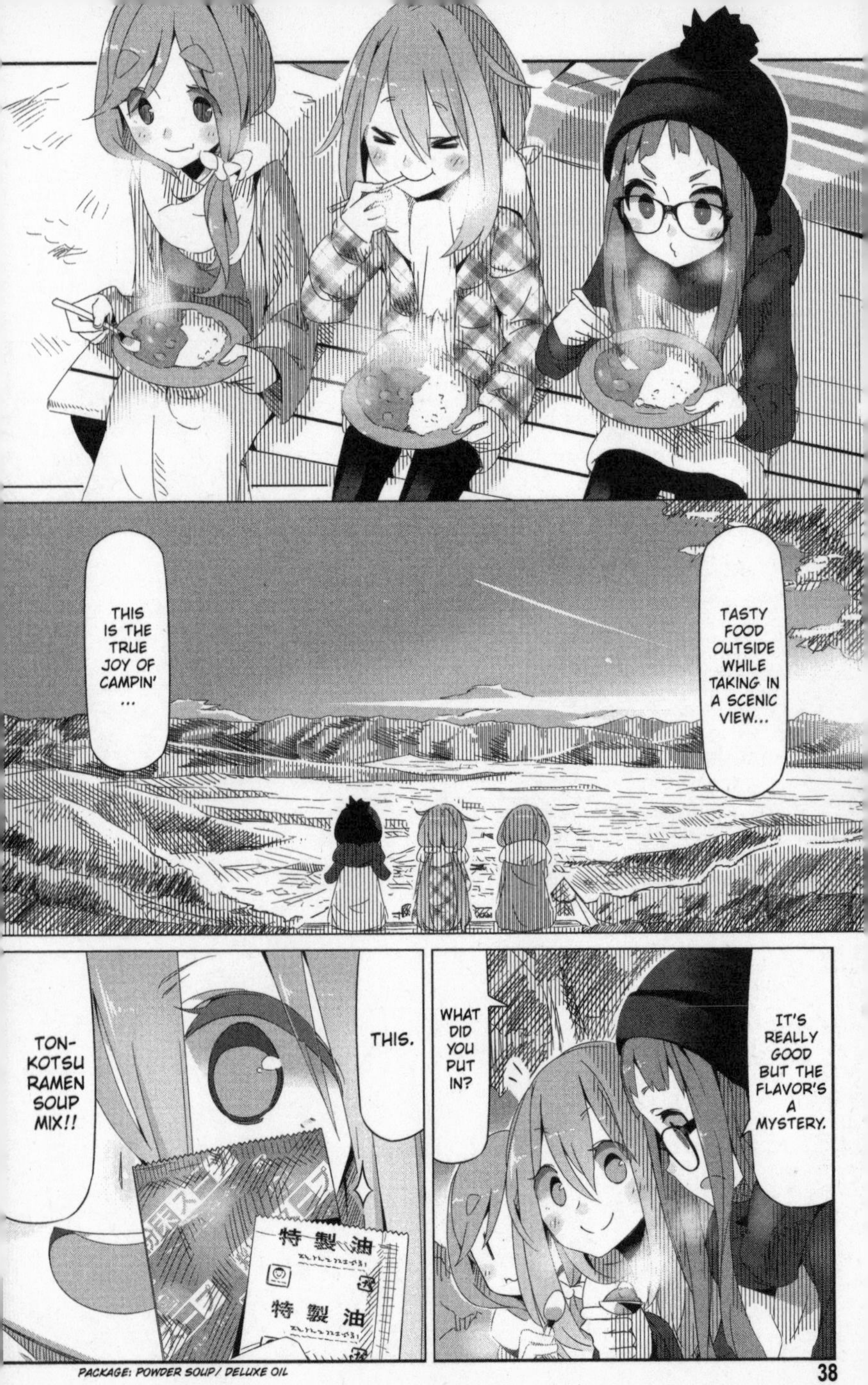
TASTY FOOD OUTSIDE WHILE TAKING IN A SCENIC VIEW...
THIS IS THE TRUE JOY OF CAMPIN'...
IT'S REALLY GOOD BUT THE FLAVOR'S A MYSTERY.
WHAT DID YOU PUT IN?
THIS.
TON-KOTSU RAMEN SOUP MIX!!
特製油
特製油

PACKAGE: POWDER SOUP/ DELUXE OIL

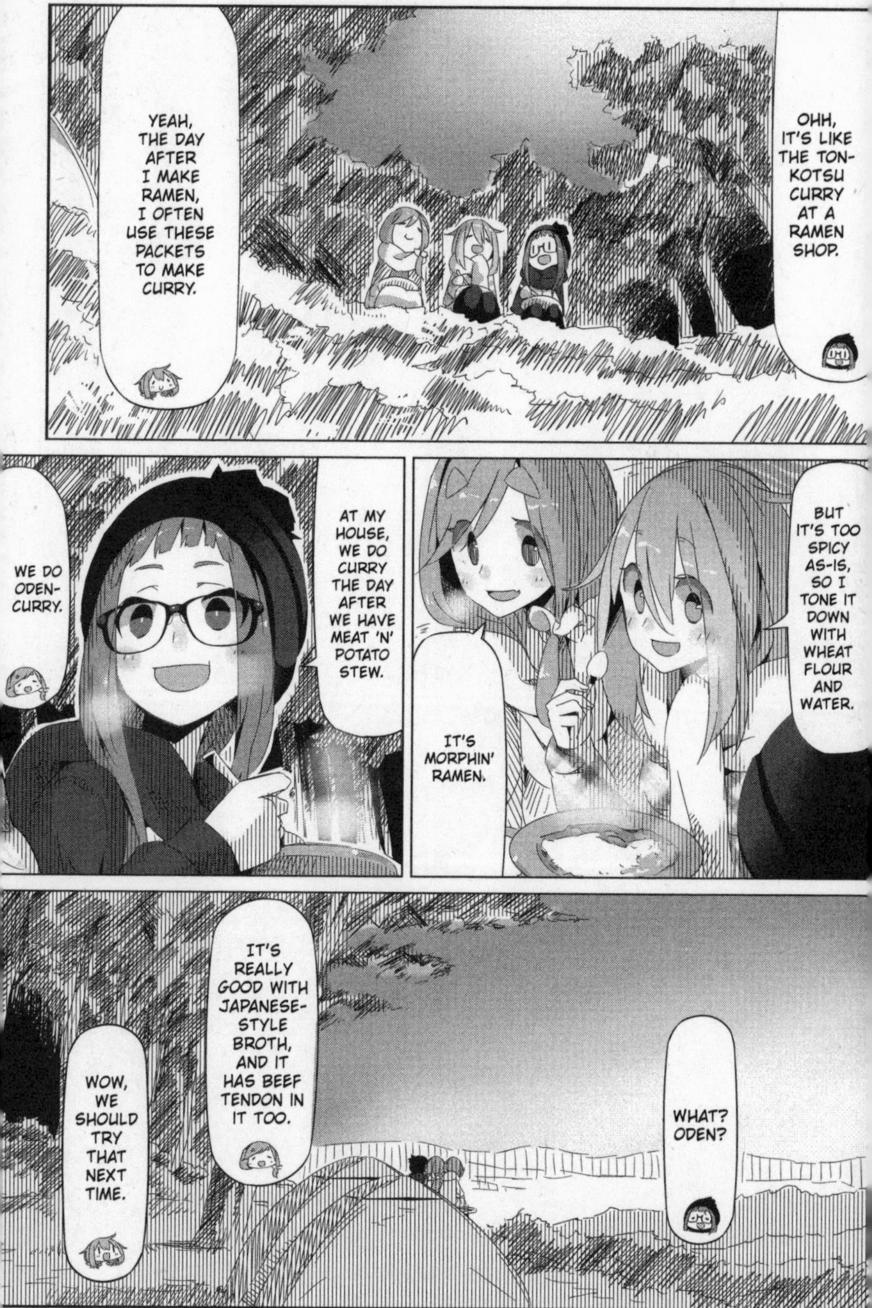
OHH, IT'S LIKE THE TON-KOTSU CURRY AT A RAMEN SHOP.
YEAH, THE DAY AFTER I MAKE RAMEN, I OFTEN USE THESE PACKETS TO MAKE CURRY.
BUT IT'S TOO SPICY AS-IS, SO I TONE IT DOWN WITH WHEAT FLOUR AND WATER.
IT'S MORPHIN' RAMEN.
AT MY HOUSE, WE DO CURRY THE DAY AFTER WE HAVE MEAT 'N' POTATO STEW.
WE DO ODEN-CURRY.
WHAT? ODEN?
IT'S REALLY GOOD WITH JAPANESE-STYLE BROTH, AND IT HAS BEEF TENDON IN IT TOO.
WOW, WE SHOULD TRY THAT NEXT TIME.

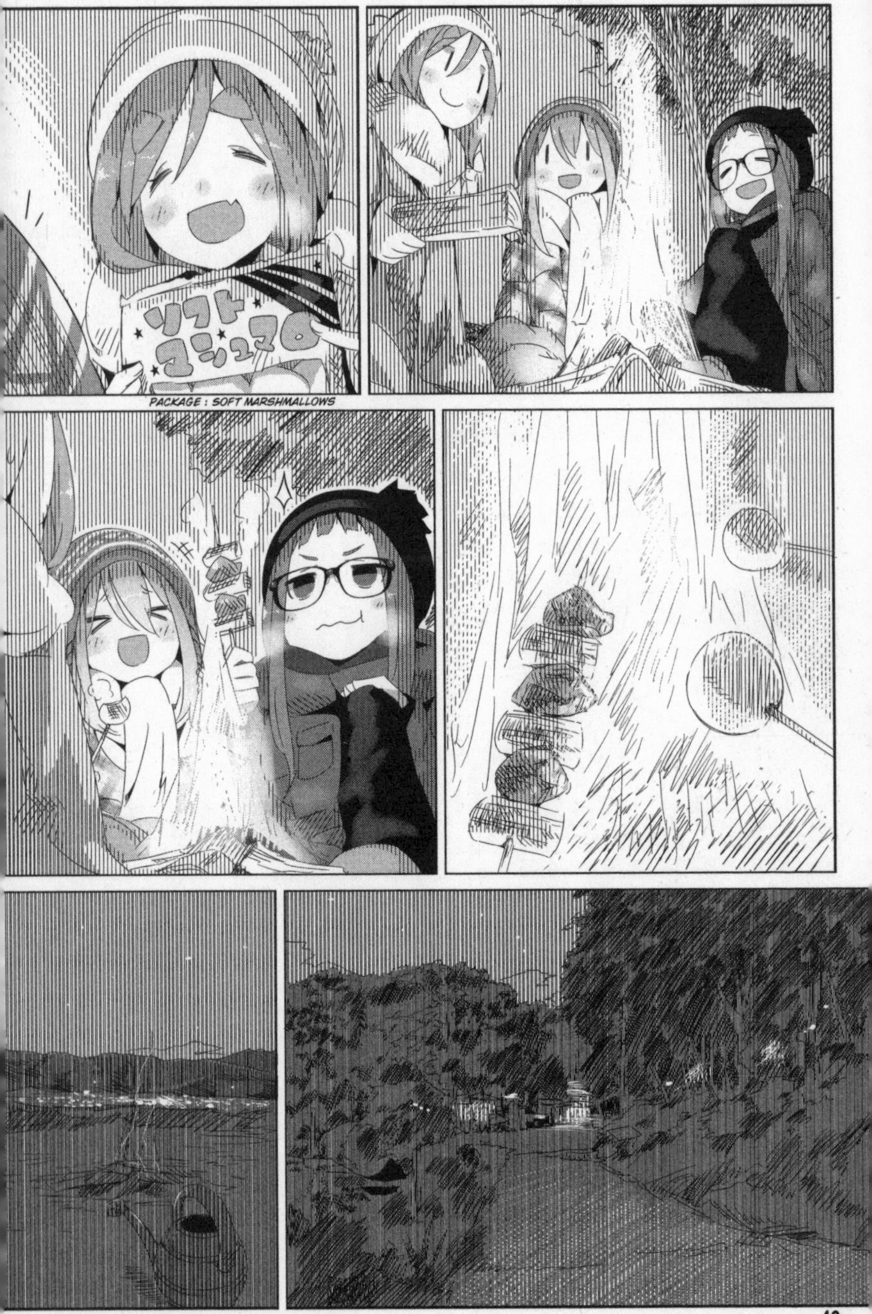
PACKAGE : SOFT MARSHMALLOWS

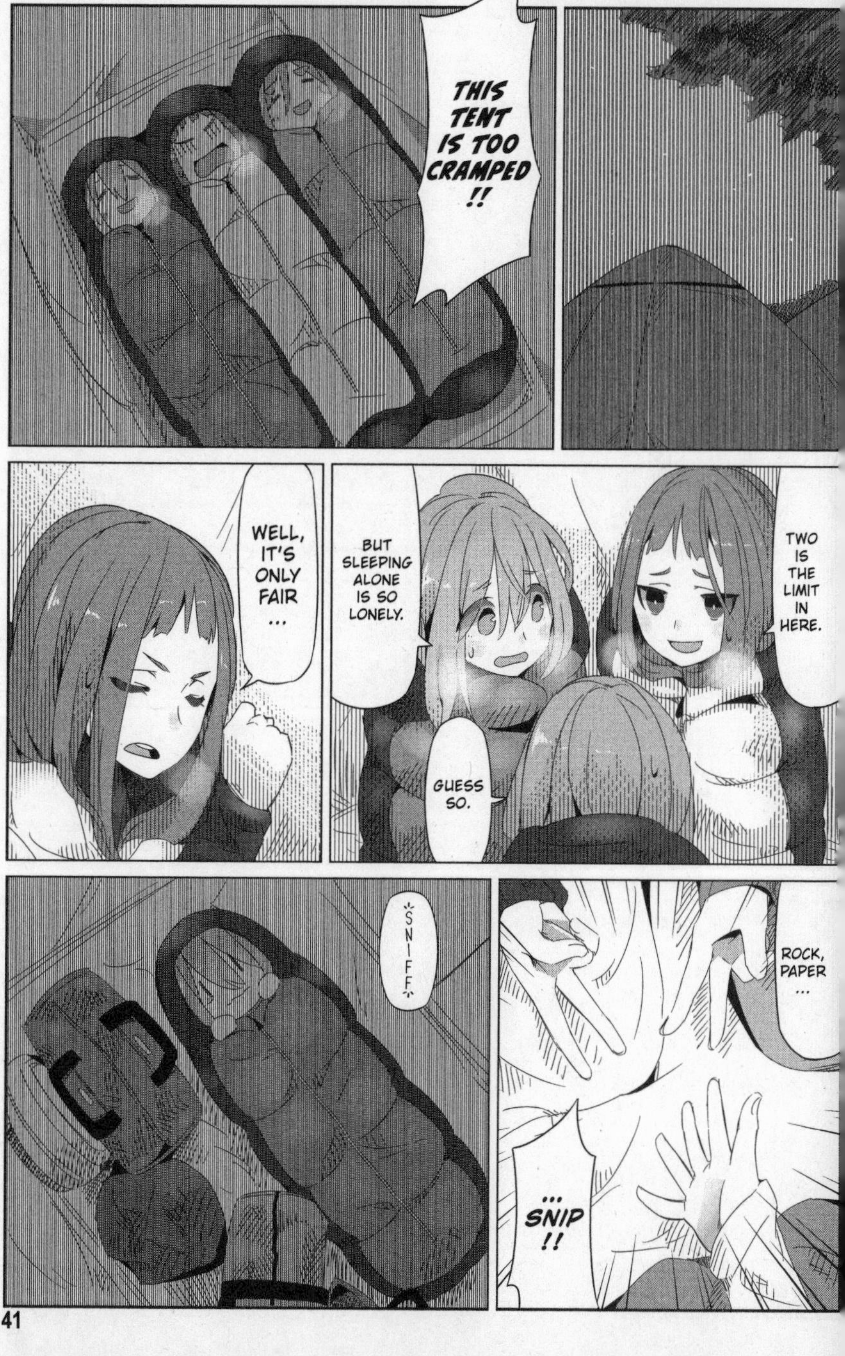
THIS TENT IS TOO CRAMPED!!
TWO IS THE LIMIT IN HERE.
BUT SLEEPING ALONE IS SO LONELY.
GUESS SO.
WELL, IT'S ONLY FAIR...
ROCK, PAPER...
...SNIP!!
SNIFF

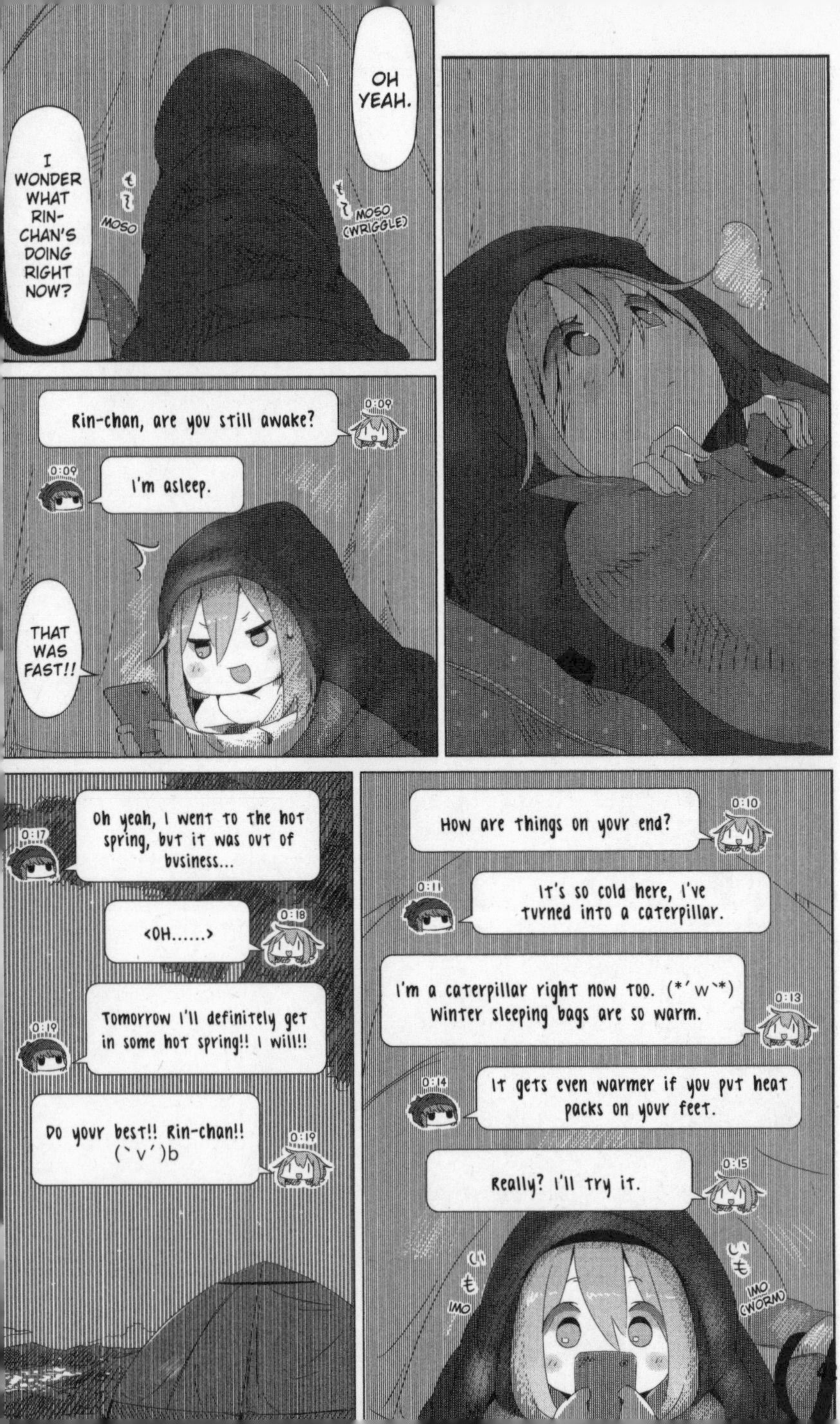

OH YEAH.
I WONDER WHAT RIN-CHAN'S DOING RIGHT NOW?
もそ MOSO (WRIGGLE)
もそ MOSO
0:09 Rin-chan, are you still awake?
0:09 I'm asleep.
THAT WAS FAST!!
0:10 How are things on your end?
0:11 It's so cold here, I've turned into a caterpillar.
0:13 I'm a caterpillar right now too. (*´w`*) Winter sleeping bags are so warm.
0:14 It gets even warmer if you put heat packs on your feet.
0:15 Really? I'll try it.
いも IMO (WORM)
いも IMO
0:17 Oh yeah, I went to the hot spring, but it was out of business...
0:18 <OH......>
0:19 Tomorrow I'll definitely get in some hot spring!! I will!!
0:19 Do your best!! Rin-chan!! (`v´)b

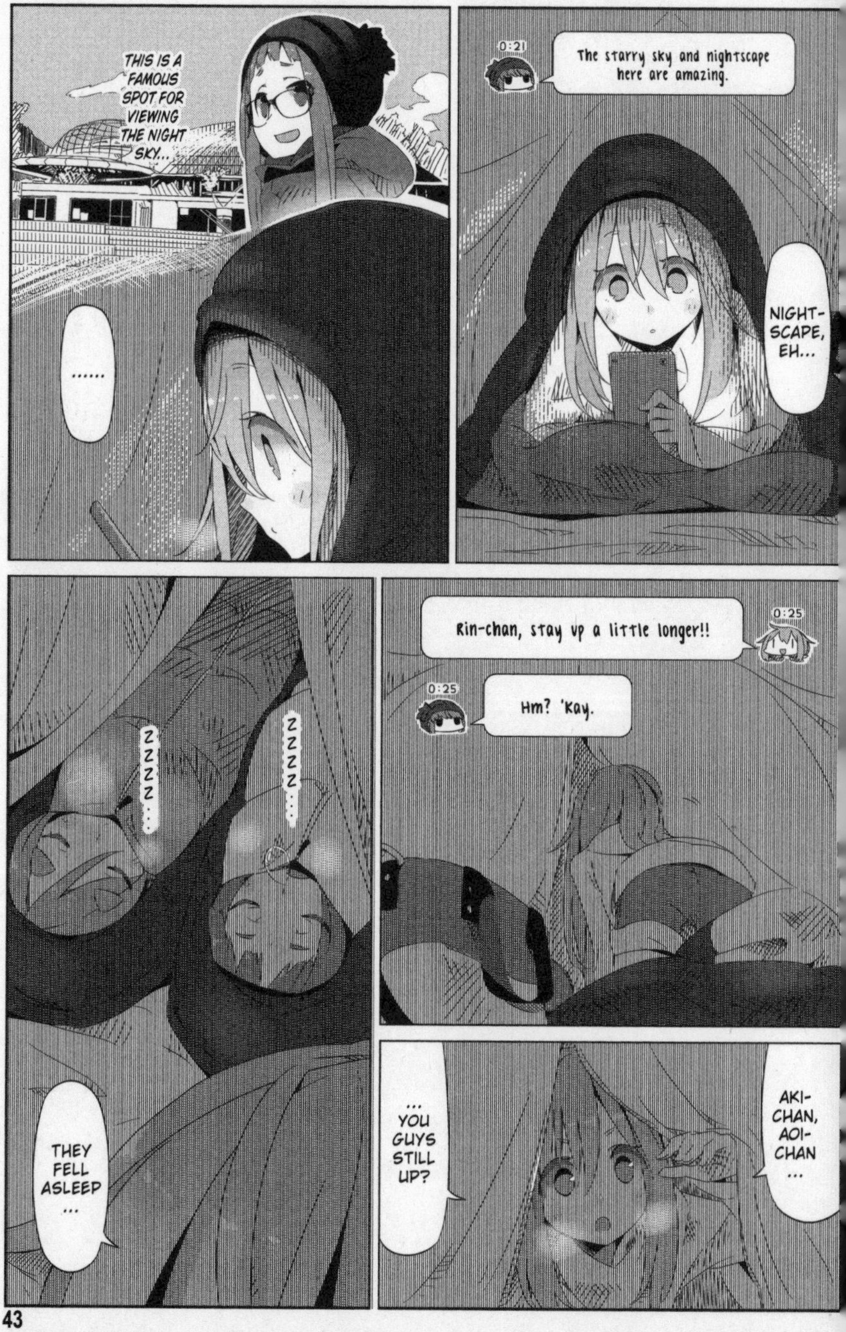
0:21
The starry sky and nightscape here are amazing.
NIGHT-SCAPE, EH...
THIS IS A FAMOUS SPOT FOR VIEWING THE NIGHT SKY...
......
0:25
Rin-chan, stay up a little longer!!
0:25
Hm? 'Kay.
AKI-CHAN, AOI-CHAN...
...YOU GUYS STILL UP?
ZZZZ...
ZZZZ...
THEY FELL ASLEEP...

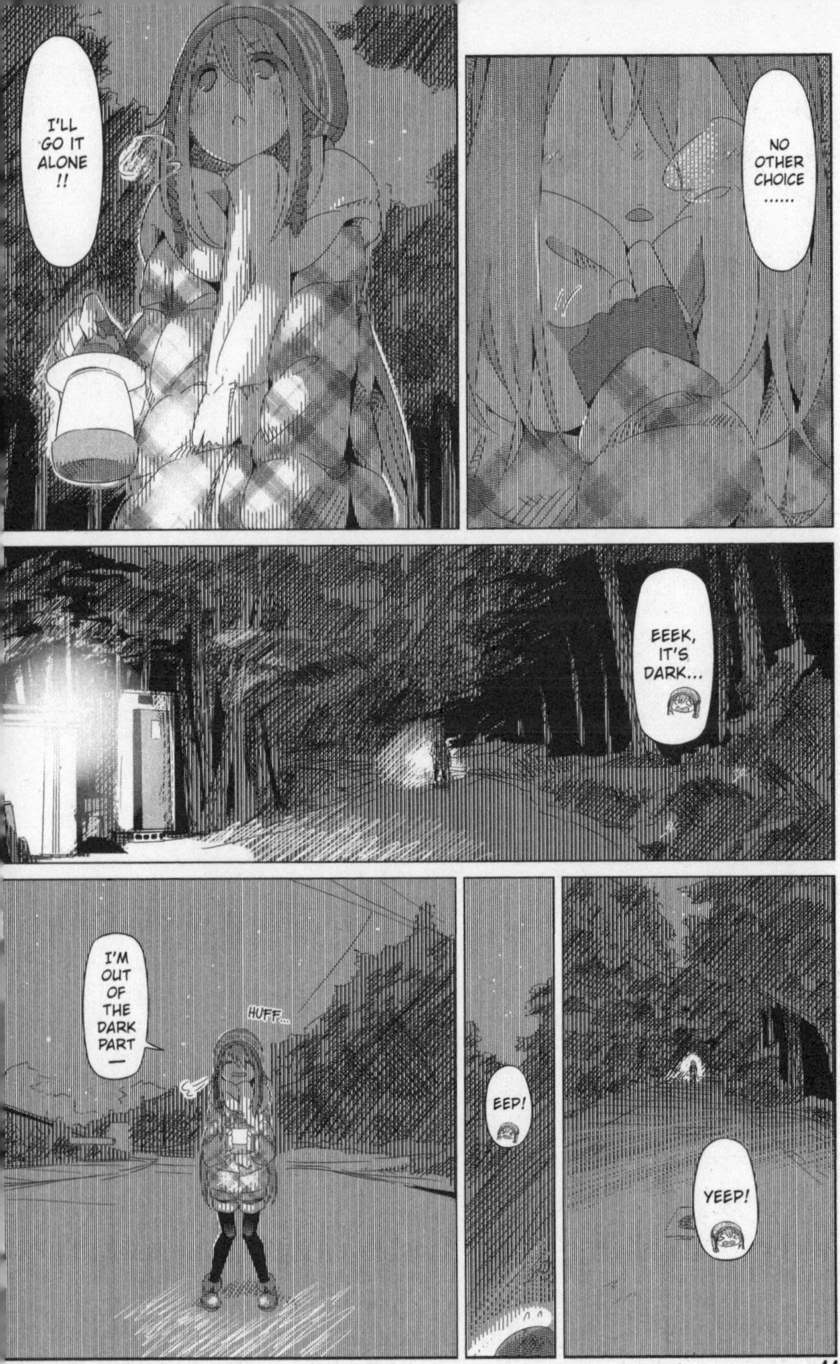
NO OTHER CHOICE ......
I'LL GO IT ALONE !!
EEEK, IT'S DARK...
YEEP!
EEP!
I'M OUT OF THE DARK PART —
HUFF...

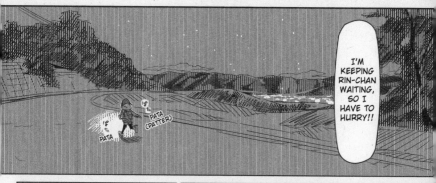

I'M KEEPING RIN-CHAN WAITING, SO I HAVE TO HURRY!!

PATA
PATA (PATTER)
PATA

HUFF...

HUFF...

MADE IT...

>BZZT<
>BZZT<

THERE IT IS... WHAT IN THE WORLD?

OKAY!

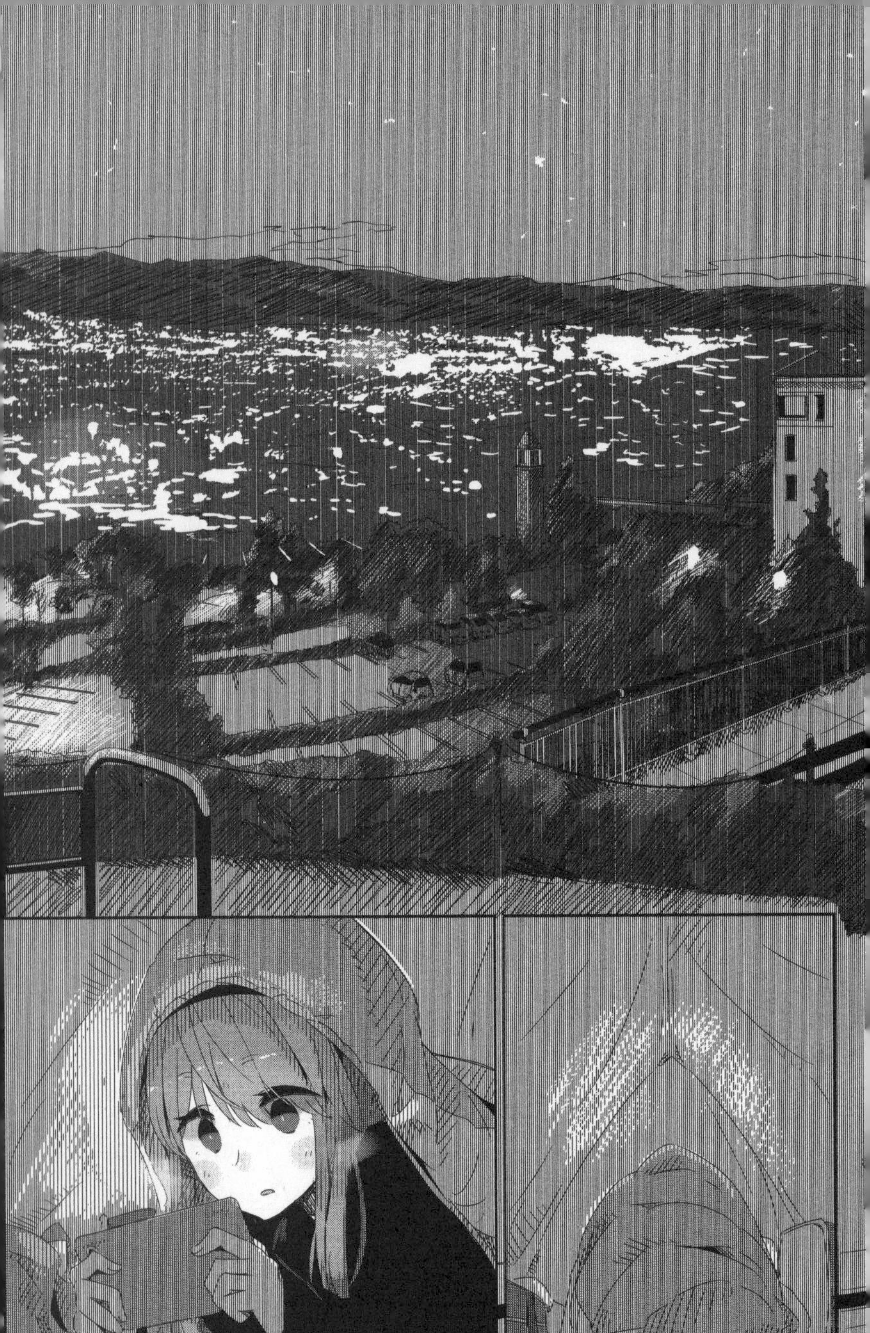

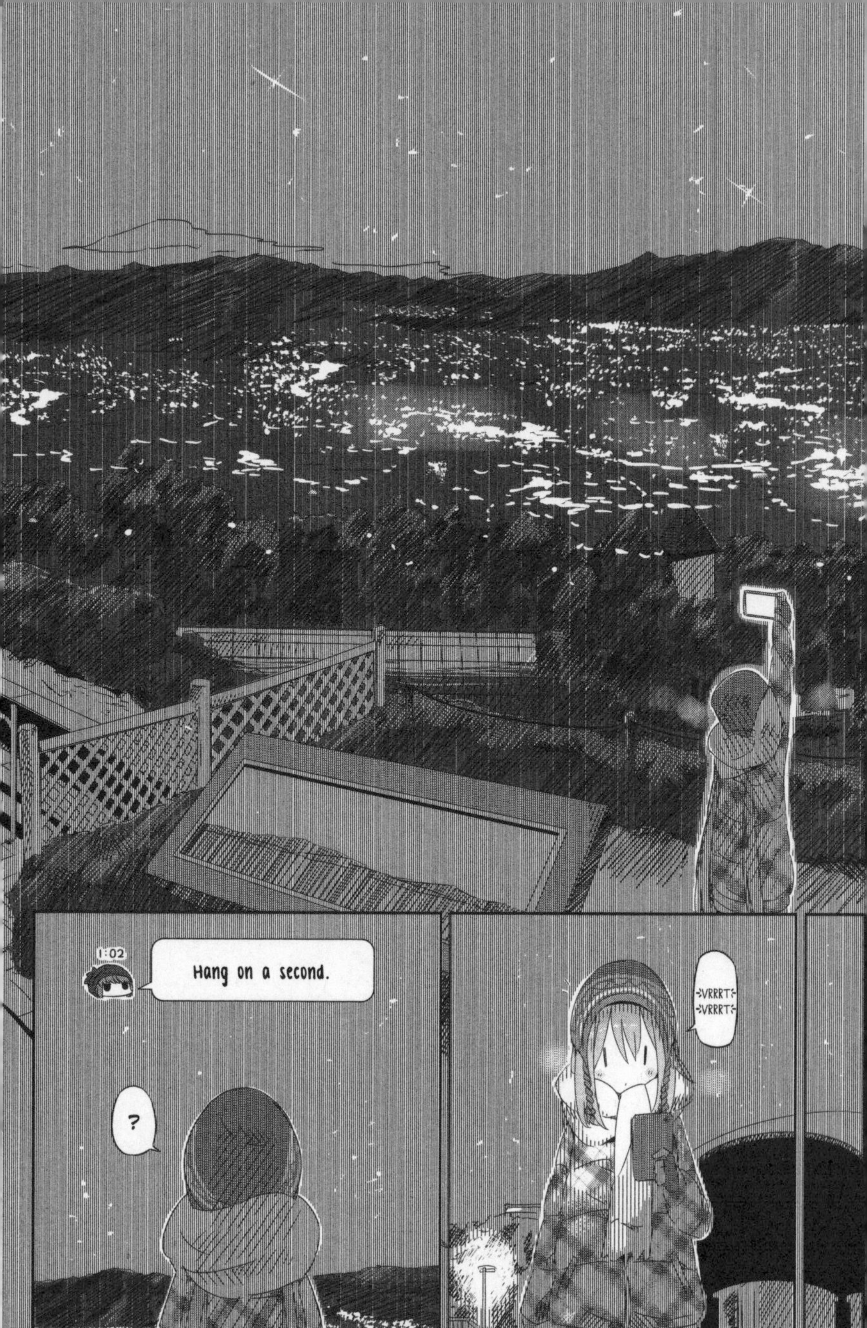
VRRRT
VRRRT
1:02
Hang on a second.
?

BRRR
...

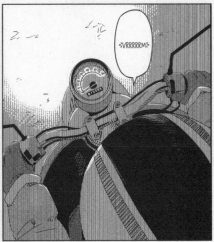

VRRRRRM

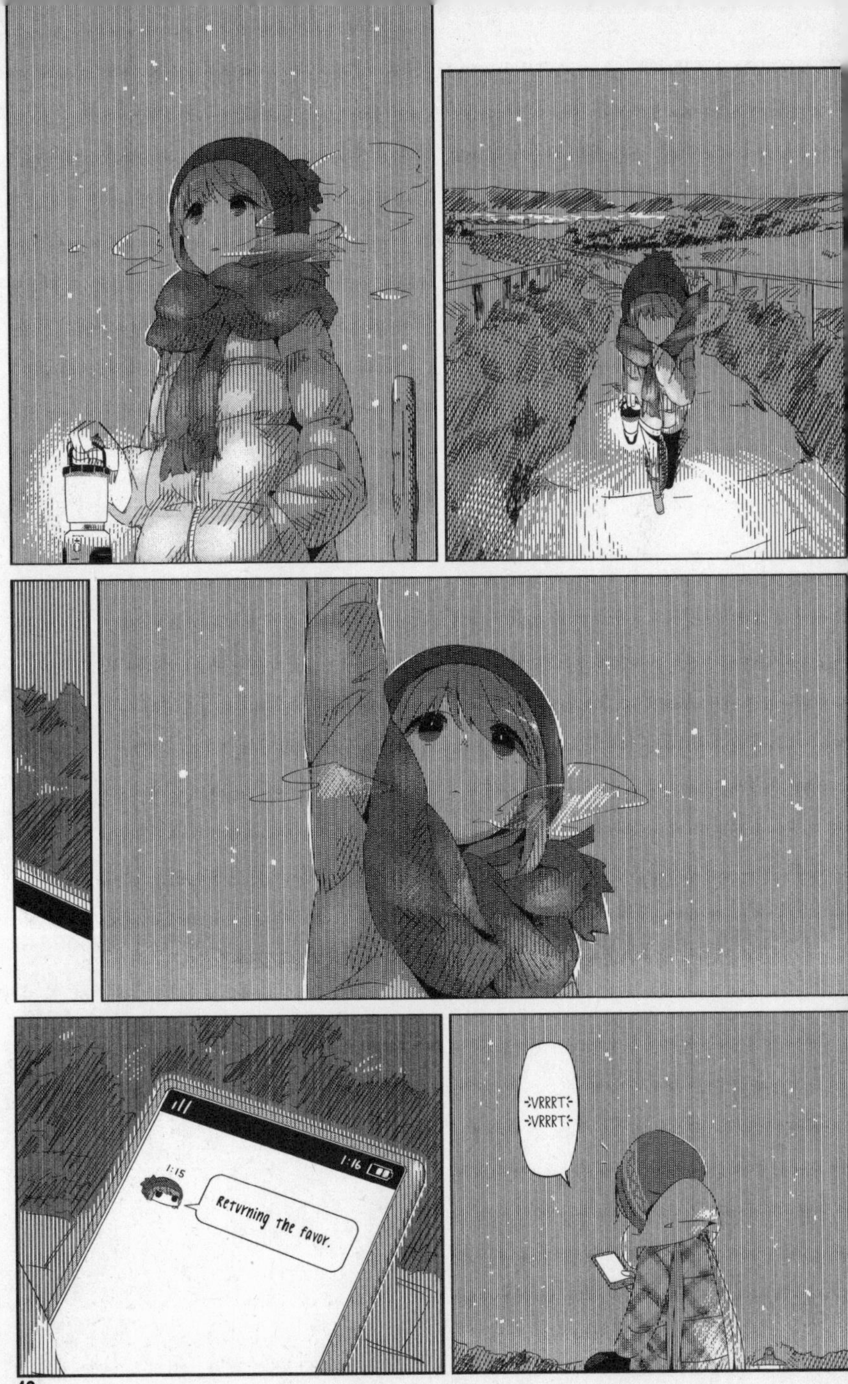

-VRRRT-
-VRRRT-
1:16
1:15
Returning the favor.

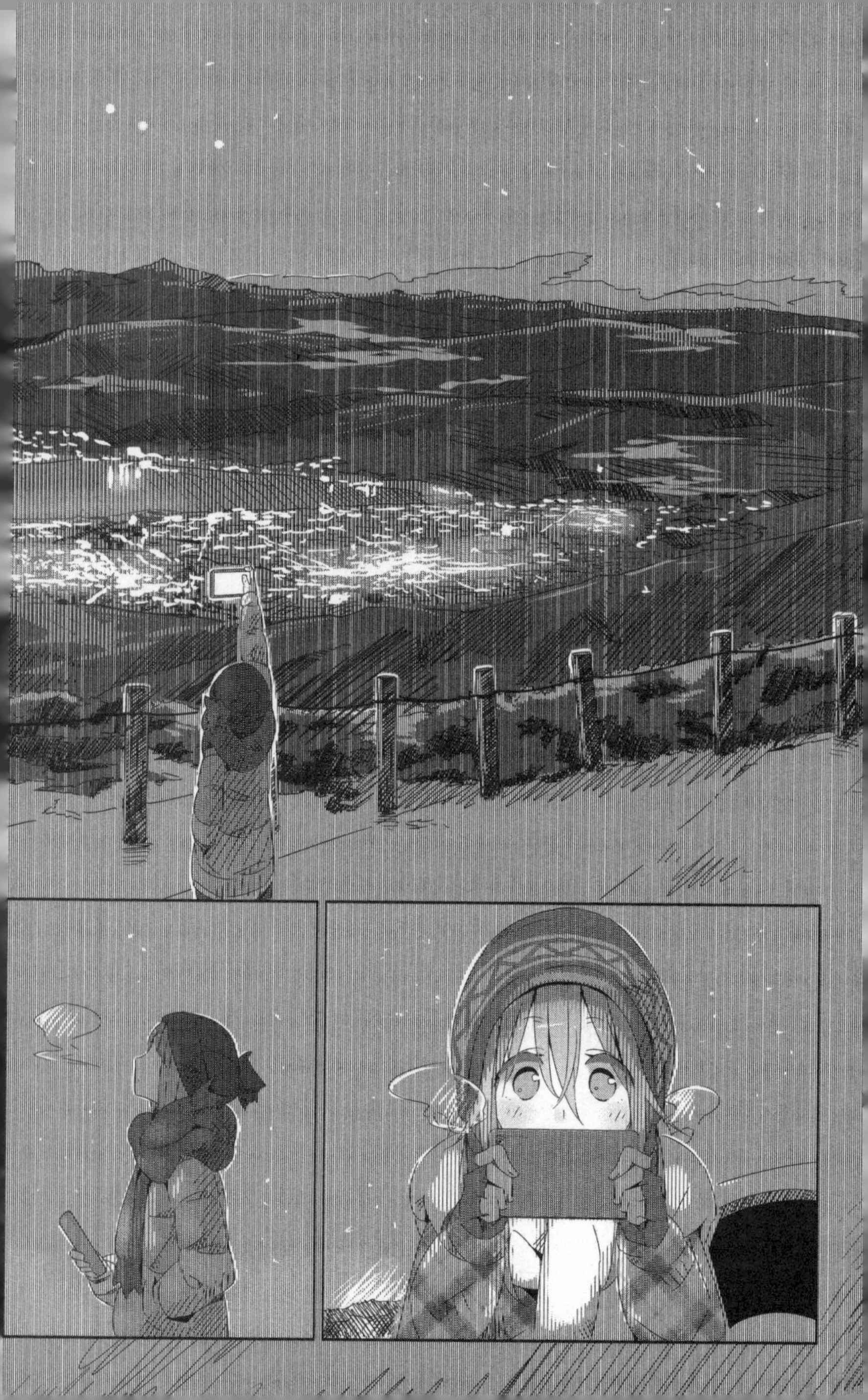

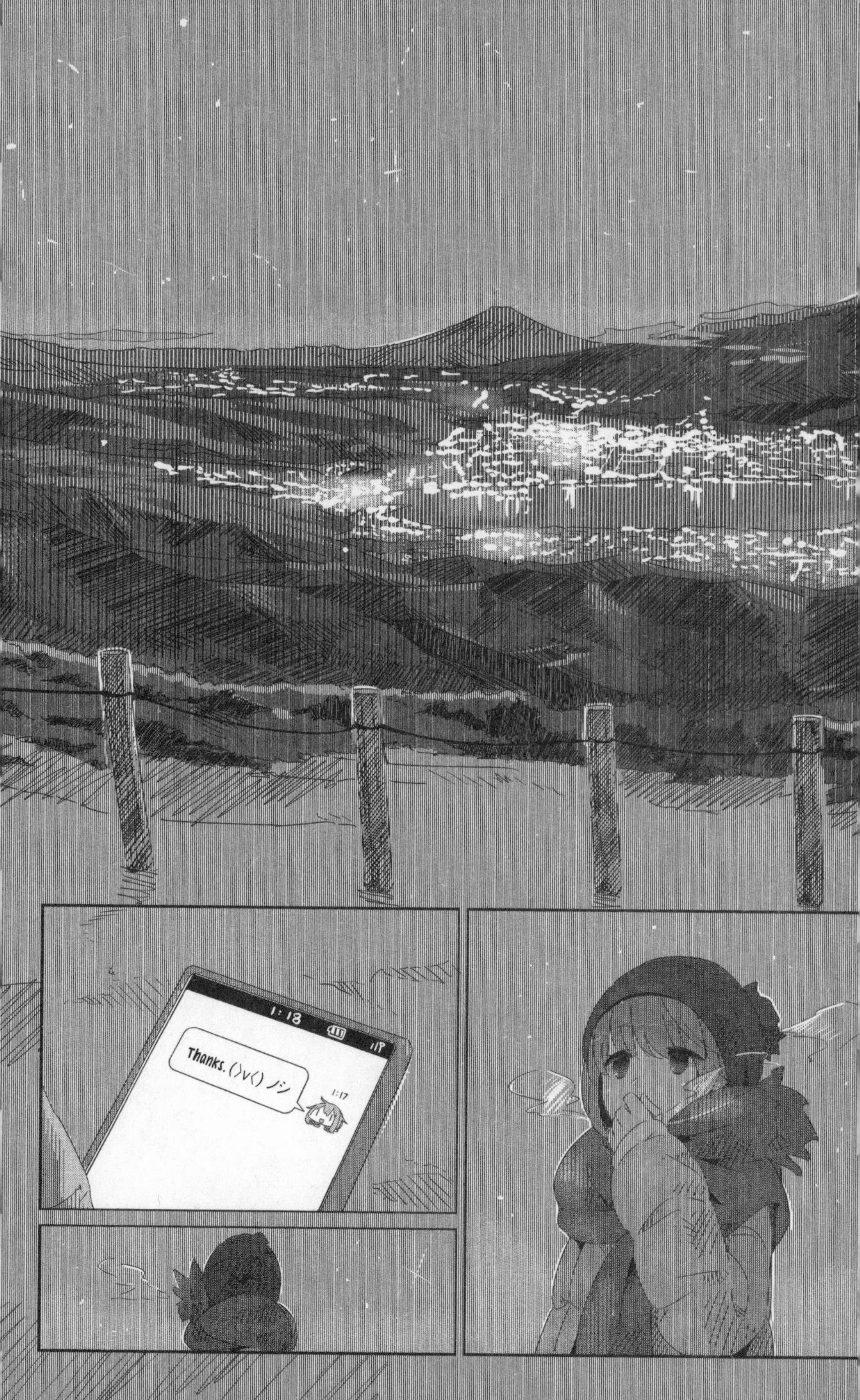
1:18
Thanks. ( )v( ) ノシ
1:17

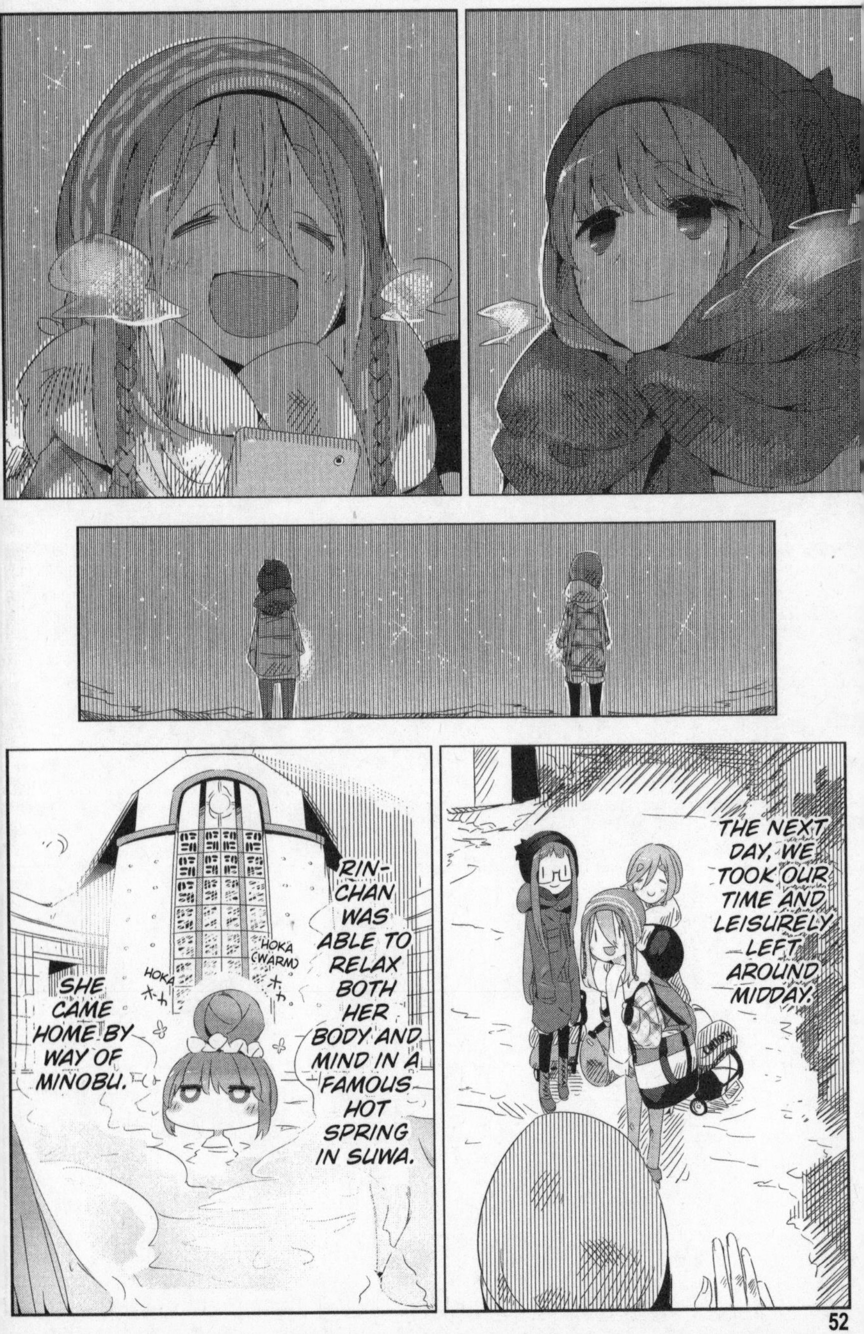
THE NEXT DAY, WE TOOK OUR TIME AND LEISURELY LEFT AROUND MIDDAY.
RIN-CHAN WAS ABLE TO RELAX BOTH HER BODY AND MIND IN A FAMOUS HOT SPRING IN SUWA.
HOKA (WARM) ホカ
HOKA ホカ
SHE CAME HOME BY WAY OF MINOBU.

CHAPTER 9 SOUVENIRS AND AFTER-SCHOOL YAKINIKU DISCOURSE

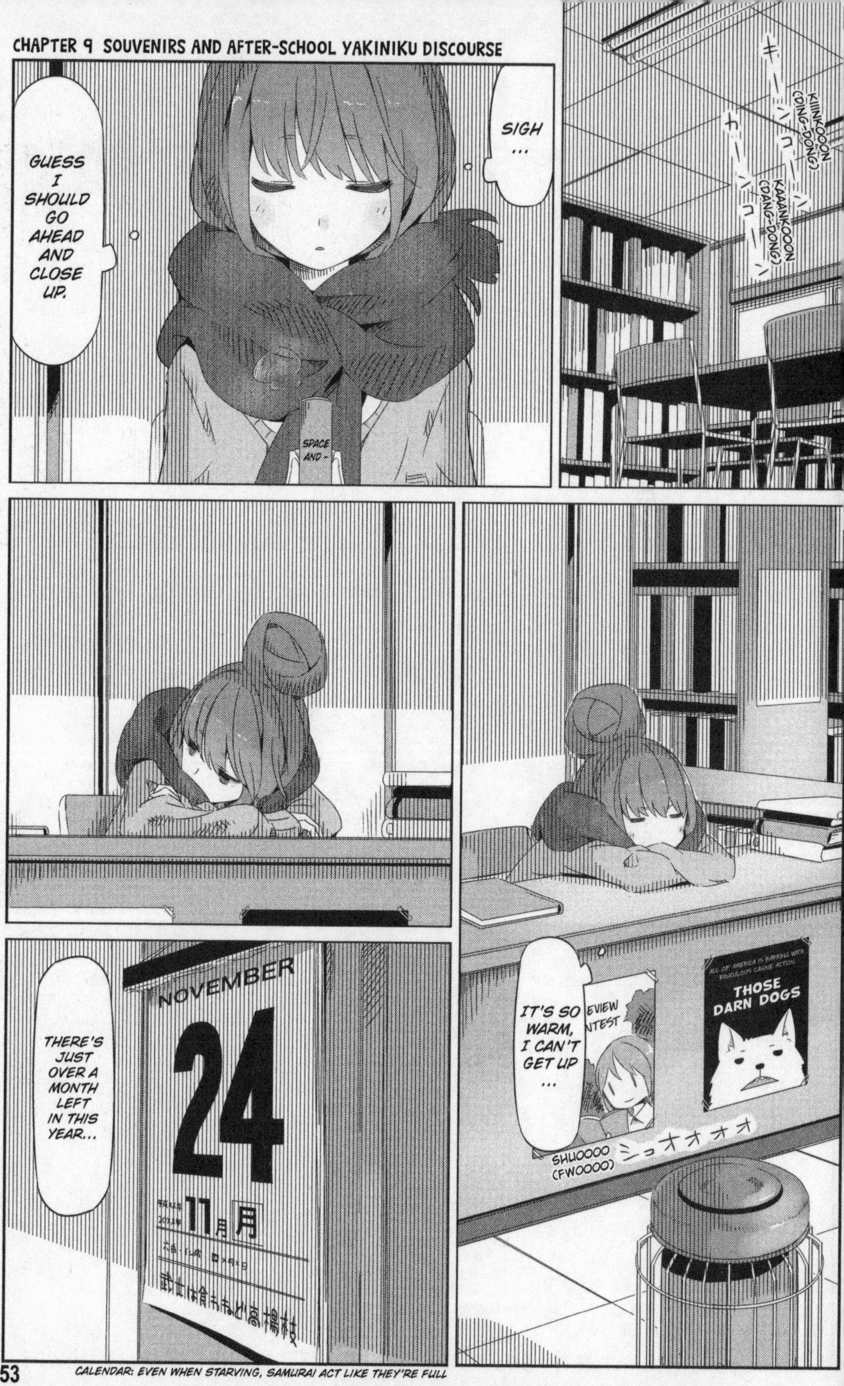
キーンコーン
KIIINKOOON (DING-DONG)
カーンコーン
KAAANKOOON (DANG-DONG)
SIGH ...
GUESS I SHOULD GO AHEAD AND CLOSE UP.
SPACE AND -
IT'S SO WARM, I CAN'T GET UP ...
ALL OF AMERICA IS BARKING WITH RIDICULOUS CANINE ACTION
THOSE DARN DOGS
EVIEW
NTEST
SHUOOOO (FWOOOO)
シュオオオオ
THERE'S JUST OVER A MONTH LEFT IN THIS YEAR...
NOVEMBER
24
11月
月

CALENDAR: EVEN WHEN STARVING, SAMURAI ACT LIKE THEY'RE FULL

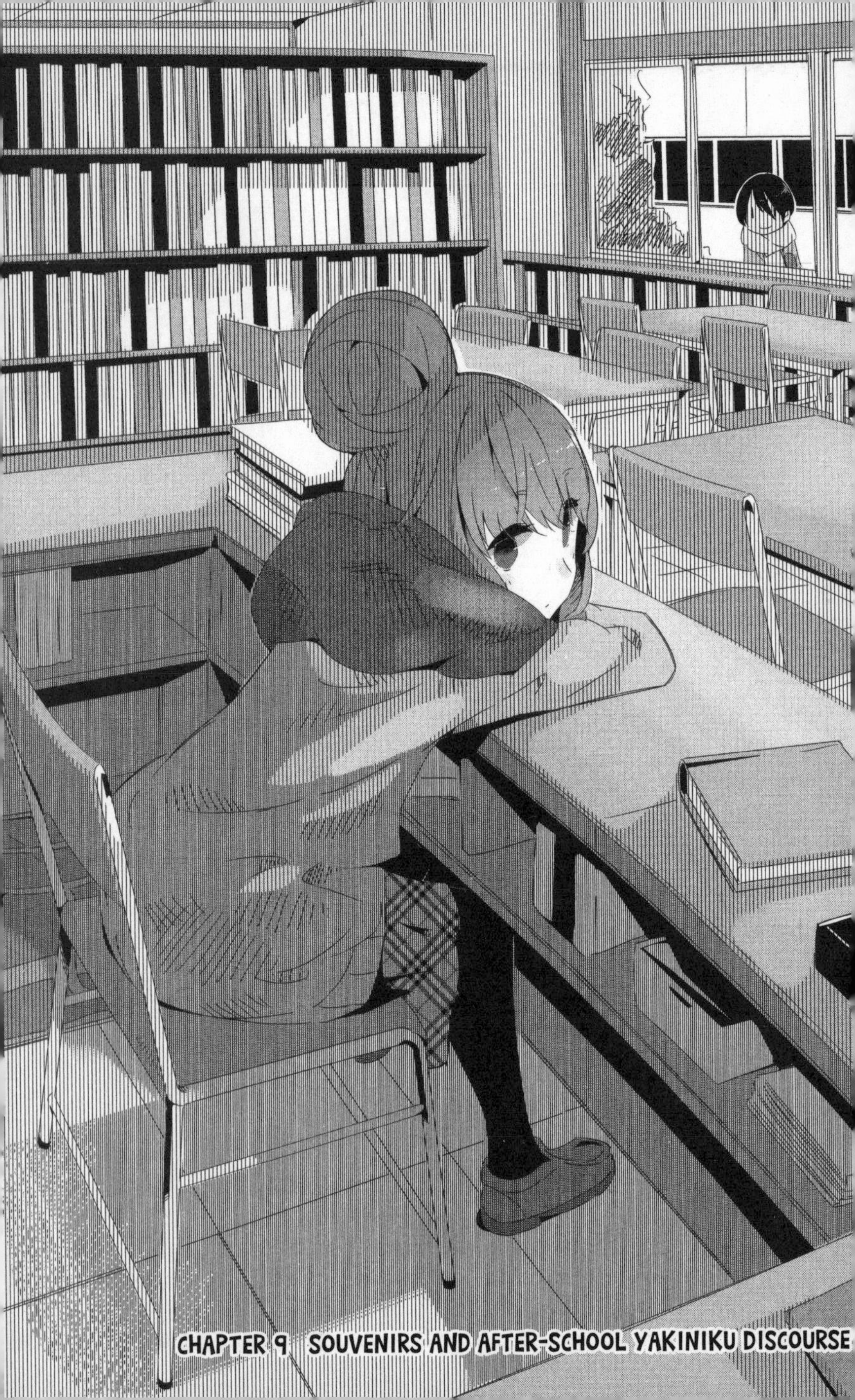

CHAPTER 9 SOUVENIRS AND AFTER-SCHOOL YAKINIKU DISCOURSE

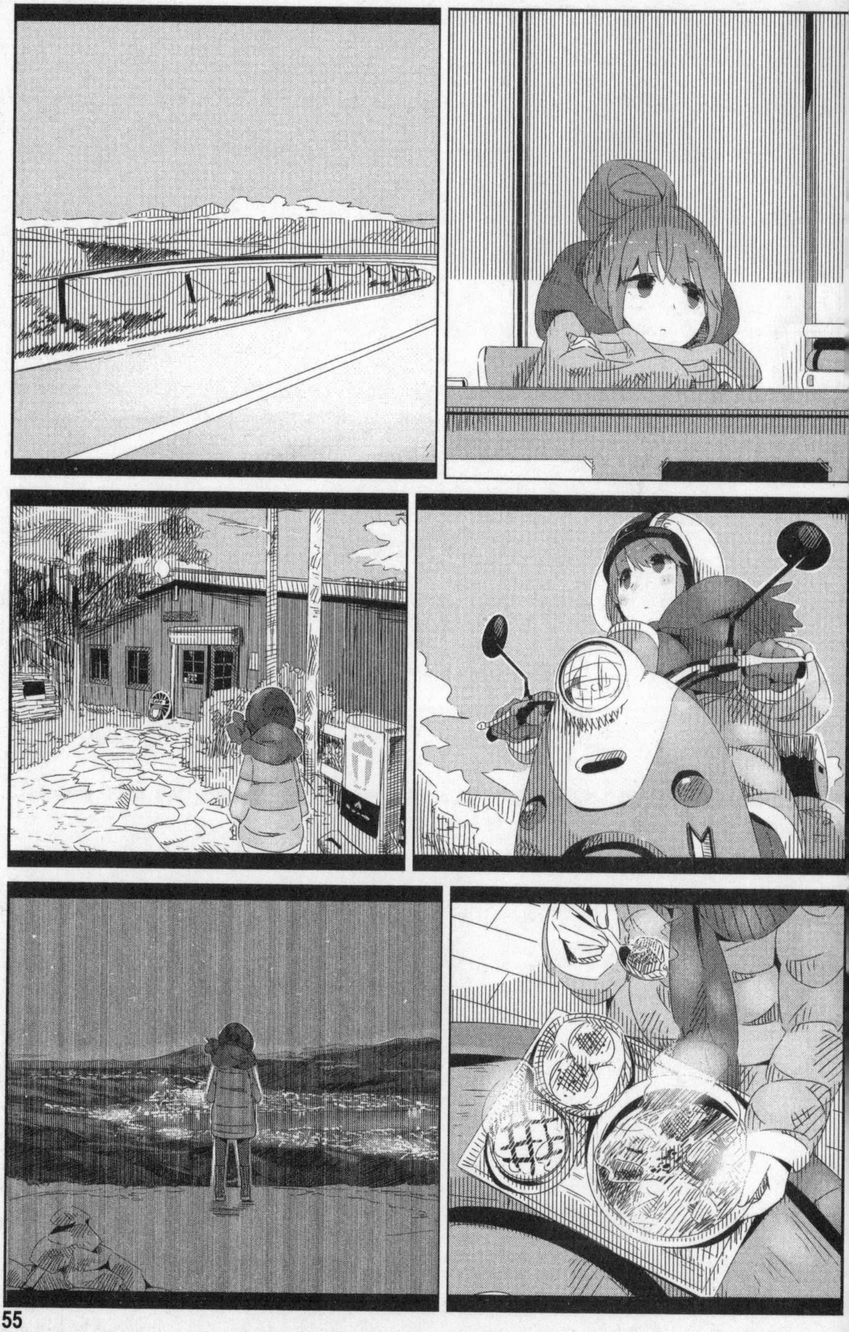

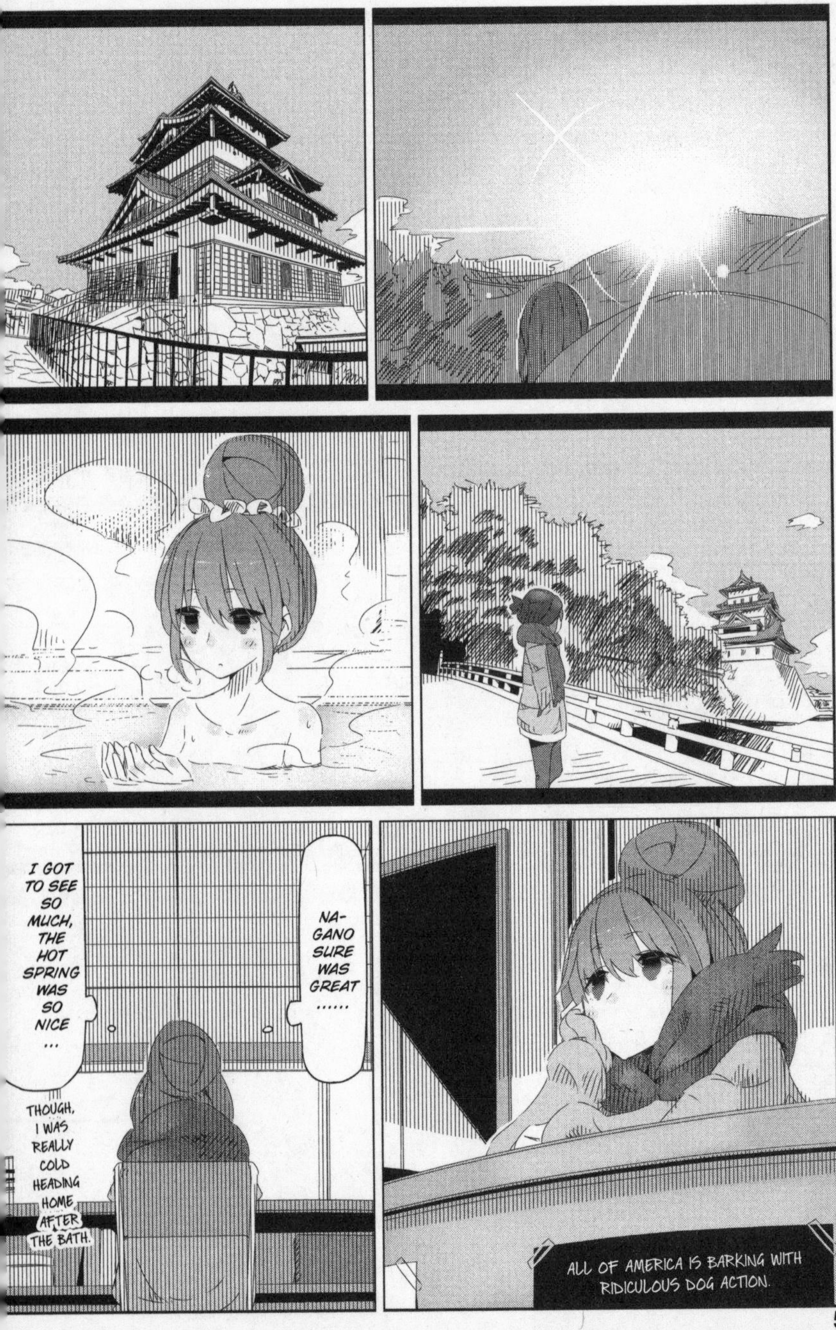
ALL OF AMERICA IS BARKING WITH RIDICULOUS DOG ACTION.
NA-GANO SURE WAS GREAT......
I GOT TO SEE SO MUCH, THE HOT SPRING WAS SO NICE ...
THOUGH, I WAS REALLY COLD HEADING HOME AFTER THE BATH.

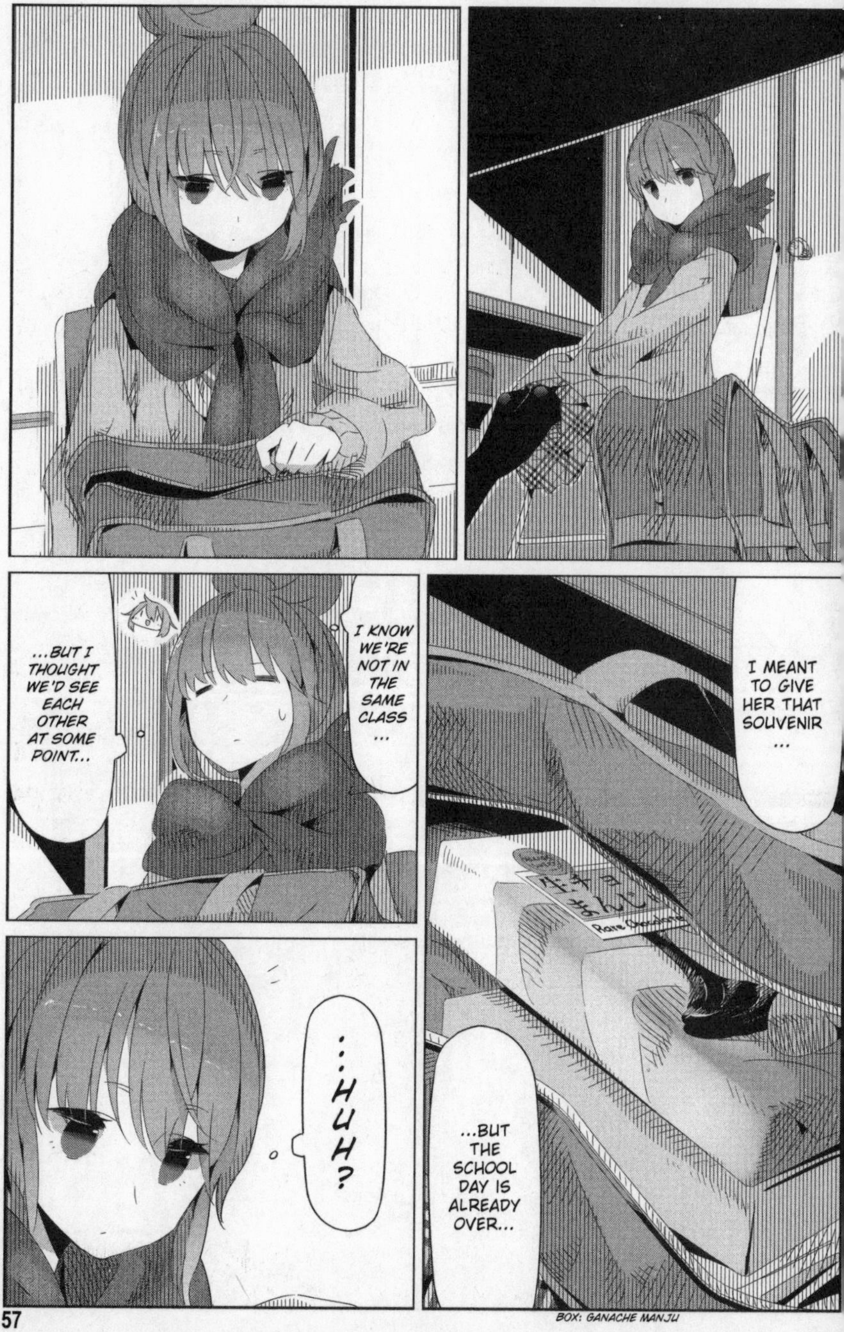
I MEANT TO GIVE HER THAT SOUVENIR...
...BUT THE SCHOOL DAY IS ALREADY OVER...
I KNOW WE'RE NOT IN THE SAME CLASS...
...BUT I THOUGHT WE'D SEE EACH OTHER AT SOME POINT...
...HUH?

BOX: GANACHE MANJU

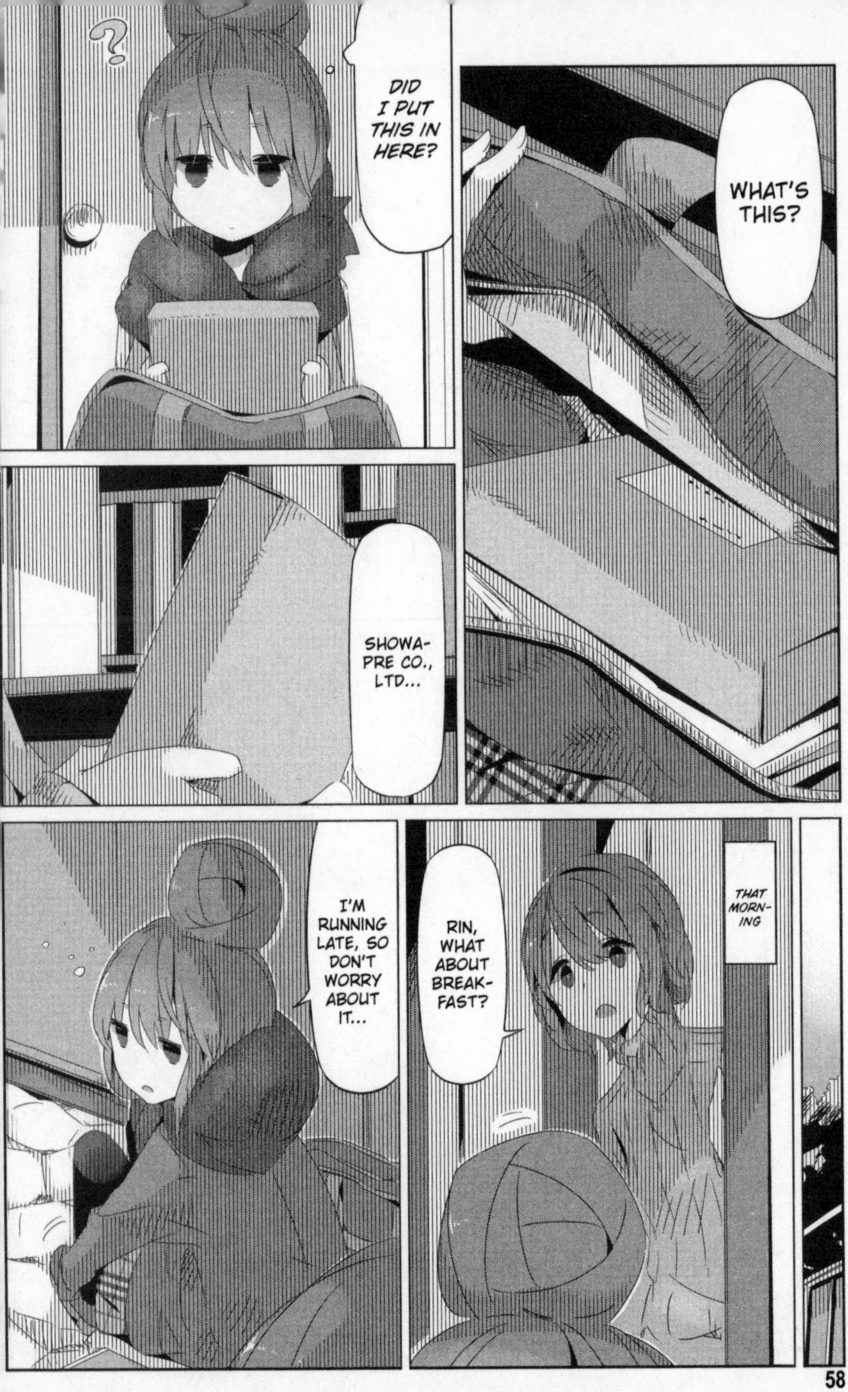
WHAT'S THIS?
DID I PUT THIS IN HERE?
SHOWA-PRE CO., LTD...
THAT MORNING
RIN, WHAT ABOUT BREAK-FAST?
I'M RUNNING LATE, SO DON'T WORRY ABOUT IT...

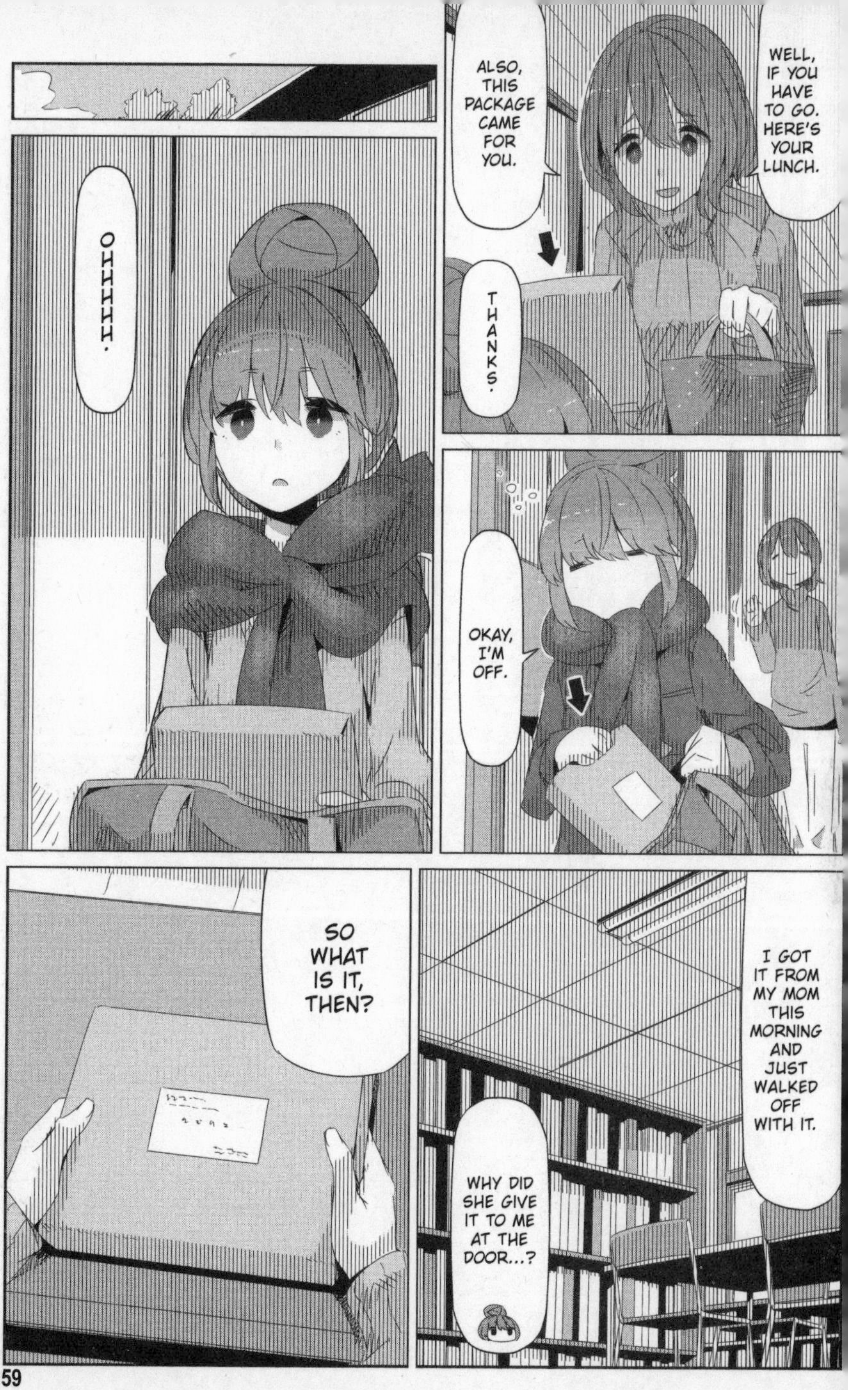
WELL, IF YOU HAVE TO GO. HERE'S YOUR LUNCH.
ALSO, THIS PACKAGE CAME FOR YOU.
THANKS.
OKAY, I'M OFF.
OHHHHH.
I GOT IT FROM MY MOM THIS MORNING AND JUST WALKED OFF WITH IT.
WHY DID SHE GIVE IT TO ME AT THE DOOR...?
SO WHAT IS IT, THEN?

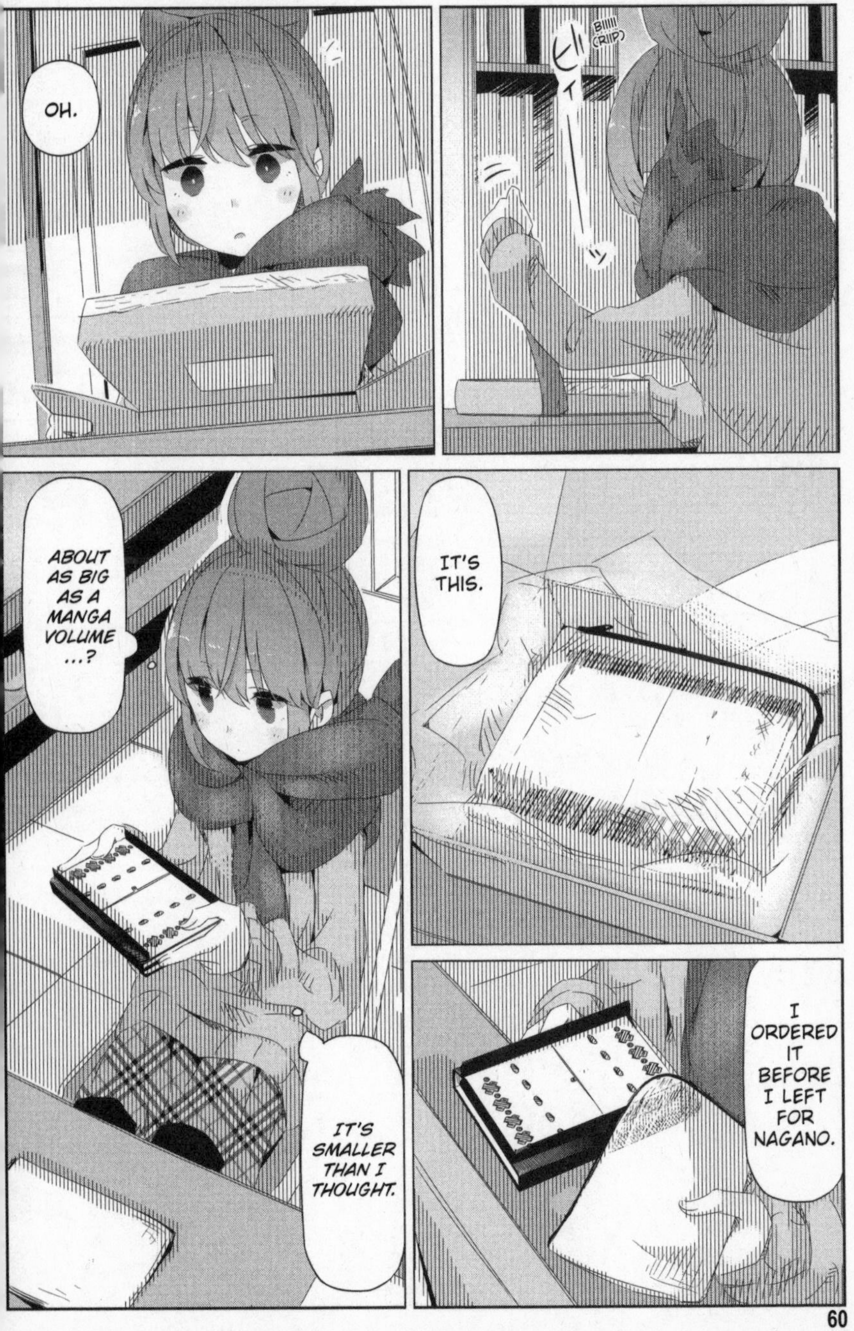
BIIIII (RIIP)
OH.
IT'S THIS.
I ORDERED IT BEFORE I LEFT FOR NAGANO.
ABOUT AS BIG AS A MANGA VOLUME ...?
IT'S SMALLER THAN I THOUGHT.

KASHA
(CLACK)

KYORO
(GLANCE?)

KYORO
(GLANCE?)

KYU
(SQUEAK)

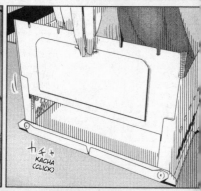

KACHA
(CLICK)

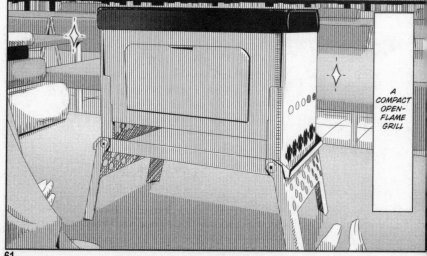

A COMPACT OPEN-FLAME GRILL

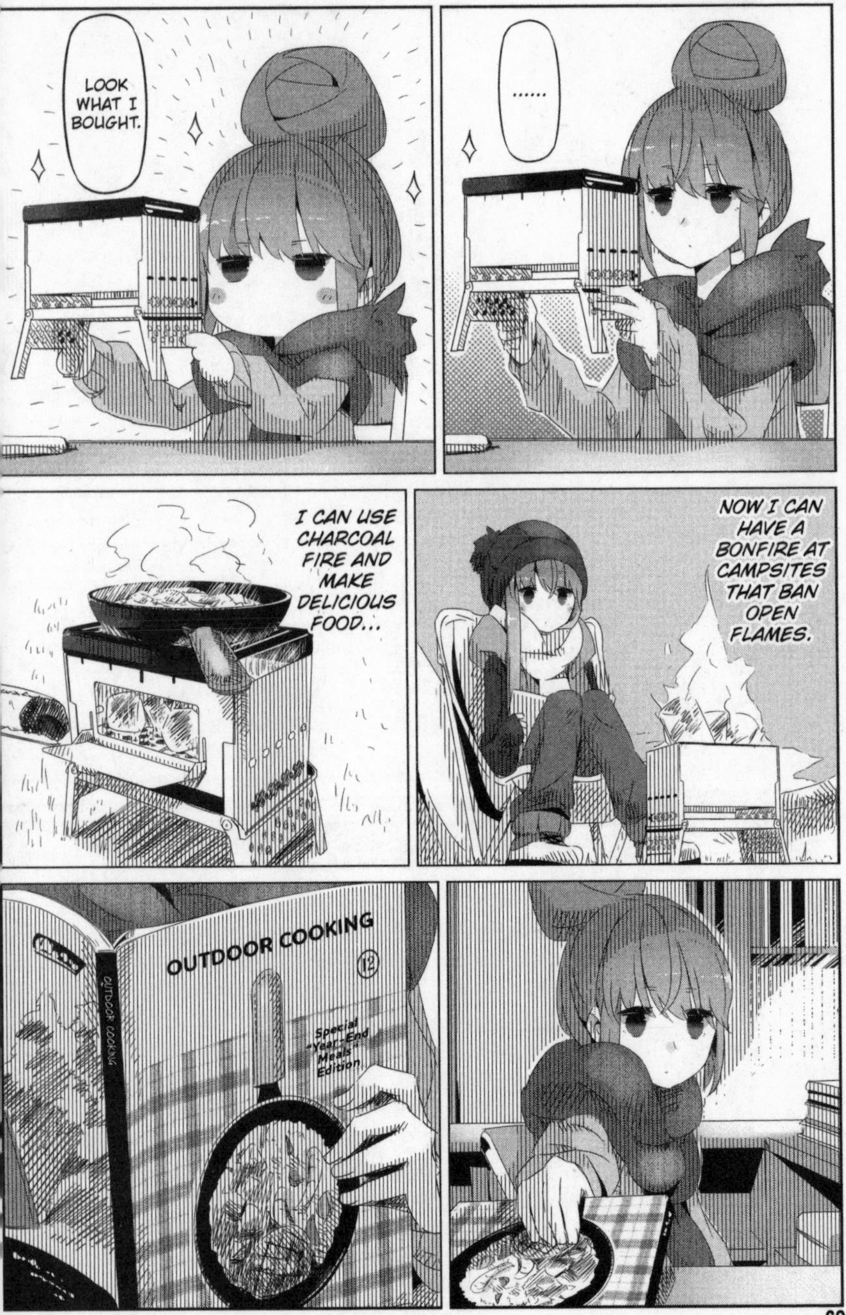
......
LOOK WHAT I BOUGHT.
NOW I CAN HAVE A BONFIRE AT CAMPSITES THAT BAN OPEN FLAMES.
I CAN USE CHARCOAL FIRE AND MAKE DELICIOUS FOOD...
OUTDOOR COOKING
12
OUTDOOR COOKING
Special "Year-End Meals" Edition

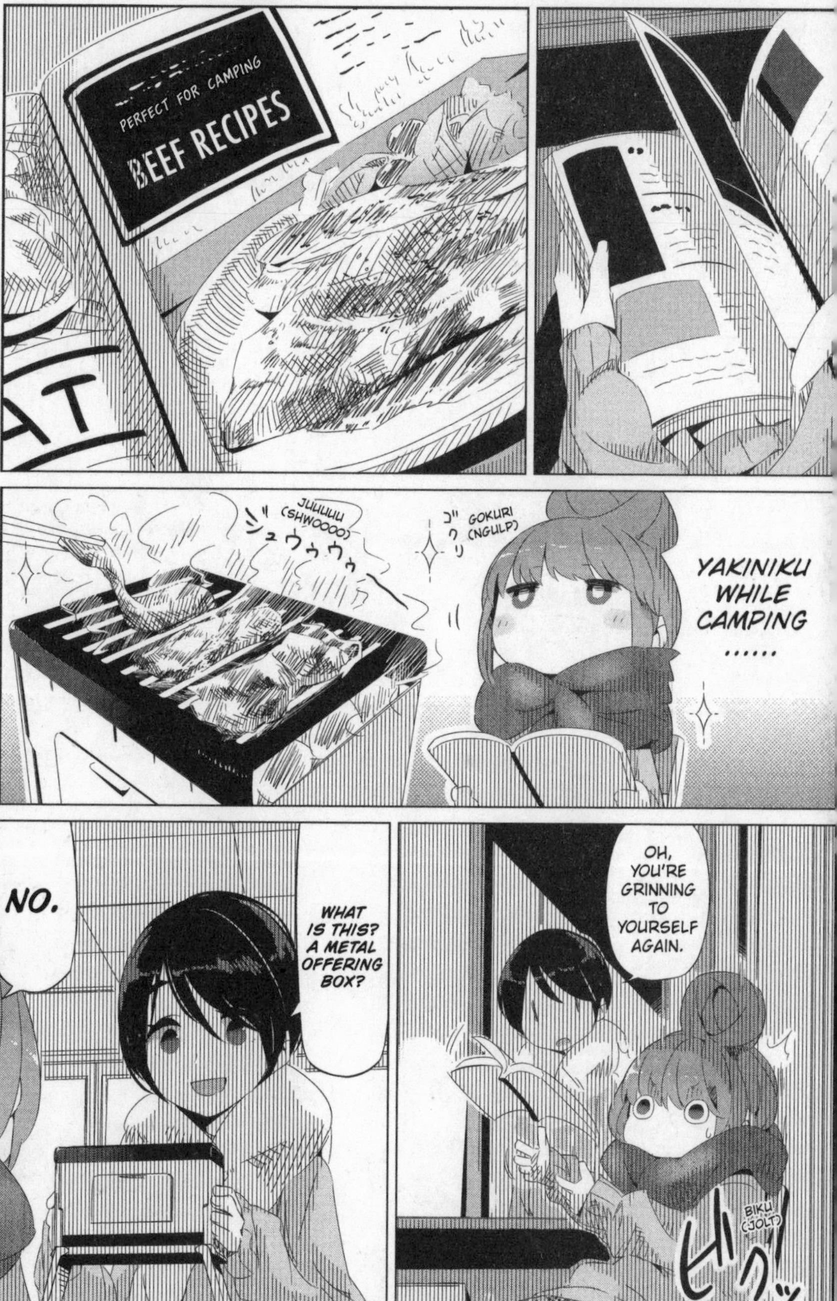
PERFECT FOR CAMPING
BEEF RECIPES
AT
YAKINIKU WHILE CAMPING ......
GOKURI (NGULP)
JUUUUU (SHWOOOO)
OH, YOU'RE GRINNING TO YOURSELF AGAIN.
BIKU (JOLT)
WHAT IS THIS? A METAL OFFERING BOX?
NO.

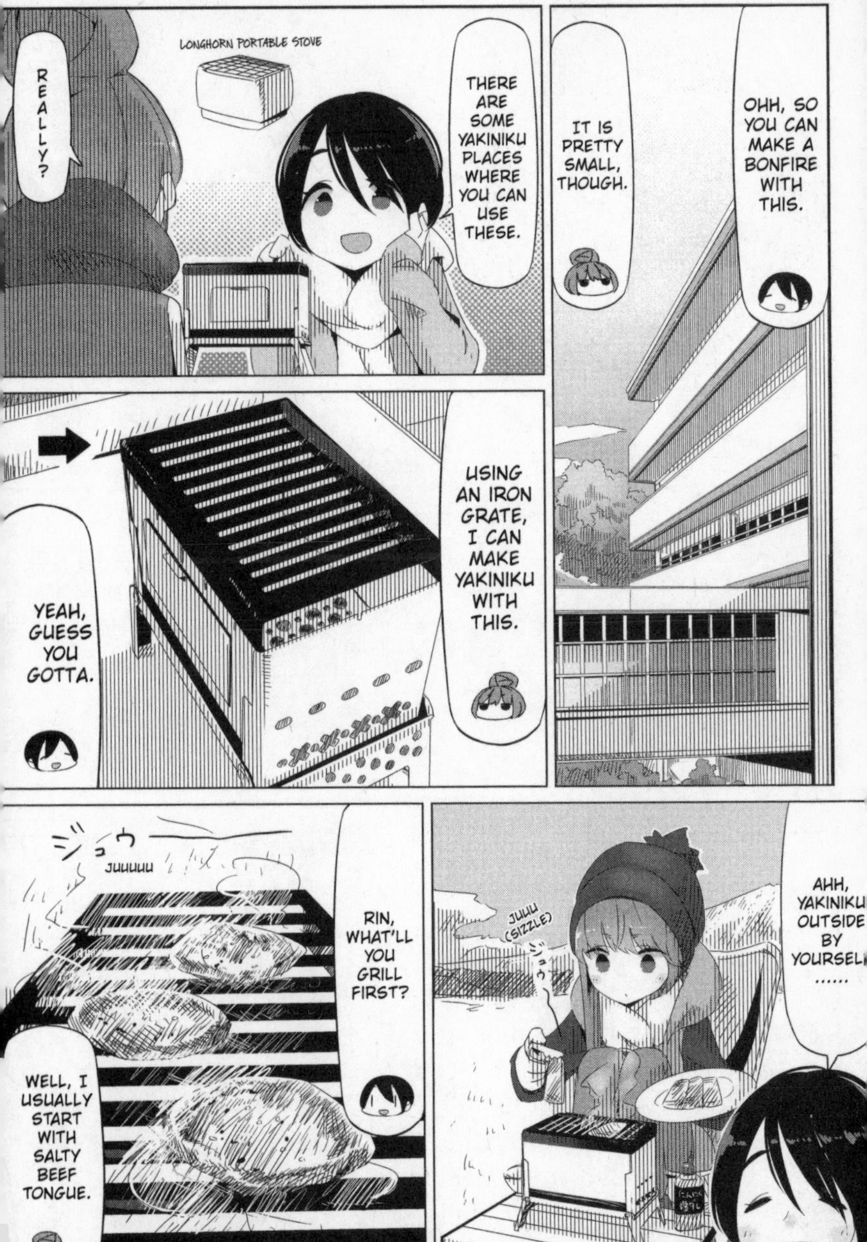
OHH, SO YOU CAN MAKE A BONFIRE WITH THIS.
IT IS PRETTY SMALL, THOUGH.
LONGHORN PORTABLE STOVE
THERE ARE SOME YAKINIKU PLACES WHERE YOU CAN USE THESE.
REALLY?
USING AN IRON GRATE, I CAN MAKE YAKINIKU WITH THIS.
YEAH, GUESS YOU GOTTA.
AHH, YAKINIKU OUTSIDE BY YOURSEL ......
ジュウ
JUUU (SIZZLE)
ジュウー
JUUUUU
RIN, WHAT'LL YOU GRILL FIRST?
WELL, I USUALLY START WITH SALTY BEEF TONGUE.

BOTTLE : GARLIC SALT SAUCE

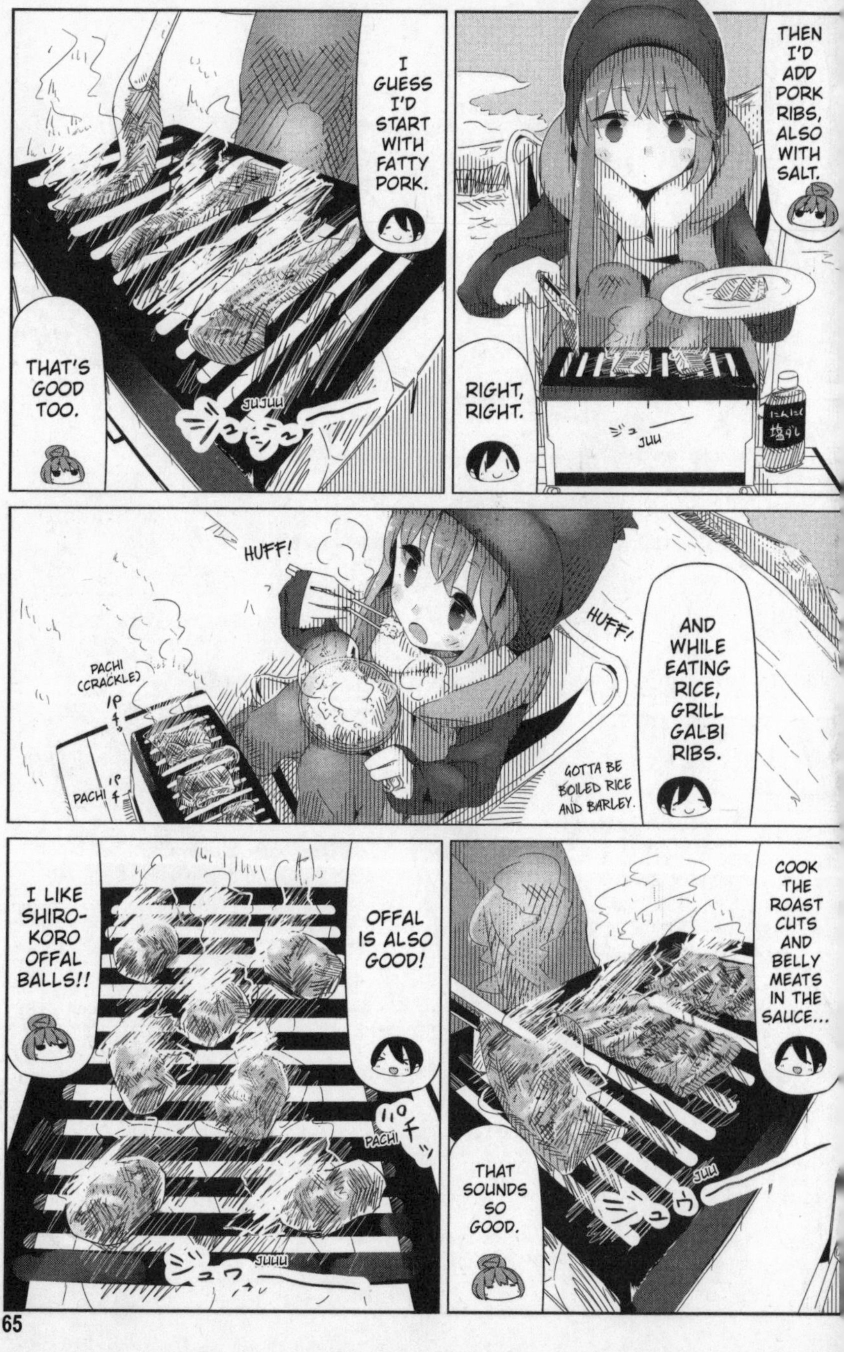
THEN I'D ADD PORK RIBS, ALSO WITH SALT.
RIGHT, RIGHT.
JUU
I GUESS I'D START WITH FATTY PORK.
THAT'S GOOD TOO.
JUJUU
AND WHILE EATING RICE, GRILL GALBI RIBS.
GOTTA BE BOILED RICE AND BARLEY.
HUFF!
HUFF!
PACHI (CRACKLE)
PACHI
COOK THE ROAST CUTS AND BELLY MEATS IN THE SAUCE...
THAT SOUNDS SO GOOD.
JUU
OFFAL IS ALSO GOOD!
I LIKE SHIRO-KORO OFFAL BALLS!!
PACHI
JUUU

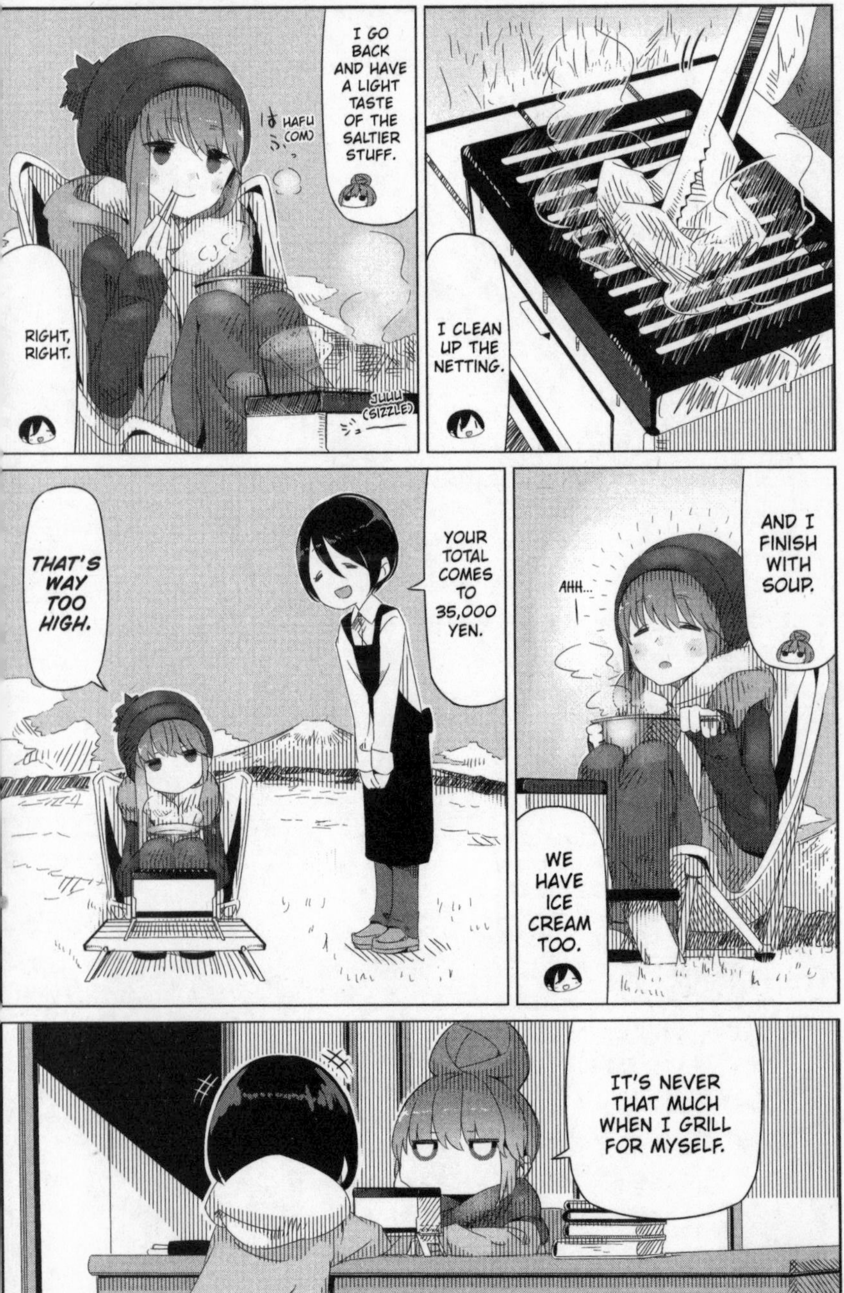
I CLEAN UP THE NETTING.
I GO BACK AND HAVE A LIGHT TASTE OF THE SALTIER STUFF.
はふ
HAFU (OM)
RIGHT, RIGHT.
ジュー
JUUU (SIZZLE)
AND I FINISH WITH SOUP.
AHH...
WE HAVE ICE CREAM TOO.
YOUR TOTAL COMES TO 35,000 YEN.
THAT'S WAY TOO HIGH.
IT'S NEVER THAT MUCH WHEN I GRILL FOR MYSELF.

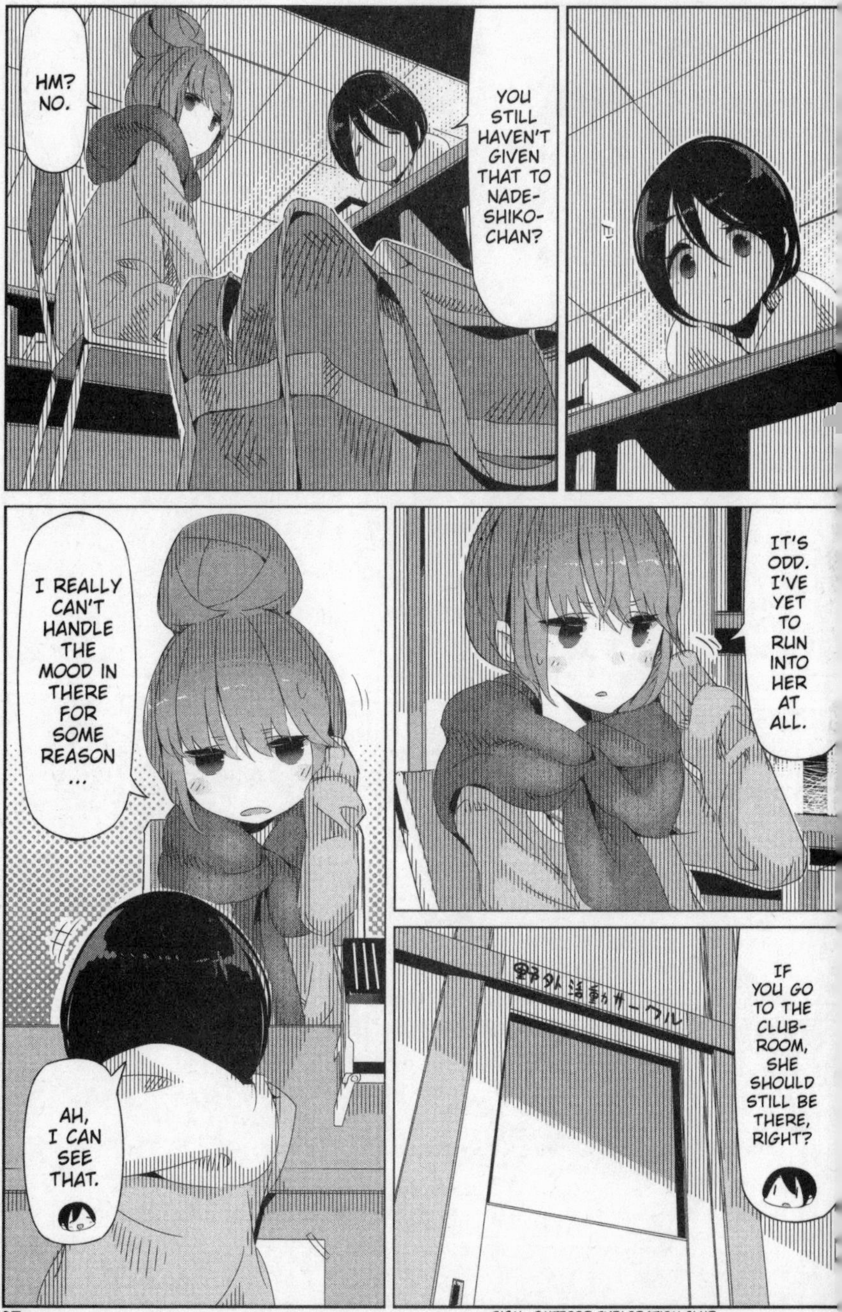
YOU STILL HAVEN'T GIVEN THAT TO NADE-SHIKO-CHAN?
HM? NO.
IT'S ODD. I'VE YET TO RUN INTO HER AT ALL.
野外活動サークル
IF YOU GO TO THE CLUB-ROOM, SHE SHOULD STILL BE THERE, RIGHT?
I REALLY CAN'T HANDLE THE MOOD IN THERE FOR SOME REASON ...
AH, I CAN SEE THAT.

SIGN : OUTDOOR EXPLORATION CLUB

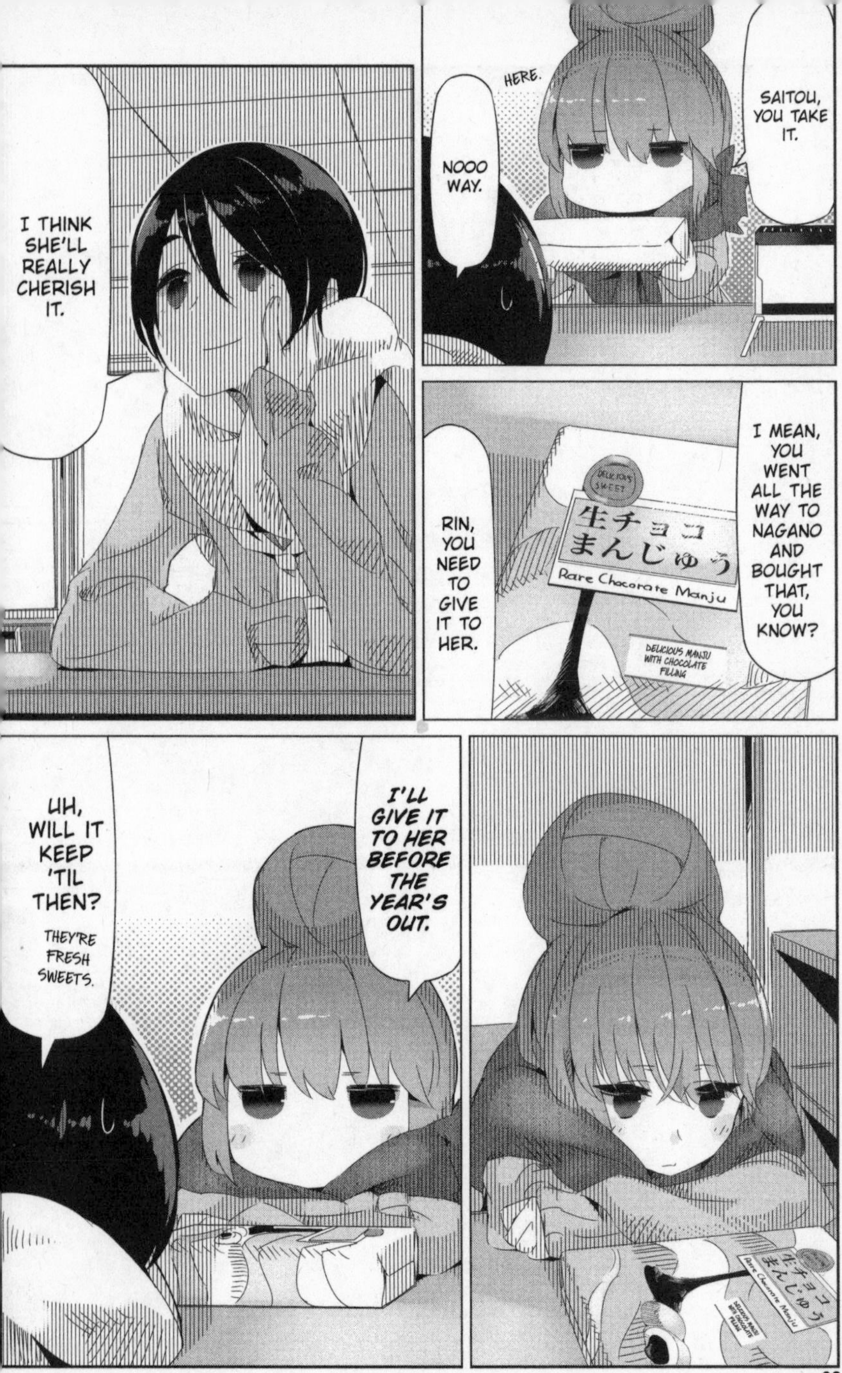
SAITOU, YOU TAKE IT.
HERE.
NOOO WAY.
I MEAN, YOU WENT ALL THE WAY TO NAGANO AND BOUGHT THAT, YOU KNOW?
DELICIOUS SWEET
生チョコまんじゅう
Rare Chocorate Manju
DELICIOUS MANJU WITH CHOCOLATE FILLING
RIN, YOU NEED TO GIVE IT TO HER.
I THINK SHE'LL REALLY CHERISH IT.
I'LL GIVE IT TO HER BEFORE THE YEAR'S OUT.
UH, WILL IT KEEP 'TIL THEN?
THEY'RE FRESH SWEETS.

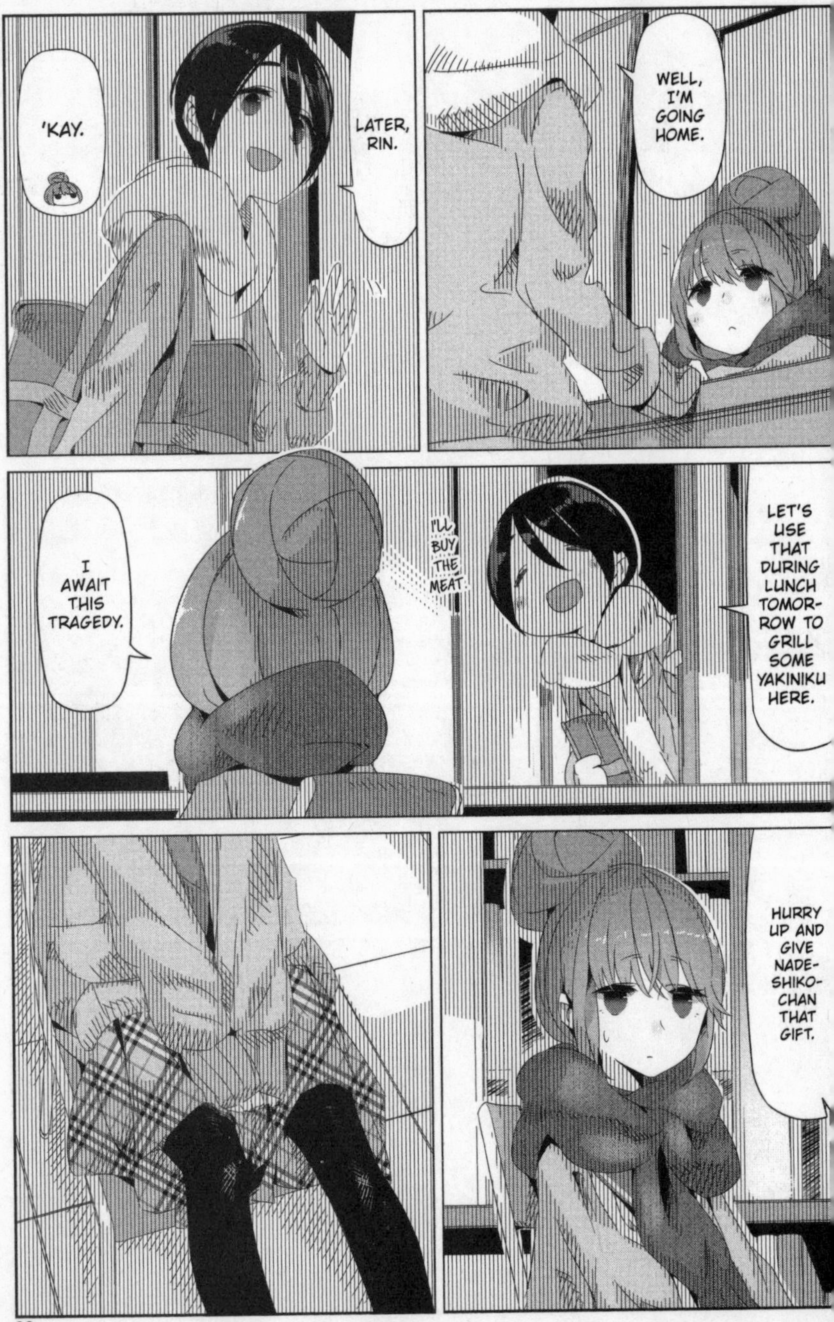
WELL, I'M GOING HOME.
LATER, RIN.
'KAY.
LET'S USE THAT DURING LUNCH TOMORROW TO GRILL SOME YAKINIKU HERE.
I'LL BUY THE MEAT.
I AWAIT THIS TRAGEDY.
HURRY UP AND GIVE NADESHIKO-CHAN THAT GIFT.

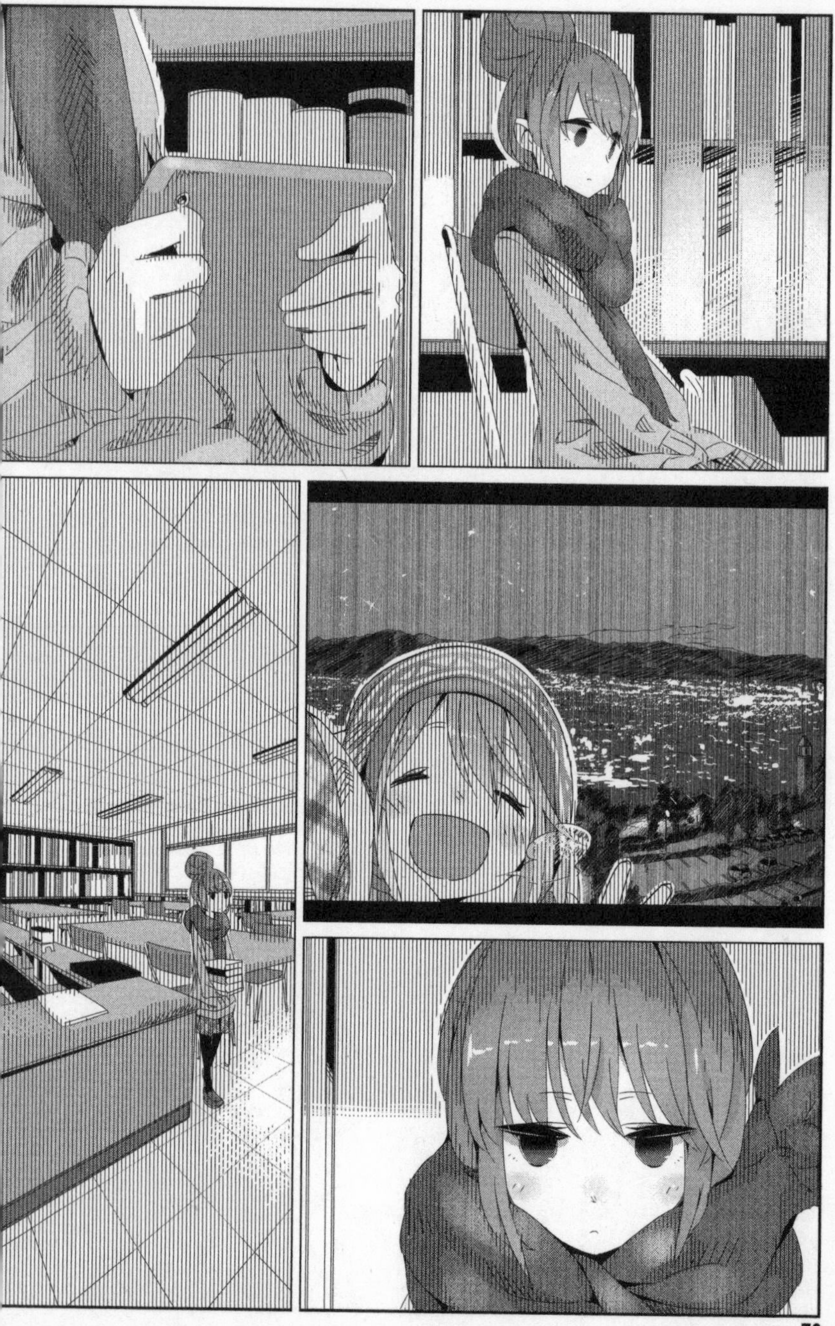

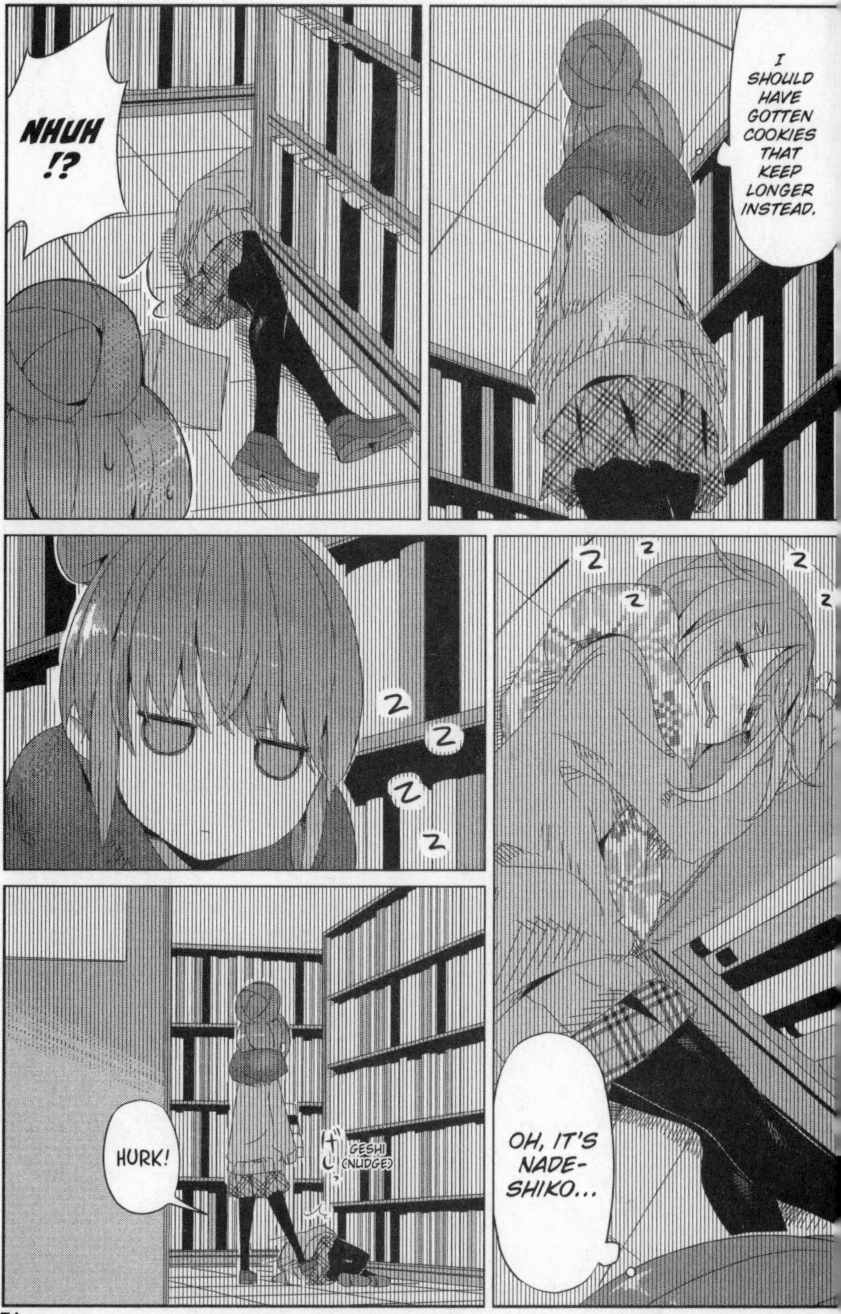
I SHOULD HAVE GOTTEN COOKIES THAT KEEP LONGER INSTEAD.
NHUH !?
Z Z Z Z Z
OH, IT'S NADE-SHIKO...
Z Z Z Z
げし GESHI (NUDGE)
HURK!

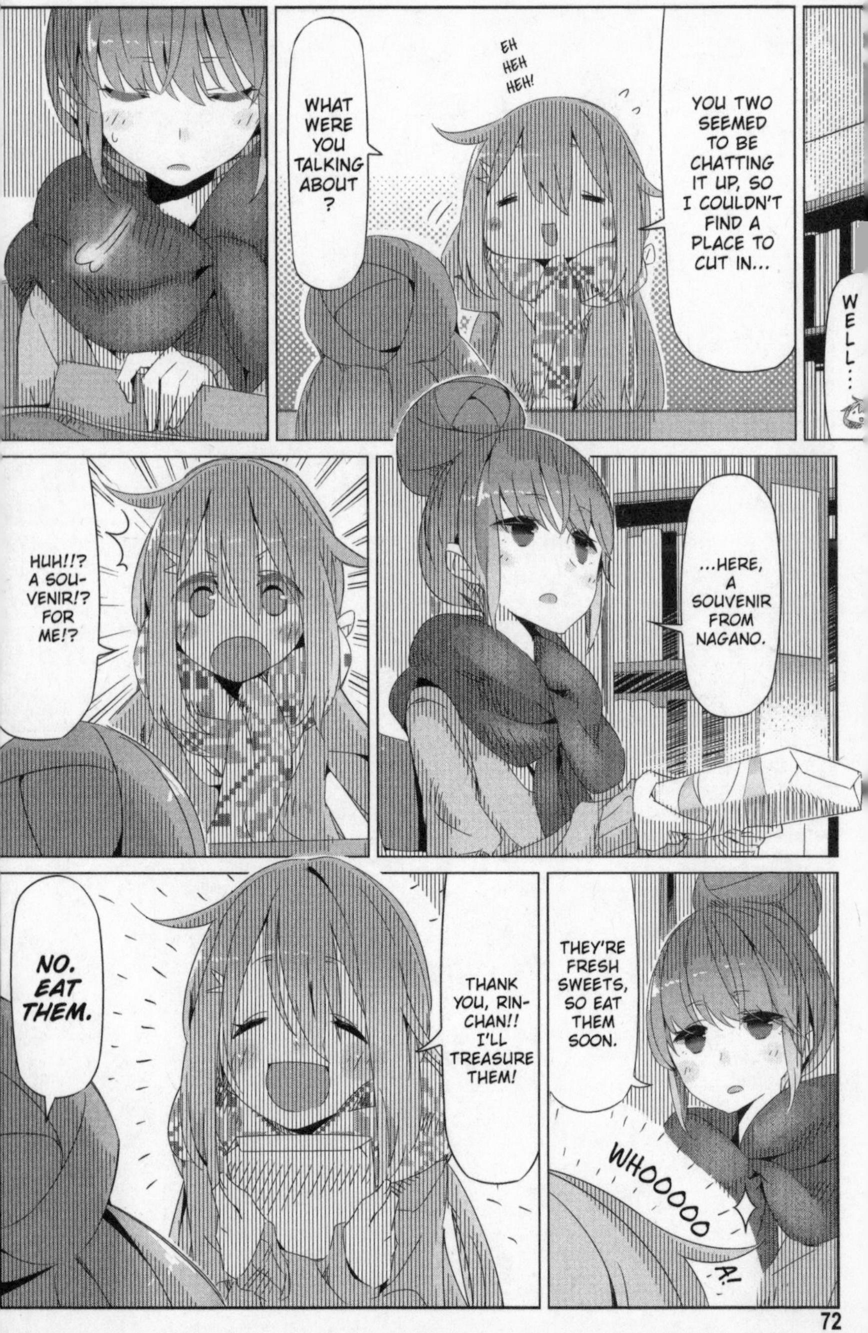

WELL...
YOU TWO SEEMED TO BE CHATTING IT UP, SO I COULDN'T FIND A PLACE TO CUT IN...
EH HEH HEH!
WHAT WERE YOU TALKING ABOUT?
...HERE, A SOUVENIR FROM NAGANO.
HUH!!? A SOU-VENIR!? FOR ME!?
THEY'RE FRESH SWEETS, SO EAT THEM SOON.
WHOOOOOA!
THANK YOU, RIN-CHAN!! I'LL TREASURE THEM!
NO. EAT THEM.

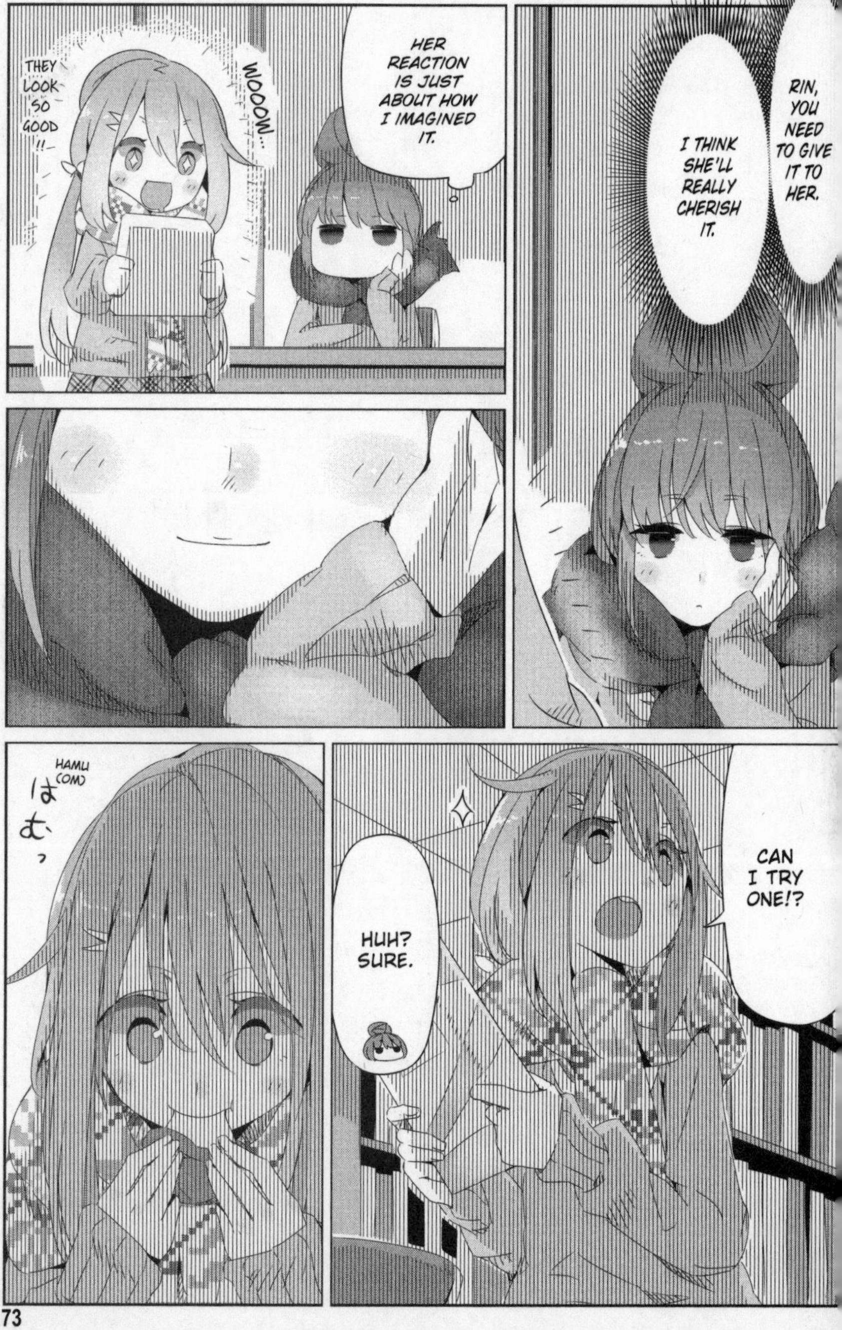
RIN, YOU NEED TO GIVE IT TO HER.
I THINK SHE'LL REALLY CHERISH IT.
HER REACTION IS JUST ABOUT HOW I IMAGINED IT.
WOOOW...
THEY LOOK SO GOOD!!
CAN I TRY ONE!?
HUH? SURE.
はむっ
HAMU (OM)

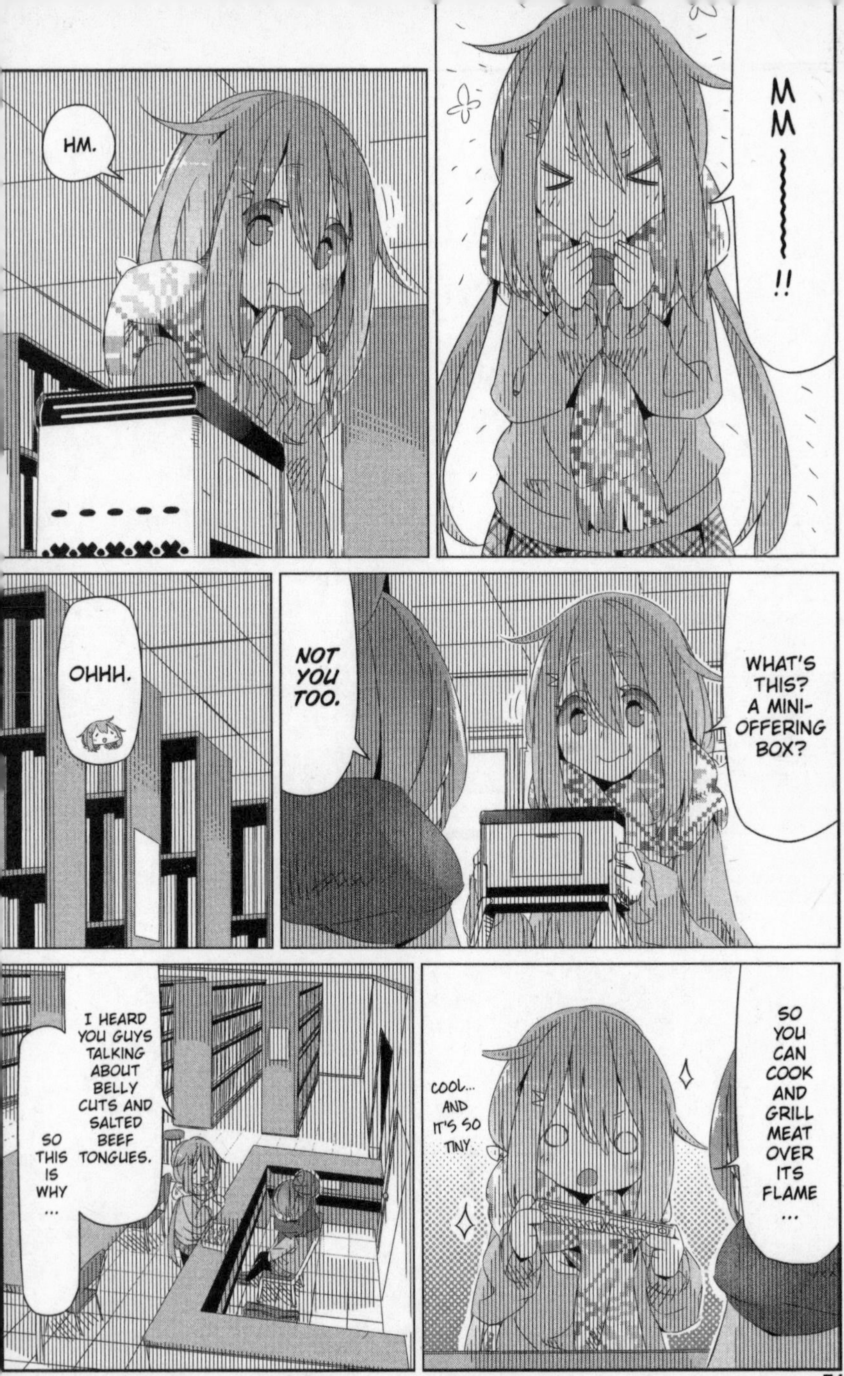
MMM~~~!!
HM.
WHAT'S THIS? A MINI-OFFERING BOX?
NOT YOU TOO.
OHHH.
SO YOU CAN COOK AND GRILL MEAT OVER ITS FLAME...
COOL... AND IT'S SO TINY.
I HEARD YOU GUYS TALKING ABOUT BELLY CUTS AND SALTED BEEF TONGUES.
SO THIS IS WHY...

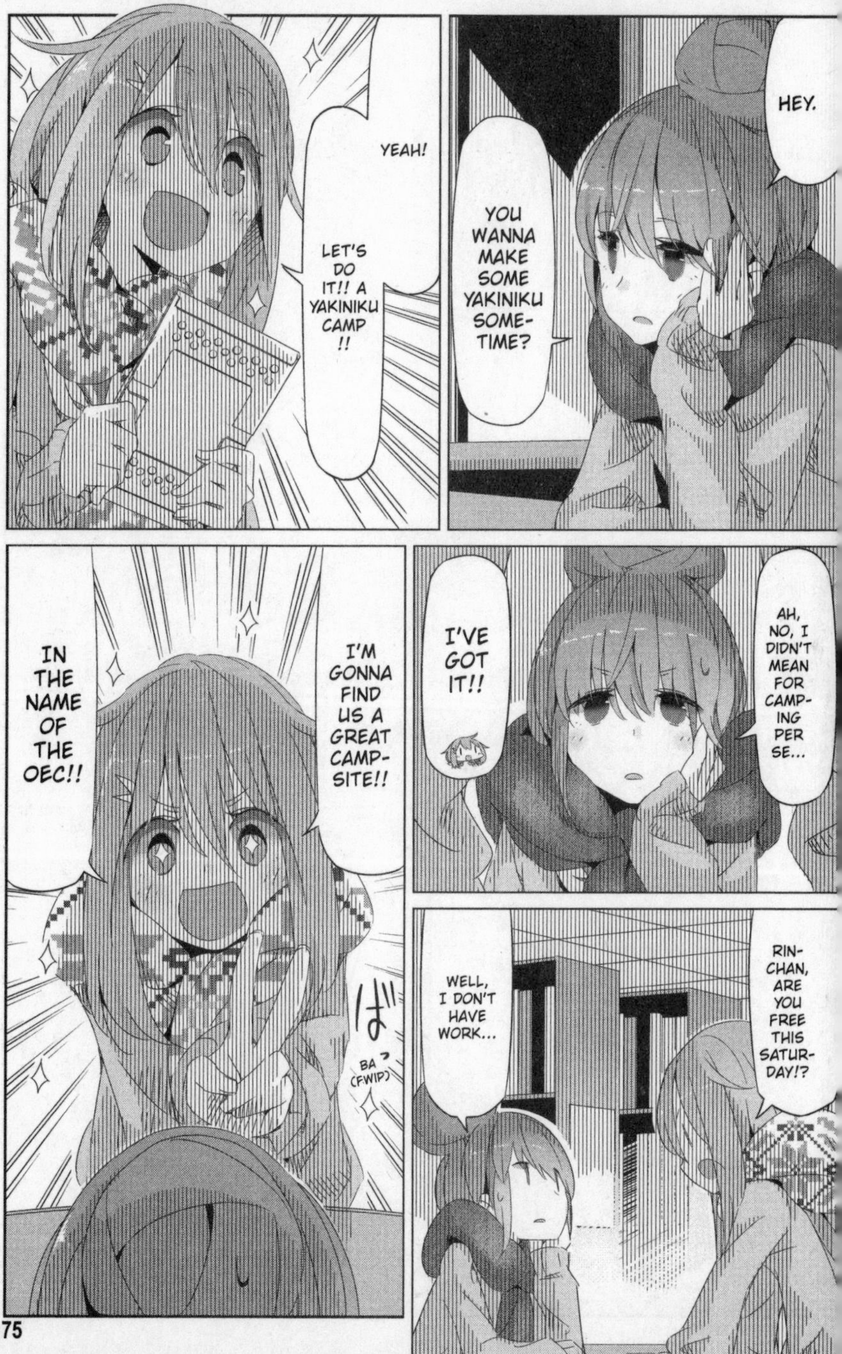
HEY.
YOU WANNA MAKE SOME YAKINIKU SOMETIME?
YEAH!
LET'S DO IT!! A YAKINIKU CAMP!!
AH, NO, I DIDN'T MEAN FOR CAMPING PER SE...
I'VE GOT IT!!
RIN-CHAN, ARE YOU FREE THIS SATURDAY!?
WELL, I DON'T HAVE WORK...
I'M GONNA FIND US A GREAT CAMPSITE!!
IN THE NAME OF THE OEC!!
ばっ
BA (FWIP)

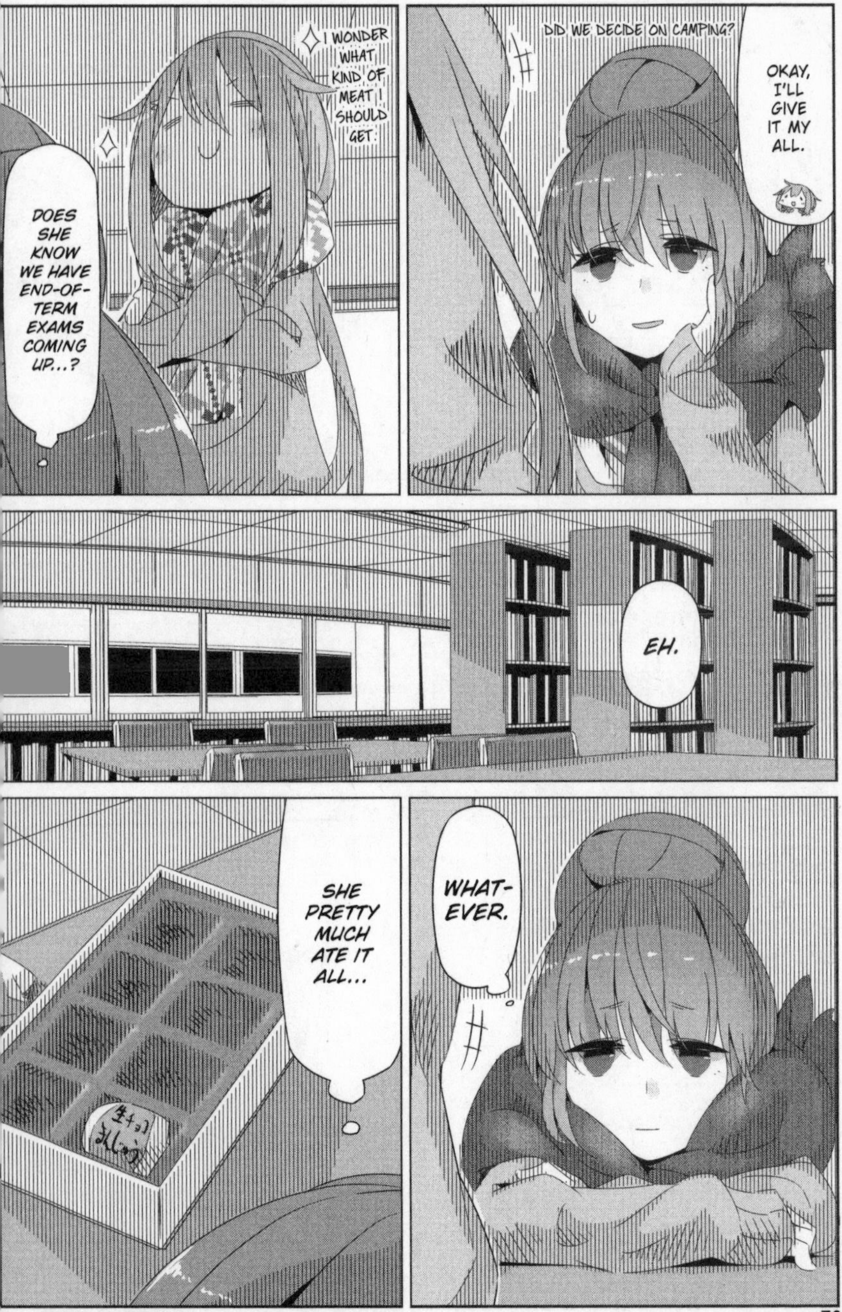
DID WE DECIDE ON CAMPING?
OKAY, I'LL GIVE IT MY ALL.
I WONDER WHAT KIND OF MEAT I SHOULD GET.
DOES SHE KNOW WE HAVE END-OF-TERM EXAMS COMING UP...?
EH.
WHAT-EVER.
SHE PRETTY MUCH ATE IT ALL...

WRAPPER: GANACHE MANJU

YAKINIKU...
ROAST CUT...
GALBI RIBS...
FATTY PORK...
じーっ
JIIIII (STARE)

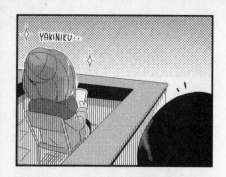

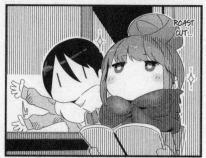

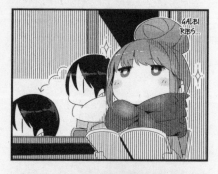

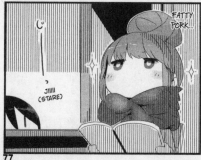

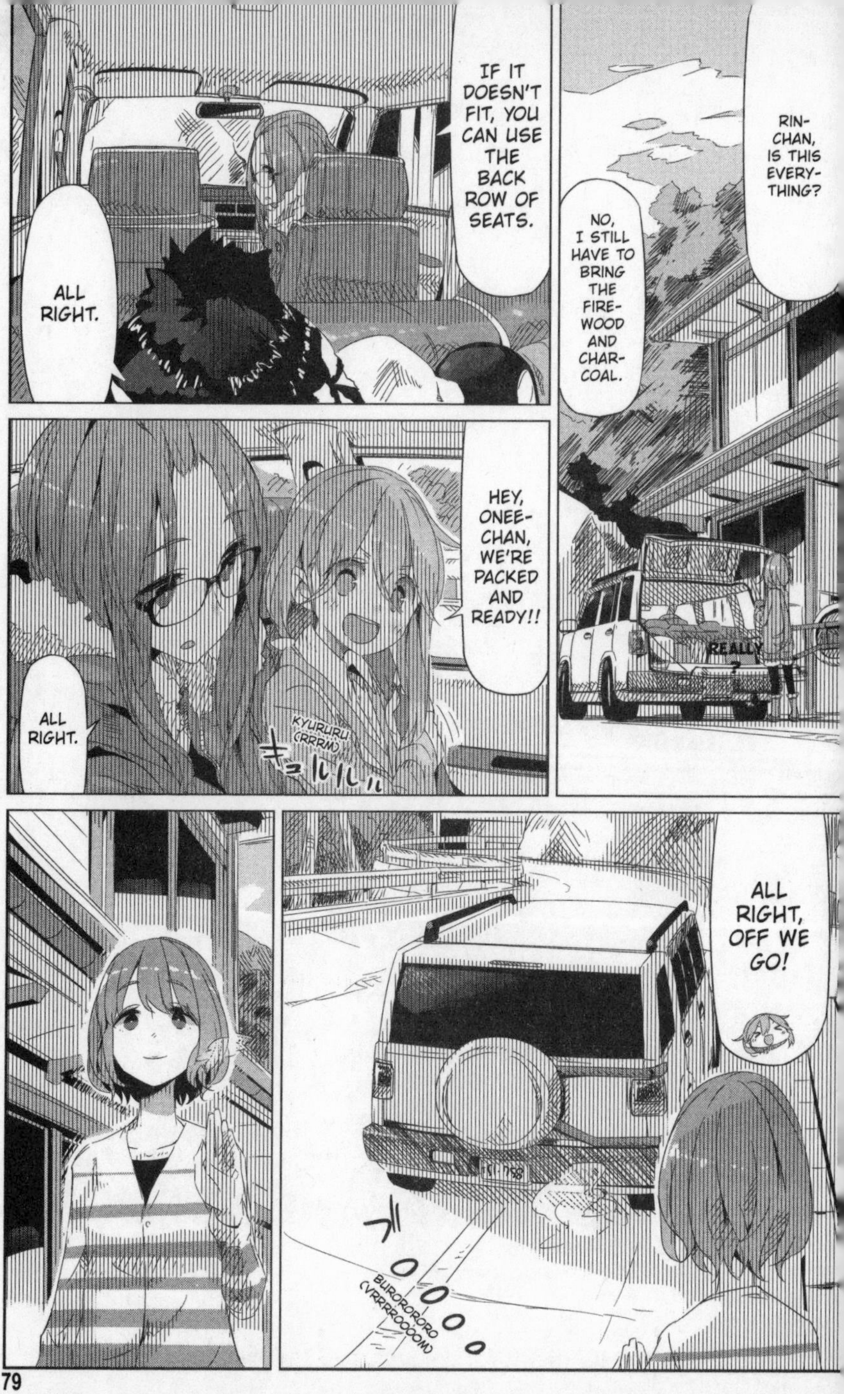
RIN-CHAN, IS THIS EVERY-THING?
NO, I STILL HAVE TO BRING THE FIRE-WOOD AND CHAR-COAL.
REALLY?
IF IT DOESN'T FIT, YOU CAN USE THE BACK ROW OF SEATS.
ALL RIGHT.
HEY, ONEE-CHAN, WE'RE PACKED AND READY!!
ALL RIGHT.
KYURURU (RRRM)
ALL RIGHT, OFF WE GO!
BURORORORO (VRRRROOOOM)

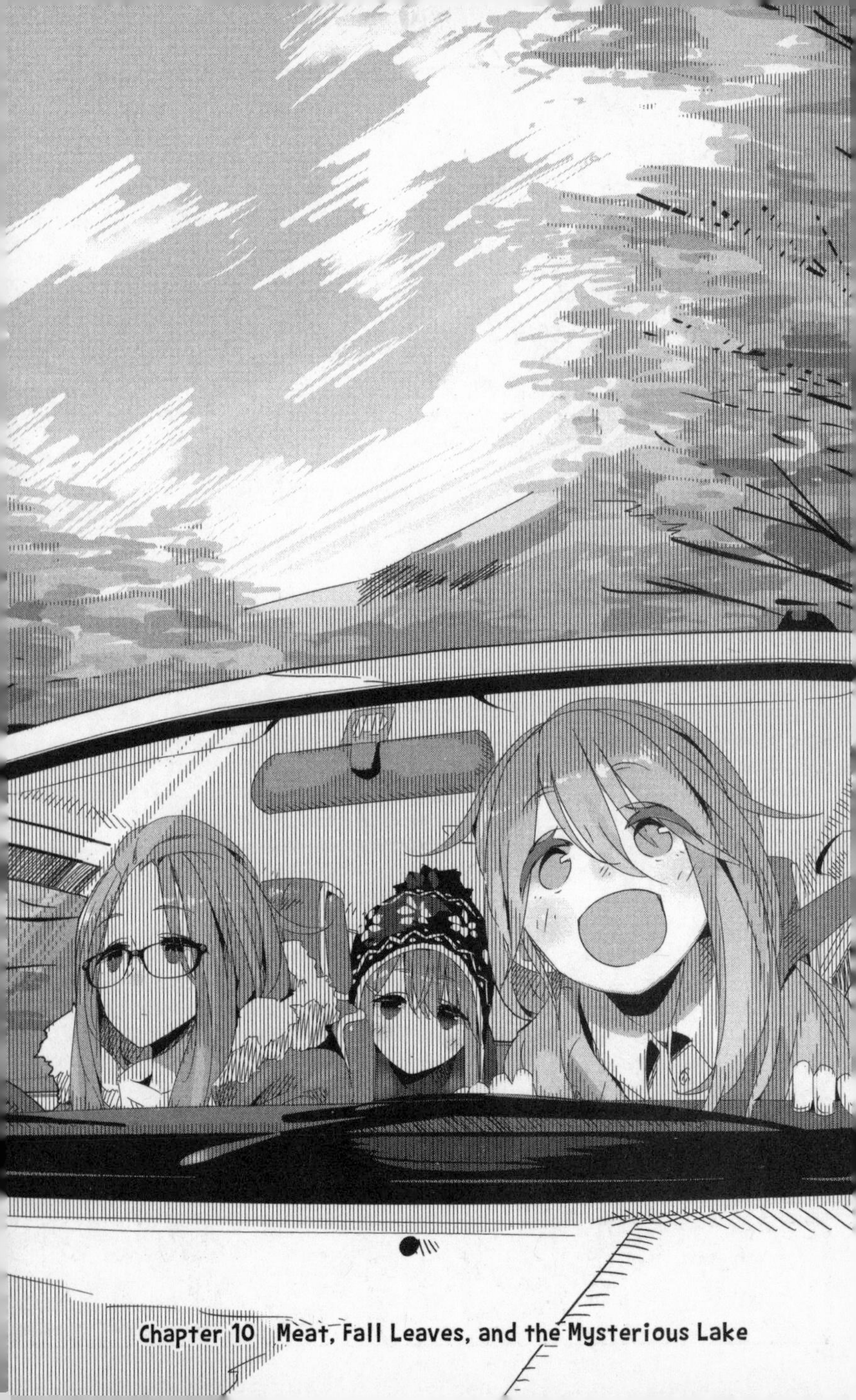

Chapter 10 Meat, Fall Leaves, and the Mysterious Lake

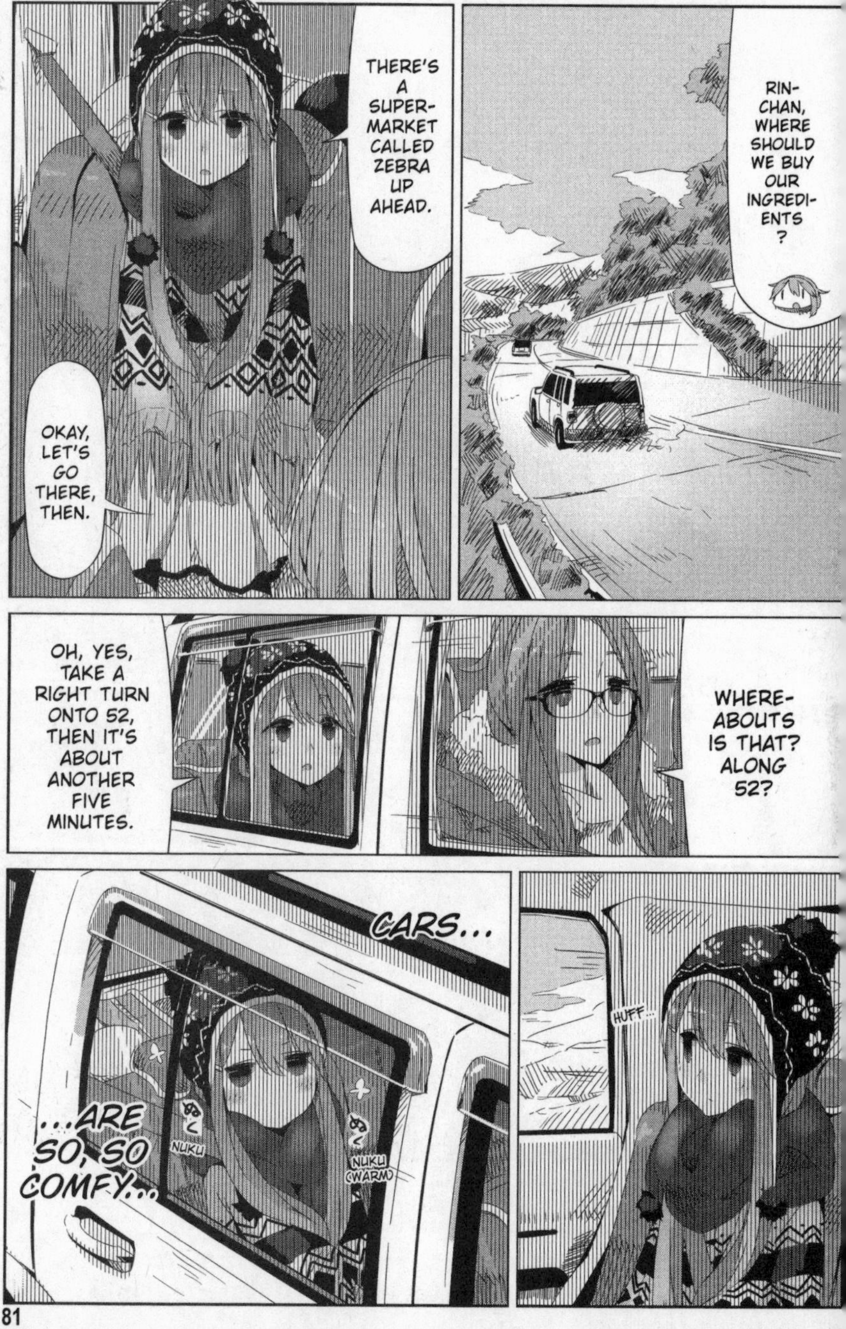
RIN-CHAN, WHERE SHOULD WE BUY OUR INGREDIENTS?
THERE'S A SUPERMARKET CALLED ZEBRA UP AHEAD.
OKAY, LET'S GO THERE, THEN.
WHEREABOUTS IS THAT? ALONG 52?
OH, YES, TAKE A RIGHT TURN ONTO 52, THEN IT'S ABOUT ANOTHER FIVE MINUTES.
HUFF...
CARS...
ぬく
NUKU (WARM)
ぬく
NUKU
...ARE SO, SO COMFY...

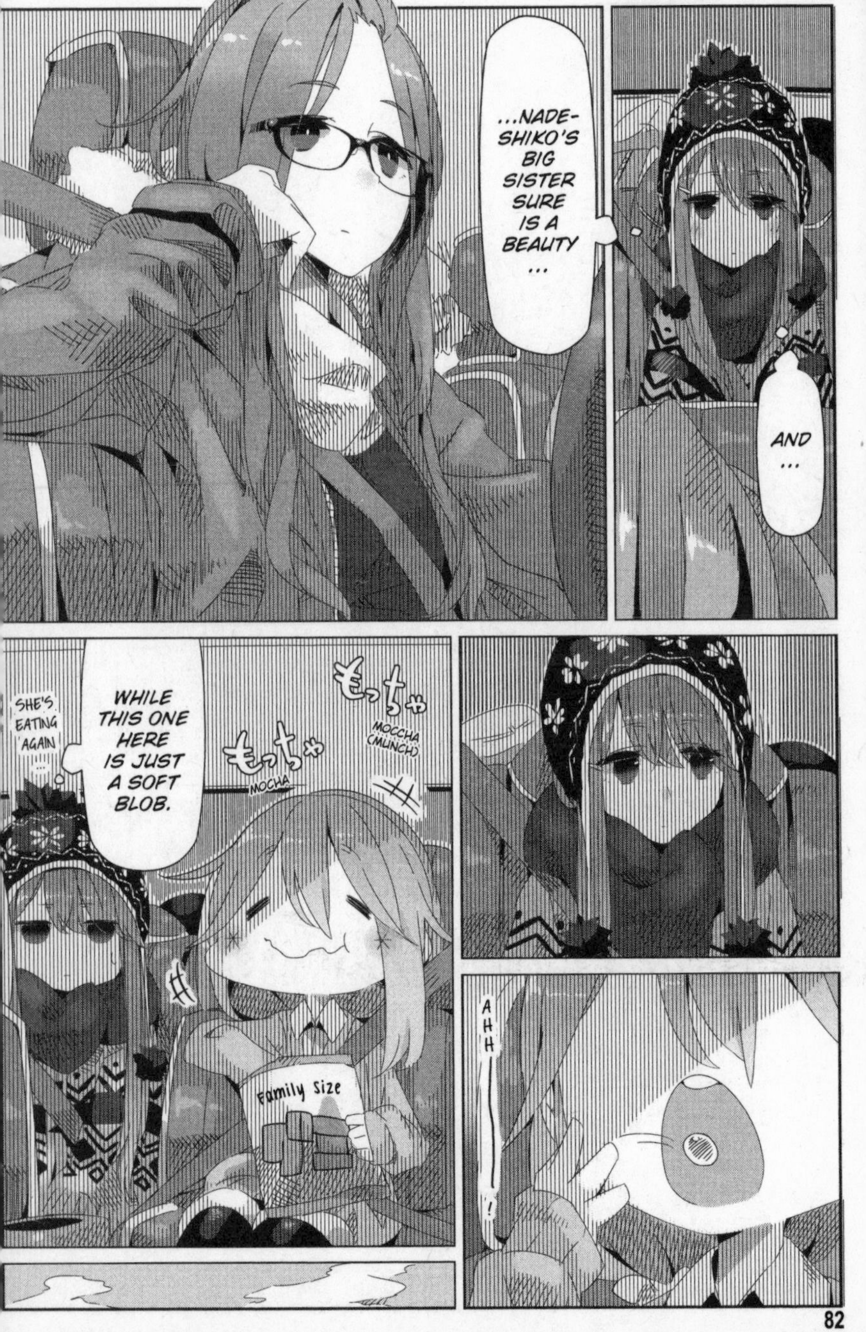
...NADE-SHIKO'S BIG SISTER SURE IS A BEAUTY ...
AND ...
もっちゃ
MOCCHA (MUNCH)
もっちゃ
MOCHA
WHILE THIS ONE HERE IS JUST A SOFT BLOB.
SHE'S EATING AGAIN ...
Family size
AHH——!

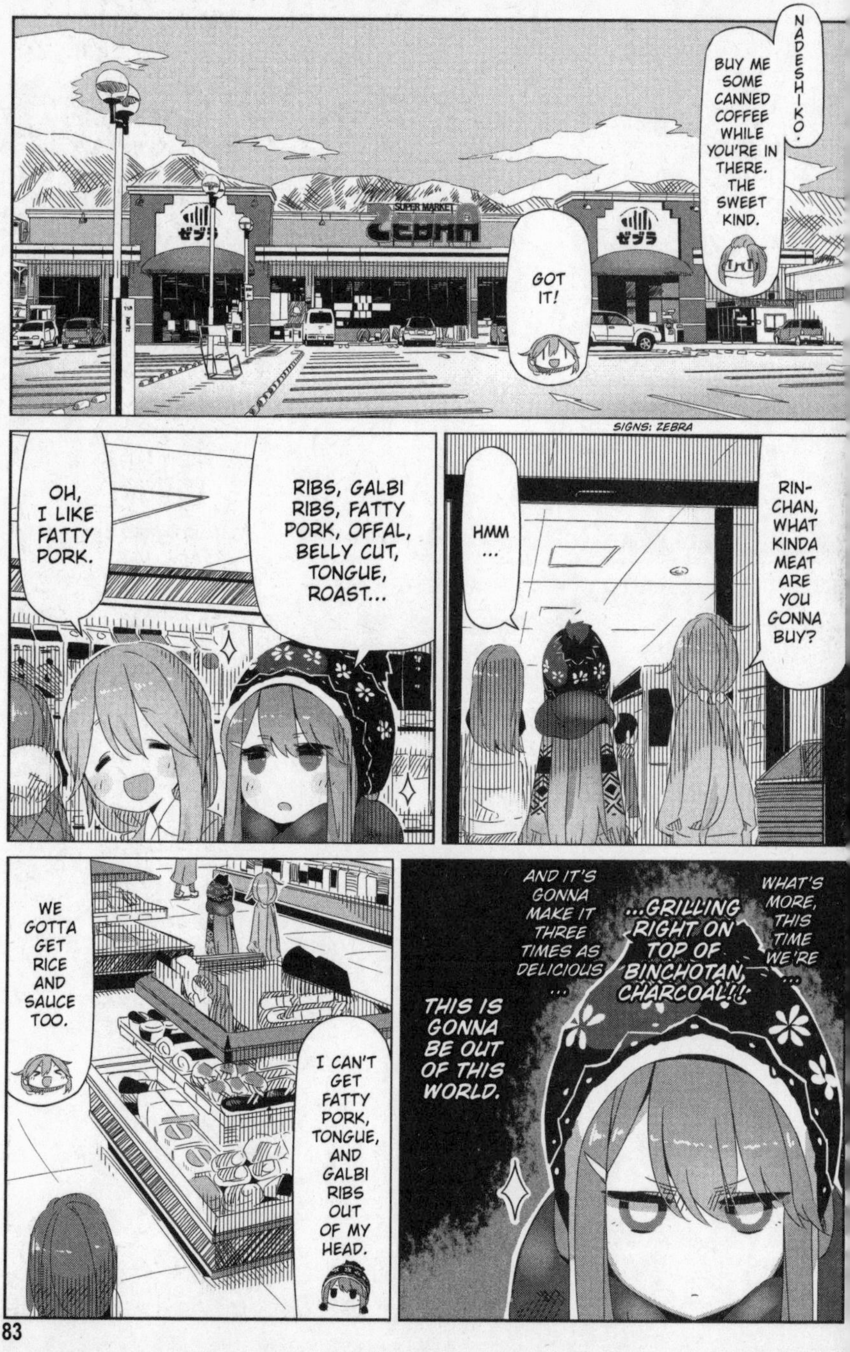
NADESHIKO.
BUY ME SOME CANNED COFFEE WHILE YOU'RE IN THERE. THE SWEET KIND.
GOT IT!
SUPER MARKET
SIGNS: ZEBRA
RIN-CHAN, WHAT KINDA MEAT ARE YOU GONNA BUY?
HMM...
RIBS, GALBI RIBS, FATTY PORK, OFFAL, BELLY CUT, TONGUE, ROAST...
OH, I LIKE FATTY PORK.
WHAT'S MORE, THIS TIME WE'RE...
...GRILLING RIGHT ON TOP OF BINCHOTAN CHARCOAL!!
AND IT'S GONNA MAKE IT THREE TIMES AS DELICIOUS...
THIS IS GONNA BE OUT OF THIS WORLD.
WE GOTTA GET RICE AND SAUCE TOO.
I CAN'T GET FATTY PORK, TONGUE, AND GALBI RIBS OUT OF MY HEAD.

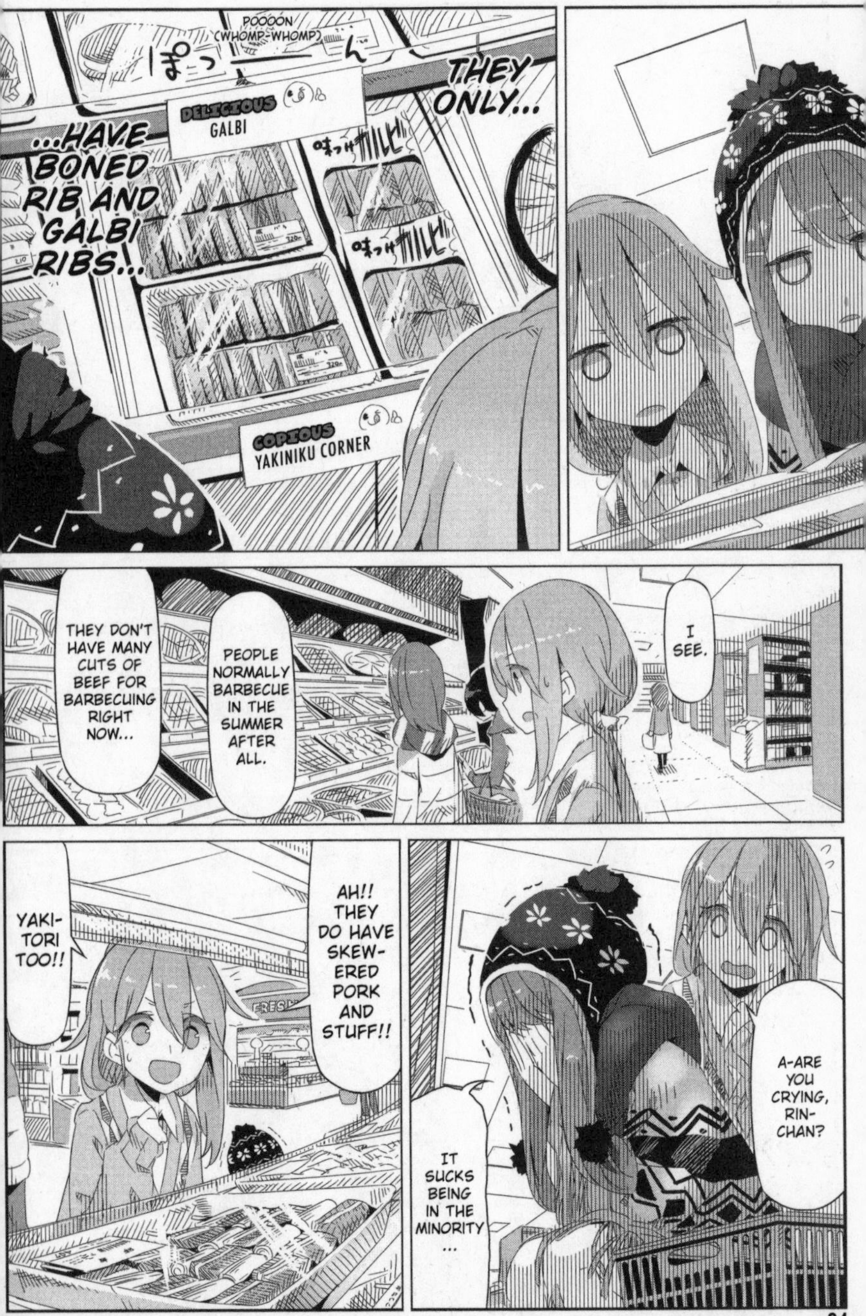
POOOON (WHOMP-WHOMP)
ぽっーーん
THEY ONLY...
...HAVE BONED RIB AND GALBI RIBS...
DELICIOUS GALBI
COPIOUS YAKINIKU CORNER
I SEE.
PEOPLE NORMALLY BARBECUE IN THE SUMMER AFTER ALL.
THEY DON'T HAVE MANY CUTS OF BEEF FOR BARBECUING RIGHT NOW...
A-ARE YOU CRYING, RIN-CHAN?
IT SUCKS BEING IN THE MINORITY...
AH!! THEY DO HAVE SKEWERED PORK AND STUFF!!
YAKI-TORI TOO!!

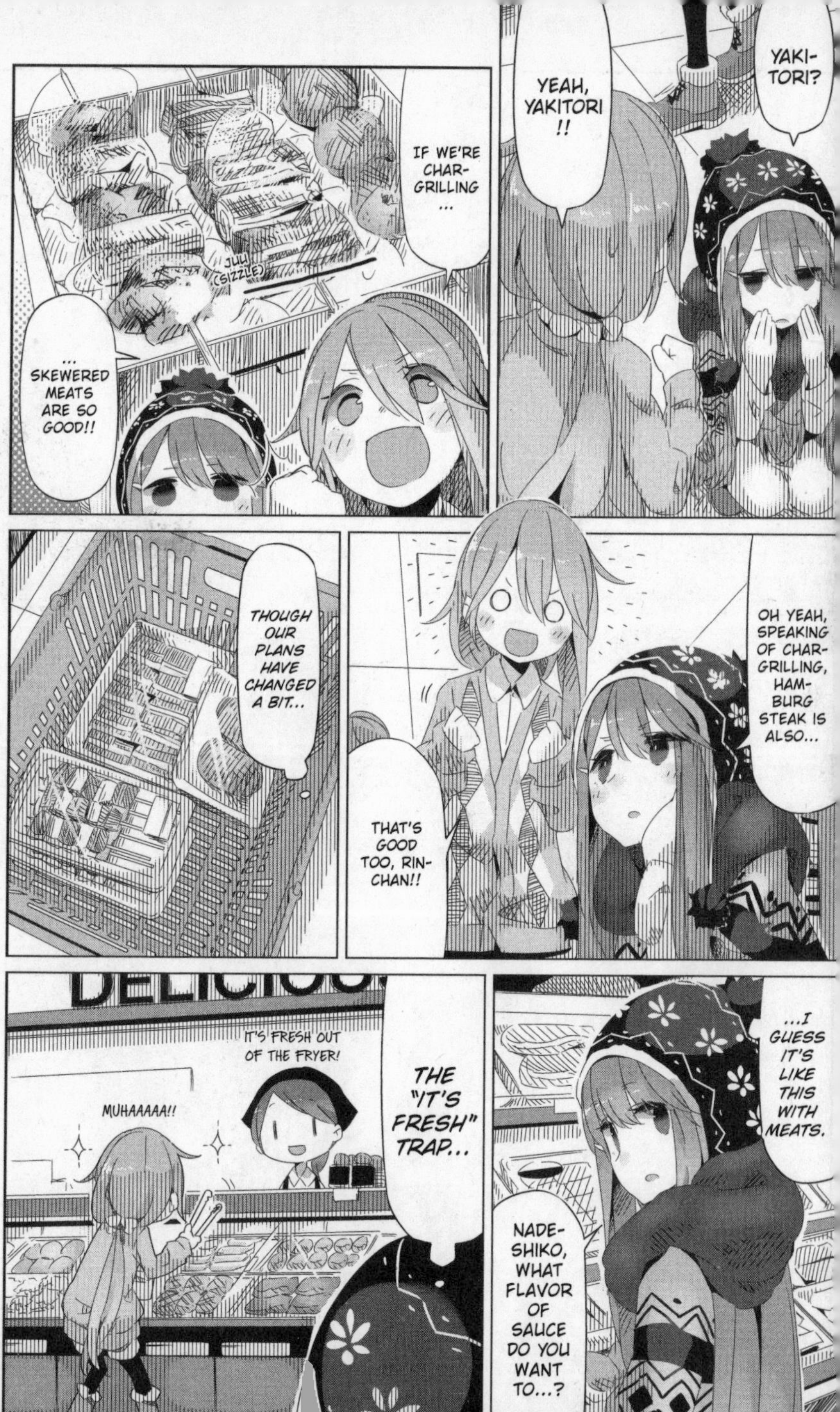
YAKI-TORI?
YEAH, YAKITORI !!
IF WE'RE CHAR-GRILLING ...
JUU (SIZZLE)
... SKEWERED MEATS ARE SO GOOD!!
OH YEAH, SPEAKING OF CHAR-GRILLING, HAM-BURG STEAK IS ALSO...
THAT'S GOOD TOO, RIN-CHAN!!
THOUGH OUR PLANS HAVE CHANGED A BIT...
...I GUESS IT'S LIKE THIS WITH MEATS.
NADE-SHIKO, WHAT FLAVOR OF SAUCE DO YOU WANT TO...?
THE "IT'S FRESH" TRAP...
IT'S FRESH OUT OF THE FRYER!
MUHAAAAA!!

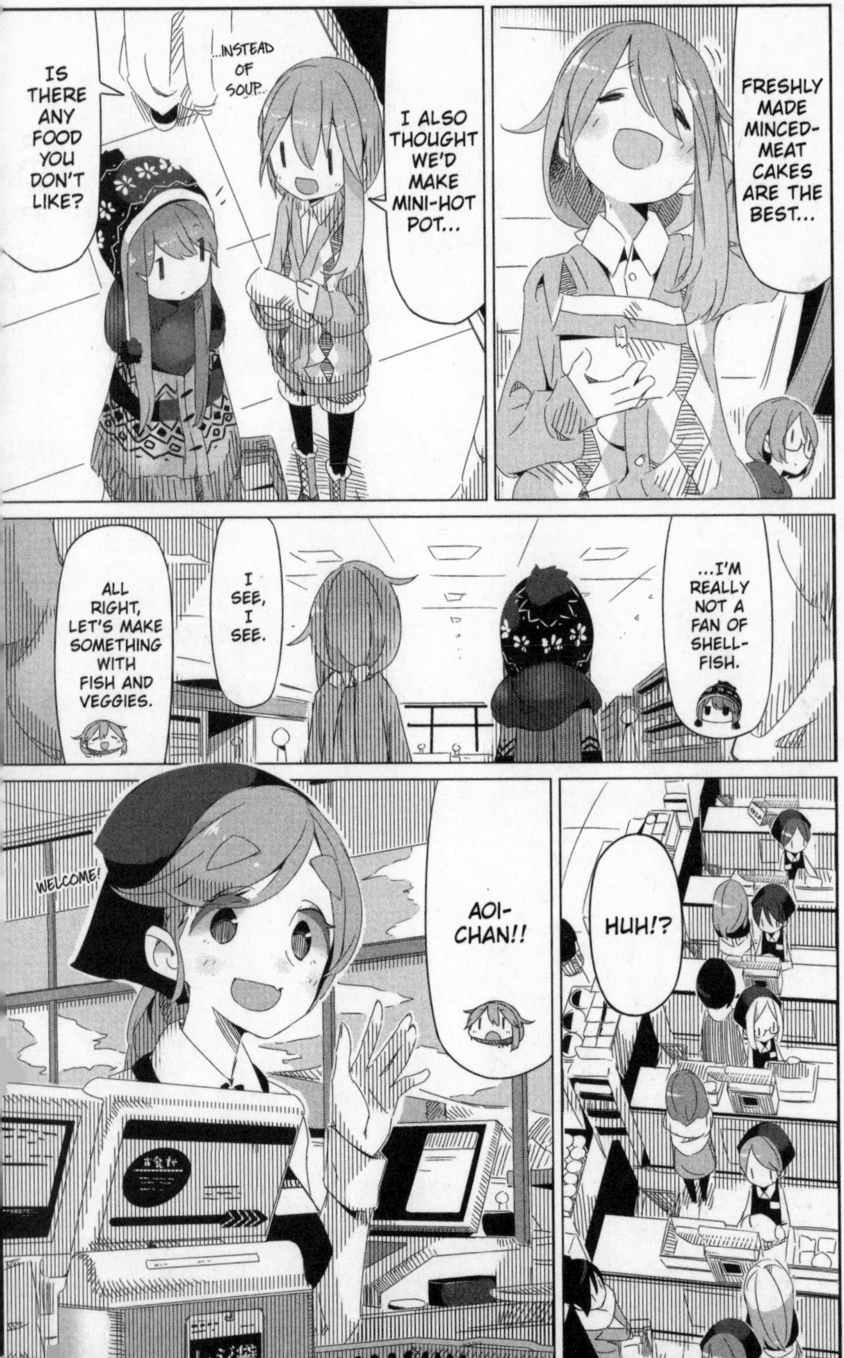
FRESHLY MADE MINCED-MEAT CAKES ARE THE BEST...
I ALSO THOUGHT WE'D MAKE MINI-HOT POT...
...INSTEAD OF SOUP...
IS THERE ANY FOOD YOU DON'T LIKE?
...I'M REALLY NOT A FAN OF SHELL-FISH.
I SEE, I SEE.
ALL RIGHT, LET'S MAKE SOMETHING WITH FISH AND VEGGIES.
HUH!?
AOI-CHAN!!
WELCOME!

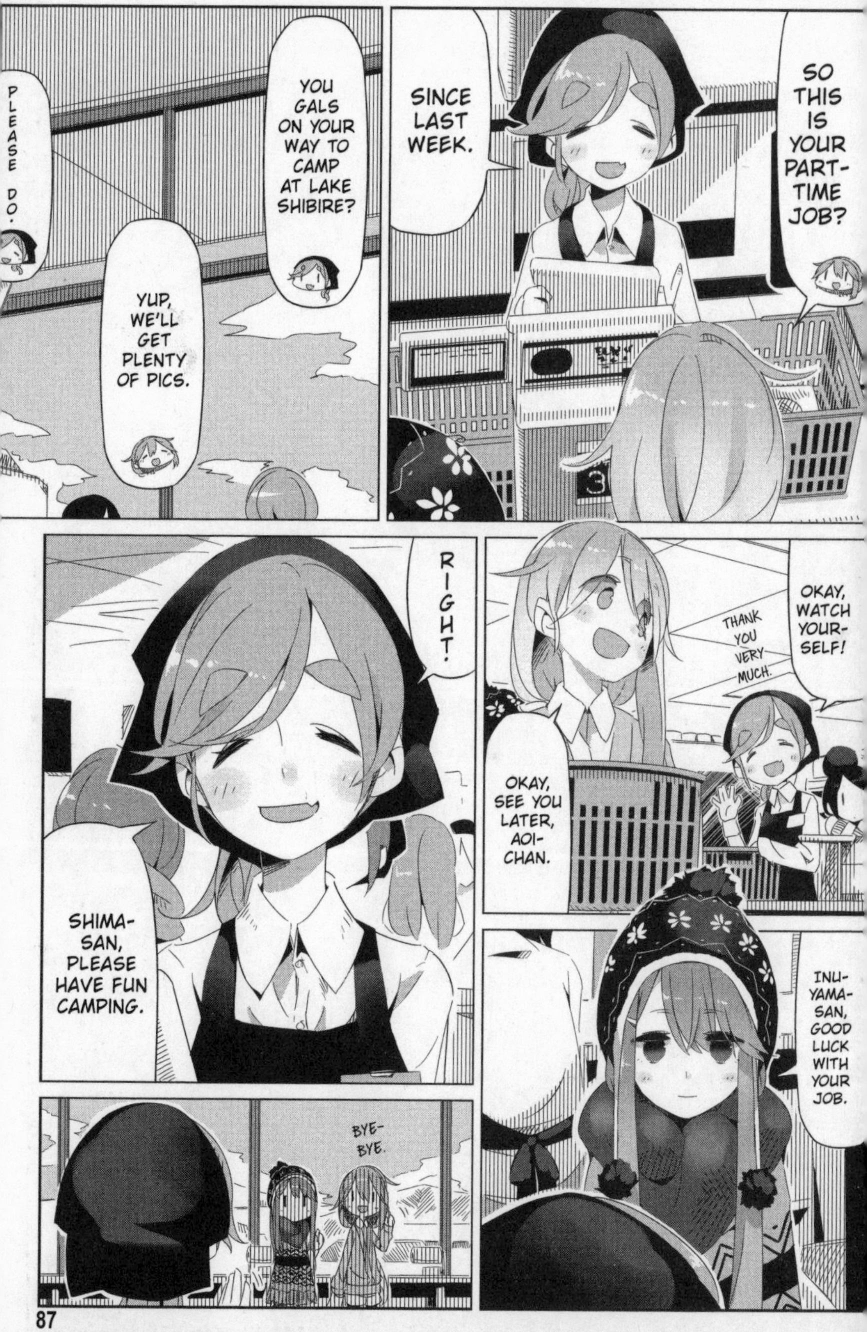
SO THIS IS YOUR PART-TIME JOB?
SINCE LAST WEEK.
YOU GALS ON YOUR WAY TO CAMP AT LAKE SHIBIRE?
YUP, WE'LL GET PLENTY OF PICS.
PLEASE DO.
OKAY, WATCH YOURSELF!
THANK YOU VERY MUCH.
OKAY, SEE YOU LATER, AOI-CHAN.
INUYAMA-SAN, GOOD LUCK WITH YOUR JOB.
RIGHT!
SHIMA-SAN, PLEASE HAVE FUN CAMPING.
BYE-BYE.

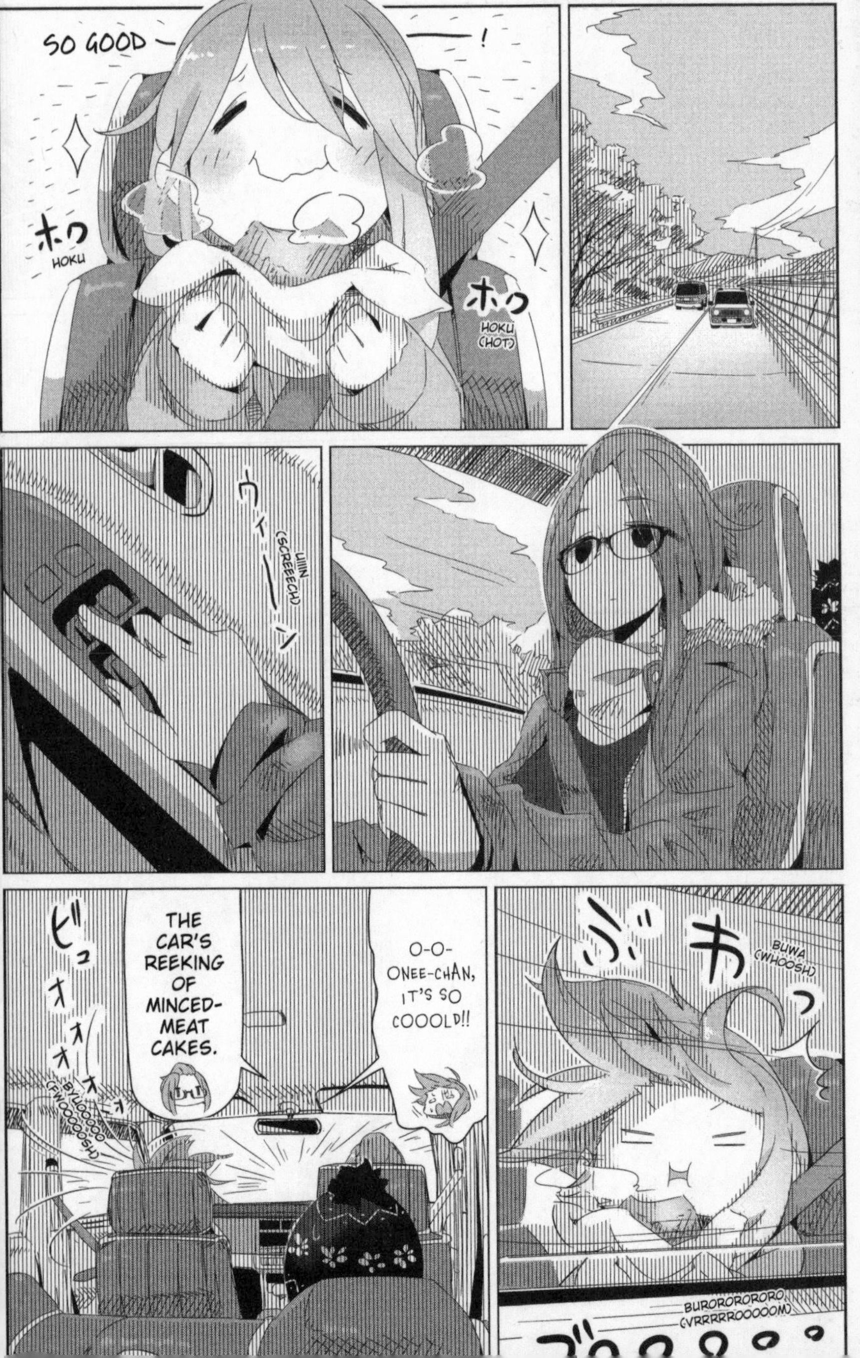

SO GOOD~ —!
ホク
HOKU (HOT)
ホク
HOKU
ウィーン
UIIIN (SCREEECH)
ぶおっ
BUWA (WHOOSH)
BURORORORORO (VRRRRROOOOOM)
O-O-ONEE-CHAN, IT'S SO COOOLD!!
THE CAR'S REEKING OF MINCED-MEAT CAKES.
BYUOOOOO (FWOOOOOSH)

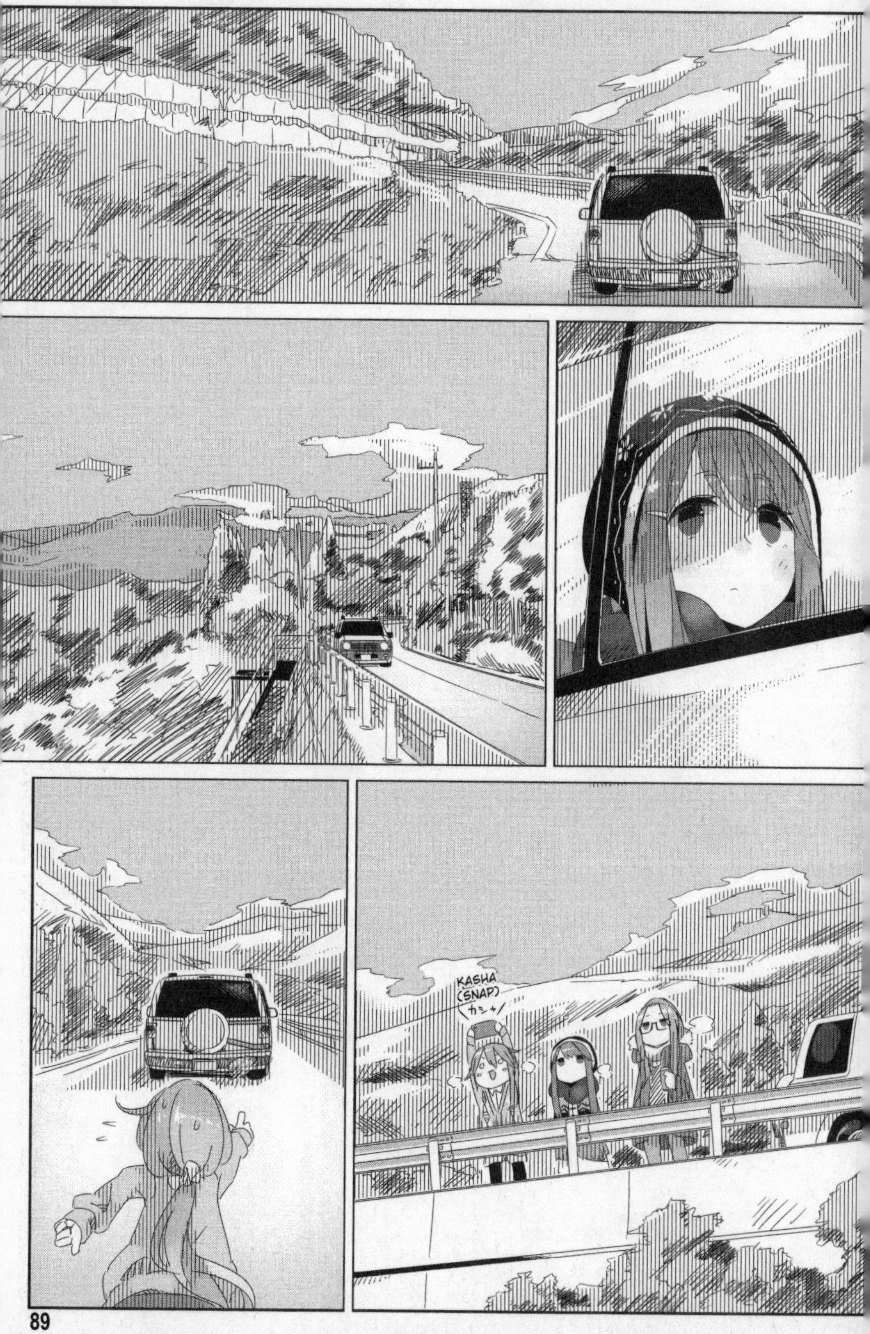
KASHA (SNAP)
カシャ

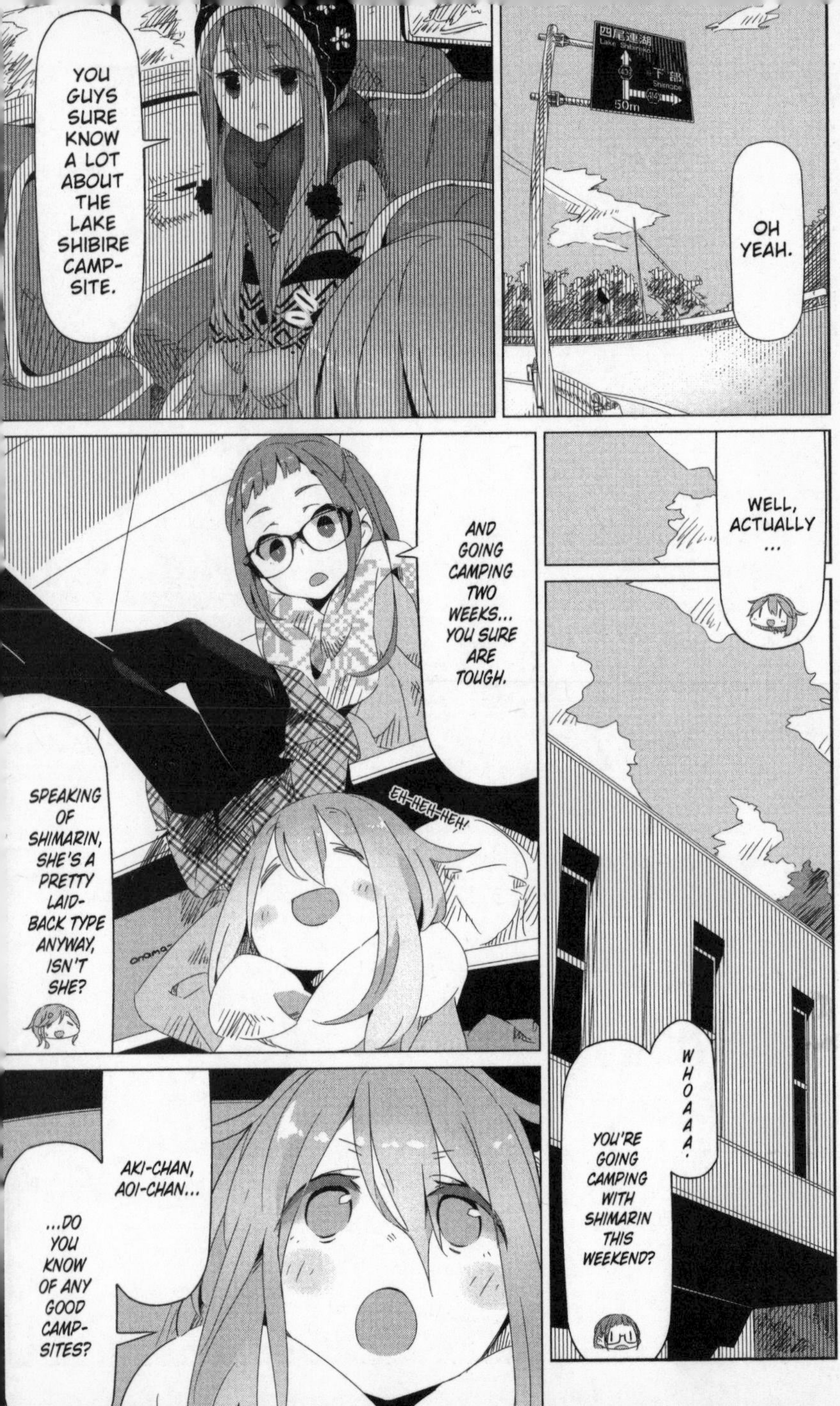
四尾連湖
Lake Shibireko
下部
Shimobe
50m
OH YEAH.
YOU GUYS SURE KNOW A LOT ABOUT THE LAKE SHIBIRE CAMP-SITE.
WELL, ACTUALLY ...
WHOAAA. YOU'RE GOING CAMPING WITH SHIMARIN THIS WEEKEND?
AND GOING CAMPING TWO WEEKS... YOU SURE ARE TOUGH.
EH-HEH-HEH!
SPEAKING OF SHIMARIN, SHE'S A PRETTY LAID-BACK TYPE ANYWAY, ISN'T SHE?
AKI-CHAN, AOI-CHAN...
...DO YOU KNOW OF ANY GOOD CAMP-SITES?

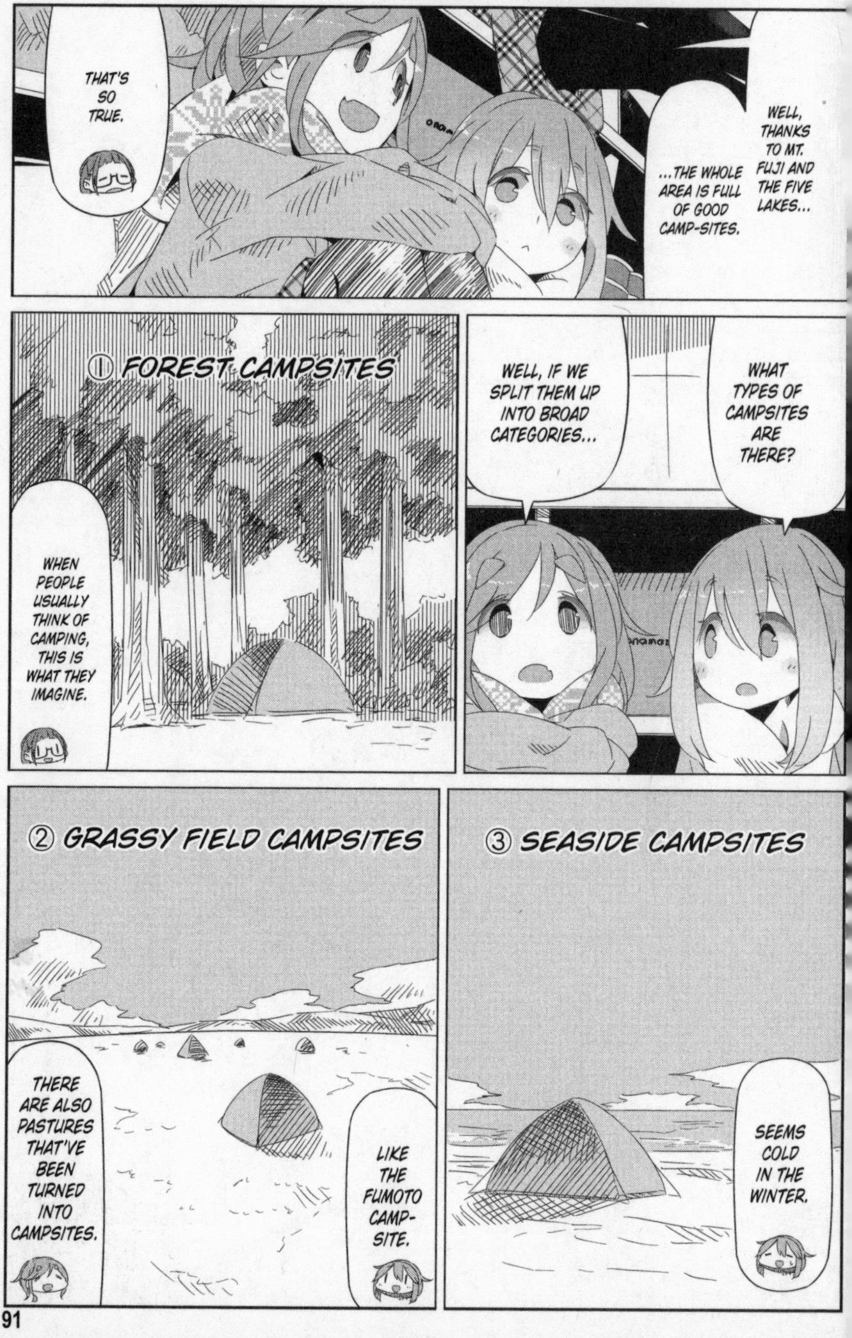
WELL, THANKS TO MT. FUJI AND THE FIVE LAKES...
...THE WHOLE AREA IS FULL OF GOOD CAMP-SITES.
THAT'S SO TRUE.
WHAT TYPES OF CAMPSITES ARE THERE?
WELL, IF WE SPLIT THEM UP INTO BROAD CATEGORIES...
① FOREST CAMPSITES
WHEN PEOPLE USUALLY THINK OF CAMPING, THIS IS WHAT THEY IMAGINE.
③ SEASIDE CAMPSITES
SEEMS COLD IN THE WINTER.
② GRASSY FIELD CAMPSITES
THERE ARE ALSO PASTURES THAT'VE BEEN TURNED INTO CAMPSITES.
LIKE THE FUMOTO CAMP-SITE.

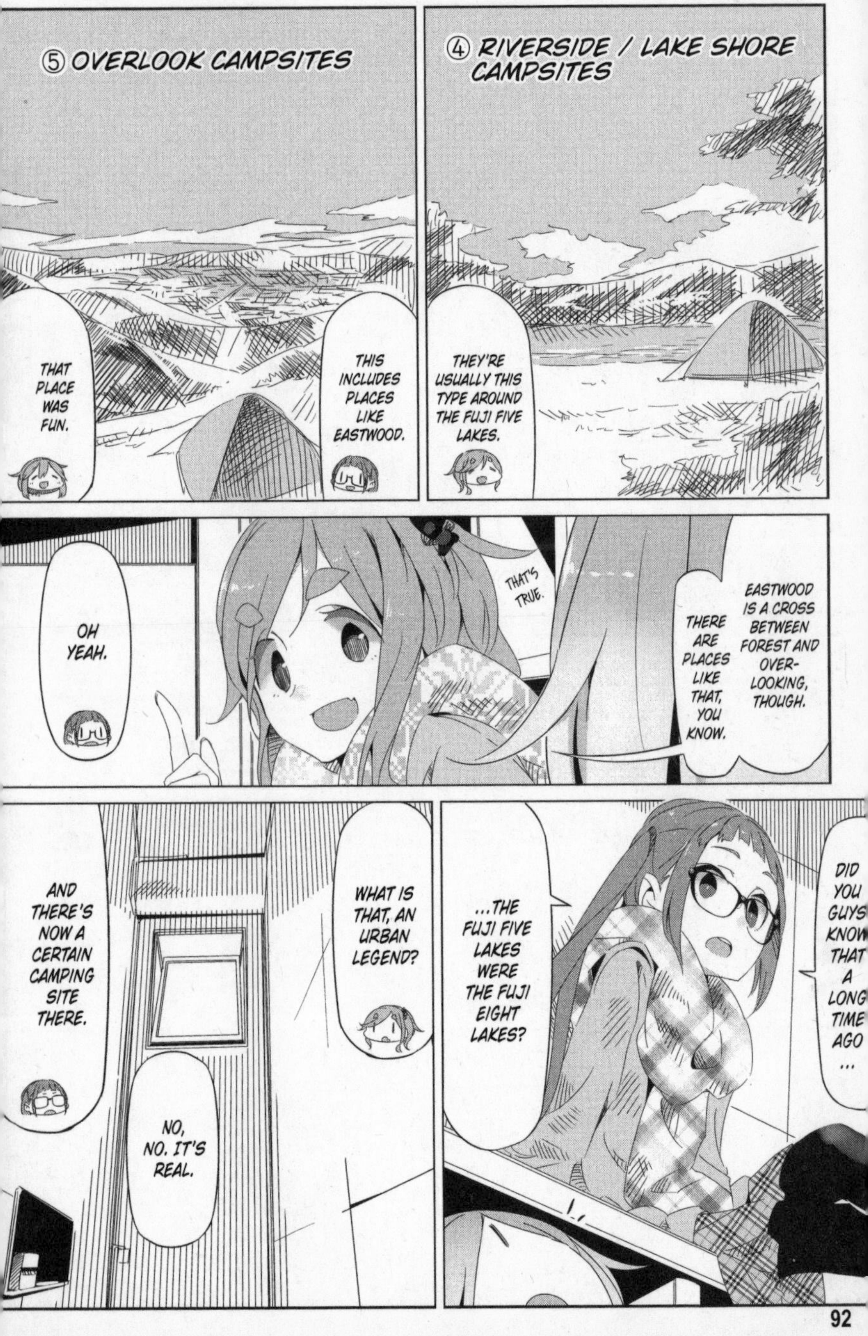
④ RIVERSIDE / LAKE SHORE CAMPSITES
THEY'RE USUALLY THIS TYPE AROUND THE FUJI FIVE LAKES.
⑤ OVERLOOK CAMPSITES
THIS INCLUDES PLACES LIKE EASTWOOD.
THAT PLACE WAS FUN.
EASTWOOD IS A CROSS BETWEEN FOREST AND OVER-LOOKING, THOUGH.
THERE ARE PLACES LIKE THAT, YOU KNOW.
THAT'S TRUE.
OH YEAH.
DID YOU GUYS KNOW THAT A LONG TIME AGO ...
...THE FUJI FIVE LAKES WERE THE FUJI EIGHT LAKES?
WHAT IS THAT, AN URBAN LEGEND?
NO, NO. IT'S REAL.
AND THERE'S NOW A CERTAIN CAMPING SITE THERE.

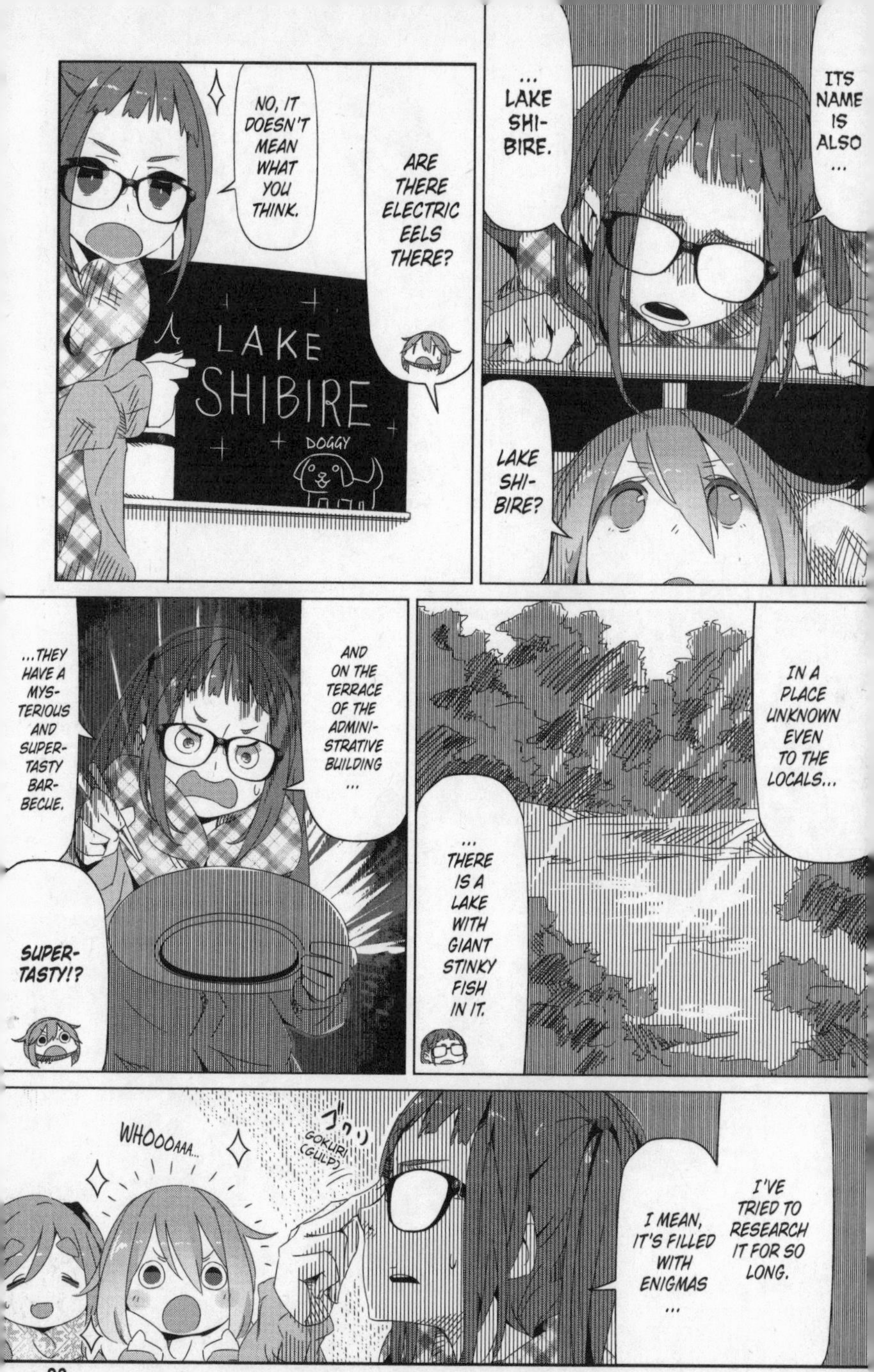
ITS NAME IS ALSO ...
... LAKE SHI-BIRE.
LAKE SHI-BIRE?
ARE THERE ELECTRIC EELS THERE?
NO, IT DOESN'T MEAN WHAT YOU THINK.
LAKE SHIBIRE
DOGGY
IN A PLACE UNKNOWN EVEN TO THE LOCALS...
... THERE IS A LAKE WITH GIANT STINKY FISH IN IT.
AND ON THE TERRACE OF THE ADMINI-STRATIVE BUILDING ...
...THEY HAVE A MYS-TERIOUS AND SUPER-TASTY BAR-BECUE.
SUPER-TASTY!?
I'VE TRIED TO RESEARCH IT FOR SO LONG.
I MEAN, IT'S FILLED WITH ENIGMAS ...
ゴクリ
GOKURI (GULP)
WHOOOAAA...

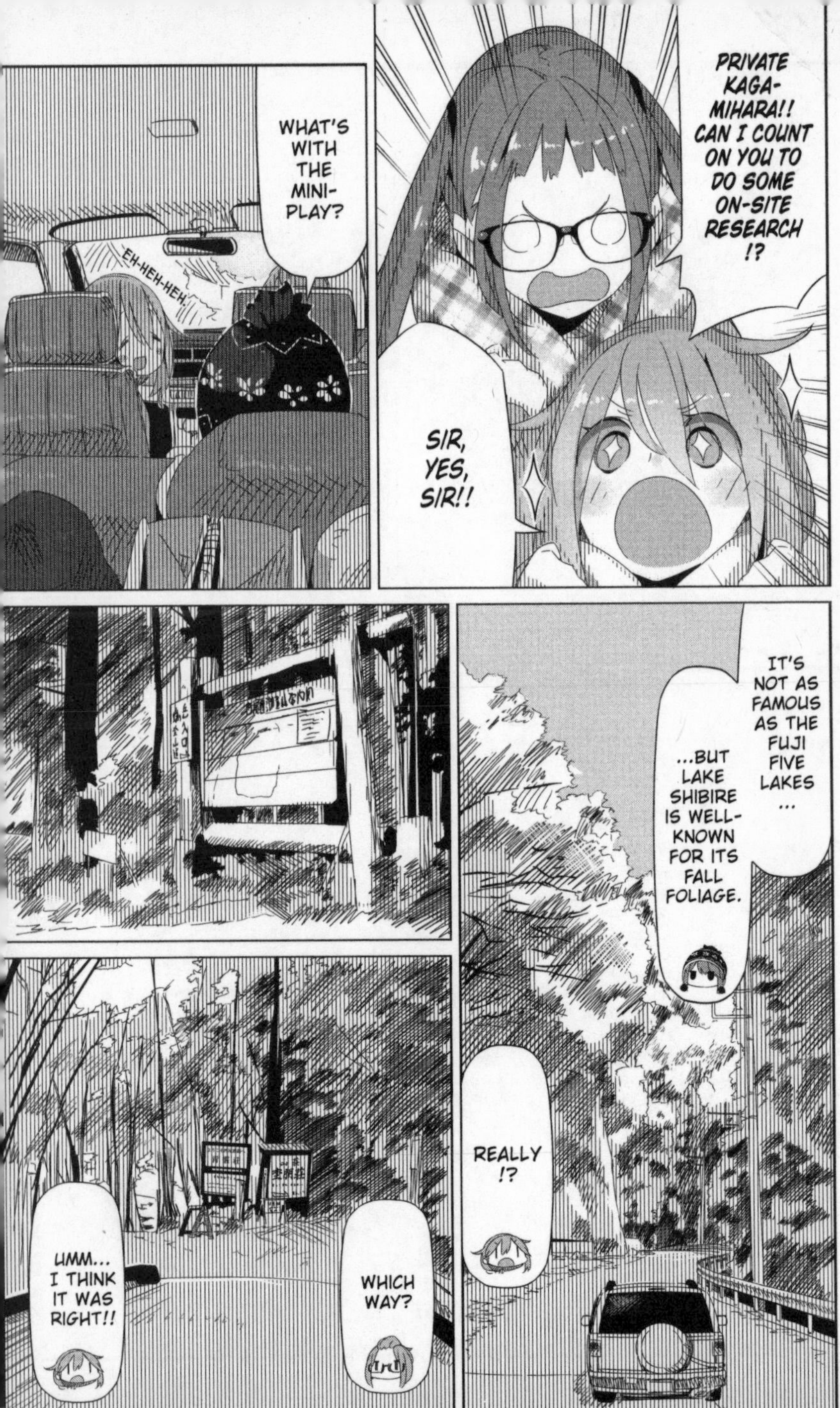
PRIVATE KAGA-MIHARA!! CAN I COUNT ON YOU TO DO SOME ON-SITE RESEARCH!?
SIR, YES, SIR!!
WHAT'S WITH THE MINI-PLAY?
EH-HEH-HEH.
IT'S NOT AS FAMOUS AS THE FUJI FIVE LAKES...
...BUT LAKE SHIBIRE IS WELL-KNOWN FOR ITS FALL FOLIAGE.
REALLY!?
WHICH WAY?
UMM... I THINK IT WAS RIGHT!!

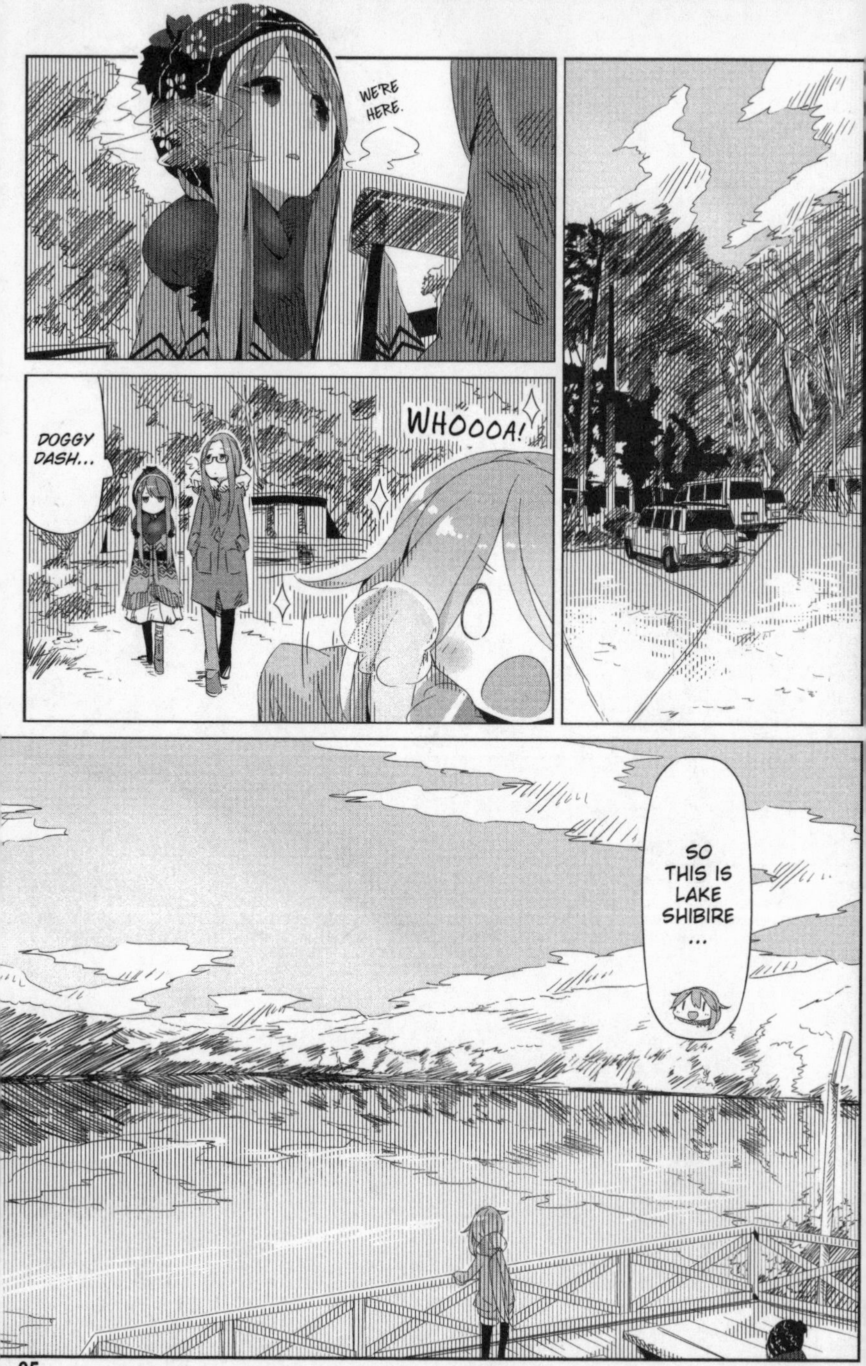
WE'RE HERE.
WHOOOA!
DOGGY DASH...
SO THIS IS LAKE SHIBIRE ...

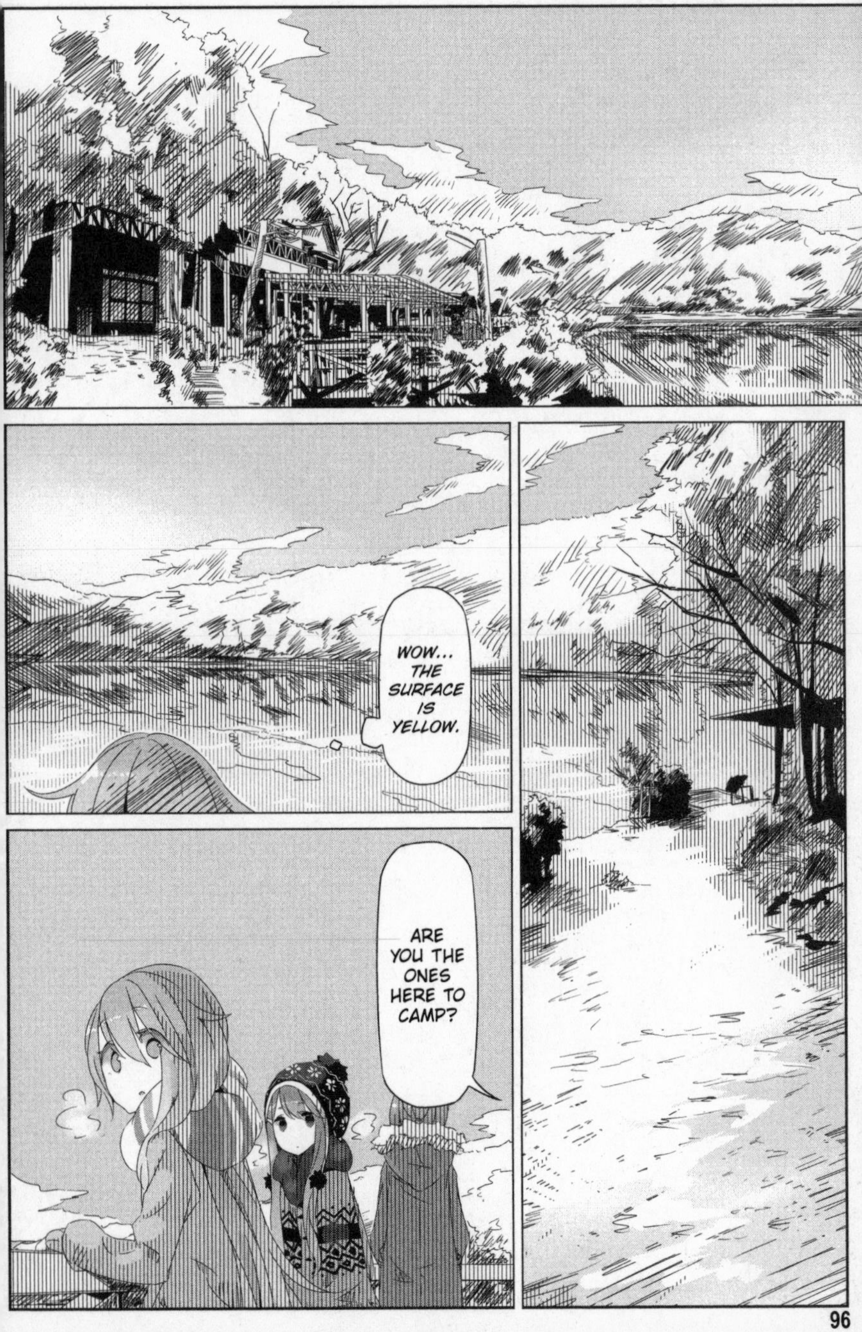
WOW... THE SURFACE IS YELLOW.
ARE YOU THE ONES HERE TO CAMP?

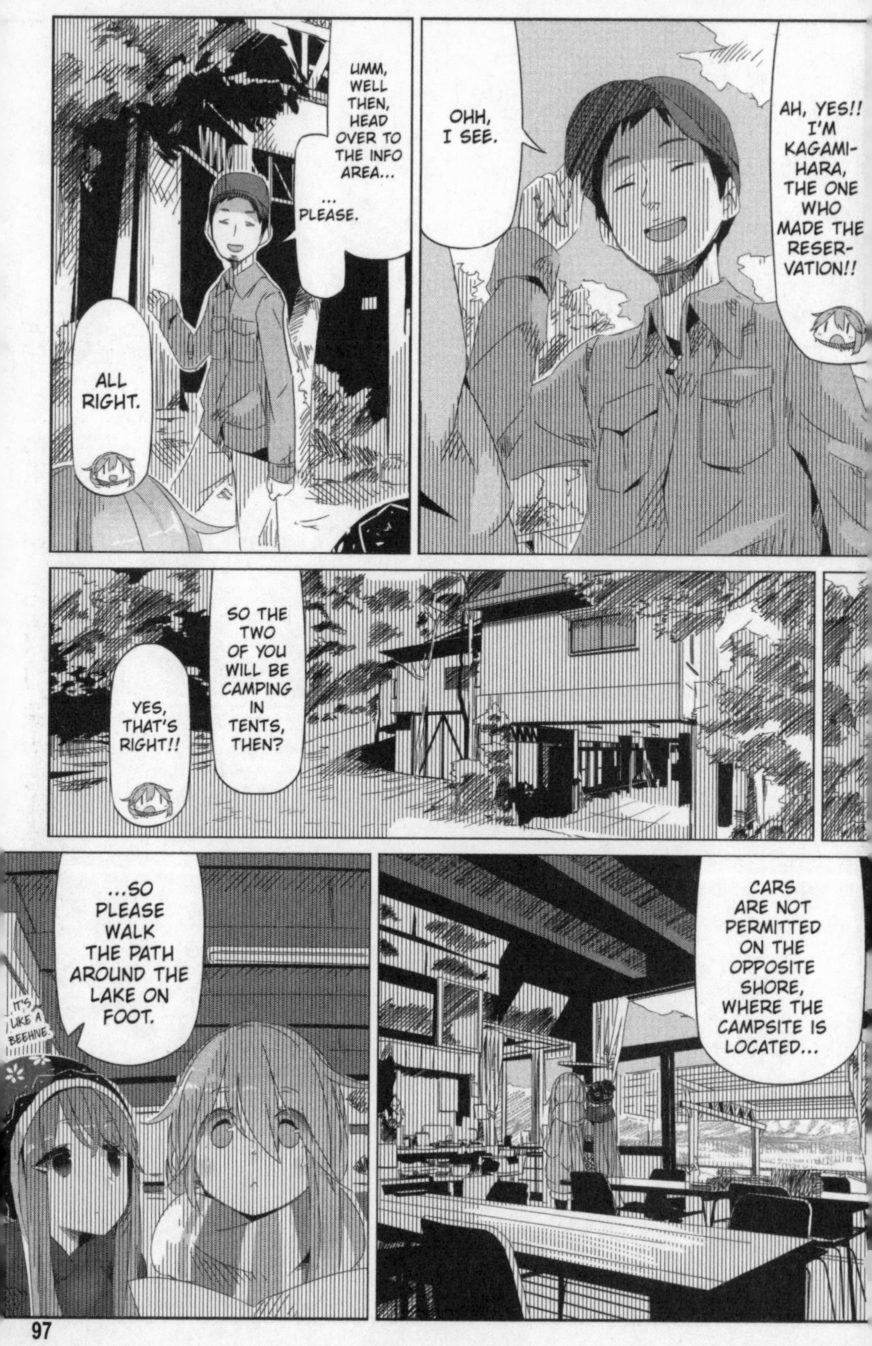
AH, YES!! I'M KAGAMIHARA, THE ONE WHO MADE THE RESERVATION!!
OHH, I SEE.
UMM, WELL THEN, HEAD OVER TO THE INFO AREA...
...PLEASE.
ALL RIGHT.
SO THE TWO OF YOU WILL BE CAMPING IN TENTS, THEN?
YES, THAT'S RIGHT!!
CARS ARE NOT PERMITTED ON THE OPPOSITE SHORE, WHERE THE CAMPSITE IS LOCATED...
...SO PLEASE WALK THE PATH AROUND THE LAKE ON FOOT.
IT'S LIKE A BEEHIVE.

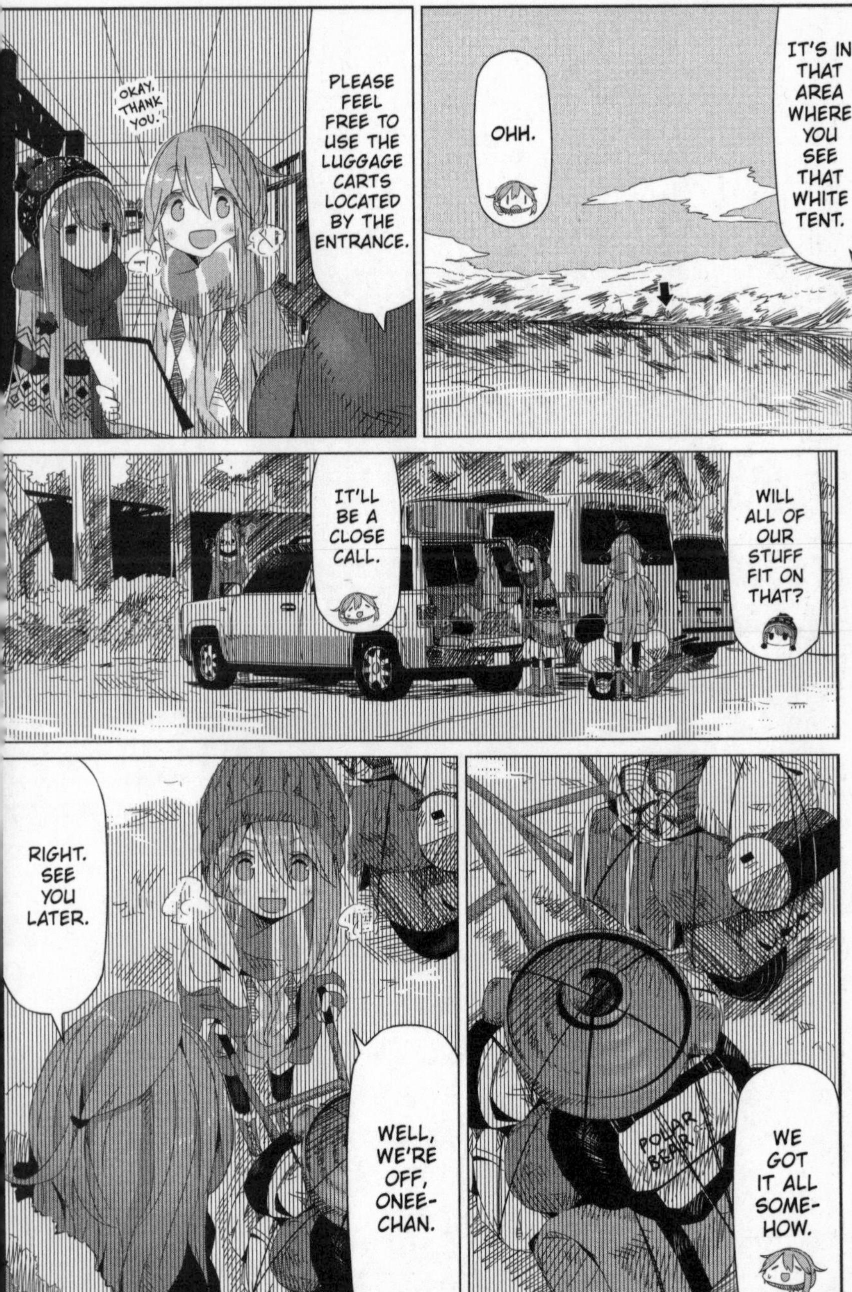
IT'S IN THAT AREA WHERE YOU SEE THAT WHITE TENT.
OHH.
PLEASE FEEL FREE TO USE THE LUGGAGE CARTS LOCATED BY THE ENTRANCE.
OKAY. THANK YOU.
WILL ALL OF OUR STUFF FIT ON THAT?
IT'LL BE A CLOSE CALL.
WE GOT IT ALL SOME-HOW.
POLAR BEAR
WELL, WE'RE OFF, ONEE-CHAN.
RIGHT. SEE YOU LATER.

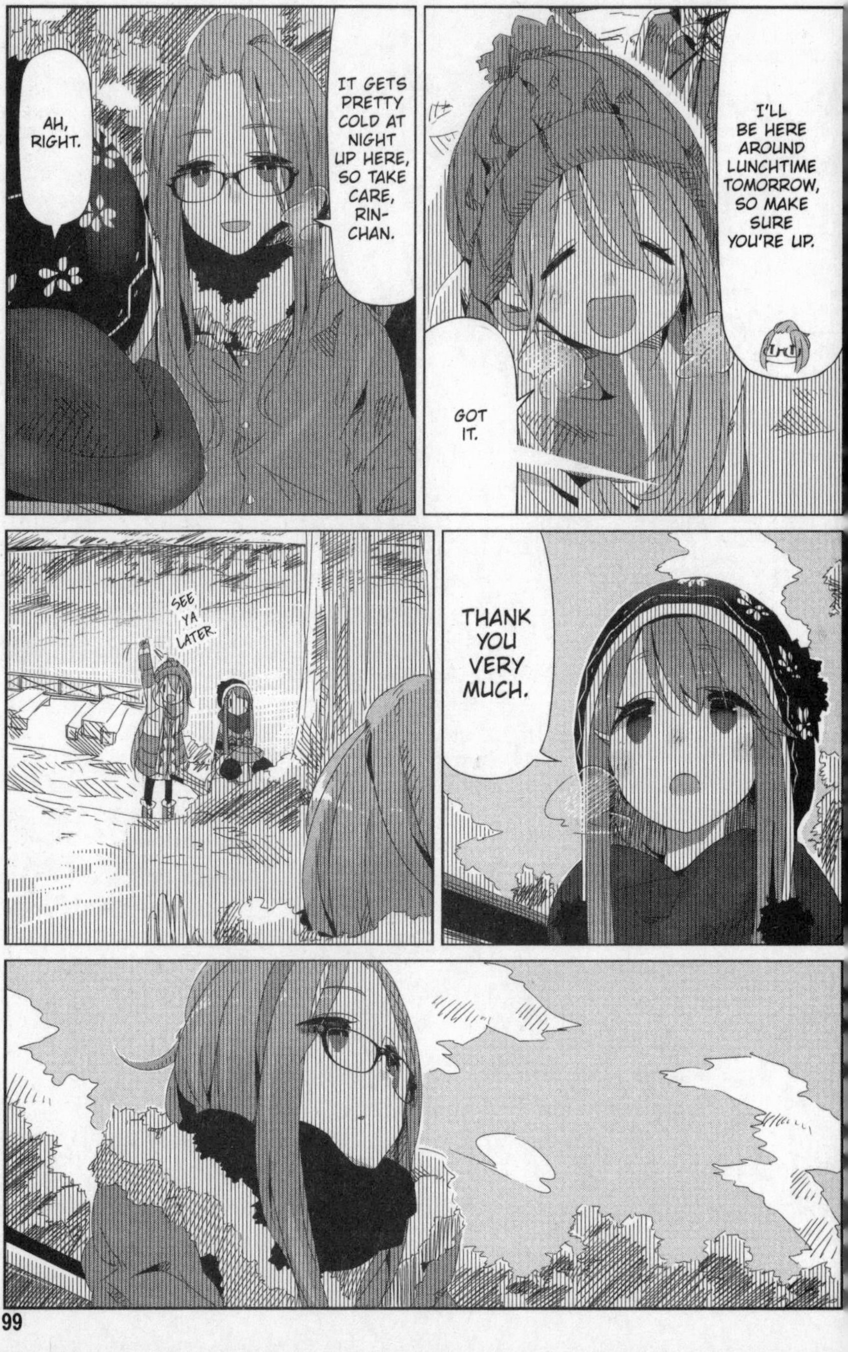
I'LL BE HERE AROUND LUNCHTIME TOMORROW, SO MAKE SURE YOU'RE UP.
GOT IT.
IT GETS PRETTY COLD AT NIGHT UP HERE, SO TAKE CARE, RIN-CHAN.
AH, RIGHT.
THANK YOU VERY MUCH.
SEE YA LATER.

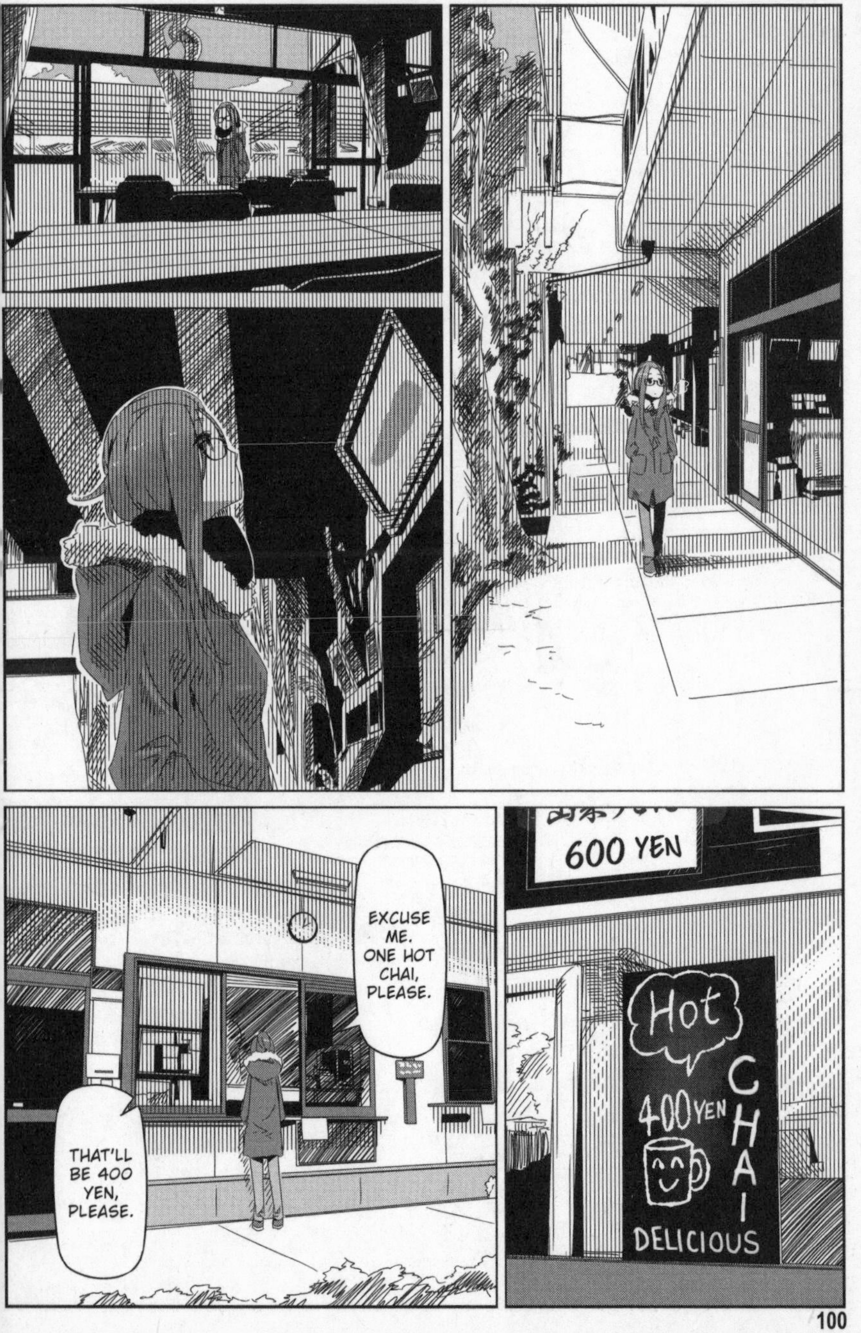
600 YEN
Hot
CHAI
400 YEN
DELICIOUS
EXCUSE ME. ONE HOT CHAI, PLEASE.
THAT'LL BE 400 YEN, PLEASE.

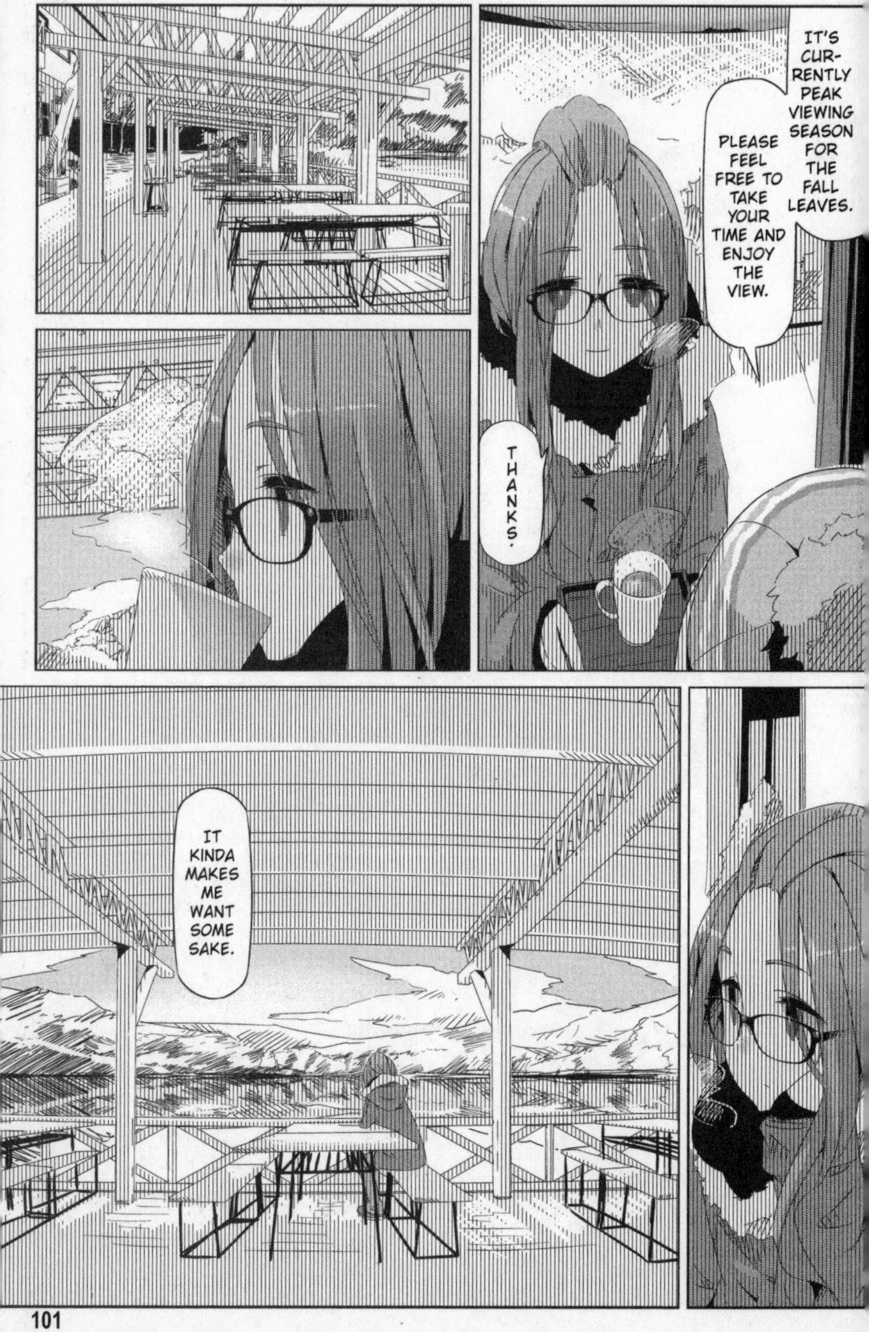
IT'S CUR-RENTLY PEAK VIEWING SEASON FOR THE FALL LEAVES.
PLEASE FEEL FREE TO TAKE YOUR TIME AND ENJOY THE VIEW.
THANKS.
IT KINDA MAKES ME WANT SOME SAKE.

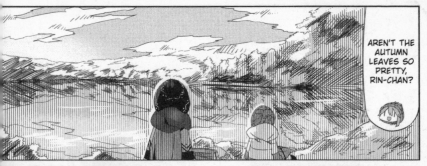

AREN'T THE AUTUMN LEAVES SO PRETTY, RIN-CHAN?
ZA (ZSH) ざっ
AND THIS IS THE PERFECT TIME TO SEE THEM.
I'LL HAVE TO THANK AKI-CHAN FOR TELLING ME ABOUT THIS PLACE!!
ZA ざっ
ZA ざっ
ざっ ZA
ざっ ZA
NOW THAT YOU MENTION IT, THE FALLING LEAVES HERE SURE DO IMPRESS.
THE LEGEND OF THE BULL-GHOST IS PRETTY FAMOUS AROUND HERE, IT SEEMS.
PIKU (FREEZE) ピクッ
GASAAA (FLOP) ガサーーッ

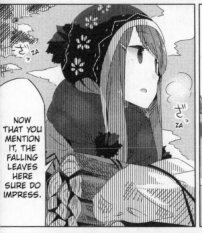

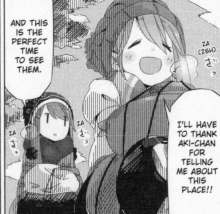

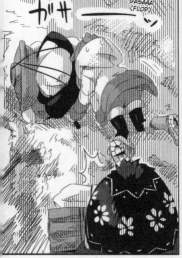

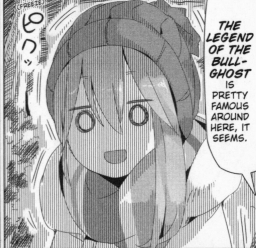

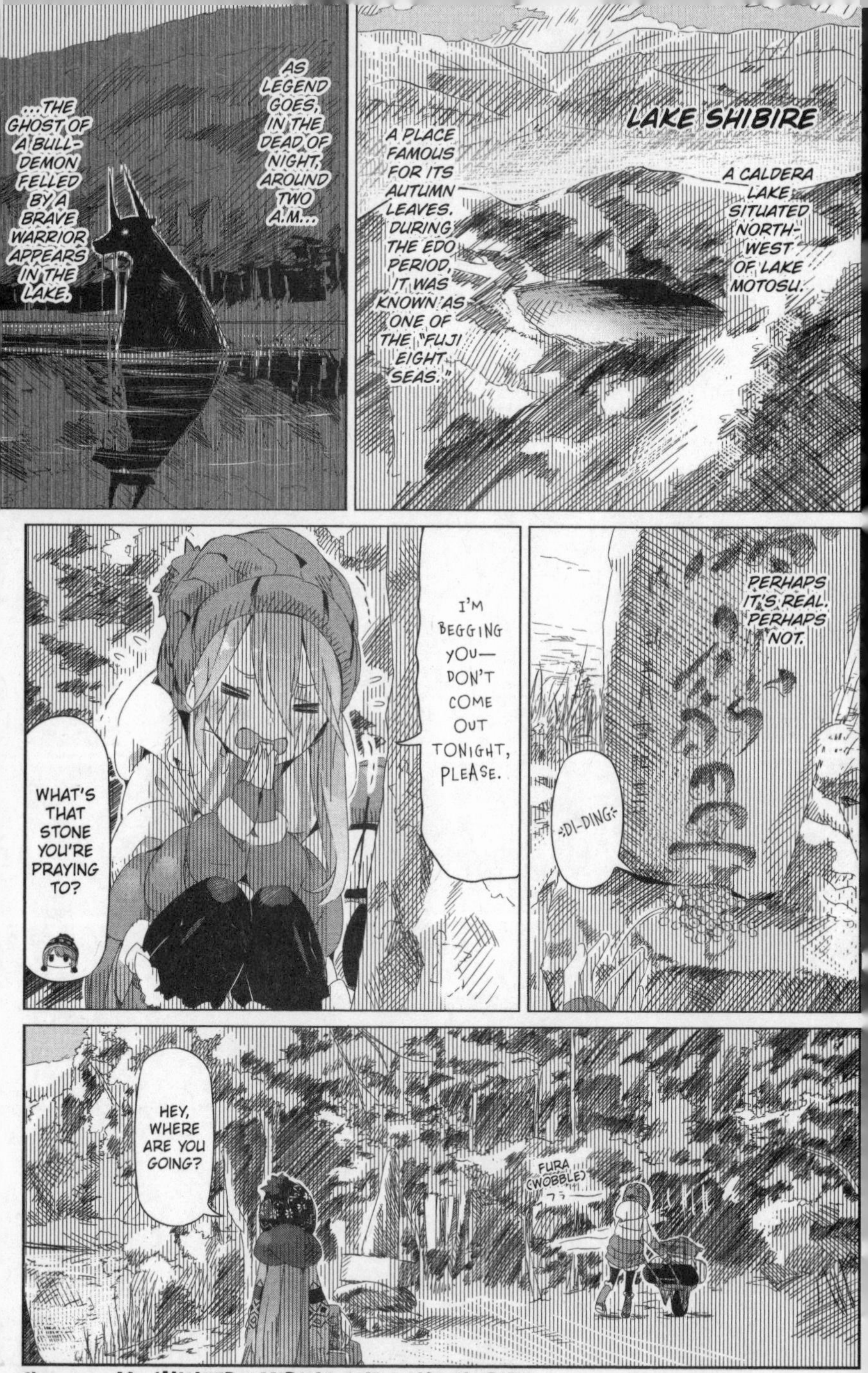
LAKE SHIBIRE
A CALDERA LAKE SITUATED NORTH-WEST OF LAKE MOTOSU.
A PLACE FAMOUS FOR ITS AUTUMN LEAVES. DURING THE EDO PERIOD, IT WAS KNOWN AS ONE OF THE "FUJI EIGHT SEAS."
AS LEGEND GOES, IN THE DEAD OF NIGHT, AROUND TWO A.M...
...THE GHOST OF A BULL-DEMON FELLED BY A BRAVE WARRIOR APPEARS IN THE LAKE.
PERHAPS IT'S REAL. PERHAPS NOT.
DI-DING
I'M BEGGING YOU—DON'T COME OUT TONIGHT, PLEASE.
WHAT'S THAT STONE YOU'RE PRAYING TO?
FURA (WOBBLE)
HEY, WHERE ARE YOU GOING?

Chapter 11 WINTER CAMPING AND LAKE SHIBIRE

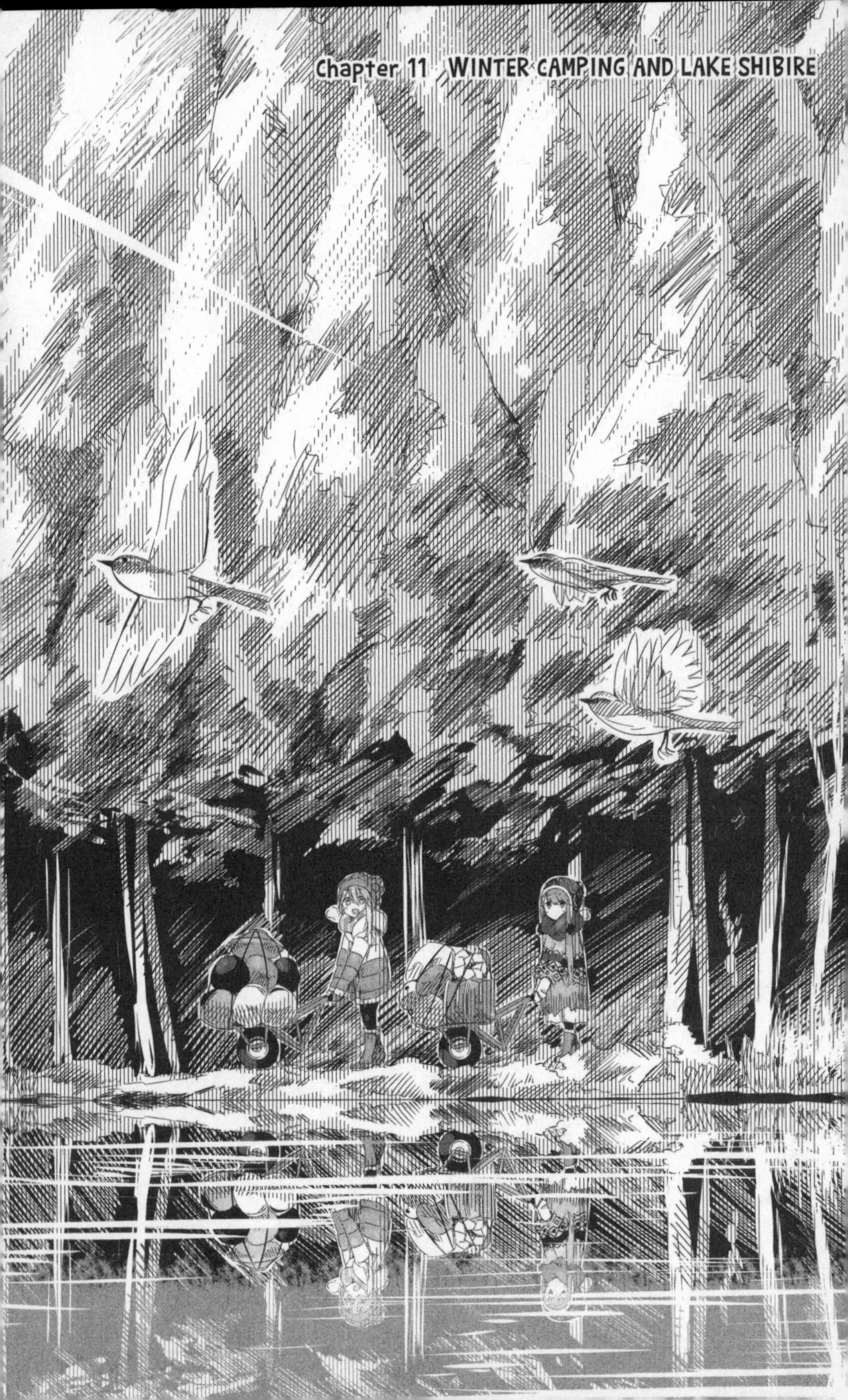
Chapter 11 WINTER CAMPING AND LAKE SHIBIRE

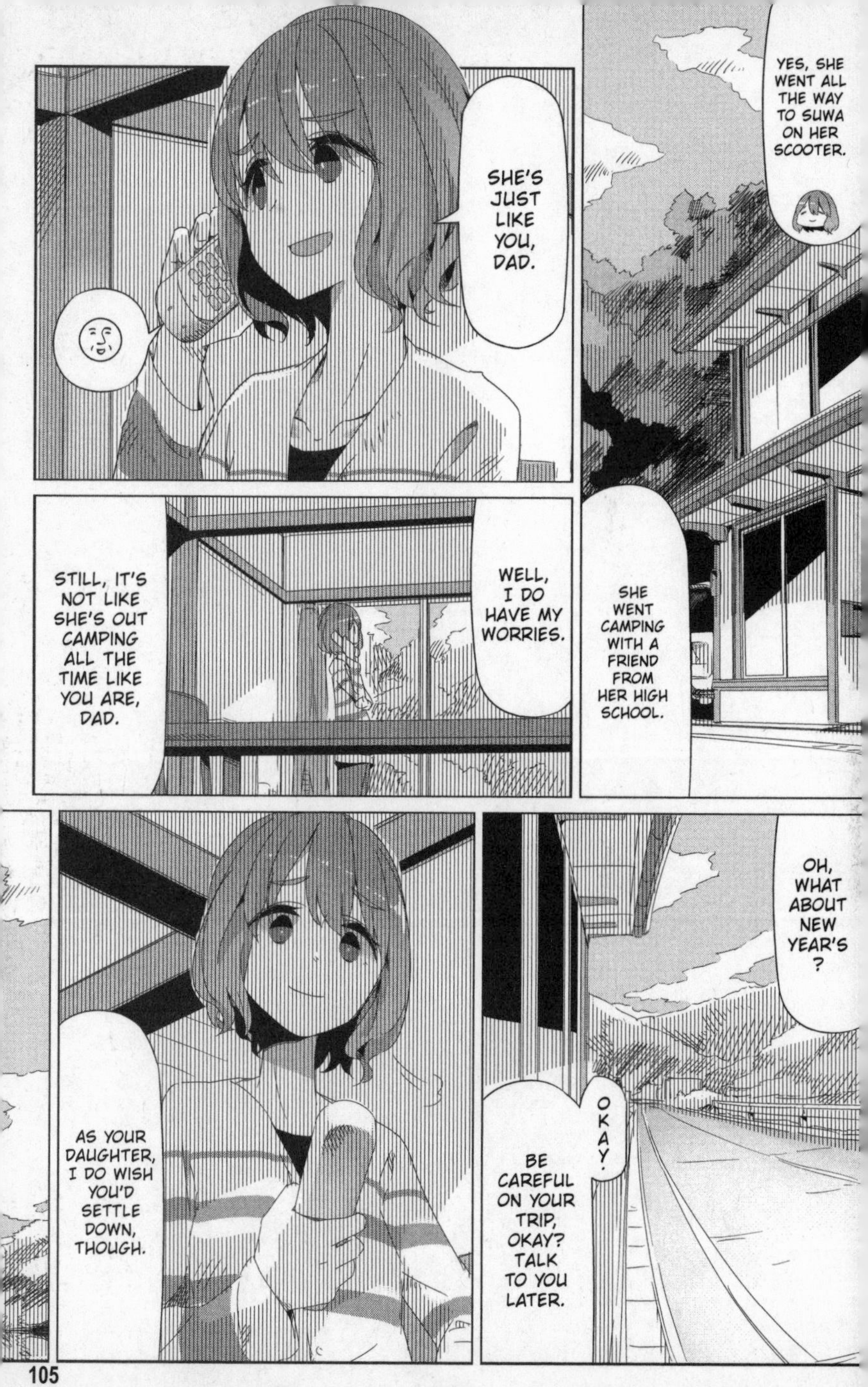
YES, SHE WENT ALL THE WAY TO SUWA ON HER SCOOTER.
SHE WENT CAMPING WITH A FRIEND FROM HER HIGH SCHOOL.
SHE'S JUST LIKE YOU, DAD.
WELL, I DO HAVE MY WORRIES.
STILL, IT'S NOT LIKE SHE'S OUT CAMPING ALL THE TIME LIKE YOU ARE, DAD.
OH, WHAT ABOUT NEW YEAR'S?
OKAY.
BE CAREFUL ON YOUR TRIP, OKAY? TALK TO YOU LATER.
AS YOUR DAUGHTER, I DO WISH YOU'D SETTLE DOWN, THOUGH.

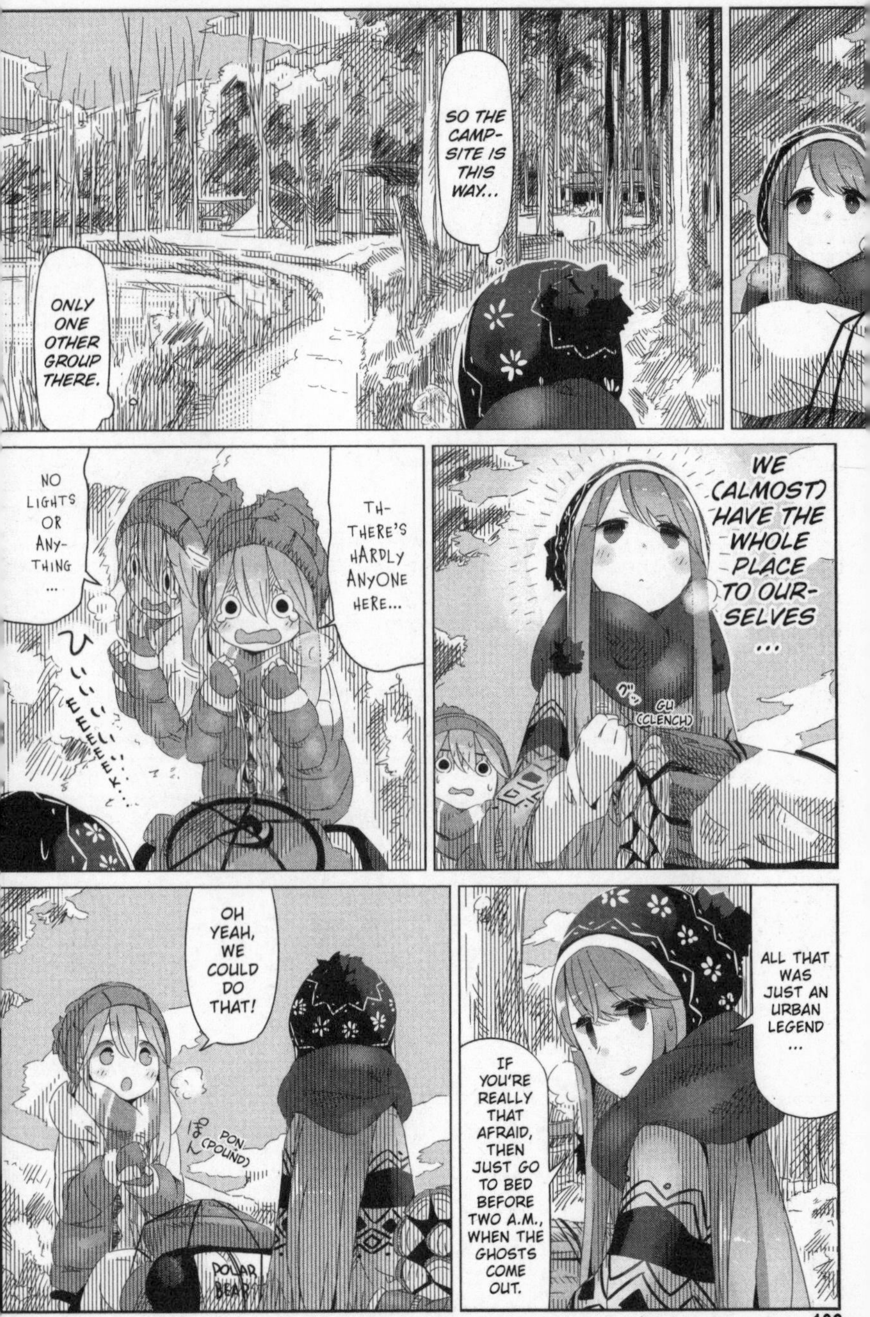
SO THE CAMP-SITE IS THIS WAY...
ONLY ONE OTHER GROUP THERE.
WE (ALMOST) HAVE THE WHOLE PLACE TO OUR-SELVES...
ぐっ GU (CLENCH)
TH-THERE'S HARDLY ANYONE HERE...
NO LIGHTS OR ANY-THING...
ひぃぃぃぃ EEEEEEK...
ALL THAT WAS JUST AN URBAN LEGEND...
IF YOU'RE REALLY THAT AFRAID, THEN JUST GO TO BED BEFORE TWO A.M., WHEN THE GHOSTS COME OUT.
OH YEAH, WE COULD DO THAT!
ぽん PON (POUND)
POLAR BEAR

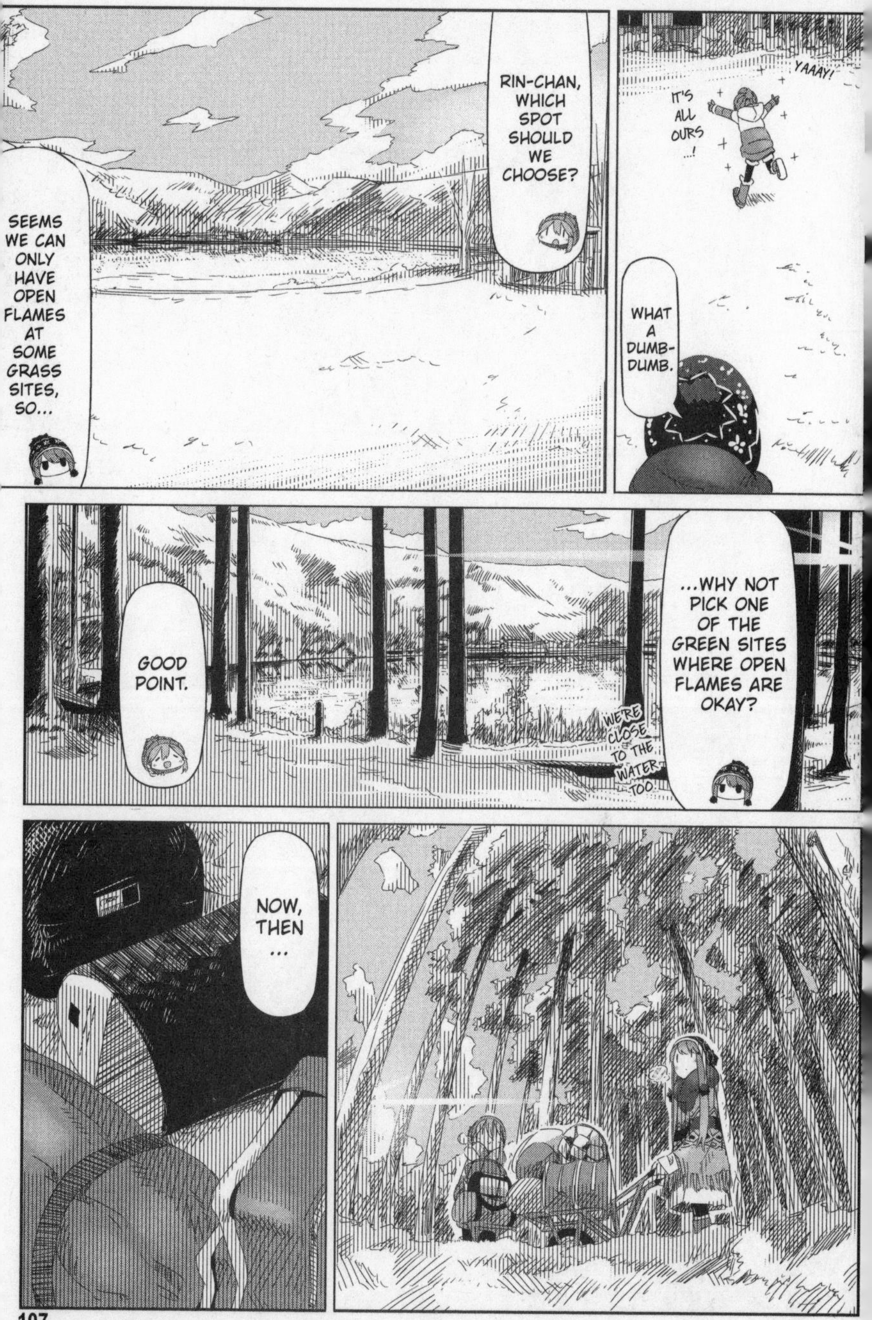
YAAAY!
IT'S ALL OURS ...!
WHAT A DUMB-DUMB.
RIN-CHAN, WHICH SPOT SHOULD WE CHOOSE?
SEEMS WE CAN ONLY HAVE OPEN FLAMES AT SOME GRASS SITES, SO...
...WHY NOT PICK ONE OF THE GREEN SITES WHERE OPEN FLAMES ARE OKAY?
WE'RE CLOSE TO THE WATER TOO.
GOOD POINT.
NOW, THEN ...

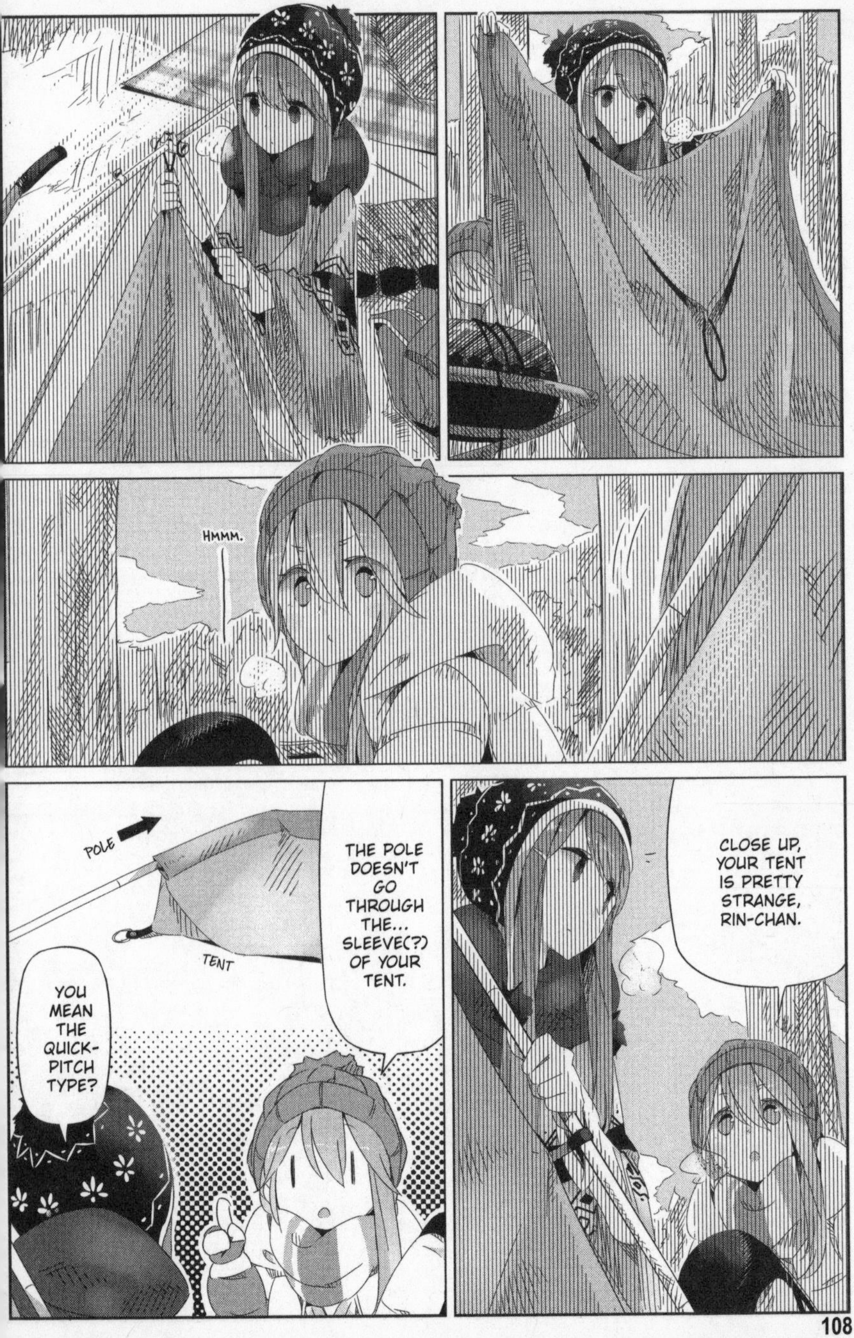
HMMM.
CLOSE UP, YOUR TENT IS PRETTY STRANGE, RIN-CHAN.
THE POLE DOESN'T GO THROUGH THE... SLEEVE(?) OF YOUR TENT.
POLE
TENT
YOU MEAN THE QUICK-PITCH TYPE?

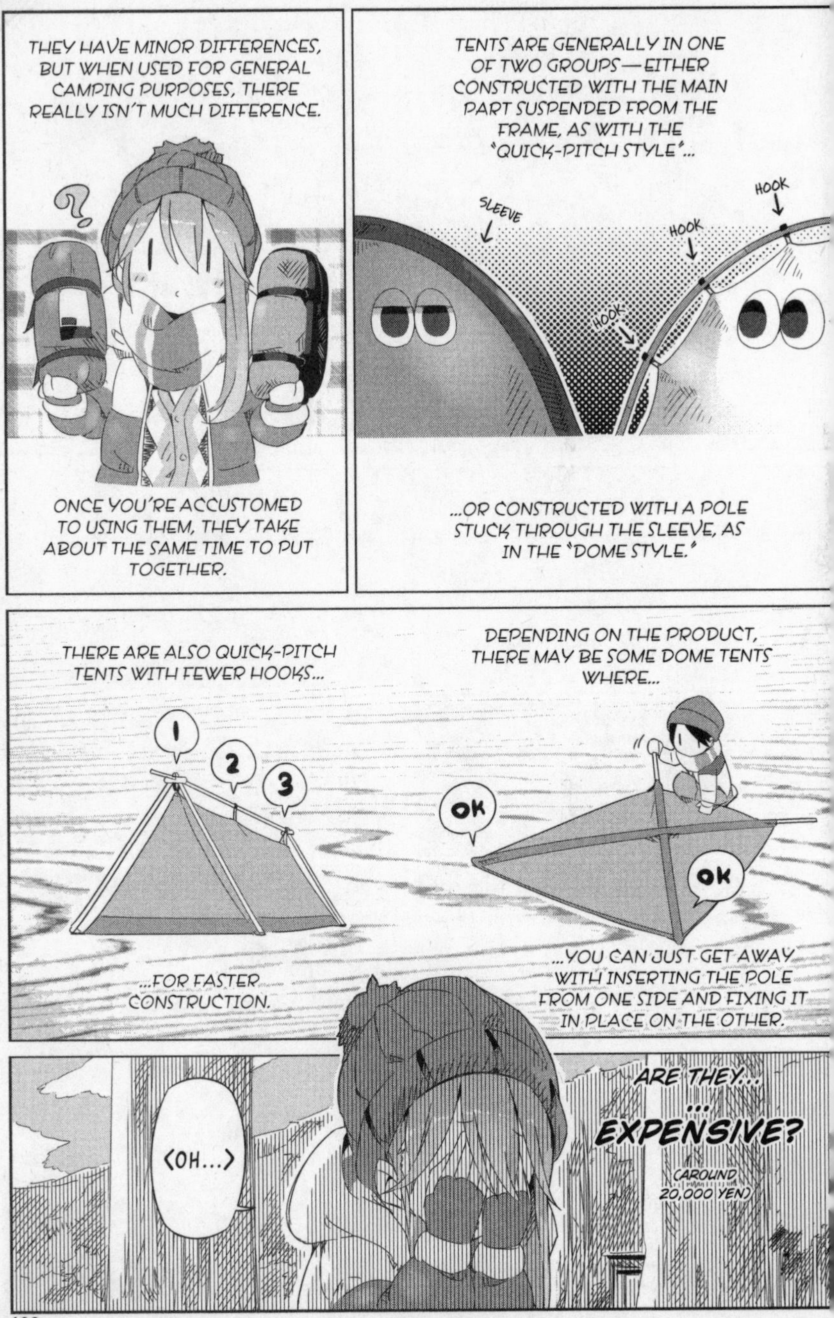

TENTS ARE GENERALLY IN ONE OF TWO GROUPS—EITHER CONSTRUCTED WITH THE MAIN PART SUSPENDED FROM THE FRAME, AS WITH THE "QUICK-PITCH STYLE"...
HOOK
HOOK
SLEEVE
HOOK
...OR CONSTRUCTED WITH A POLE STUCK THROUGH THE SLEEVE, AS IN THE "DOME STYLE."
THEY HAVE MINOR DIFFERENCES, BUT WHEN USED FOR GENERAL CAMPING PURPOSES, THERE REALLY ISN'T MUCH DIFFERENCE.
ONCE YOU'RE ACCUSTOMED TO USING THEM, THEY TAKE ABOUT THE SAME TIME TO PUT TOGETHER.
DEPENDING ON THE PRODUCT, THERE MAY BE SOME DOME TENTS WHERE...
OK
OK
...YOU CAN JUST GET AWAY WITH INSERTING THE POLE FROM ONE SIDE AND FIXING IT IN PLACE ON THE OTHER.
THERE ARE ALSO QUICK-PITCH TENTS WITH FEWER HOOKS...
1
2
3
...FOR FASTER CONSTRUCTION.
ARE THEY... ...EXPENSIVE?
(AROUND 20,000 YEN)
<OH...>

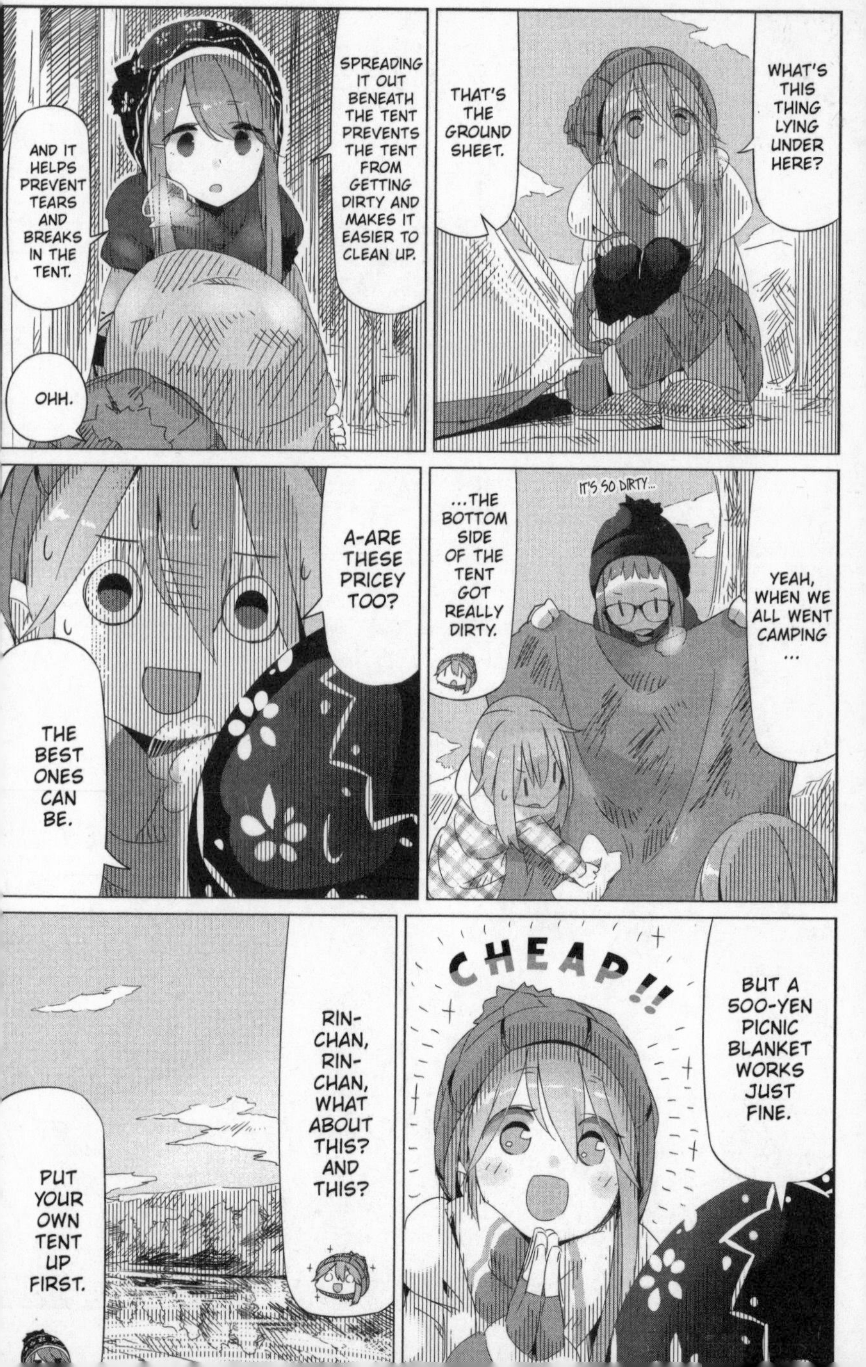
WHAT'S THIS THING LYING UNDER HERE?
THAT'S THE GROUND SHEET.
SPREADING IT OUT BENEATH THE TENT PREVENTS THE TENT FROM GETTING DIRTY AND MAKES IT EASIER TO CLEAN UP.
AND IT HELPS PREVENT TEARS AND BREAKS IN THE TENT.
OHH.
YEAH, WHEN WE ALL WENT CAMPING ...
...THE BOTTOM SIDE OF THE TENT GOT REALLY DIRTY.
IT'S SO DIRTY...
A-ARE THESE PRICEY TOO?
THE BEST ONES CAN BE.
BUT A 500-YEN PICNIC BLANKET WORKS JUST FINE.
CHEAP!!
RIN-CHAN, RIN-CHAN, WHAT ABOUT THIS? AND THIS?
PUT YOUR OWN TENT UP FIRST.

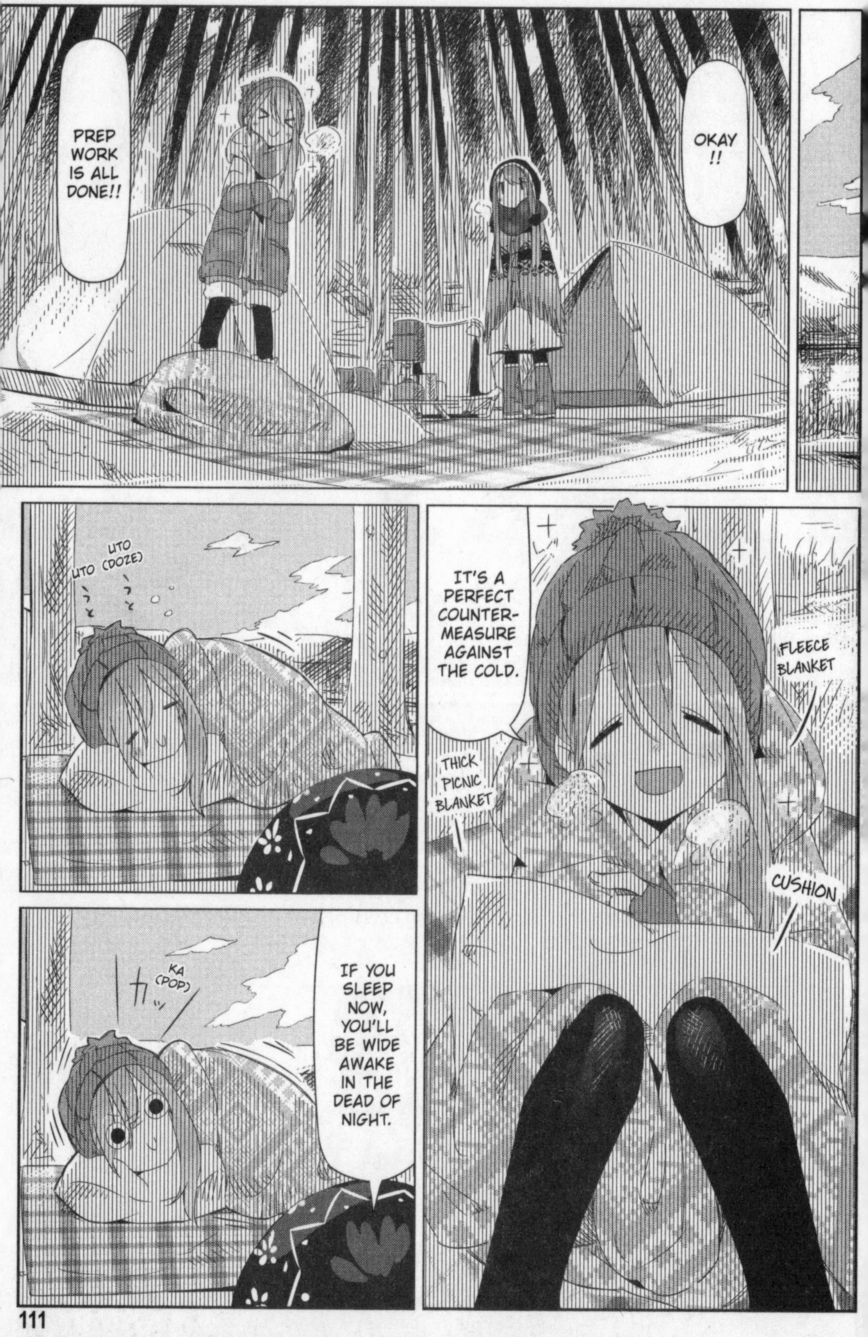
OKAY !!
PREP WORK IS ALL DONE!!
IT'S A PERFECT COUNTER-MEASURE AGAINST THE COLD.
FLEECE BLANKET
THICK PICNIC BLANKET
CUSHION
UTO UTO (DOZE)
KA (POP)
IF YOU SLEEP NOW, YOU'LL BE WIDE AWAKE IN THE DEAD OF NIGHT.

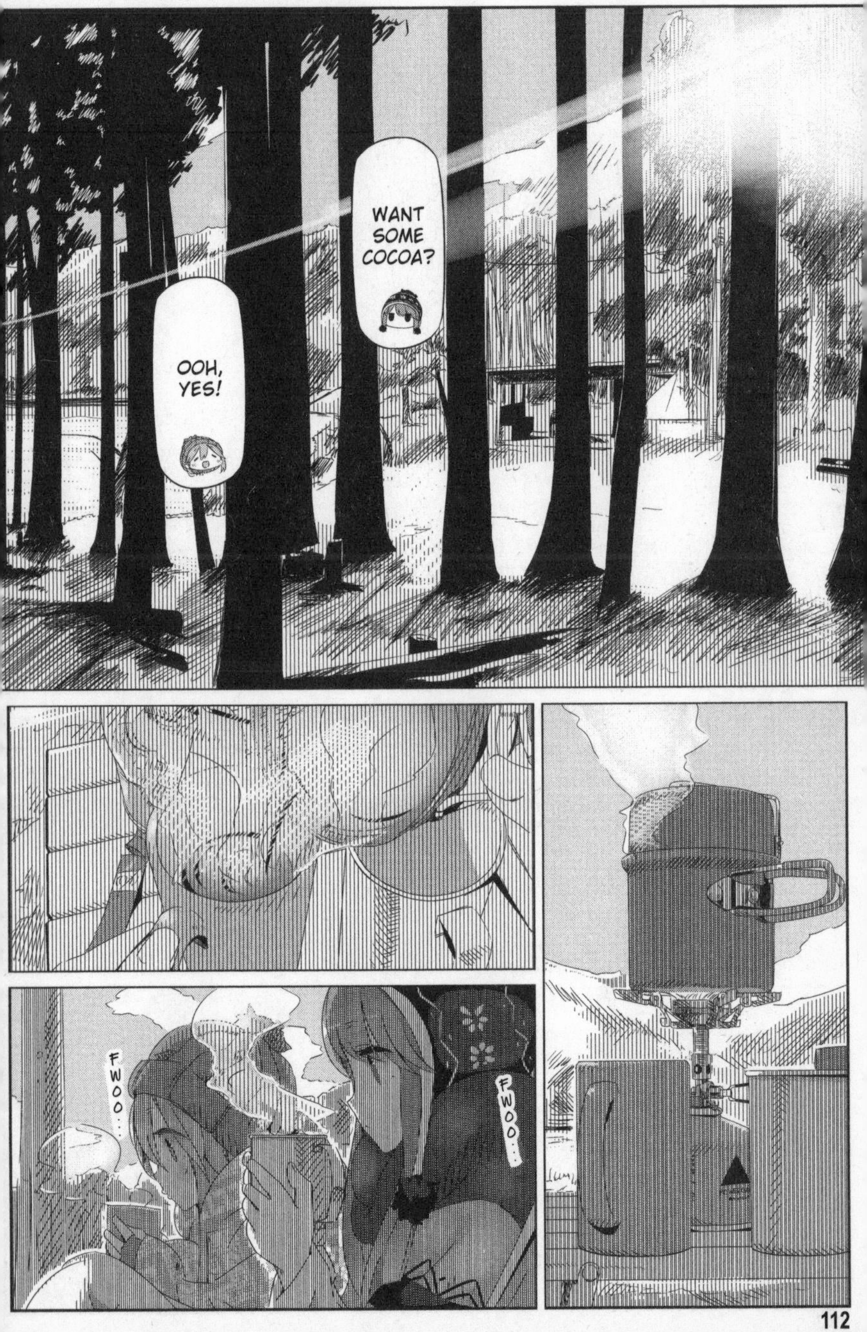
WANT SOME COCOA?
OOH, YES!
FWOO...
FWOO...

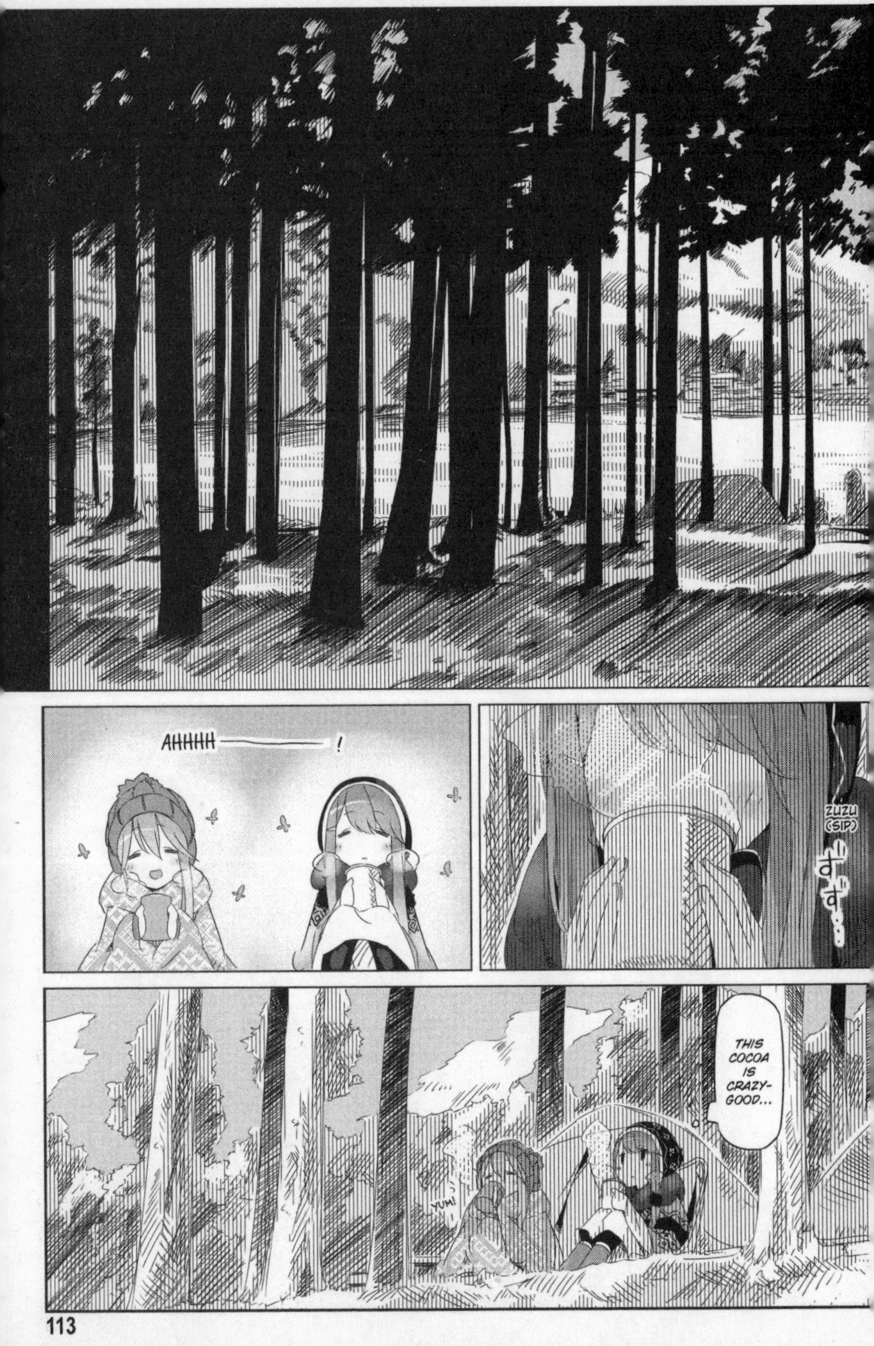
ZUZU (SIP)
ずず…
AHHHH——!
THIS COCOA IS CRAZY-GOOD...
YUM!

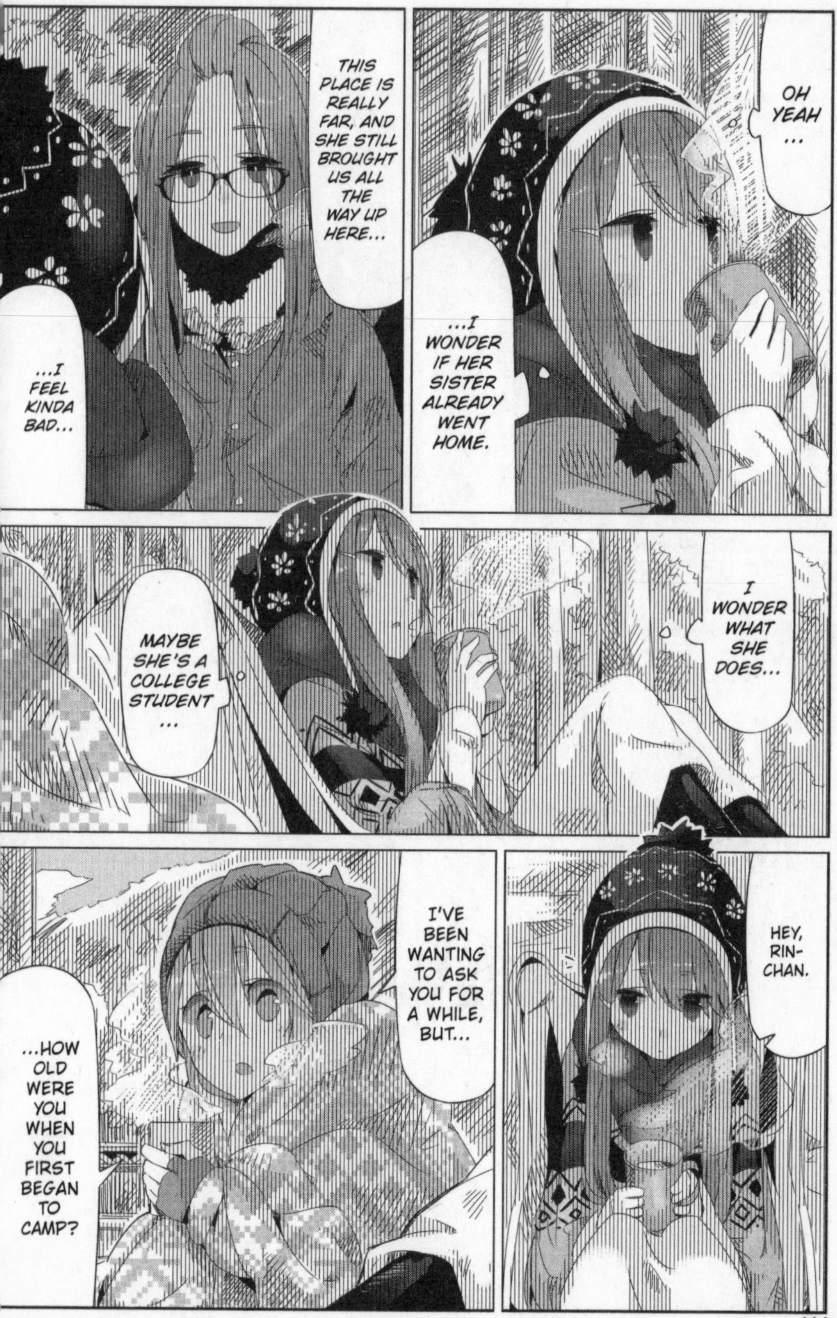
OH YEAH ...
...I WONDER IF HER SISTER ALREADY WENT HOME.
THIS PLACE IS REALLY FAR, AND SHE STILL BROUGHT US ALL THE WAY UP HERE...
...I FEEL KINDA BAD...
I WONDER WHAT SHE DOES...
MAYBE SHE'S A COLLEGE STUDENT ...
HEY, RIN-CHAN.
I'VE BEEN WANTING TO ASK YOU FOR A WHILE, BUT...
...HOW OLD WERE YOU WHEN YOU FIRST BEGAN TO CAMP?

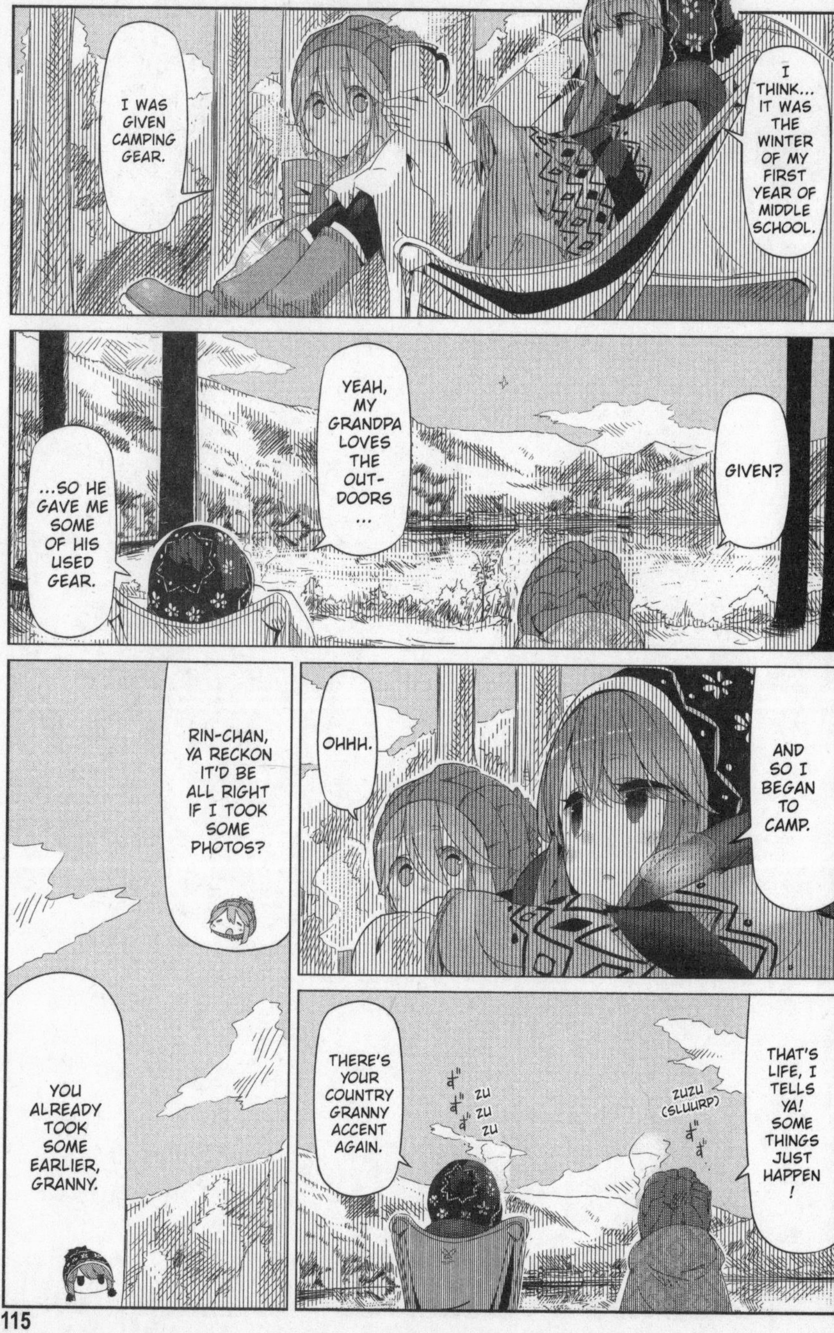

I THINK... IT WAS THE WINTER OF MY FIRST YEAR OF MIDDLE SCHOOL.
I WAS GIVEN CAMPING GEAR.
GIVEN?
YEAH, MY GRANDPA LOVES THE OUT-DOORS...
...SO HE GAVE ME SOME OF HIS USED GEAR.
AND SO I BEGAN TO CAMP.
OHHH.
THAT'S LIFE, I TELLS YA! SOME THINGS JUST HAPPEN!
ZUZU (SLUURP)
ZU ZU ZU
THERE'S YOUR COUNTRY GRANNY ACCENT AGAIN.
RIN-CHAN, YA RECKON IT'D BE ALL RIGHT IF I TOOK SOME PHOTOS?
YOU ALREADY TOOK SOME EARLIER, GRANNY.

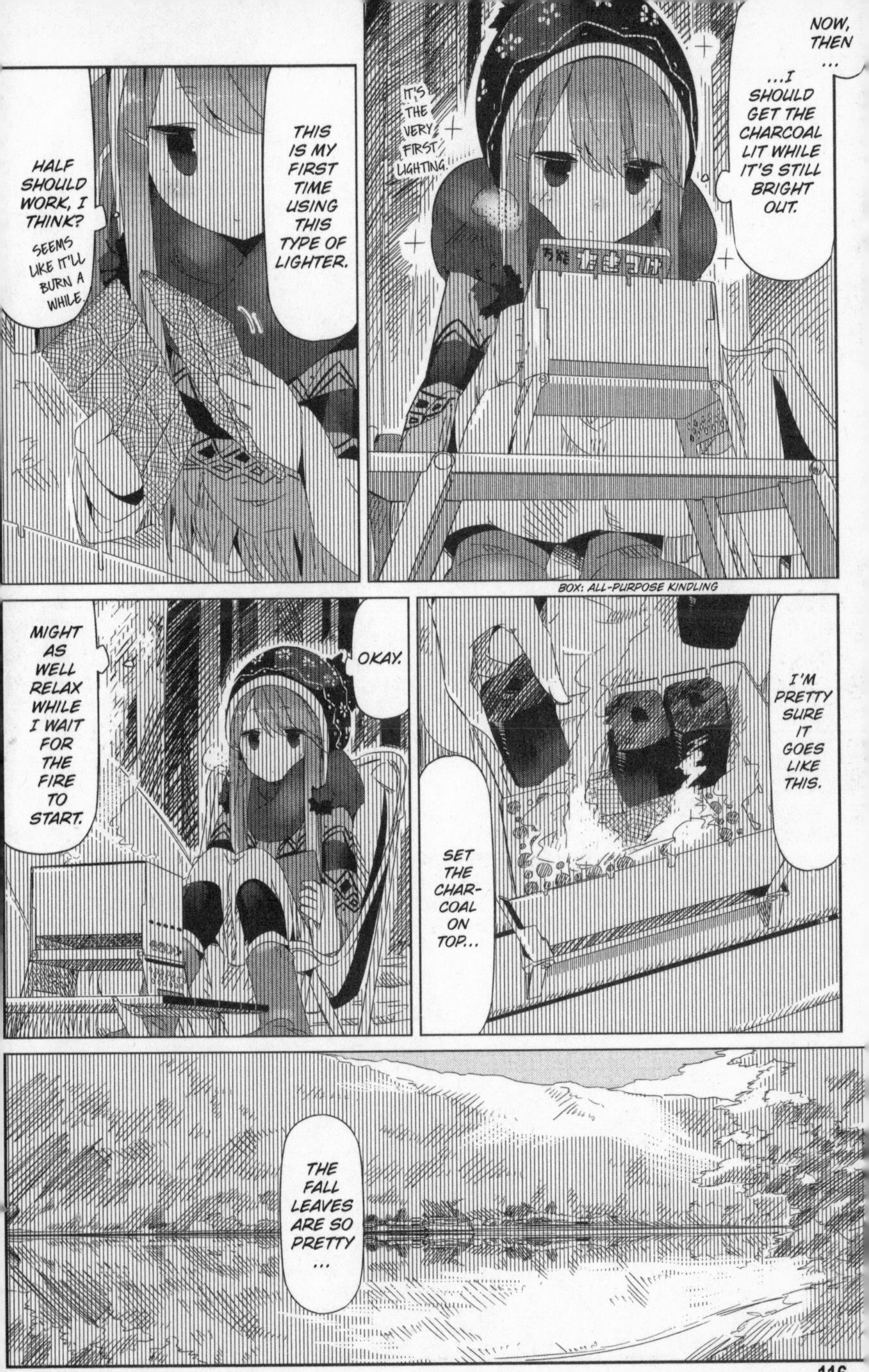
NOW, THEN...
...I SHOULD GET THE CHARCOAL LIT WHILE IT'S STILL BRIGHT OUT.
IT'S THE VERY FIRST LIGHTING.
BOX: ALL-PURPOSE KINDLING
THIS IS MY FIRST TIME USING THIS TYPE OF LIGHTER.
HALF SHOULD WORK, I THINK?
SEEMS LIKE IT'LL BURN A WHILE.
I'M PRETTY SURE IT GOES LIKE THIS.
SET THE CHAR-COAL ON TOP...
OKAY.
MIGHT AS WELL RELAX WHILE I WAIT FOR THE FIRE TO START.
THE FALL LEAVES ARE SO PRETTY...

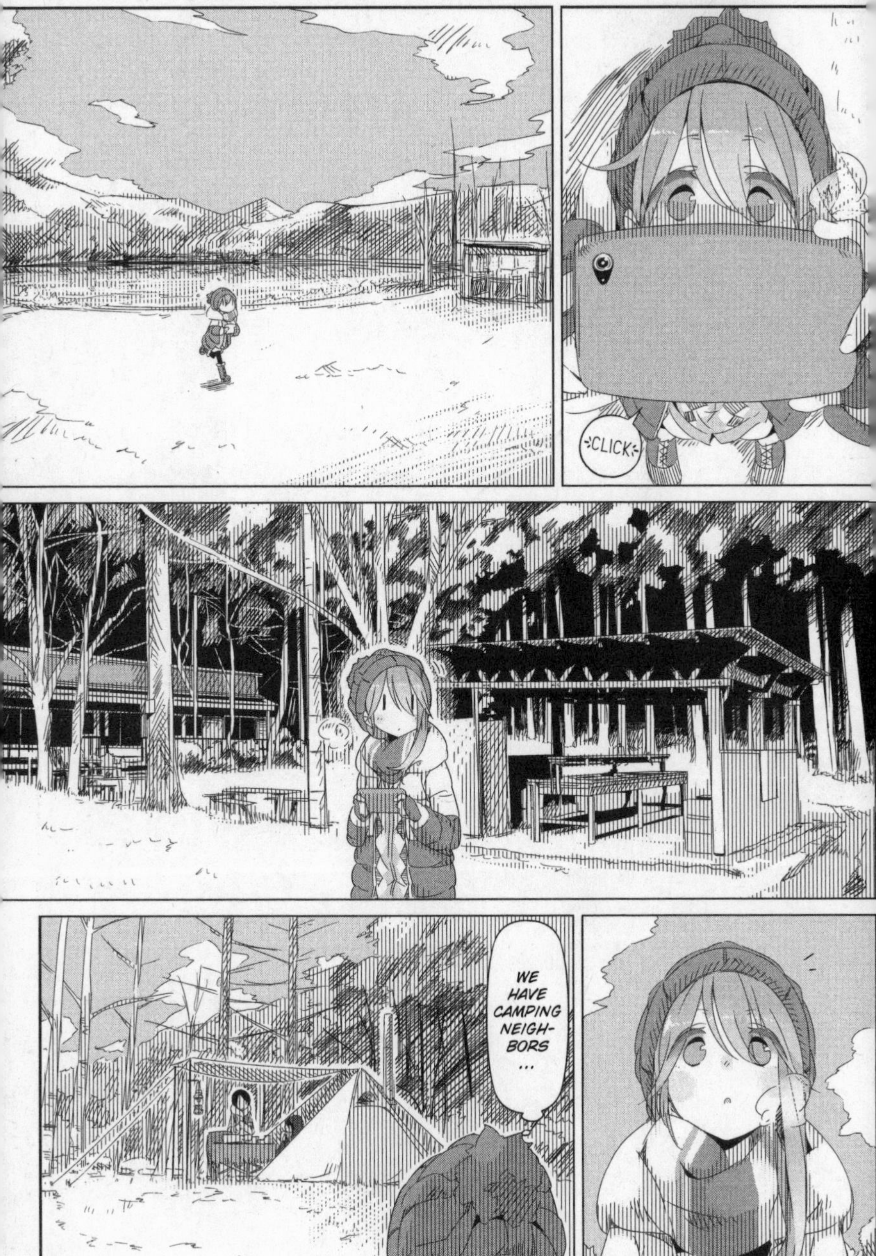
CLICK
WE HAVE CAMPING NEIGH-BORS ...

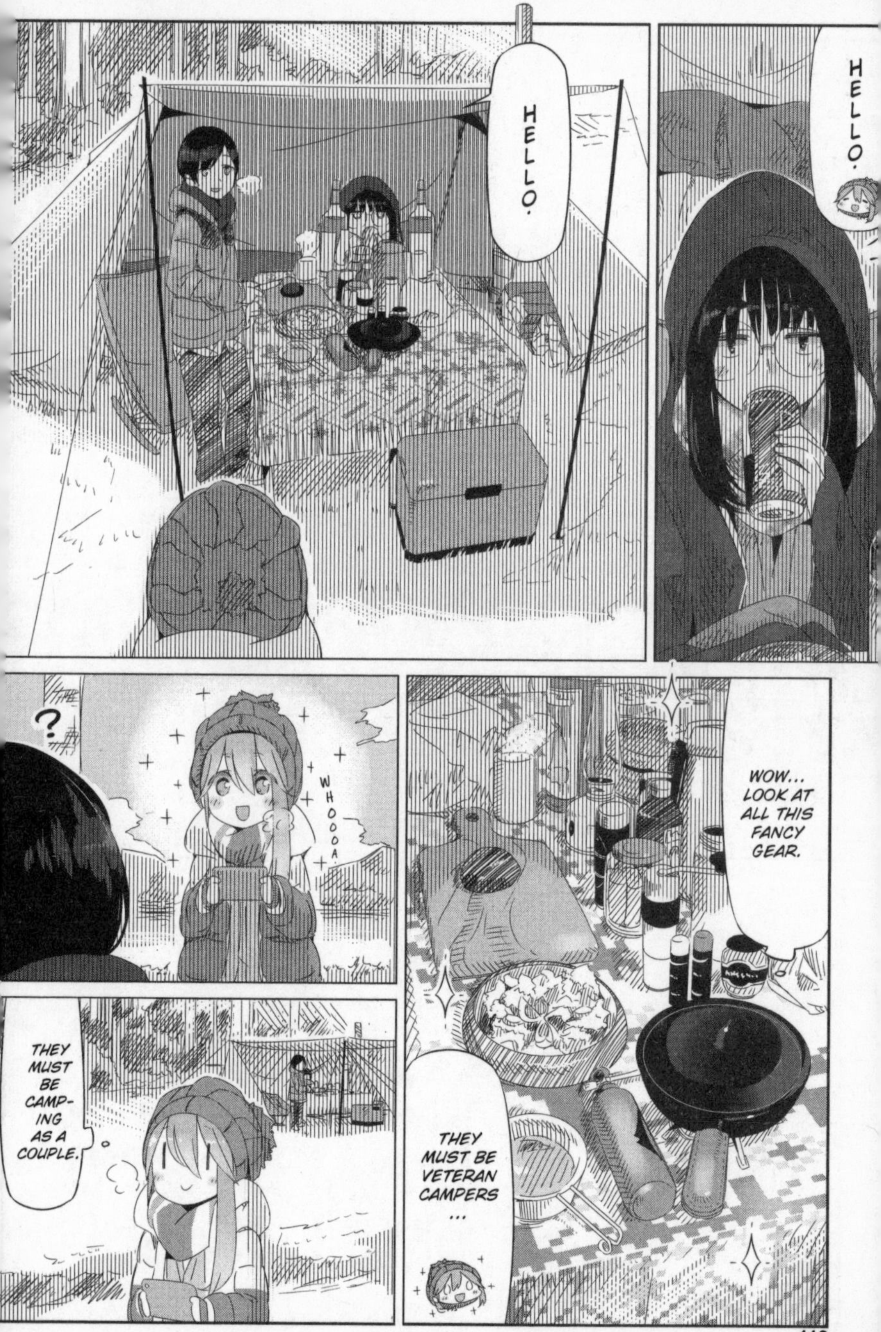

HELLO.
HELLO.
WOW... LOOK AT ALL THIS FANCY GEAR.
?
WHOOOOA
THEY MUST BE VETERAN CAMPERS...
THEY MUST BE CAMP-ING AS A COUPLE.

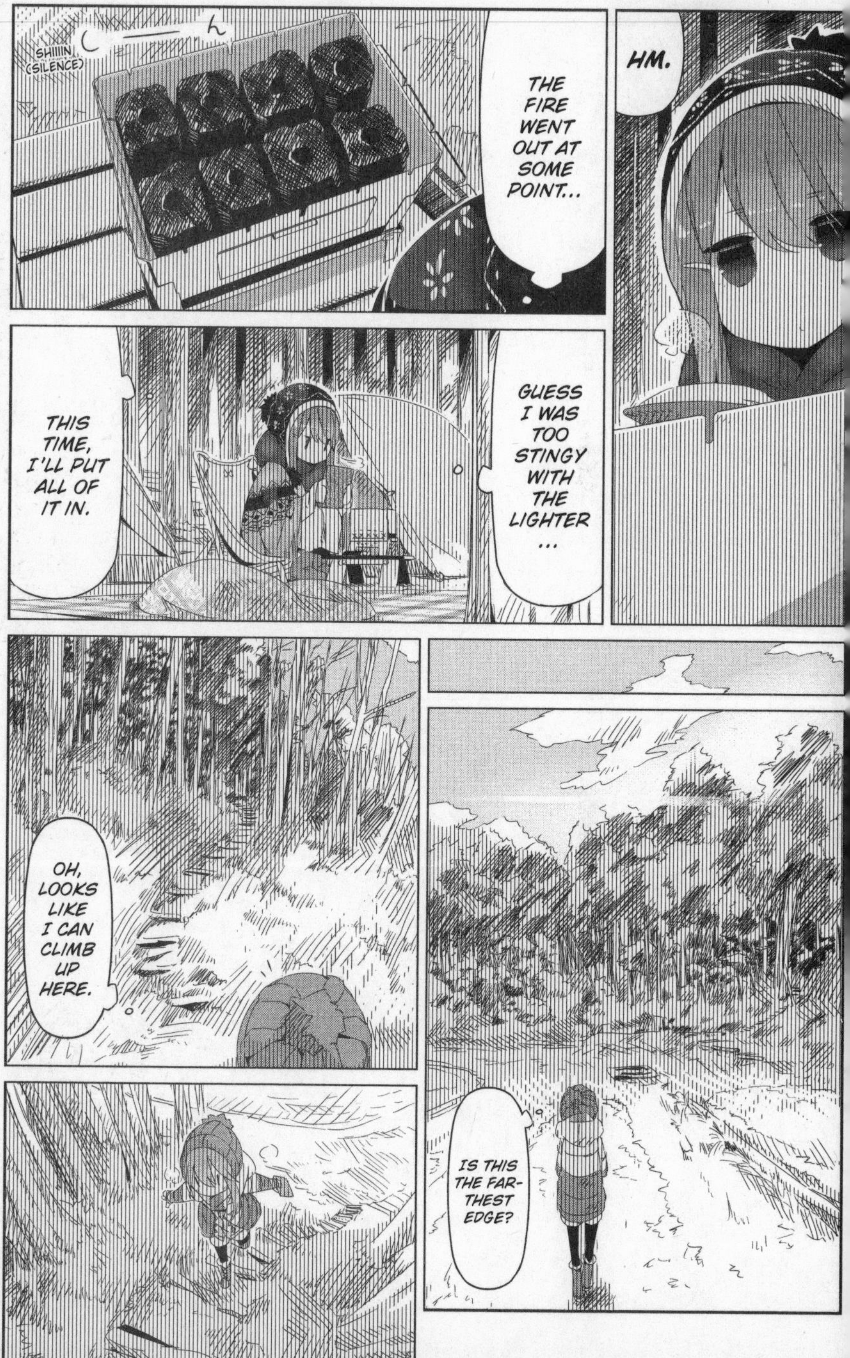
HM.
SHIIIN (SILENCE)
THE FIRE WENT OUT AT SOME POINT...
GUESS I WAS TOO STINGY WITH THE LIGHTER...
THIS TIME, I'LL PUT ALL OF IT IN.
IS THIS THE FAR-THEST EDGE?
OH, LOOKS LIKE I CAN CLIMB UP HERE.

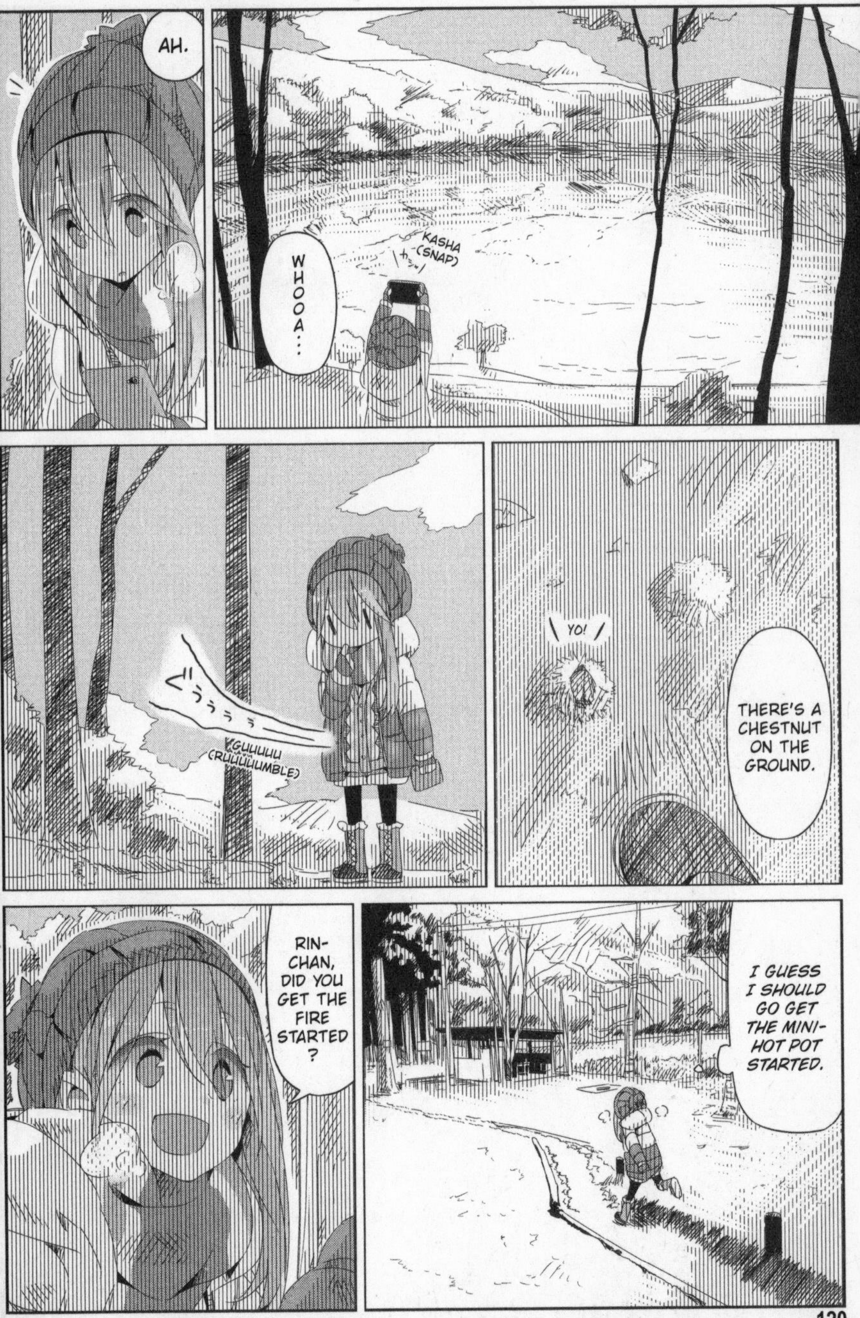
WHOOA...
KASHA (SNAP)
AH.
YO!
THERE'S A CHESTNUT ON THE GROUND.
ぐぅぅぅぅ
GUUUUU (RUUUUUMBLE)
I GUESS I SHOULD GO GET THE MINI-HOT POT STARTED.
RIN-CHAN, DID YOU GET THE FIRE STARTED?

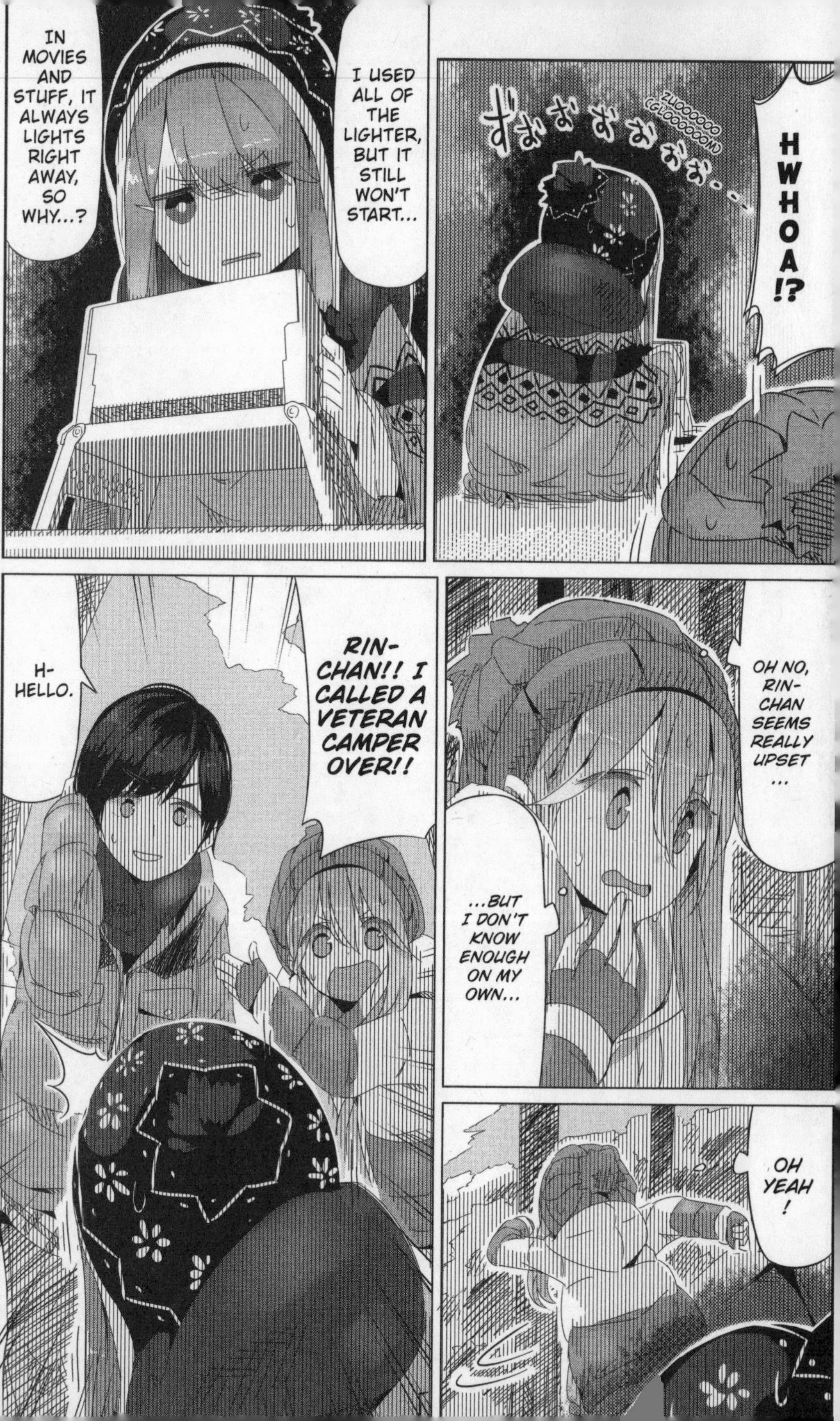
HWHOA!?
ずおおおおおお…
ZUOOOOOO (GLOOOOOOM)
I USED ALL OF THE LIGHTER, BUT IT STILL WON'T START…
IN MOVIES AND STUFF, IT ALWAYS LIGHTS RIGHT AWAY, SO WHY…?
OH NO, RIN-CHAN SEEMS REALLY UPSET…
…BUT I DON'T KNOW ENOUGH ON MY OWN…
OH YEAH!
RIN-CHAN!! I CALLED A VETERAN CAMPER OVER!!
H-HELLO.

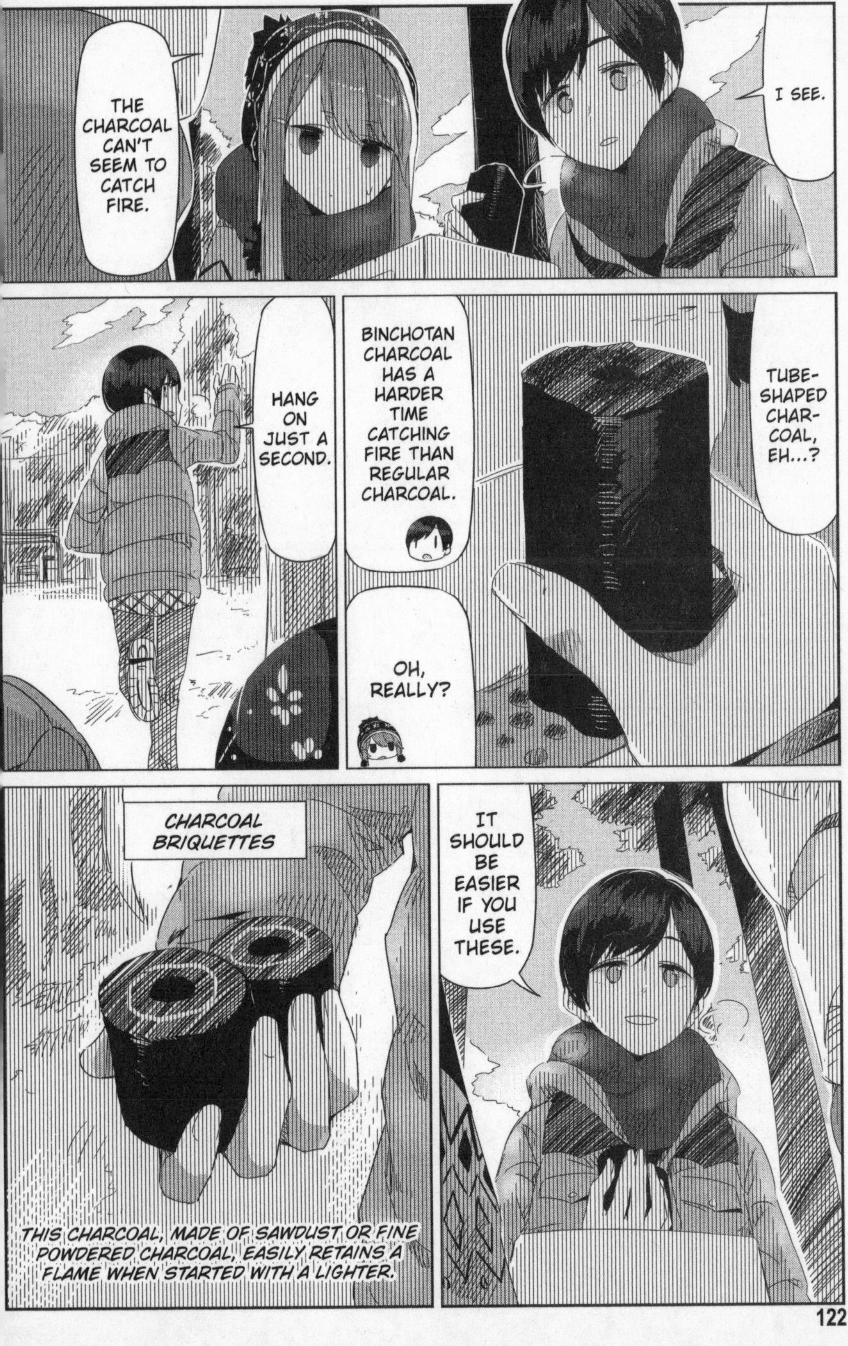
I SEE.
THE CHARCOAL CAN'T SEEM TO CATCH FIRE.
TUBE-SHAPED CHAR-COAL, EH...?
BINCHOTAN CHARCOAL HAS A HARDER TIME CATCHING FIRE THAN REGULAR CHARCOAL.
OH, REALLY?
HANG ON JUST A SECOND.
IT SHOULD BE EASIER IF YOU USE THESE.
CHARCOAL BRIQUETTES
THIS CHARCOAL, MADE OF SAWDUST OR FINE POWDERED CHARCOAL, EASILY RETAINS A FLAME WHEN STARTED WITH A LIGHTER.

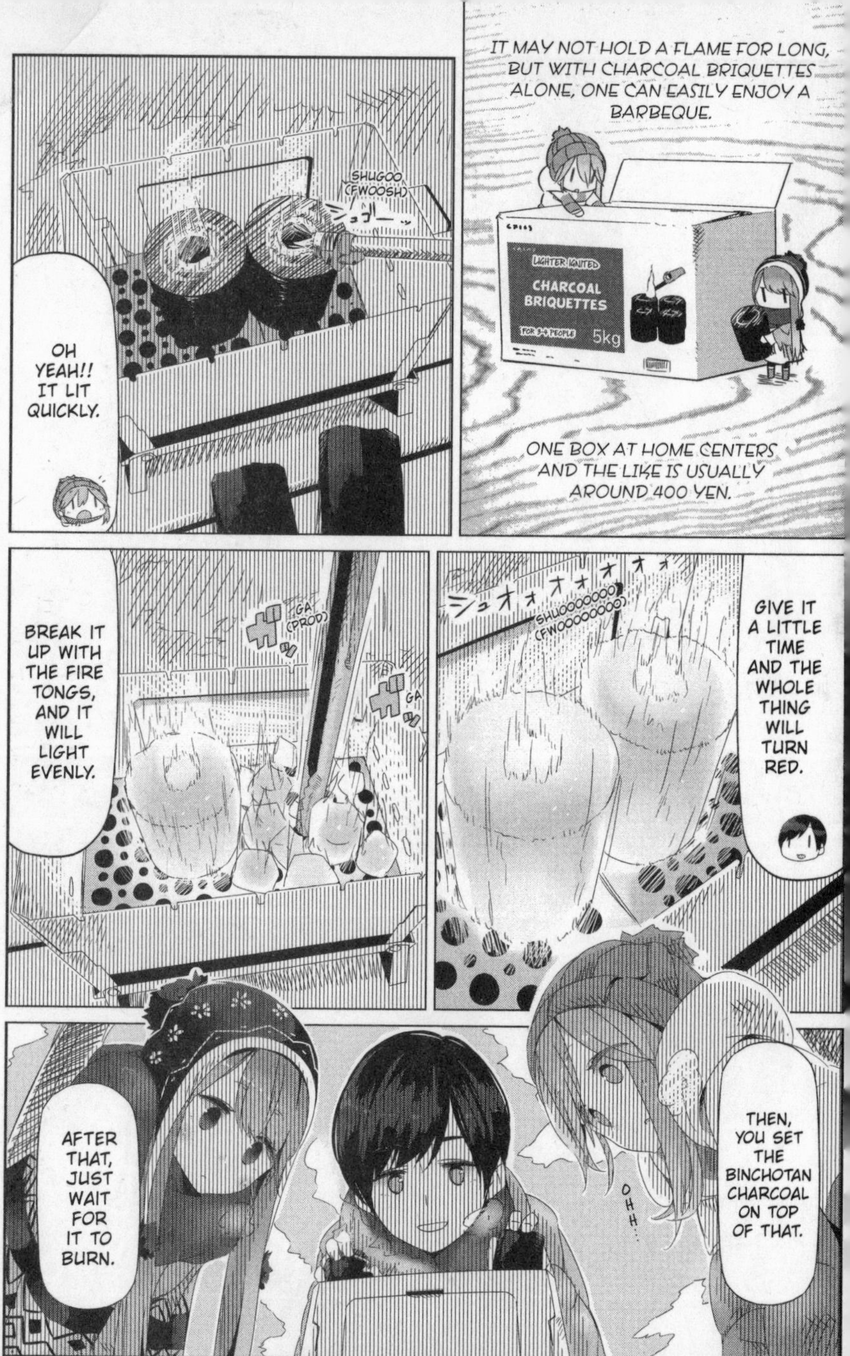
IT MAY NOT HOLD A FLAME FOR LONG, BUT WITH CHARCOAL BRIQUETTES ALONE, ONE CAN EASILY ENJOY A BARBEQUE.
LIGHTER IGNITED
CHARCOAL BRIQUETTES
FOR 3-4 PEOPLE
5kg
ONE BOX AT HOME CENTERS AND THE LIKE IS USUALLY AROUND 400 YEN.
SHUGOO (FWOOSH)
シュゴー
OH YEAH!! IT LIT QUICKLY.
シュオォオオオォォ
SHUOOOOOOO (FWOOOOOOOO)
GIVE IT A LITTLE TIME AND THE WHOLE THING WILL TURN RED.
GA (PROD)
GA
BREAK IT UP WITH THE FIRE TONGS, AND IT WILL LIGHT EVENLY.
THEN, YOU SET THE BINCHOTAN CHARCOAL ON TOP OF THAT.
OHH...
AFTER THAT, JUST WAIT FOR IT TO BURN.

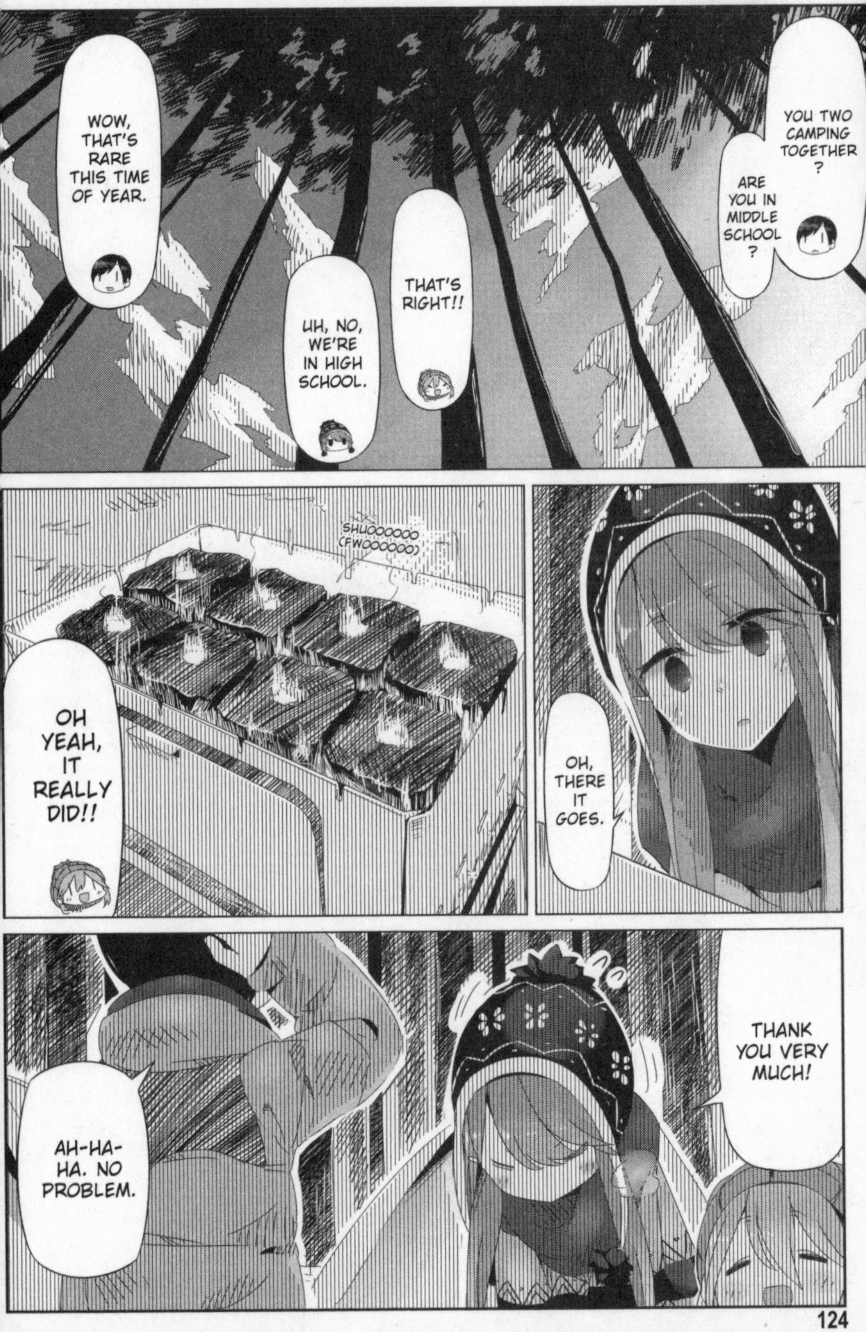
YOU TWO CAMPING TOGETHER?
ARE YOU IN MIDDLE SCHOOL?
THAT'S RIGHT!!
UH, NO, WE'RE IN HIGH SCHOOL.
WOW, THAT'S RARE THIS TIME OF YEAR.
OH, THERE IT GOES.
SHUOOOOOO (FWOOOOOOO)
OH YEAH, IT REALLY DID!!
THANK YOU VERY MUCH!
AH-HA-HA. NO PROBLEM.

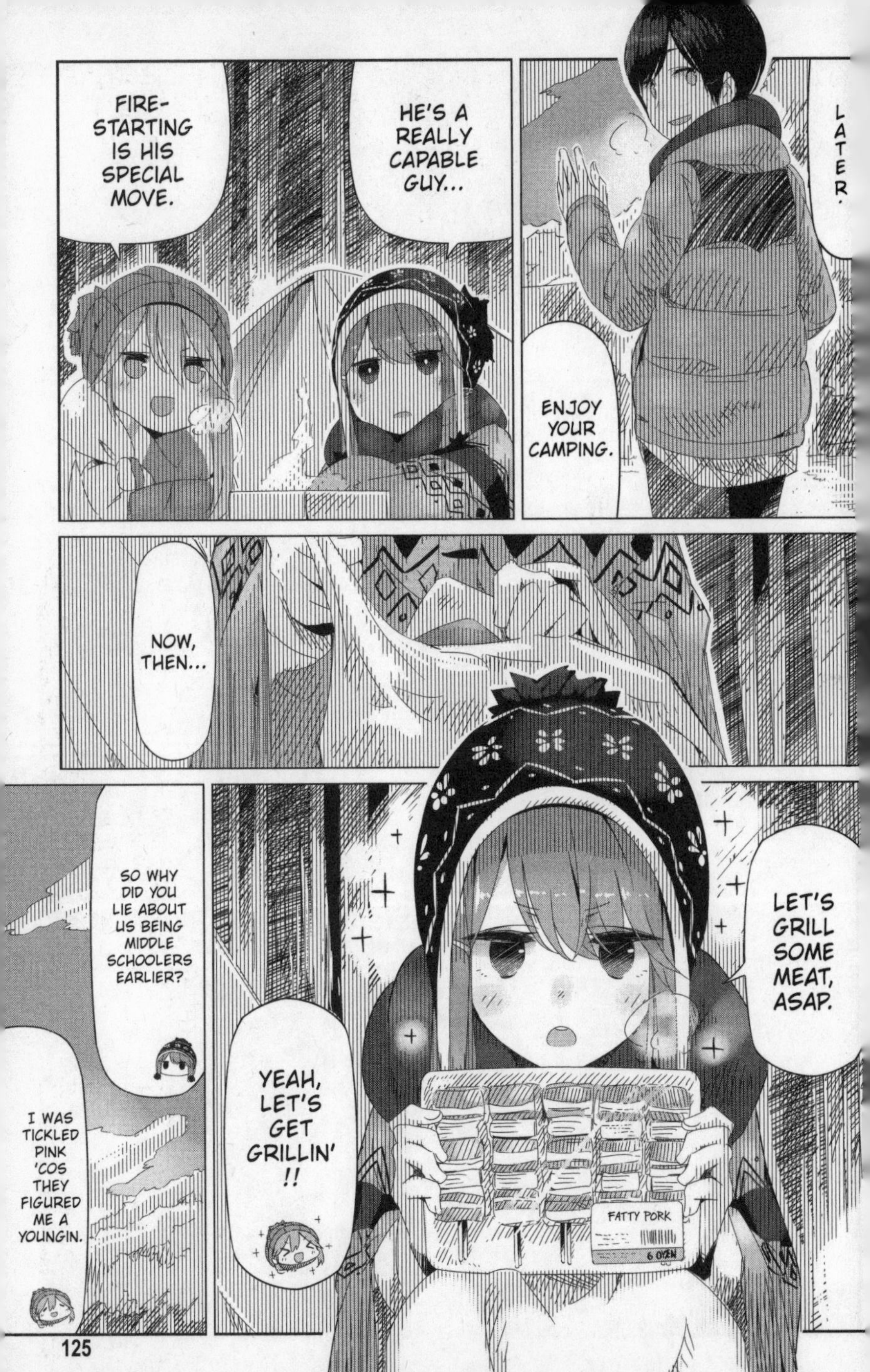
LATER.
ENJOY YOUR CAMPING.
HE'S A REALLY CAPABLE GUY...
FIRE-STARTING IS HIS SPECIAL MOVE.
NOW, THEN...
LET'S GRILL SOME MEAT, ASAP.
YEAH, LET'S GET GRILLIN' !!
FATTY PORK
SO WHY DID YOU LIE ABOUT US BEING MIDDLE SCHOOLERS EARLIER?
I WAS TICKLED PINK 'COS THEY FIGURED ME A YOUNGIN.

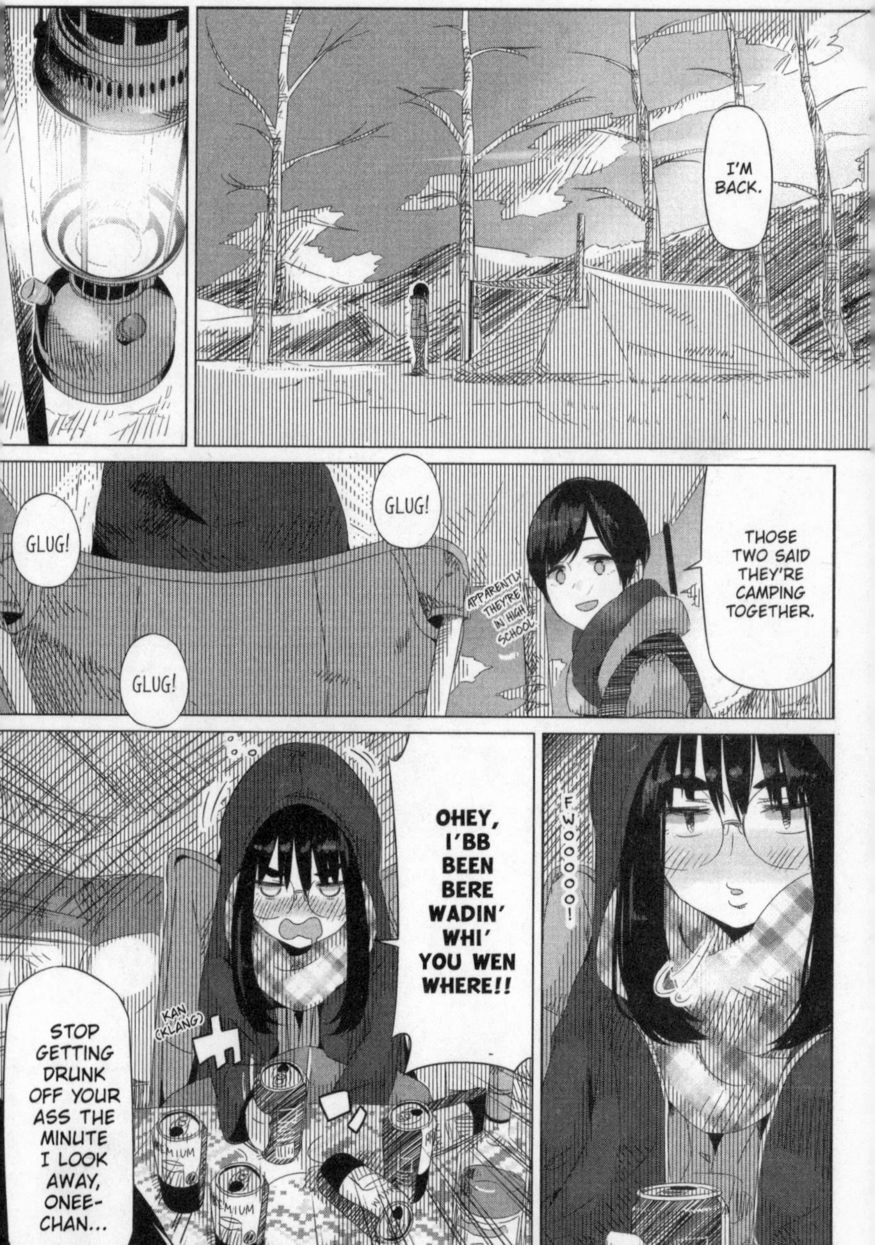
I'M BACK.
THOSE TWO SAID THEY'RE CAMPING TOGETHER.
APPARENTLY THEY'RE IN HIGH SCHOOL
GLUG!
GLUG!
GLUG!
FWOOOOOO!
OHEY, I'BB BEEN BERE WADIN' WHI' YOU WEN WHERE!!
KAN (KLANG)
STOP GETTING DRUNK OFF YOUR ASS THE MINUTE I LOOK AWAY, ONEE-CHAN...

Chapter 12 Nighttime on the Lake with Fellow Campers

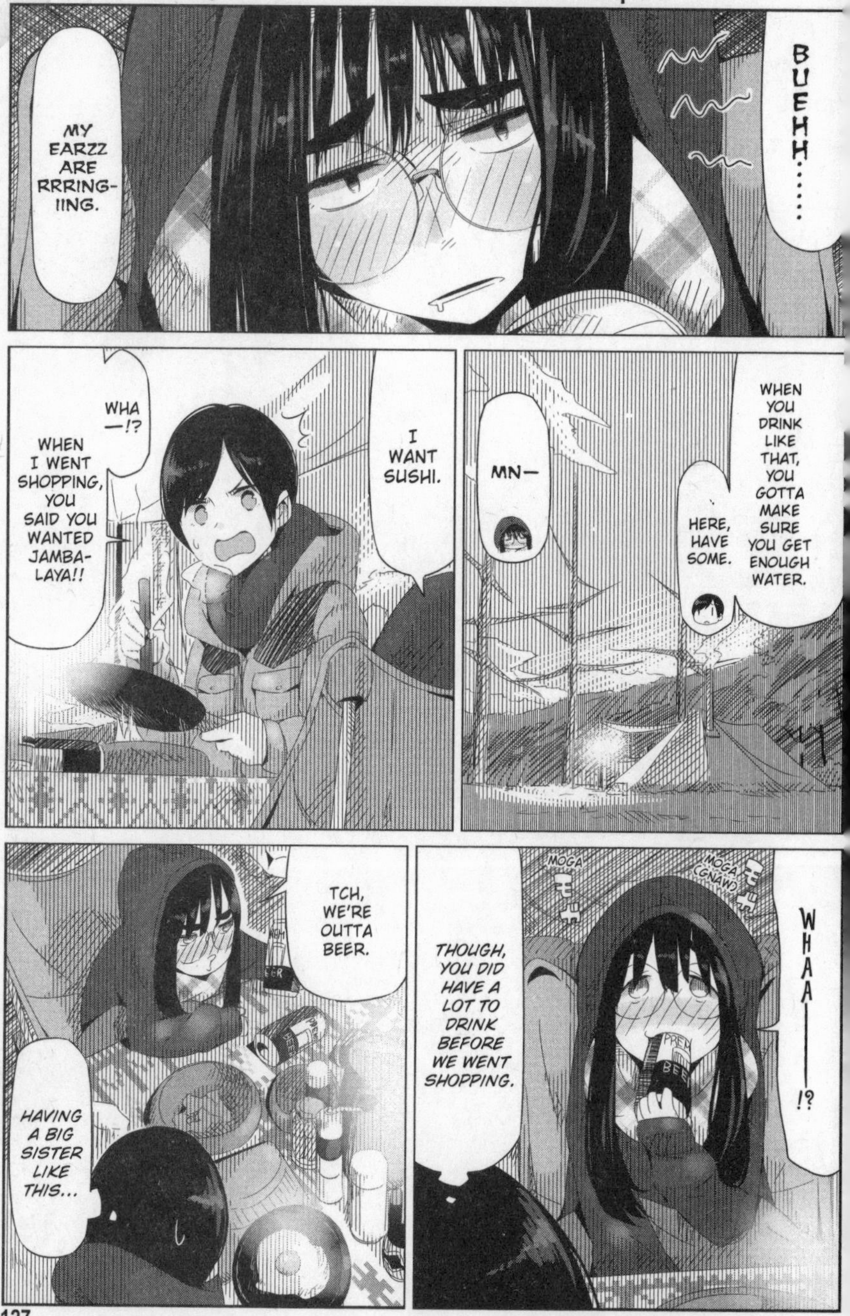
BUEHH......
MY EARZZ ARE RRRING-IING.
WHEN YOU DRINK LIKE THAT, YOU GOTTA MAKE SURE YOU GET ENOUGH WATER.
HERE, HAVE SOME.
MN—
I WANT SUSHI.
WHA—!?
WHEN I WENT SHOPPING, YOU SAID YOU WANTED JAMBA-LAYA!!
MOGA
MOGA (GNAW)
WHAA—!?
THOUGH, YOU DID HAVE A LOT TO DRINK BEFORE WE WENT SHOPPING.
TCH, WE'RE OUTTA BEER.
HAVING A BIG SISTER LIKE THIS...

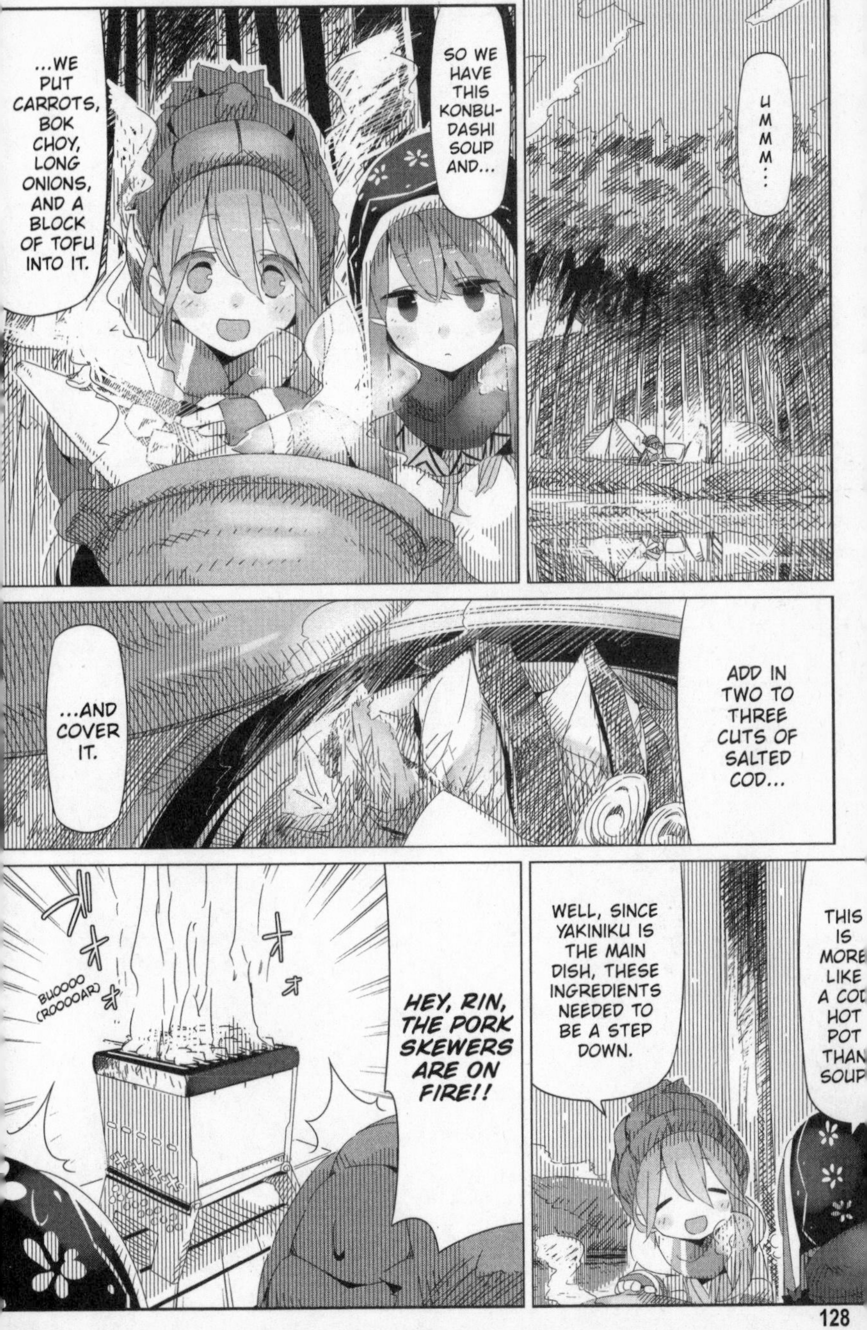
UMMM...
SO WE HAVE THIS KONBU-DASHI SOUP AND...
...WE PUT CARROTS, BOK CHOY, LONG ONIONS, AND A BLOCK OF TOFU INTO IT.
ADD IN TWO TO THREE CUTS OF SALTED COD...
...AND COVER IT.
THIS IS MORE LIKE A COD HOT POT THAN SOUP
WELL, SINCE YAKINIKU IS THE MAIN DISH, THESE INGREDIENTS NEEDED TO BE A STEP DOWN.
HEY, RIN, THE PORK SKEWERS ARE ON FIRE!!
BUOOOO (ROOOOAR)

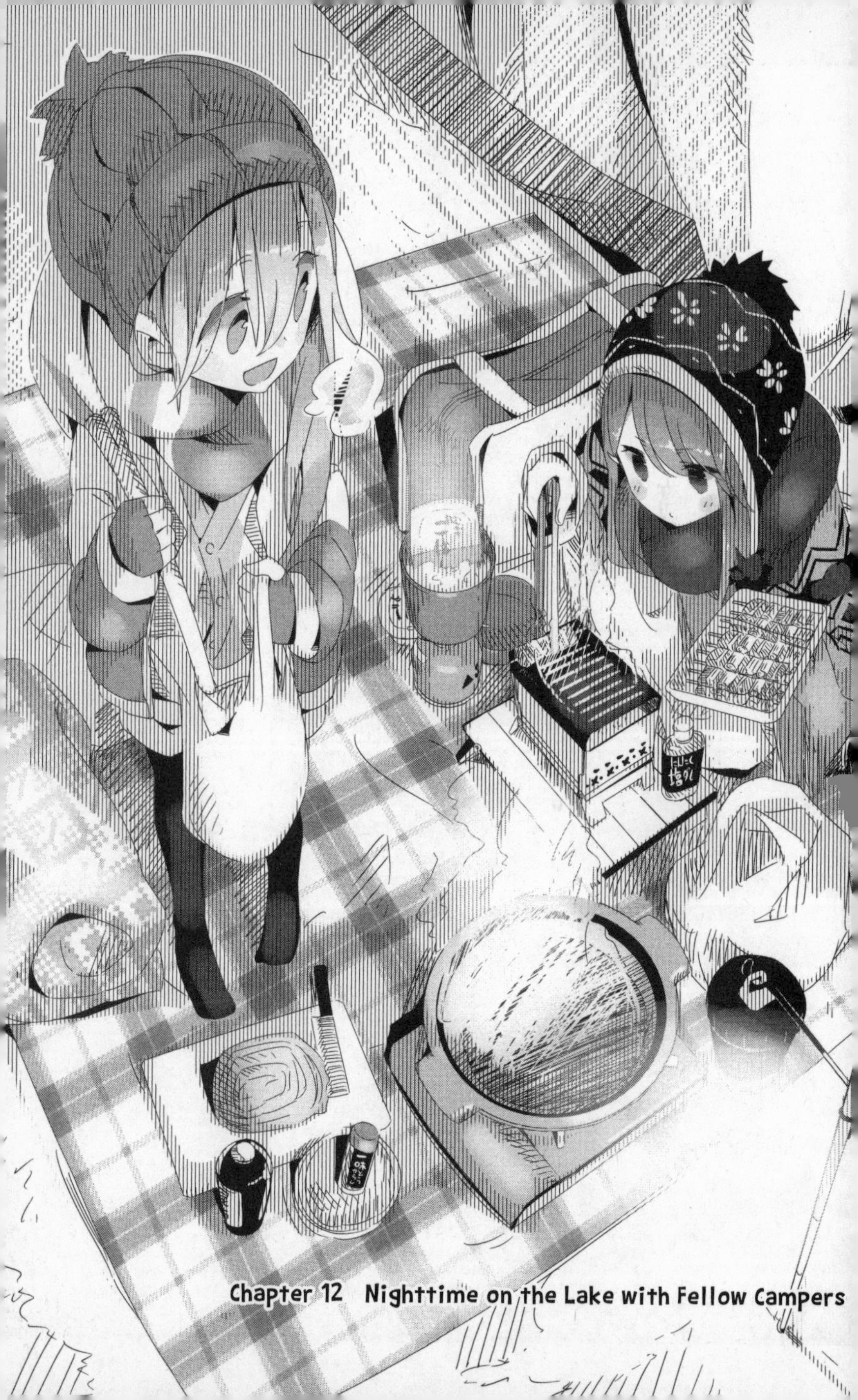

Chapter 12 Nighttime on the Lake with Fellow Campers

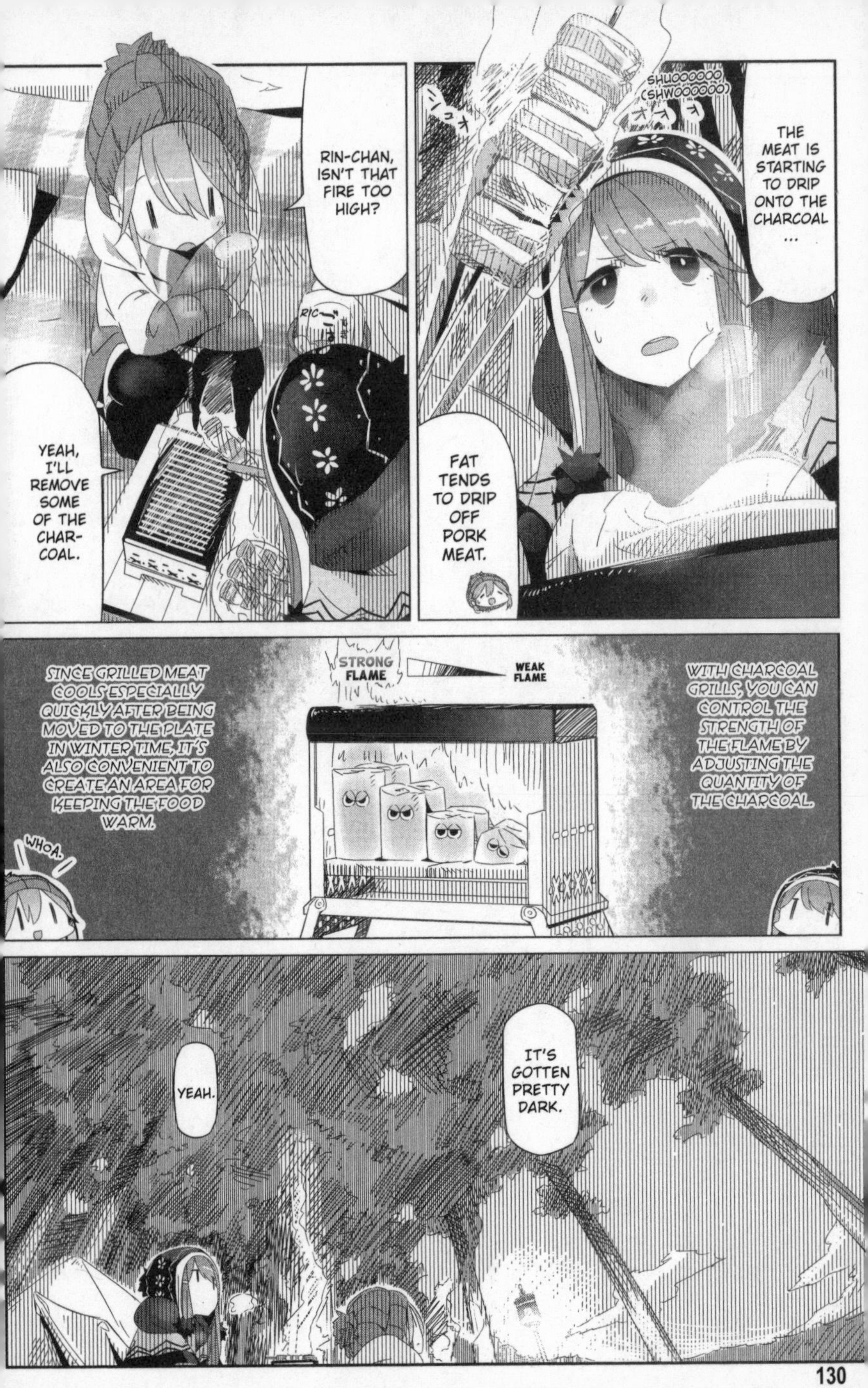
SHUOOOOOO (SHWOOOOOO)
THE MEAT IS STARTING TO DRIP ONTO THE CHARCOAL ...
FAT TENDS TO DRIP OFF PORK MEAT.
RIN-CHAN, ISN'T THAT FIRE TOO HIGH?
RIC-
YEAH, I'LL REMOVE SOME OF THE CHAR-COAL.
WITH CHARCOAL GRILLS, YOU CAN CONTROL THE STRENGTH OF THE FLAME BY ADJUSTING THE QUANTITY OF THE CHARCOAL.
STRONG FLAME
WEAK FLAME
SINCE GRILLED MEAT COOLS ESPECIALLY QUICKLY AFTER BEING MOVED TO THE PLATE IN WINTER TIME, IT'S ALSO CONVENIENT TO CREATE AN AREA FOR KEEPING THE FOOD WARM.
WHOA.
IT'S GOTTEN PRETTY DARK.
YEAH.

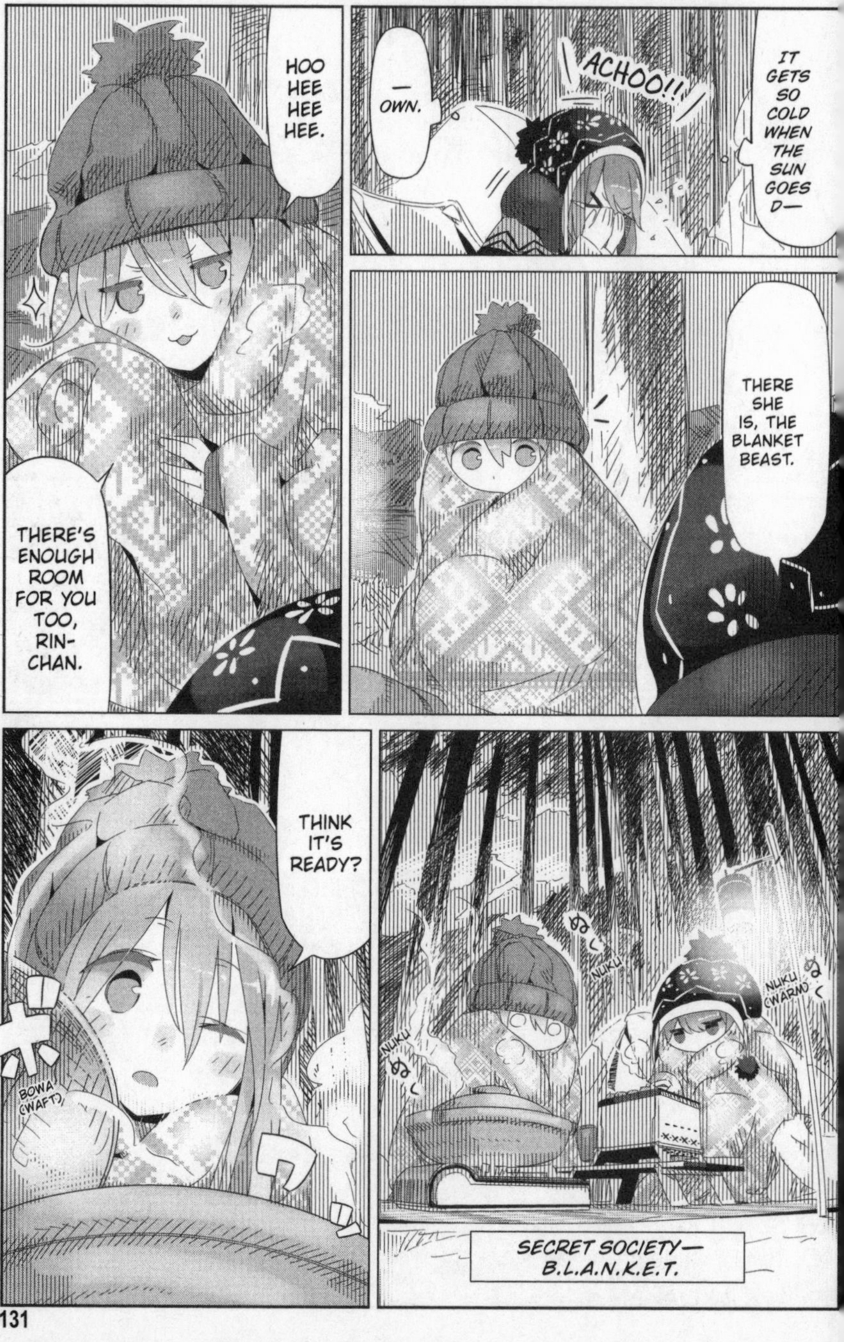
IT GETS SO COLD WHEN THE SUN GOES D—
ACHOO!!
—OWN.
THERE SHE IS, THE BLANKET BEAST.
HOO HEE HEE HEE.
THERE'S ENOUGH ROOM FOR YOU TOO, RIN-CHAN.
NUKU (WARM)
NUKU
NUKU
SECRET SOCIETY— B.L.A.N.K.E.T.
THINK IT'S READY?
BOWA (WAFT)

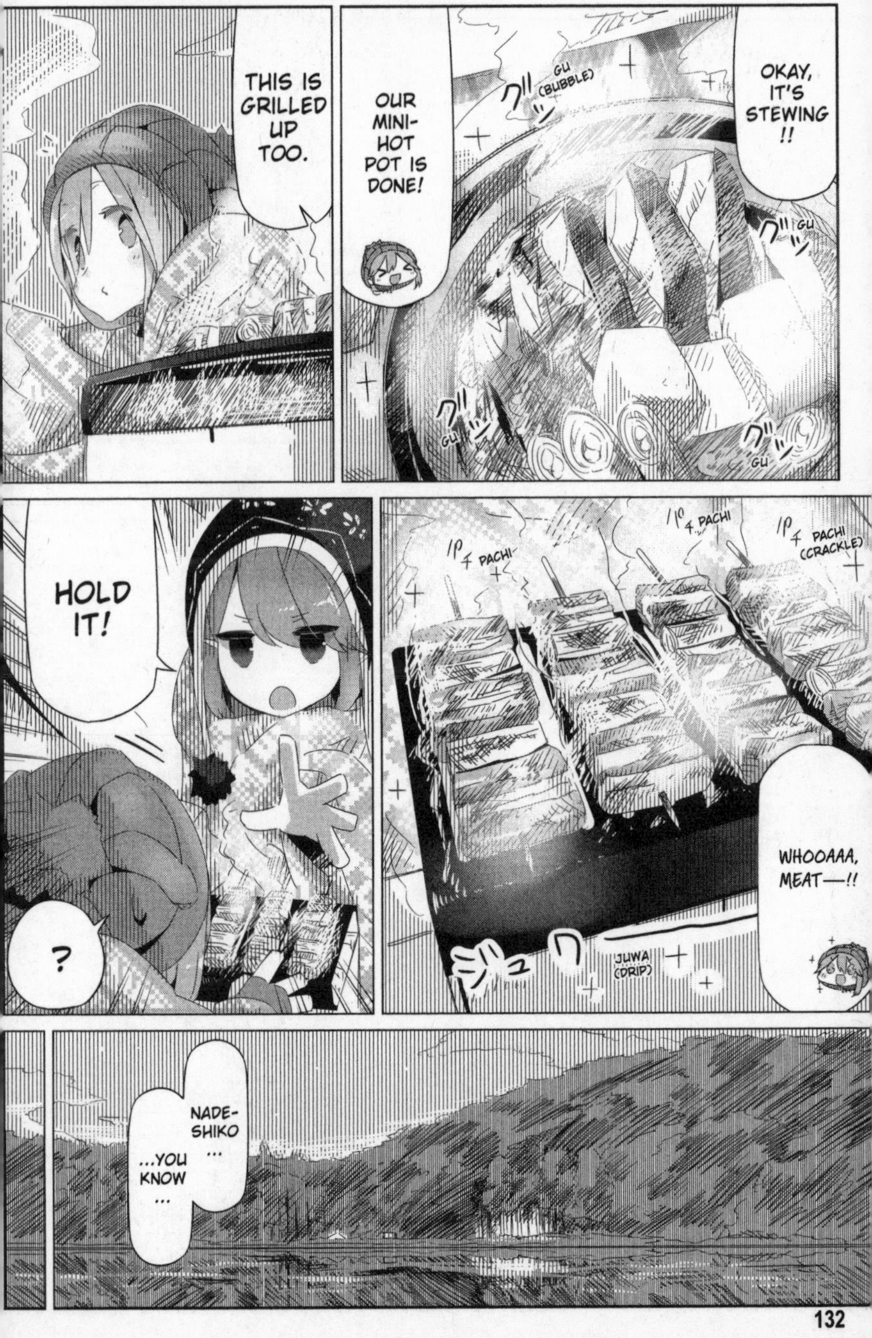
OKAY, IT'S STEWING!!
GU (BUBBLE)
GU
GU
GU
OUR MINI-HOT POT IS DONE!
THIS IS GRILLED UP TOO.
PACHI (CRACKLE)
PACHI
PACHI
WHOOAAA, MEAT—!!
JUWA (DRIP)
HOLD IT!
?
NADE-SHIKO...
...YOU KNOW...

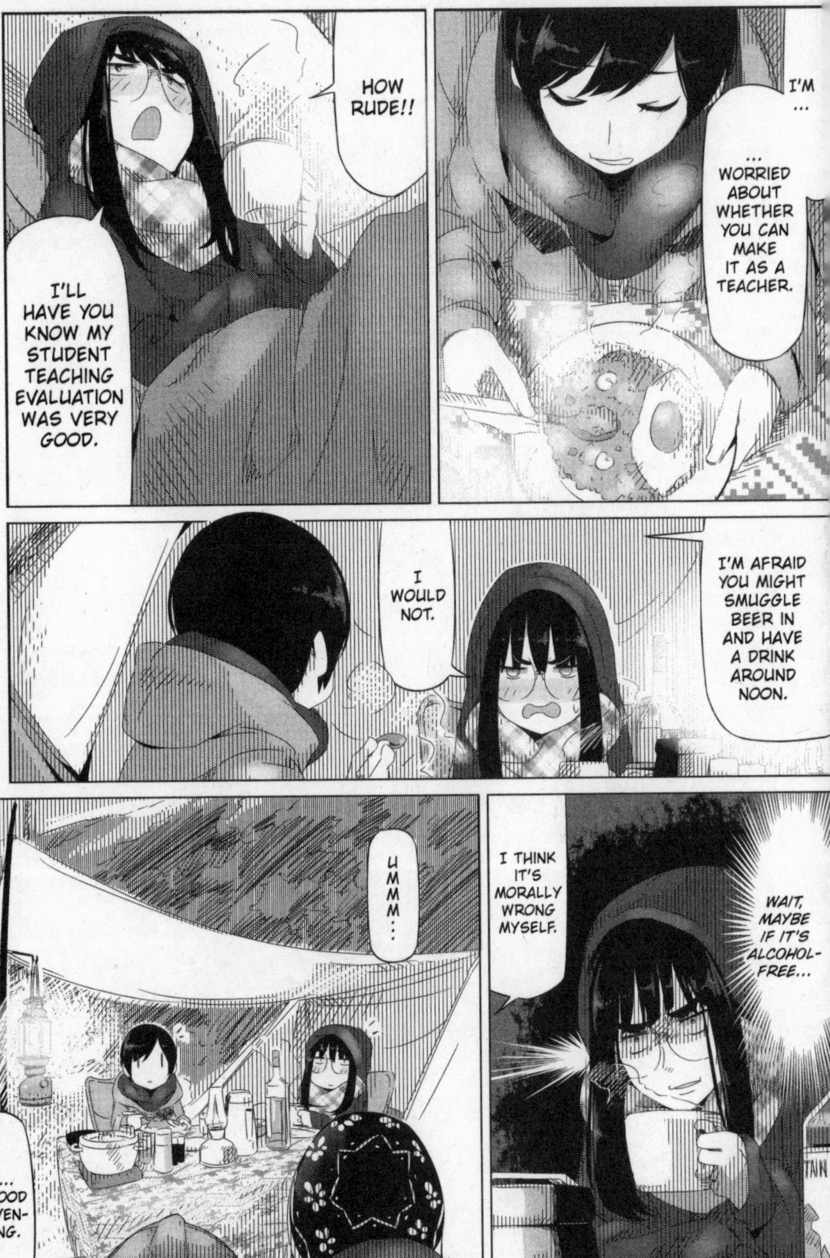
I'M ...
... WORRIED ABOUT WHETHER YOU CAN MAKE IT AS A TEACHER.
HOW RUDE!!
I'LL HAVE YOU KNOW MY STUDENT TEACHING EVALUATION WAS VERY GOOD.
I'M AFRAID YOU MIGHT SMUGGLE BEER IN AND HAVE A DRINK AROUND NOON.
I WOULD NOT.
WAIT, MAYBE IF IT'S ALCOHOL-FREE...
I THINK IT'S MORALLY WRONG MYSELF.
UMMM...
... GOOD EVEN-ING.

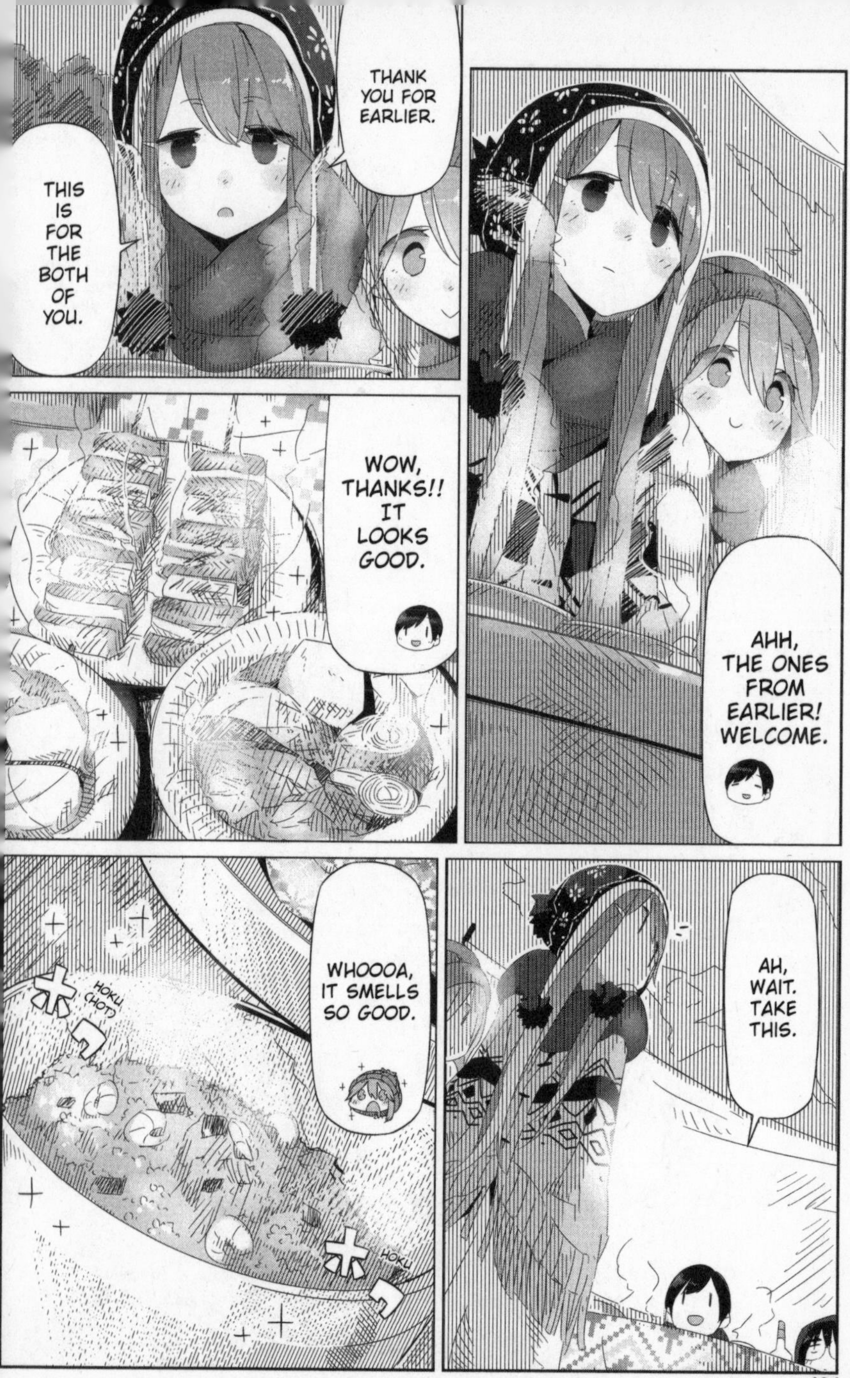
AHH, THE ONES FROM EARLIER! WELCOME.
THANK YOU FOR EARLIER.
THIS IS FOR THE BOTH OF YOU.
WOW, THANKS!! IT LOOKS GOOD.
AH, WAIT. TAKE THIS.
WHOOOA, IT SMELLS SO GOOD.
HOKU (HOT)
HOKU

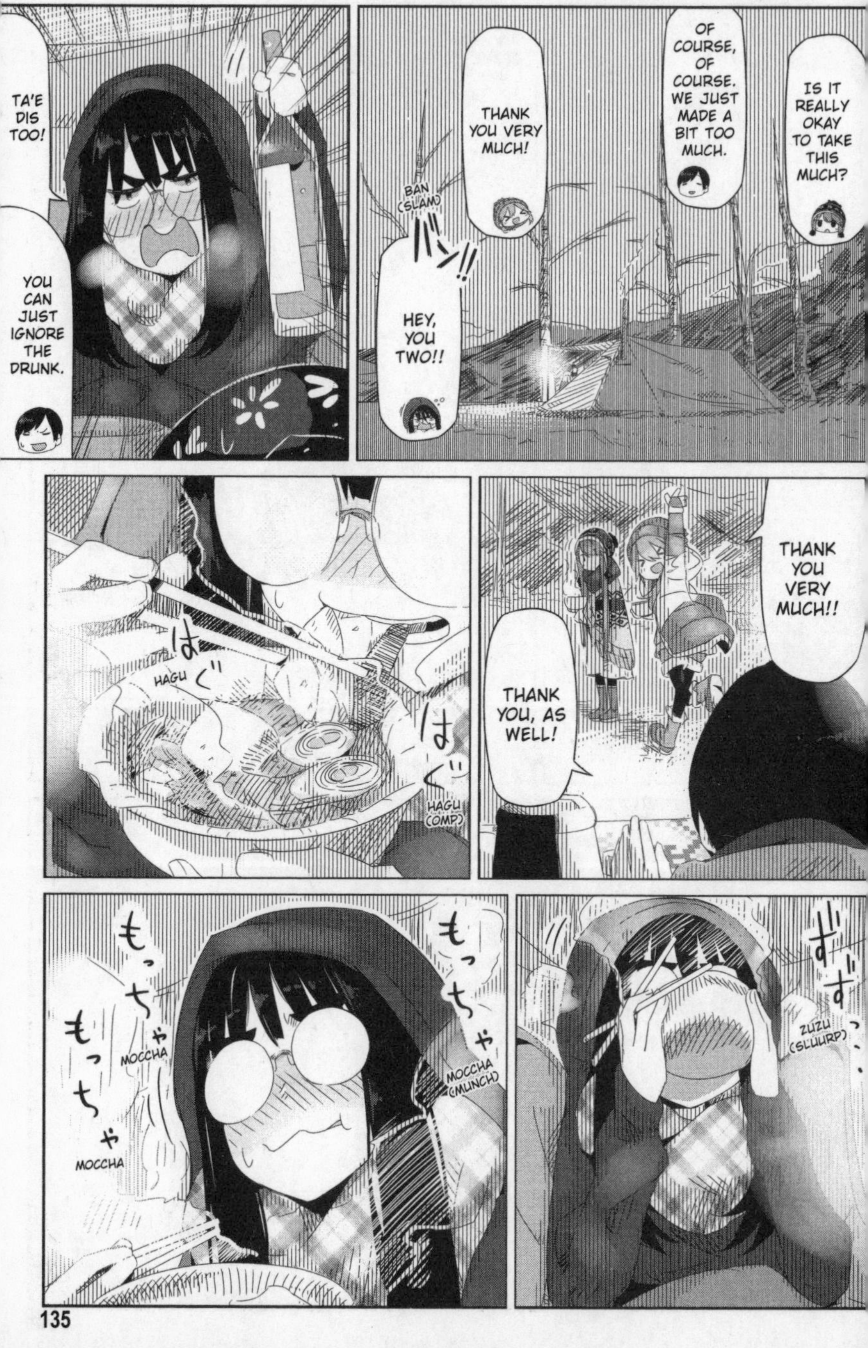
IS IT REALLY OKAY TO TAKE THIS MUCH?
OF COURSE, OF COURSE. WE JUST MADE A BIT TOO MUCH.
THANK YOU VERY MUCH!
バン!!
BAN (SLAM)
HEY, YOU TWO!!
TA'E DIS TOO!
YOU CAN JUST IGNORE THE DRUNK.
THANK YOU VERY MUCH!!
THANK YOU, AS WELL!
はぐ
HAGU
はぐ
HAGU (COMP)
ずず
ZUZU (SLUURP)
もっちゃ
MOCCHA (MUNCH)
もっちゃ
MOCCHA
もっちゃ
MOCCHA

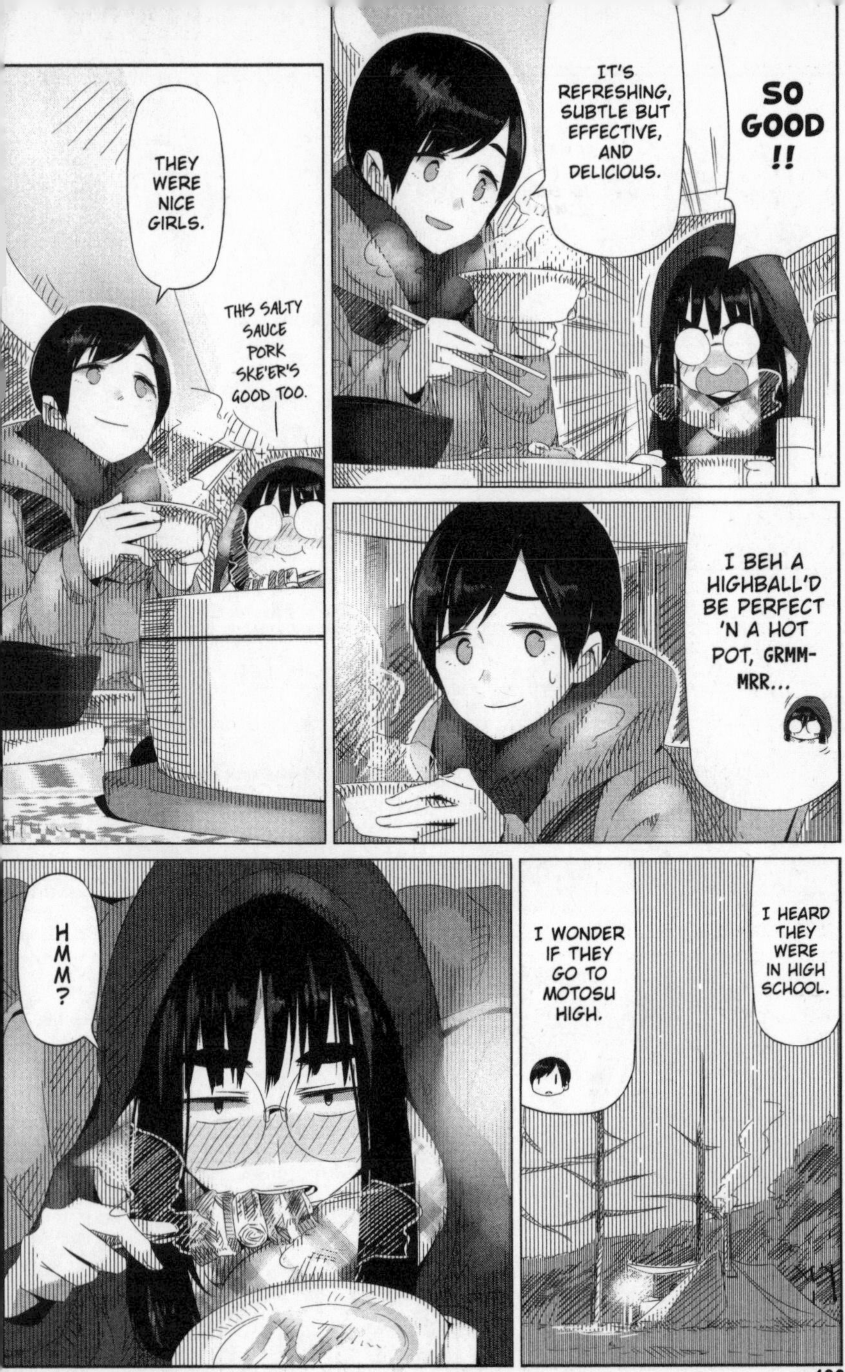
SO GOOD!!
IT'S REFRESHING, SUBTLE BUT EFFECTIVE, AND DELICIOUS.
I BEH A HIGHBALL'D BE PERFECT 'N A HOT POT, GRMM-MRR...
THEY WERE NICE GIRLS.
THIS SALTY SAUCE PORK SKE'ER'S GOOD TOO.
I HEARD THEY WERE IN HIGH SCHOOL.
I WONDER IF THEY GO TO MOTOSU HIGH.
HMM?

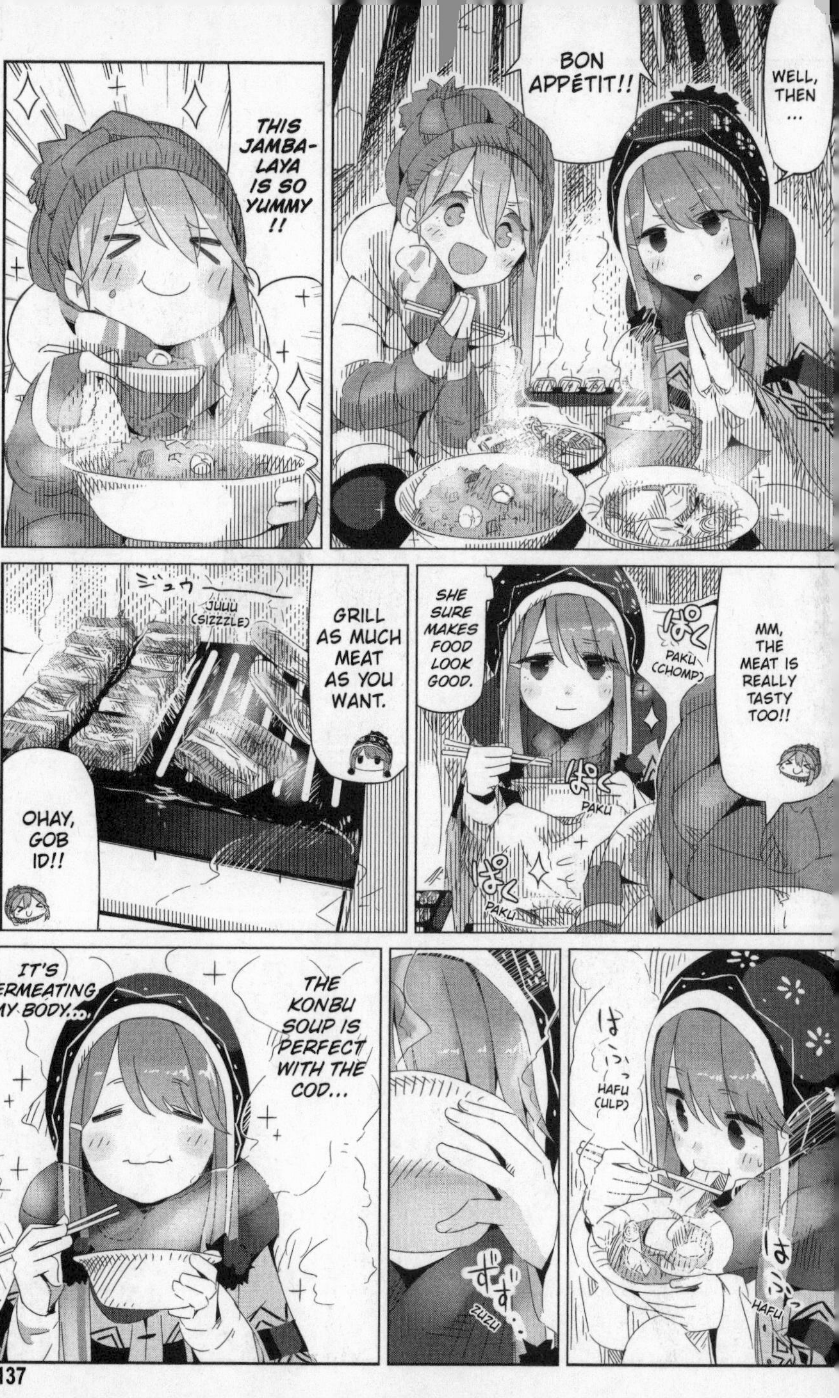
WELL, THEN ...
BON APPÉTIT!!
THIS JAMBALAYA IS SO YUMMY!!
MM, THE MEAT IS REALLY TASTY TOO!!
ぱく
PAKU (CHOMP)
ぱく
PAKU
ぱく
PAKU
SHE SURE MAKES FOOD LOOK GOOD.
ジュウ～
JUUU (SIZZZLE)
GRILL AS MUCH MEAT AS YOU WANT.
OHAY, GOB ID!!
はふっ
HAFU (ULP)
はふっ
HAFU
ずず…
ZUZU
THE KONBU SOUP IS PERFECT WITH THE COD...
IT'S PERMEATING MY BODY...

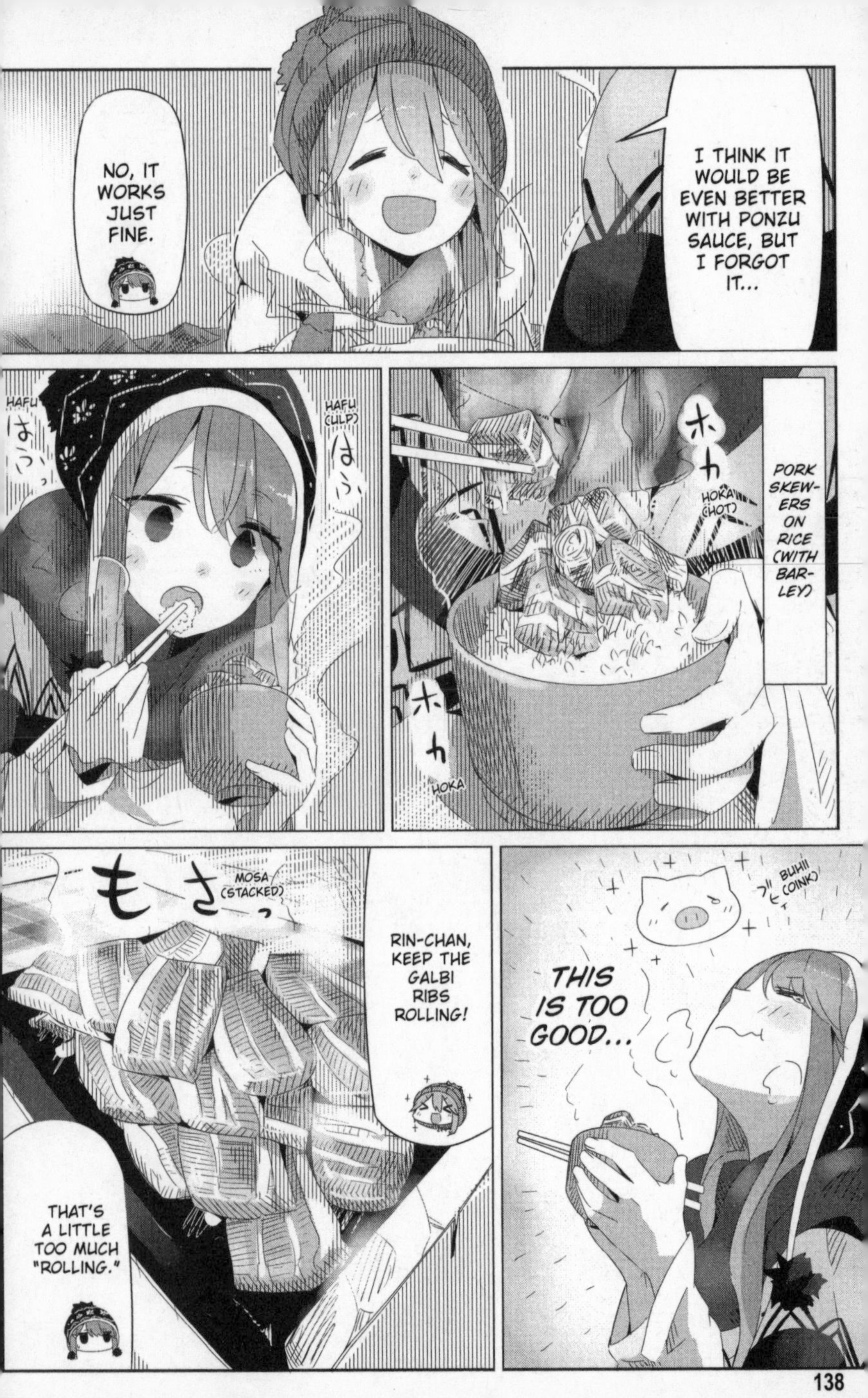
I THINK IT WOULD BE EVEN BETTER WITH PONZU SAUCE, BUT I FORGOT IT...
NO, IT WORKS JUST FINE.
PORK SKEWERS ON RICE (WITH BARLEY)
ホカ
HOKA (HOT)
ホカ
HOKA
はふ
HAFU (ULP)
はふ
HAFU
ブヒ
BUHII (COINK)
THIS IS TOO GOOD...
もさっ
MOSA (STACKED)
RIN-CHAN, KEEP THE GALBI RIBS ROLLING!
THAT'S A LITTLE TOO MUCH "ROLLING."

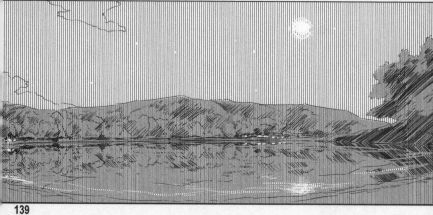

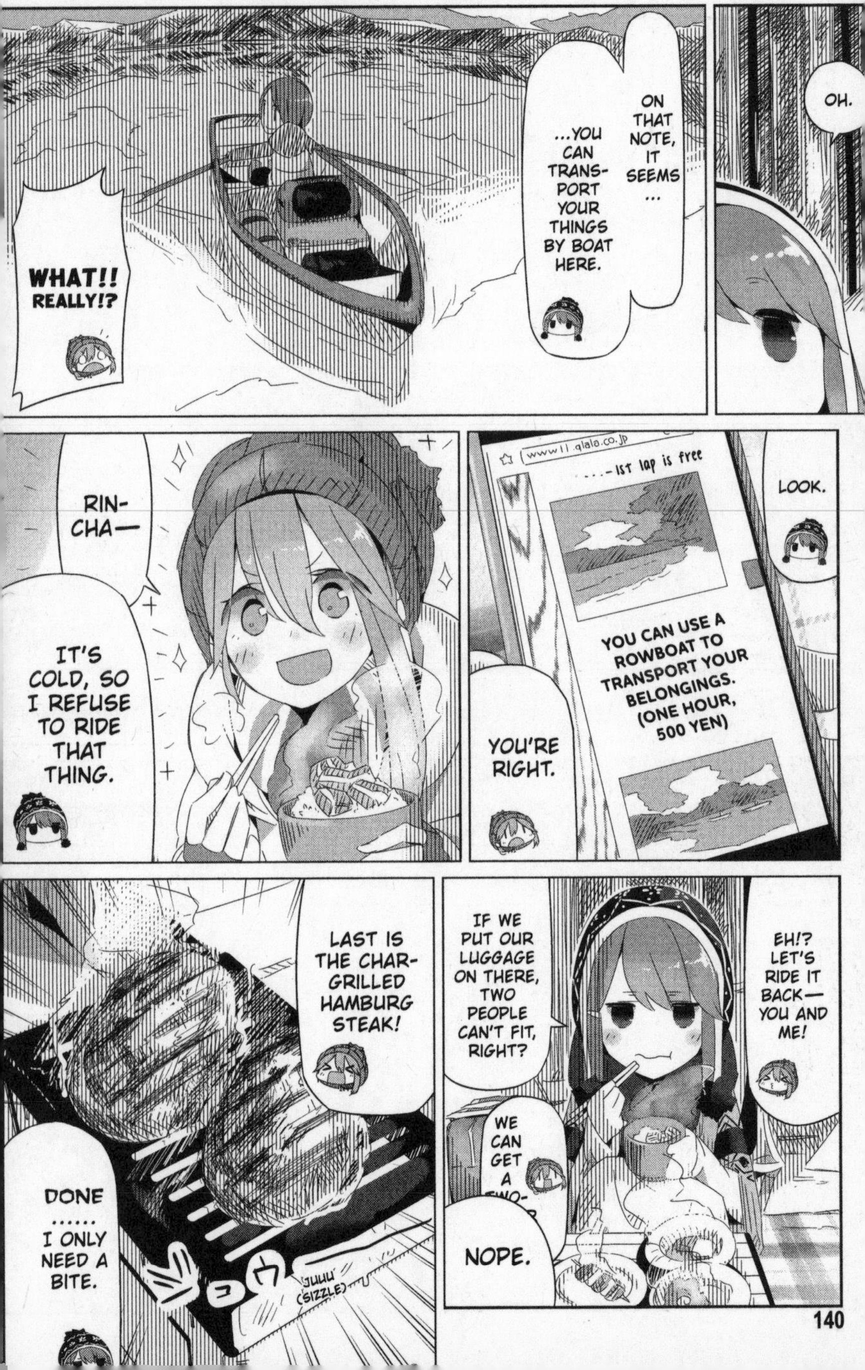
OH.
ON THAT NOTE, IT SEEMS...
...YOU CAN TRANSPORT YOUR THINGS BY BOAT HERE.
WHAT!! REALLY!?
LOOK.
www11.qlala.co.jp
...-1st lap is free
YOU CAN USE A ROWBOAT TO TRANSPORT YOUR BELONGINGS. (ONE HOUR, 500 YEN)
YOU'RE RIGHT.
RIN-CHA—
IT'S COLD, SO I REFUSE TO RIDE THAT THING.
EH!? LET'S RIDE IT BACK—YOU AND ME!
IF WE PUT OUR LUGGAGE ON THERE, TWO PEOPLE CAN'T FIT, RIGHT?
WE CAN GET A
NOPE.
LAST IS THE CHAR-GRILLED HAMBURG STEAK!
JUUU (SIZZLE)
DONE...... I ONLY NEED A BITE.

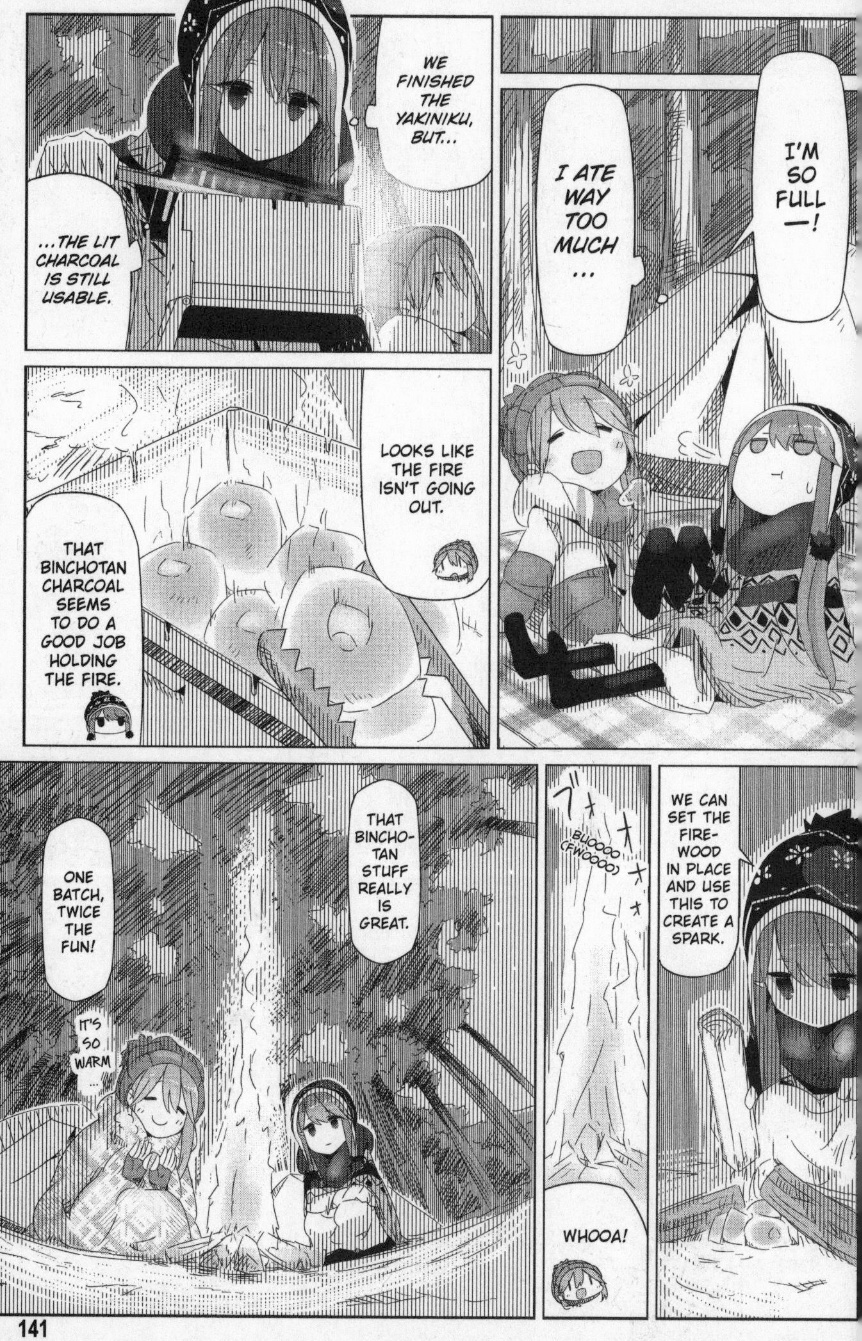
I'M SO FULL—!
I ATE WAY TOO MUCH...
WE FINISHED THE YAKINIKU, BUT...
...THE LIT CHARCOAL IS STILL USABLE.
LOOKS LIKE THE FIRE ISN'T GOING OUT.
THAT BINCHOTAN CHARCOAL SEEMS TO DO A GOOD JOB HOLDING THE FIRE.
WE CAN SET THE FIREWOOD IN PLACE AND USE THIS TO CREATE A SPARK.
BUOOOO (FWOOOO)
WHOOA!
THAT BINCHOTAN STUFF REALLY IS GREAT.
ONE BATCH, TWICE THE FUN!
IT'S SO WARM...

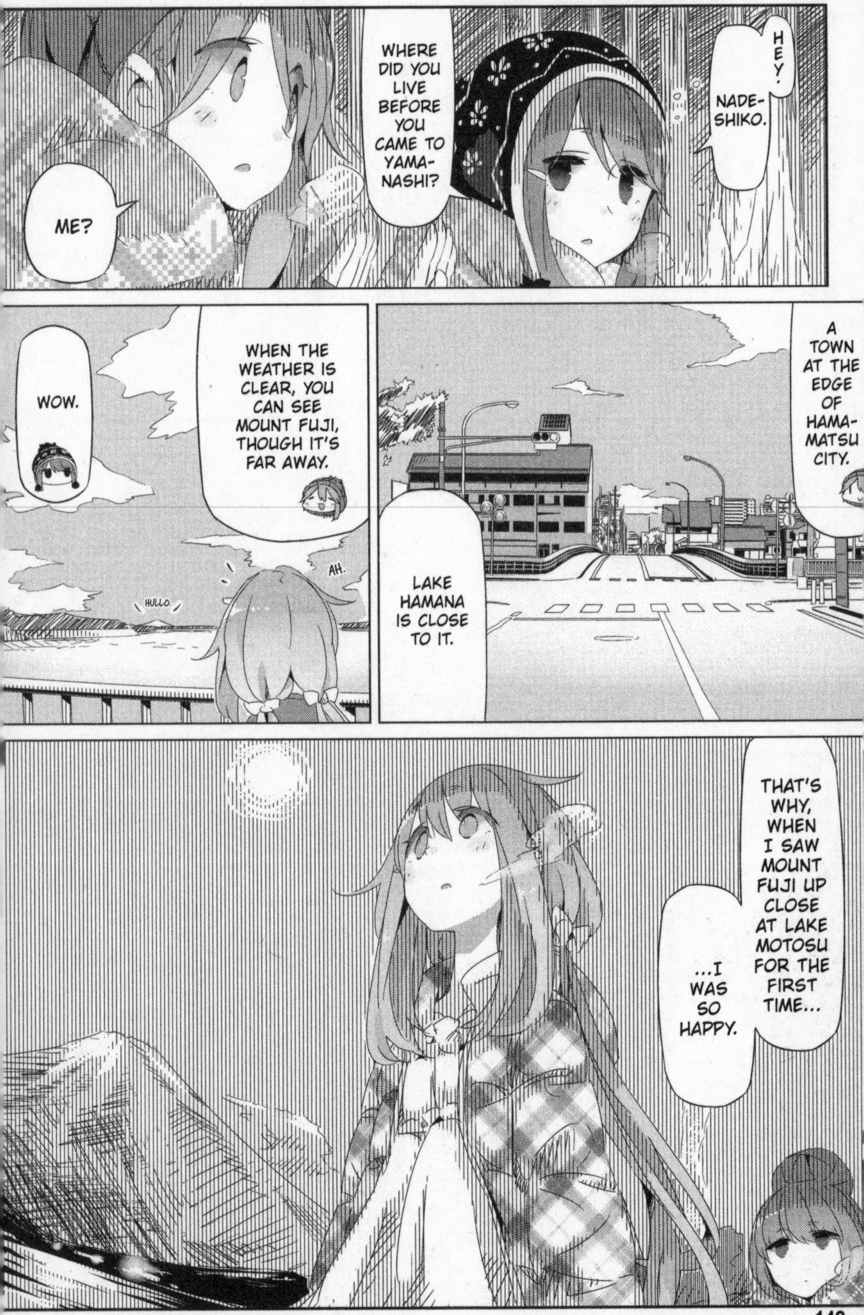
HEY. NADESHIKO.
WHERE DID YOU LIVE BEFORE YOU CAME TO YAMANASHI?
ME?
A TOWN AT THE EDGE OF HAMAMATSU CITY.
LAKE HAMANA IS CLOSE TO IT.
WHEN THE WEATHER IS CLEAR, YOU CAN SEE MOUNT FUJI, THOUGH IT'S FAR AWAY.
AH.
HULLO.
WOW.
THAT'S WHY, WHEN I SAW MOUNT FUJI UP CLOSE AT LAKE MOTOSU FOR THE FIRST TIME...
...I WAS SO HAPPY.

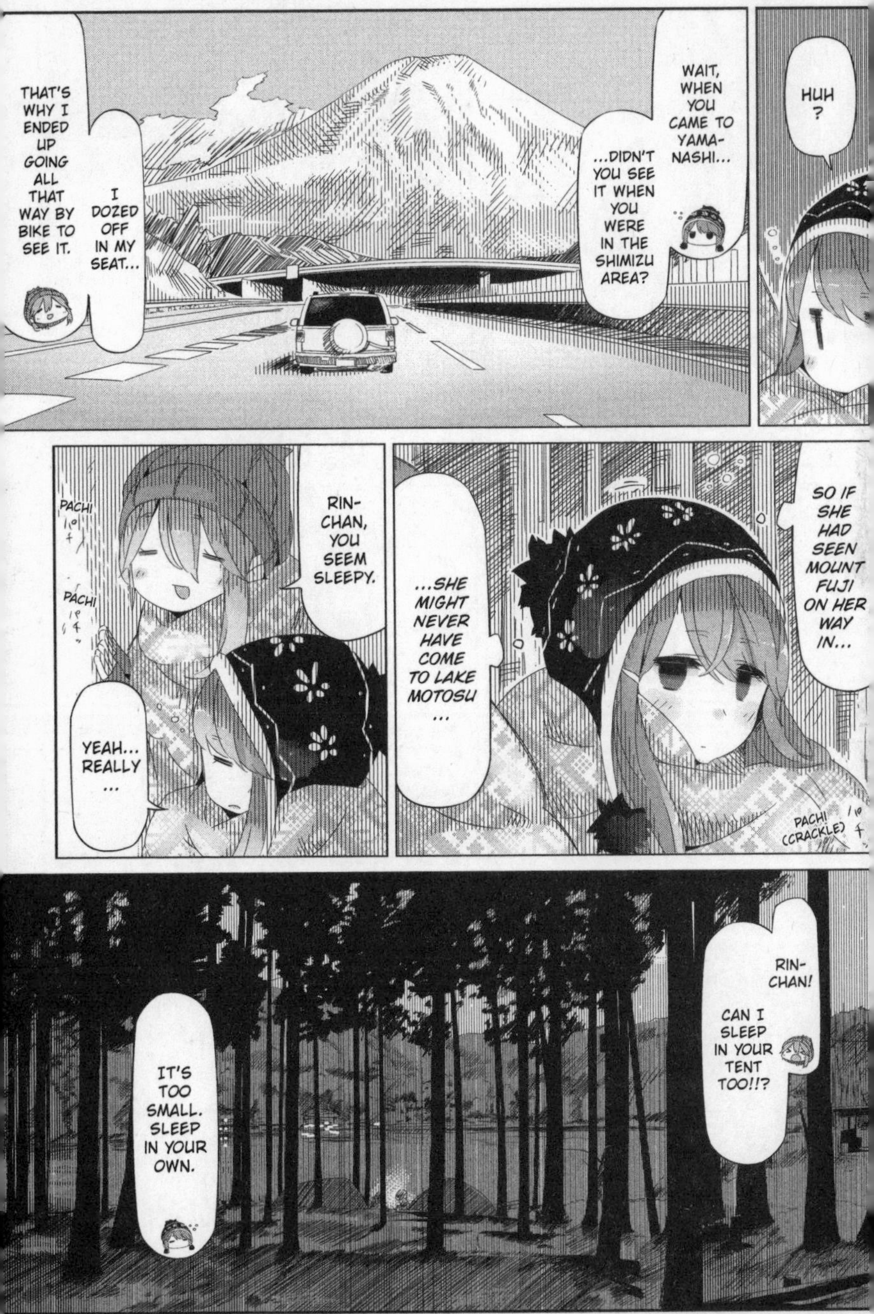
HUH?
WAIT, WHEN YOU CAME TO YAMANASHI...
...DIDN'T YOU SEE IT WHEN YOU WERE IN THE SHIMIZU AREA?
I DOZED OFF IN MY SEAT...
THAT'S WHY I ENDED UP GOING ALL THAT WAY BY BIKE TO SEE IT.
SO IF SHE HAD SEEN MOUNT FUJI ON HER WAY IN...
...SHE MIGHT NEVER HAVE COME TO LAKE MOTOSU...
PACHI (CRACKLE)
RIN-CHAN, YOU SEEM SLEEPY.
PACHI
PACHI
YEAH... REALLY...
RIN-CHAN!
CAN I SLEEP IN YOUR TENT TOO!!?
IT'S TOO SMALL. SLEEP IN YOUR OWN.

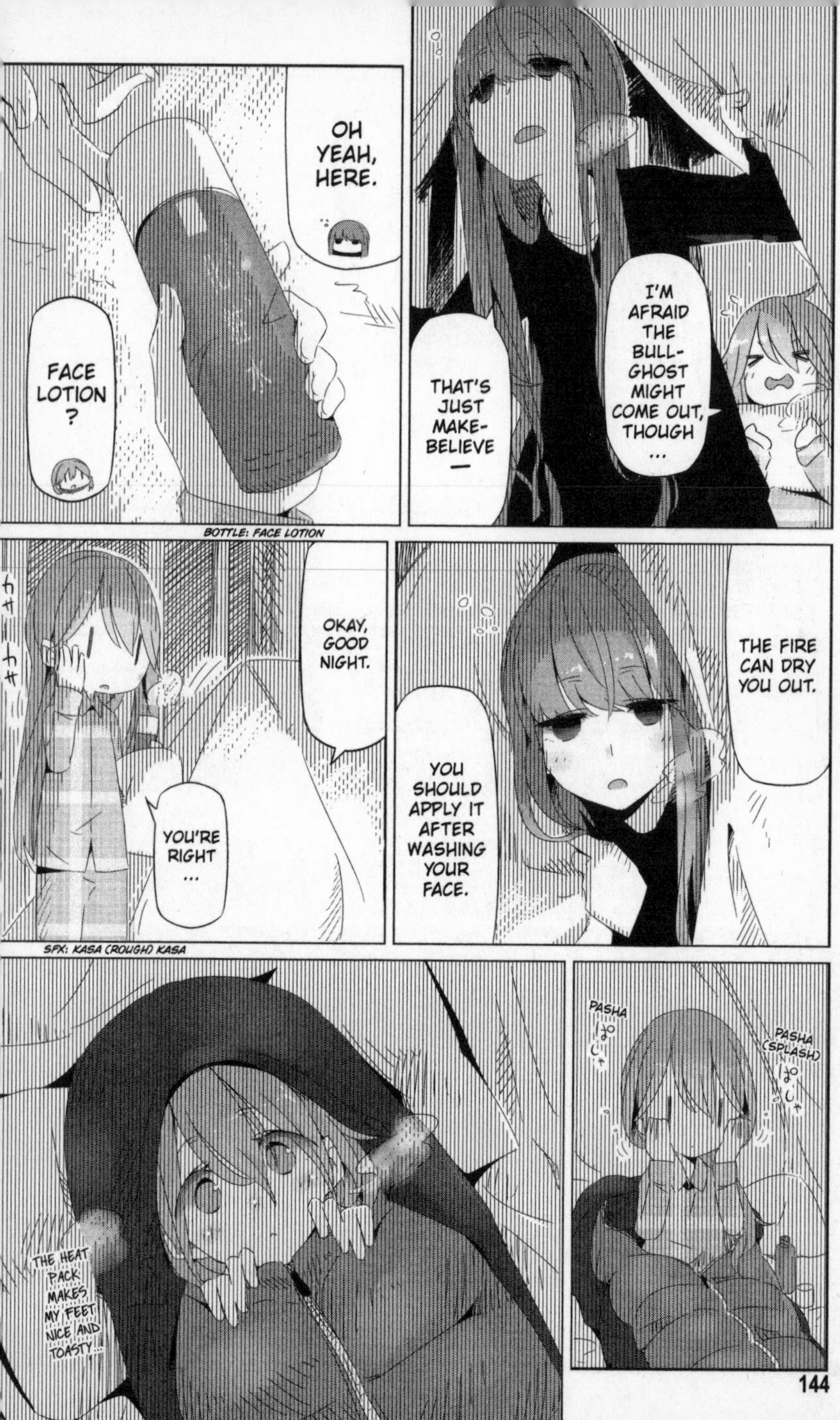
I'M AFRAID THE BULL-GHOST MIGHT COME OUT, THOUGH ...
THAT'S JUST MAKE-BELIEVE —
OH YEAH, HERE.
FACE LOTION ?
BOTTLE: FACE LOTION
THE FIRE CAN DRY YOU OUT.
YOU SHOULD APPLY IT AFTER WASHING YOUR FACE.
OKAY, GOOD NIGHT.
YOU'RE RIGHT ...
カサカサ
SFX: KASA (ROUGH) KASA
PASHA
ぱしゃ
PASHA (SPLASH)
ぱしゃ
THE HEAT PACK MAKES MY FEET NICE AND TOASTY...

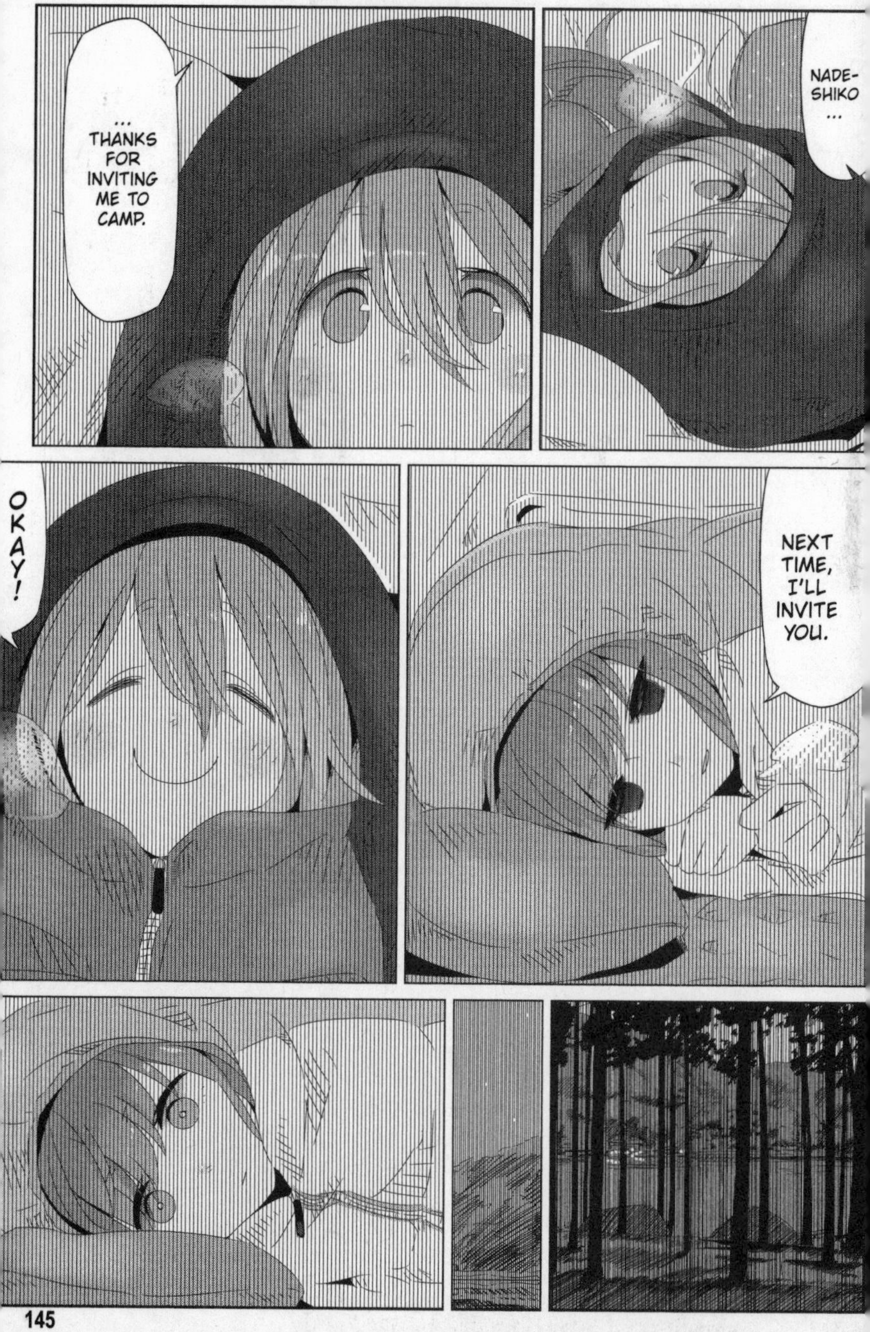
NADE-SHIKO ...
... THANKS FOR INVITING ME TO CAMP.
NEXT TIME, I'LL INVITE YOU.
OKAY!

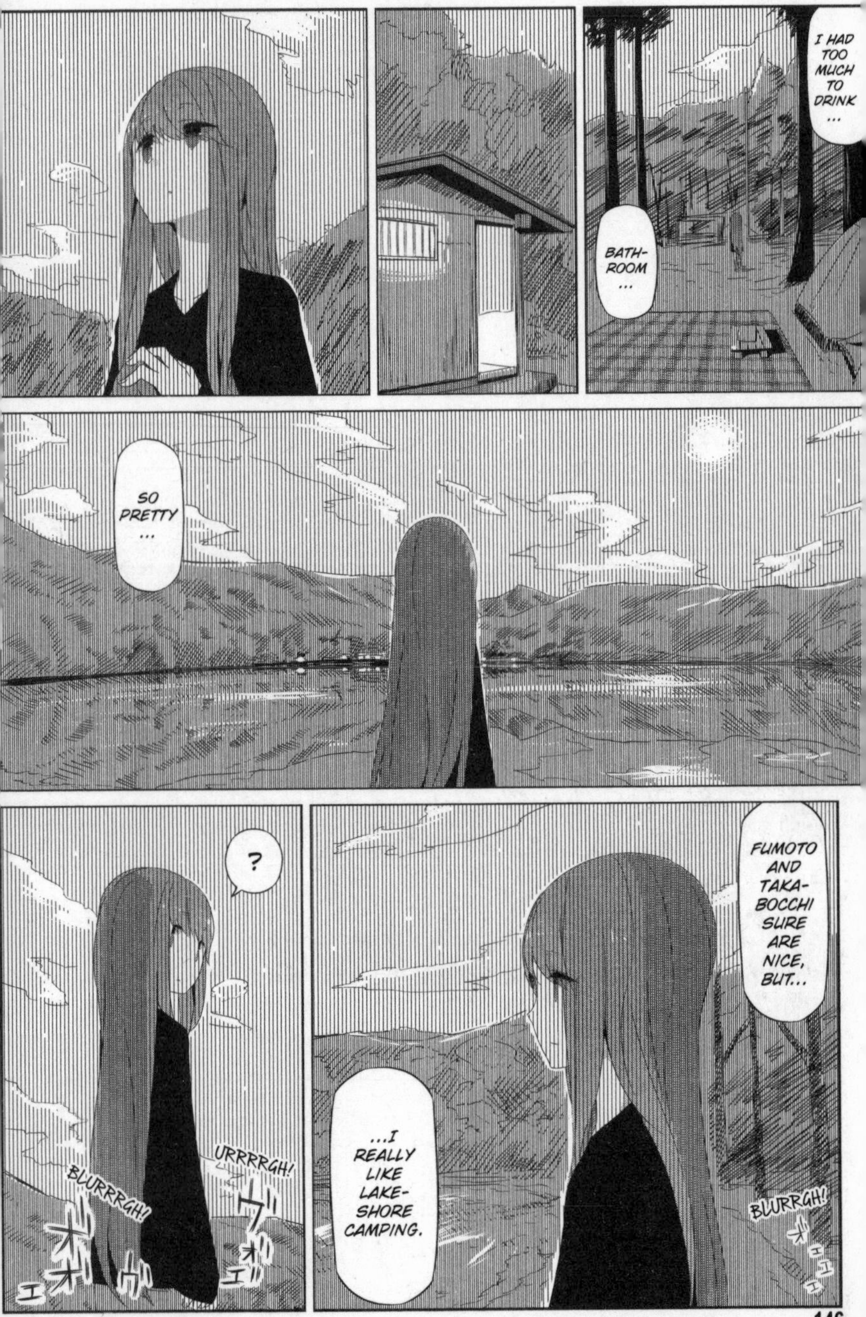
I HAD TOO MUCH TO DRINK...
BATH-ROOM...
SO PRETTY...
FUMOTO AND TAKA-BOCCHI SURE ARE NICE, BUT...
...I REALLY LIKE LAKE-SHORE CAMPING.
BLURRGH!
?
URRRRGH!
BLURRRGH!

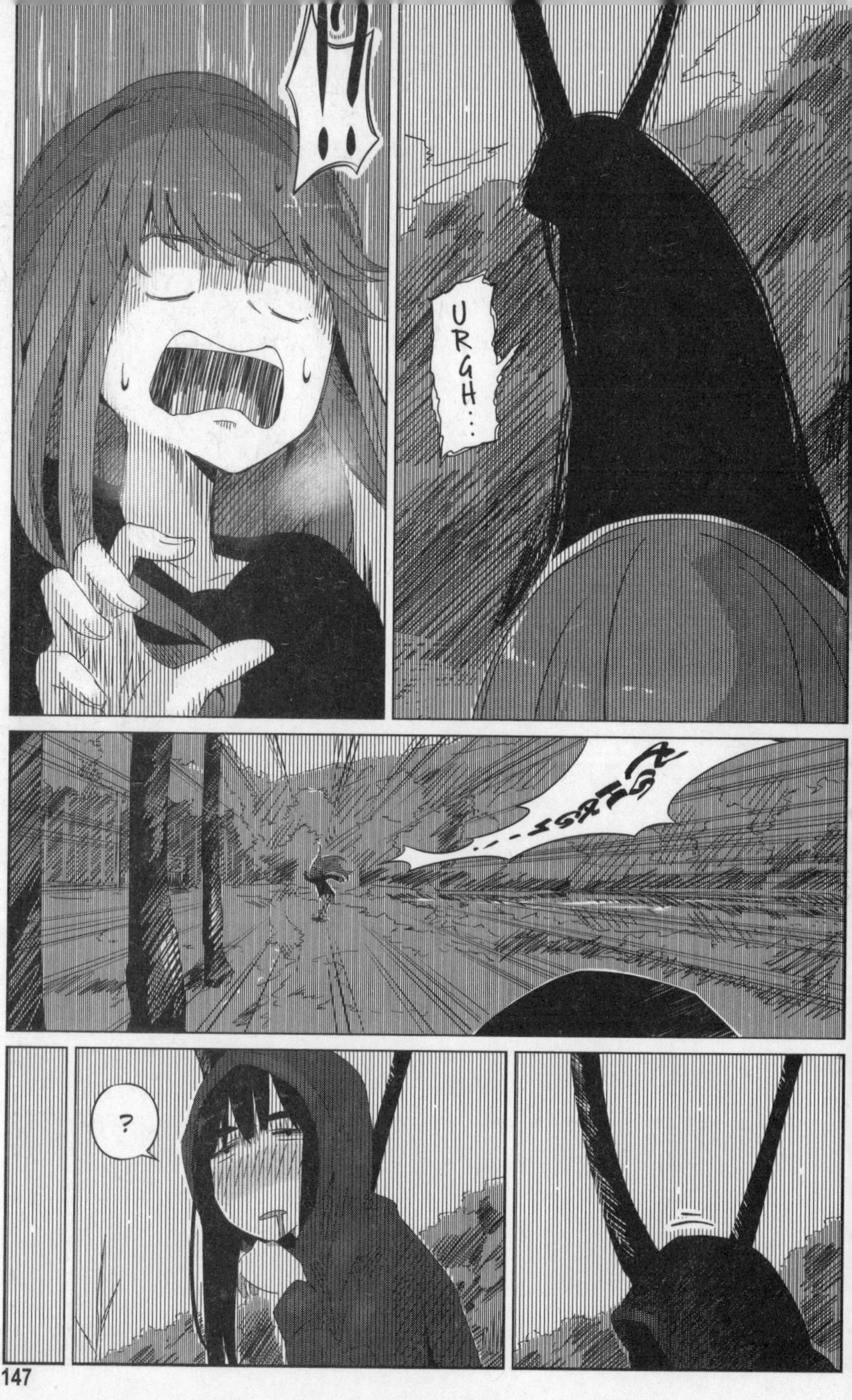
URGH...
!!
AGHASS--!
?

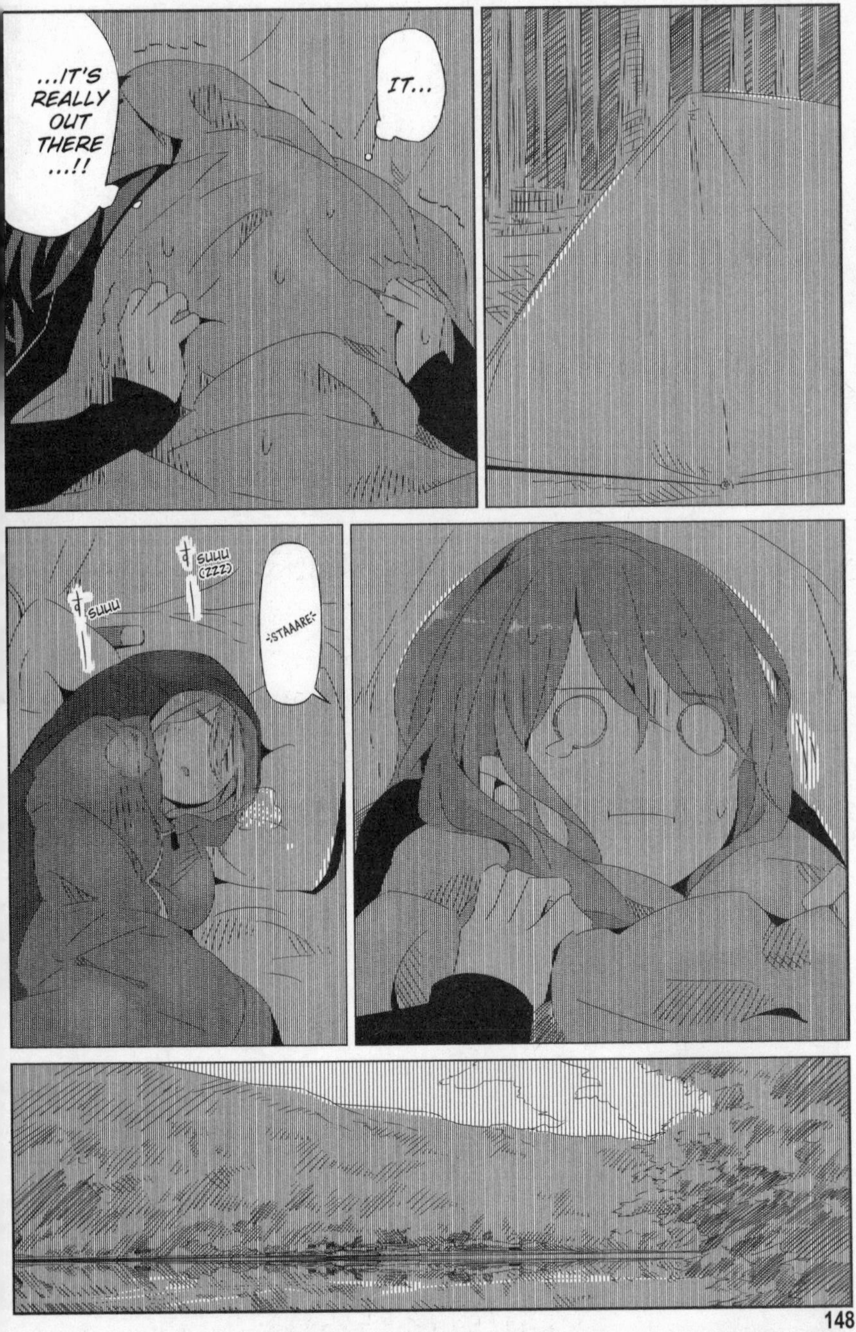
IT...
...IT'S REALLY OUT THERE...!!
STAAARE
す suuu (zzz)
す suuu

PACHI
(BLINK)

SUUU
す
ー

SUUU
す

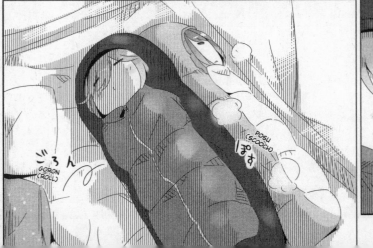

ごろん
GORON
(ROLL)

POSU
(SCOOCH)
ぽす

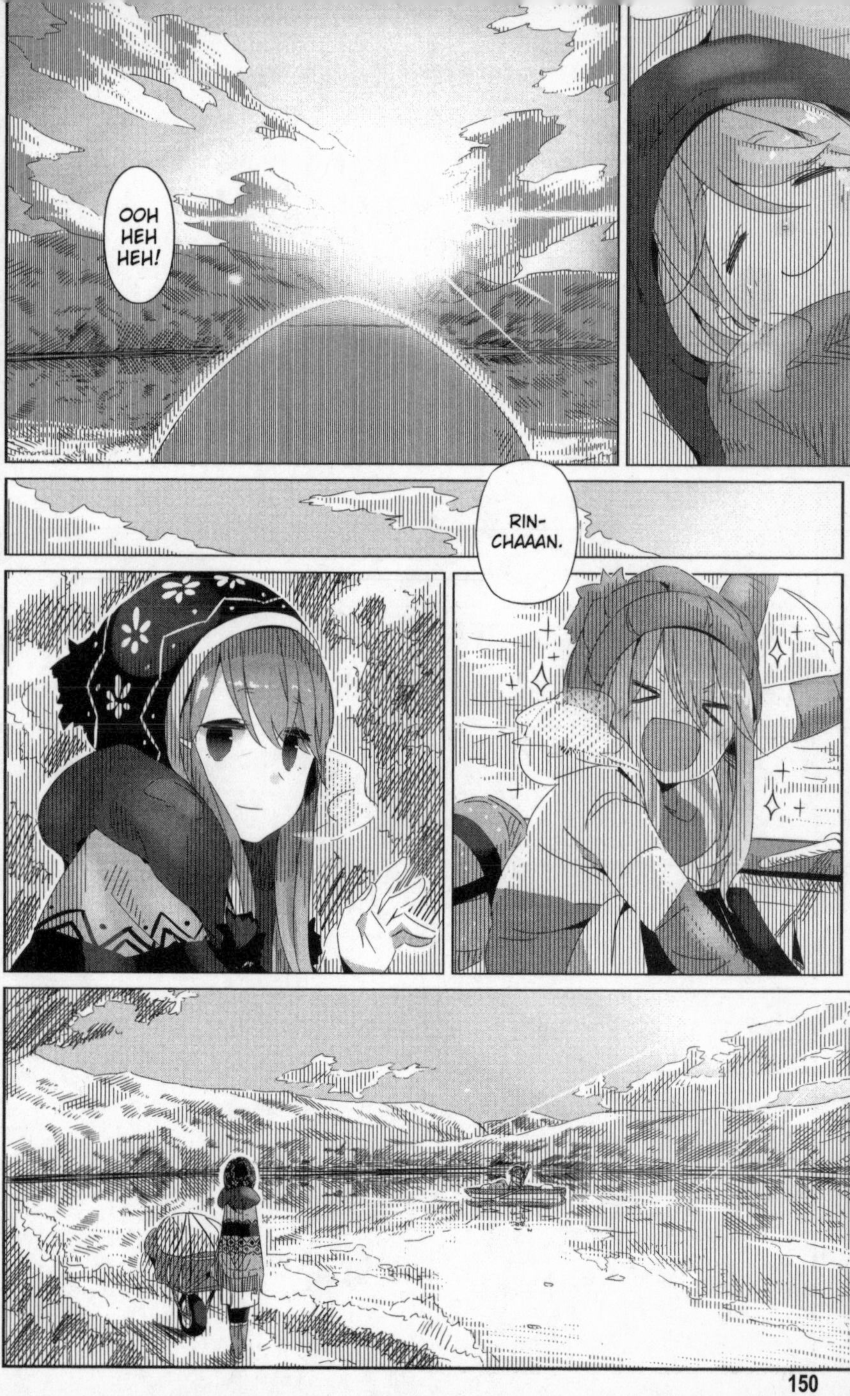
OOH HEH HEH!
RIN-CHAAAN.

THAT BOAT RIDE WAS SO FUN.
WEL-COME BACK.
NEXT TIME WE COME HERE, WE SHOULD RIDE TOGETHER !!
ONCE IT GETS WARM OUT.
BUT THAT PROMISE WAS NEVER TO BE KEPT.
NOT LONG AFTER ...
...SHE GOT SICK OF CAMPING.
HEY! NO I DIDN'T !!

TRANSLATION NOTES

100 yen is approximately $1 USD.

PAGE 3
Achichi: Means "ow, hot, hot, hot!" in Japanese.

PAGE 7
Tsukimi soba, _tsukimi_ udon: Noodle dishes with an egg yolk in them to represent the moon. _Tsukimi_ means "moon-viewing," and moon-viewing festivities are often held in mid-autumn.

PAGE 8
Fried hot-spring egg: _Ontama-age_ in Japanese, it's a popular dish at the real life Hottarakashi Hot Springs in Yamanashi, Japan. "Hottokeya Hot Spring" appears to be based on this locale.

PAGE 10
Takabocchi: A high-altitude area in Nagano Prefecture made up of Mount Takabocchi and the surrounding Takabocchi Plateau.

PAGE 17
"Climbing 'Bocchi all alone…": This is a pun based on how _bocchi_ can be short for both Takabocchi and _hitoribocchi_, or "alone."

PAGE 58
Showapre Co., Ltd: Based on an actual manufacturer of camping gear.

PAGE 83
Binchotan: A type of charcoal traditionally used in Japanese cooking.

PAGE 91
Fuji Five Lakes: The name of the area around the base of Mount Fuji, which is surrounded by five lakes created by Fuji's past volcanic eruptions.

PAGE 93
Electric eels: Lake Shibire sounds indentitcal to _shibire_, which means "to tingle"—like when getting shocked by electric eels.

PAGE 161
Tsunayoshi Tokugawa: A Japanese shogun so famous for passing several measures protecting dogs that he received the nickname "dog shogun."

INSIDE COVER
Aichi, Shizuoka, Gifu: Three neighboring prefectures in Japan.

Mikawa Dialect: A dialect unique to the eastern part of Aichi Prefecture. The "Jandarariiin" her grandparents say refers to the three sentence-endings unique to Mikawa dialect—_jan_, _dara_, and _rin_.

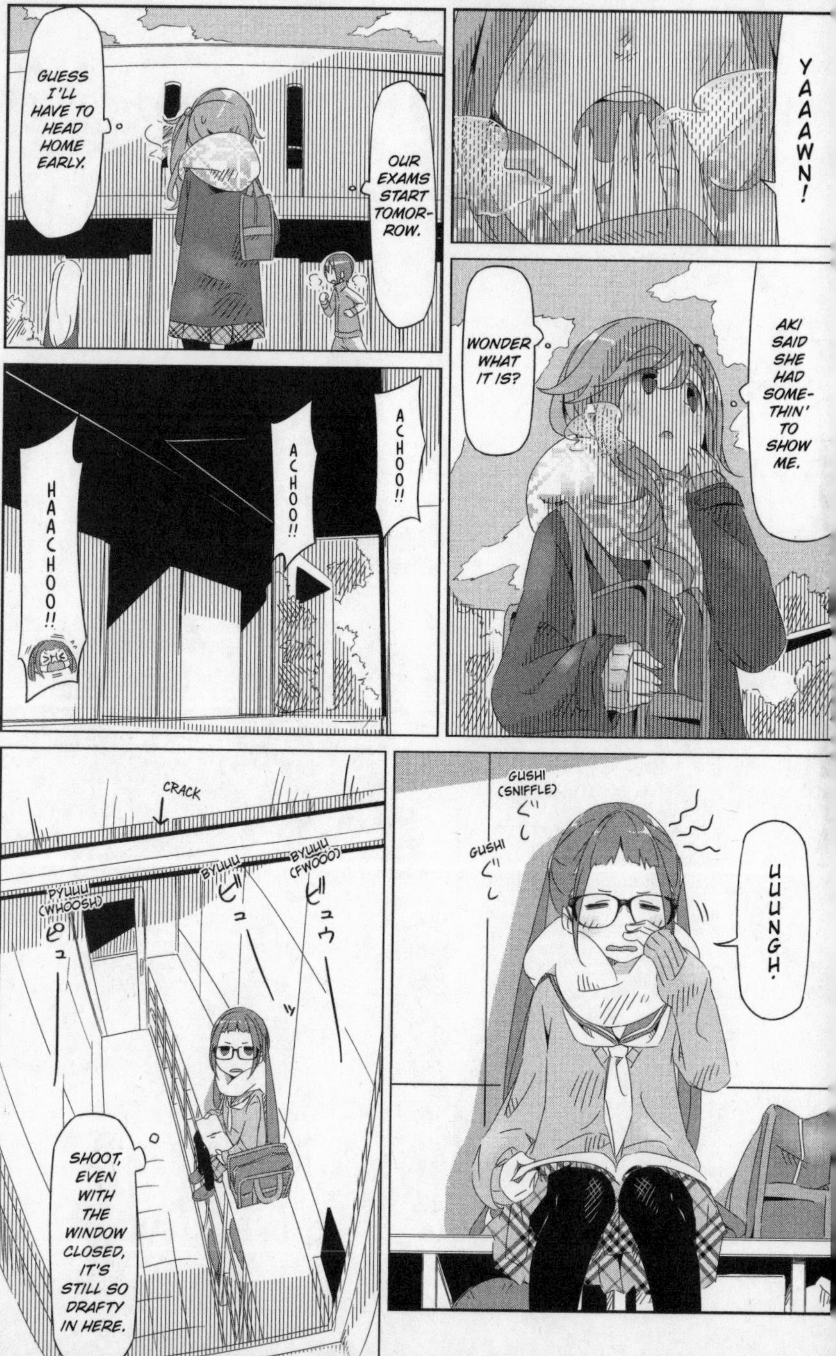
YAAAAWN!
OUR EXAMS START TOMORROW.
GUESS I'LL HAVE TO HEAD HOME EARLY.
AKI SAID SHE HAD SOMETHIN' TO SHOW ME.
WONDER WHAT IT IS?
ACHOO!!
ACHOO!!
HAACHOO!!
GUSHI (SNIFFLE)
GUSHI
UUUNGH.
CRACK
BYUUU (FWOOO)
BYUUU
PYUUU (WHOOSH)
SHOOT, EVEN WITH THE WINDOW CLOSED, IT'S STILL SO DRAFTY IN HERE.

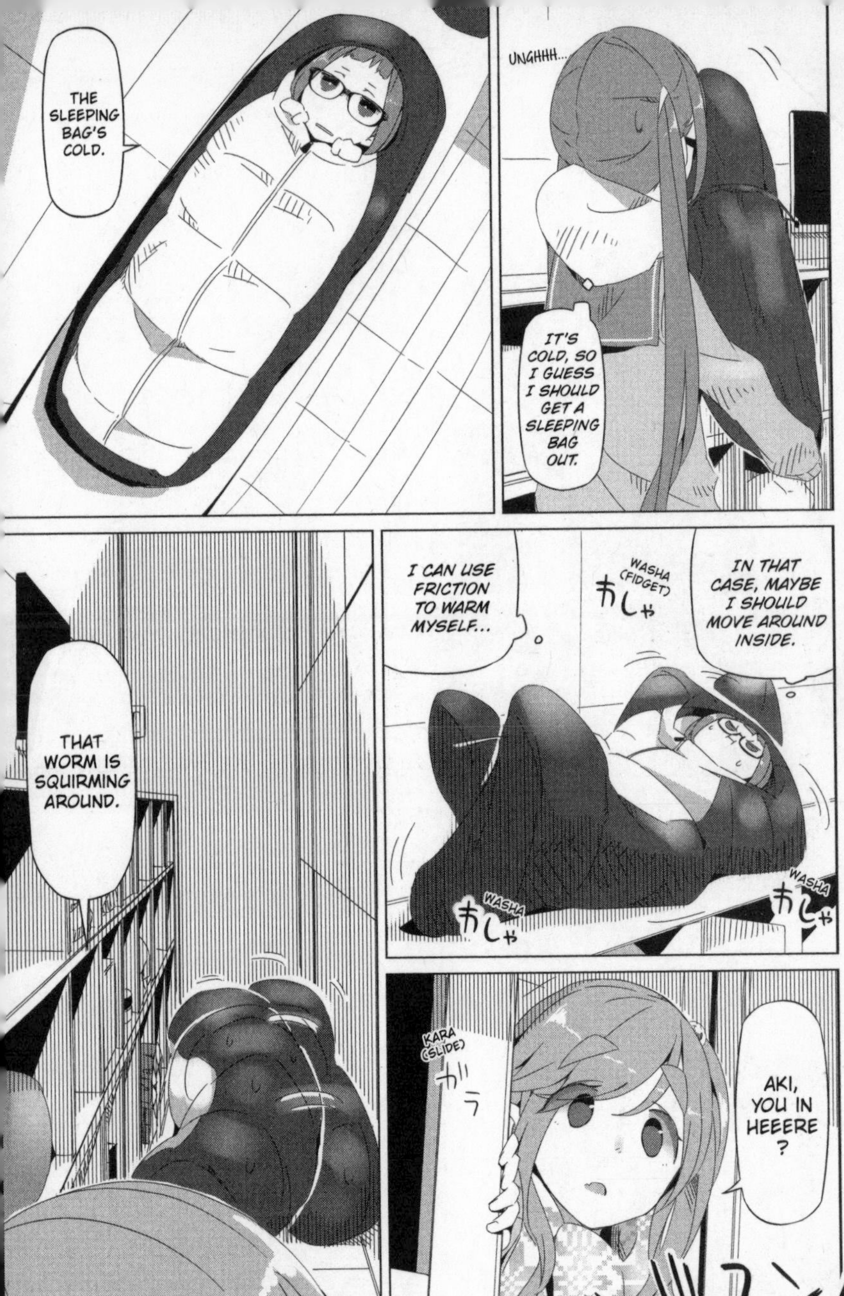
UNGHHH...
IT'S COLD, SO I GUESS I SHOULD GET A SLEEPING BAG OUT.
THE SLEEPING BAG'S COLD.
IN THAT CASE, MAYBE I SHOULD MOVE AROUND INSIDE.
WASHA (FIDGET)
わしゃ
I CAN USE FRICTION TO WARM MYSELF...
WASHA
わしゃ
WASHA
わしゃ
AKI, YOU IN HEEERE?
KARA (SLIDE)
ガラ
ドスン
DOSUN (FLOP)
THAT WORM IS SQUIRMING AROUND.

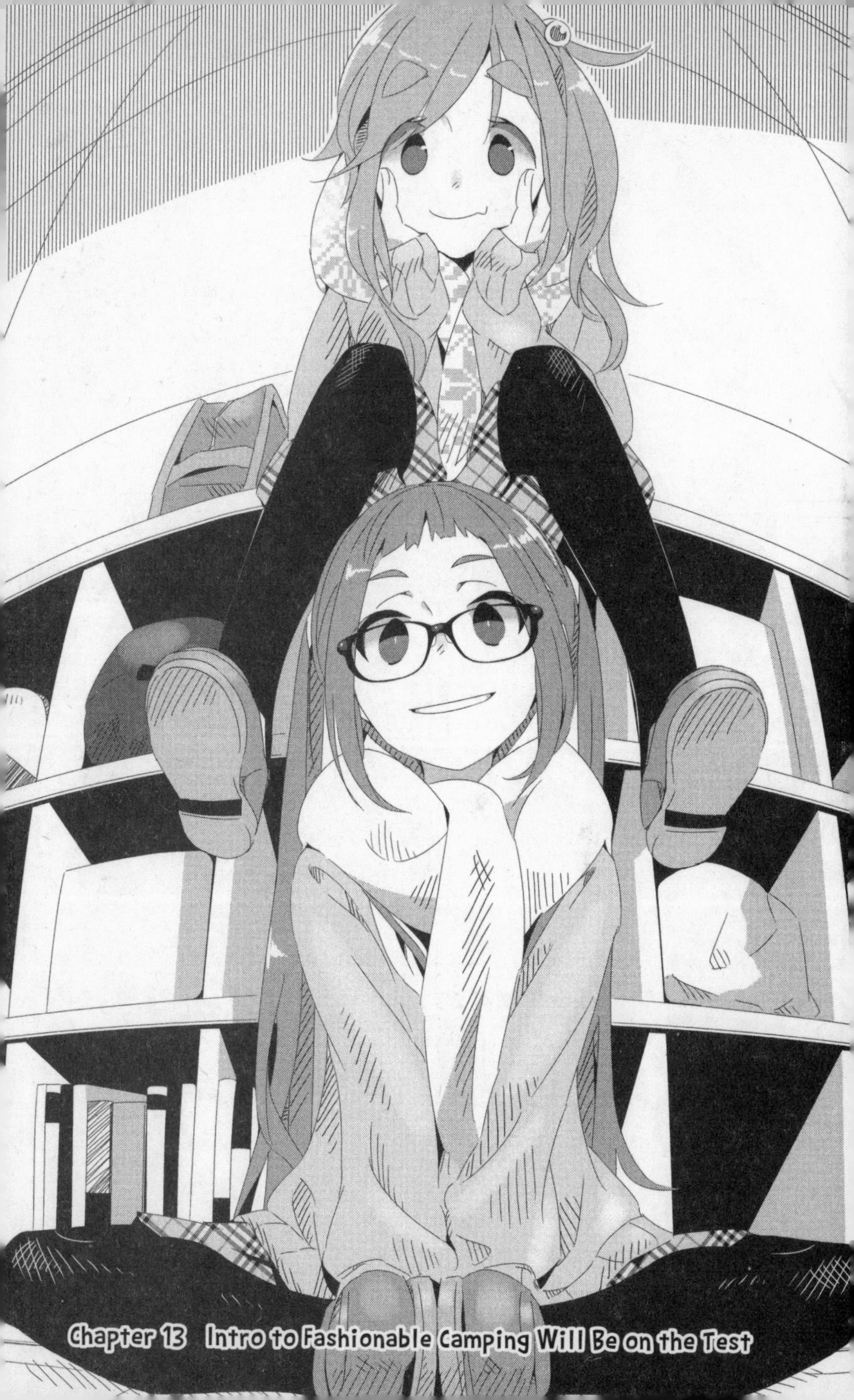

Chapter 13 Intro to Fashionable Camping Will Be on the Test

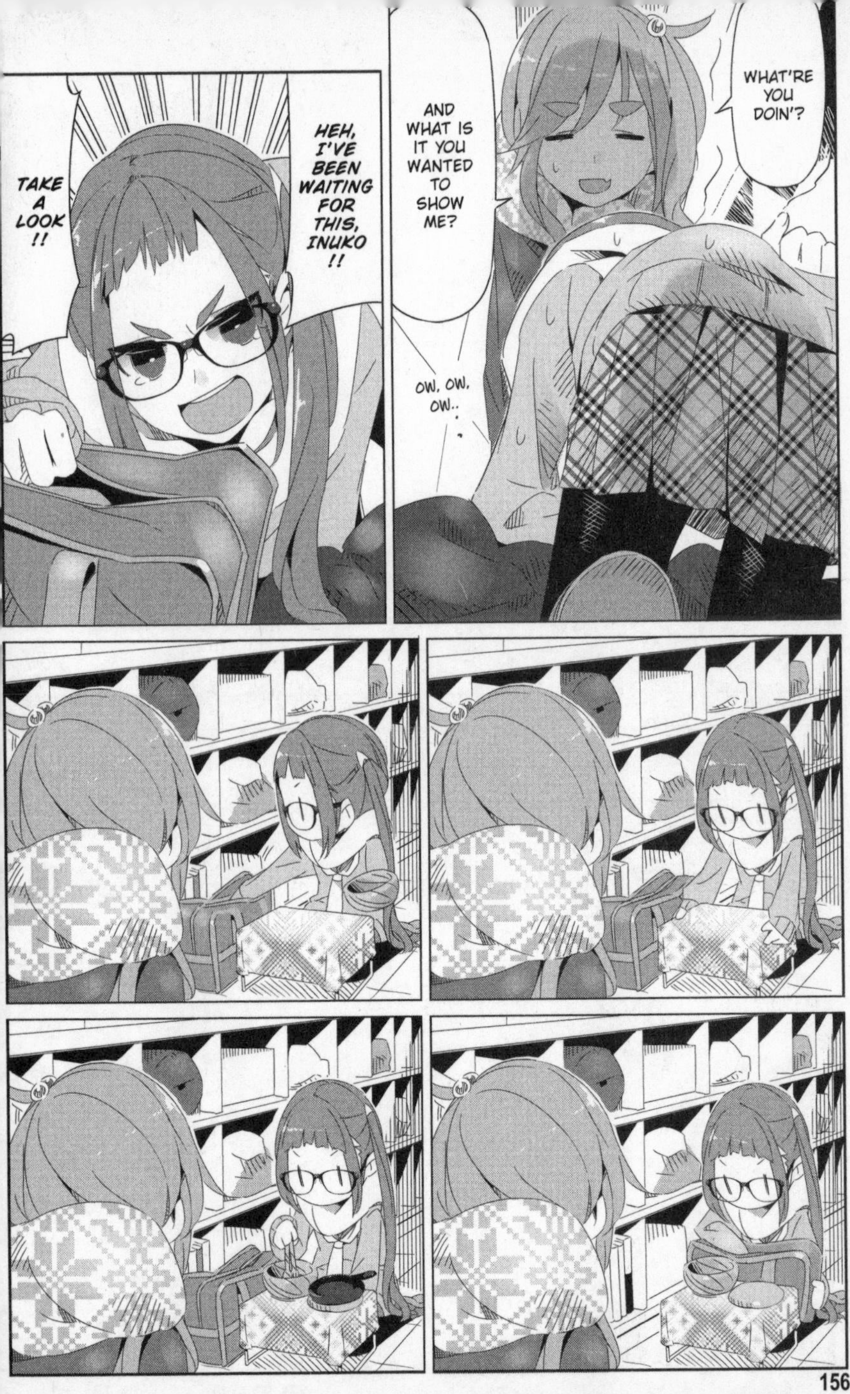
WHAT'RE YOU DOIN'?
AND WHAT IS IT YOU WANTED TO SHOW ME?
OW, OW, OW..
HEH, I'VE BEEN WAITING FOR THIS, INUKO!!
TAKE A LOOK!!

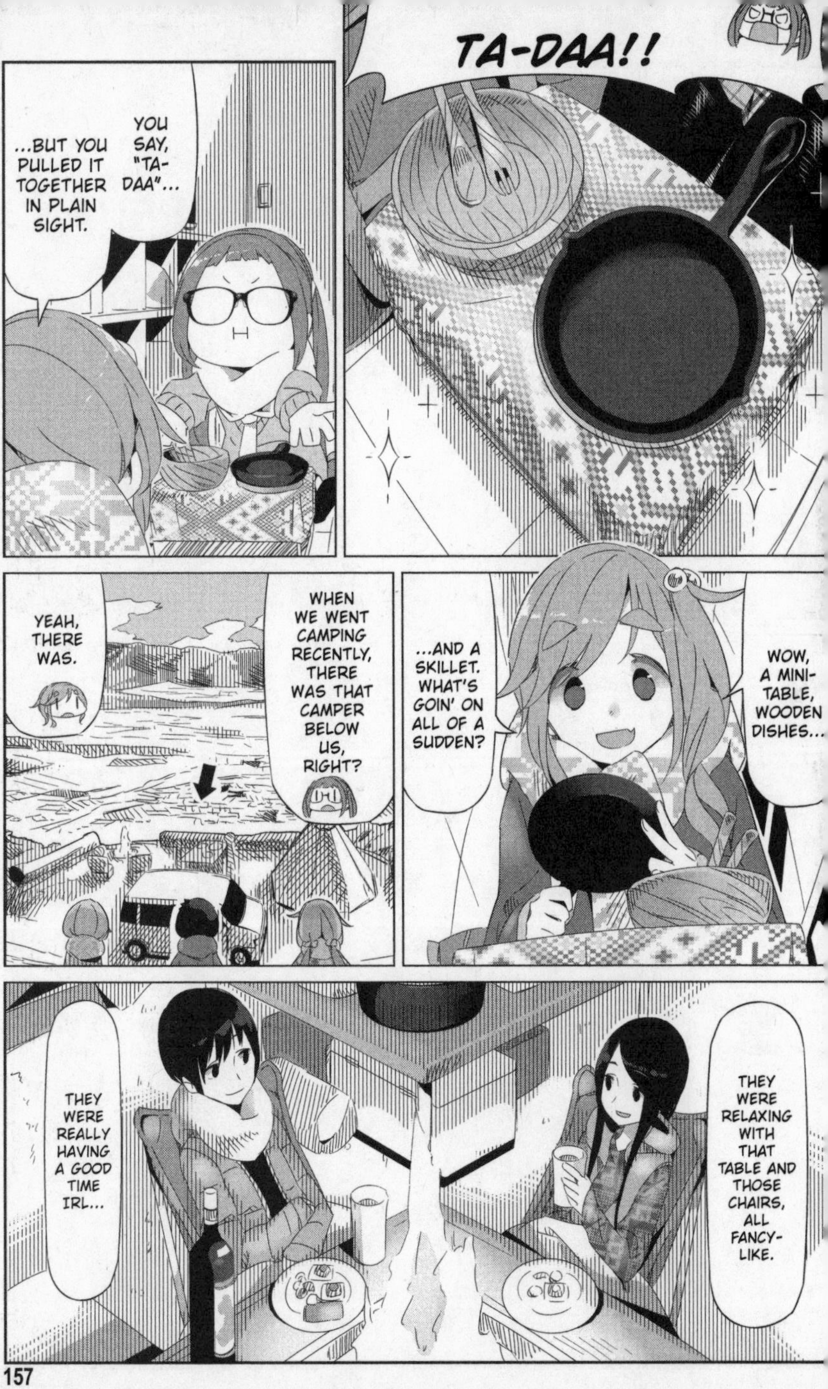
TA-DAA!!
YOU SAY, "TA-DAA"...
...BUT YOU PULLED IT TOGETHER IN PLAIN SIGHT.
WOW, A MINI-TABLE, WOODEN DISHES...
...AND A SKILLET. WHAT'S GOIN' ON ALL OF A SUDDEN?
WHEN WE WENT CAMPING RECENTLY, THERE WAS THAT CAMPER BELOW US, RIGHT?
YEAH, THERE WAS.
THEY WERE RELAXING WITH THAT TABLE AND THOSE CHAIRS, ALL FANCY-LIKE.
THEY WERE REALLY HAVING A GOOD TIME IRL...

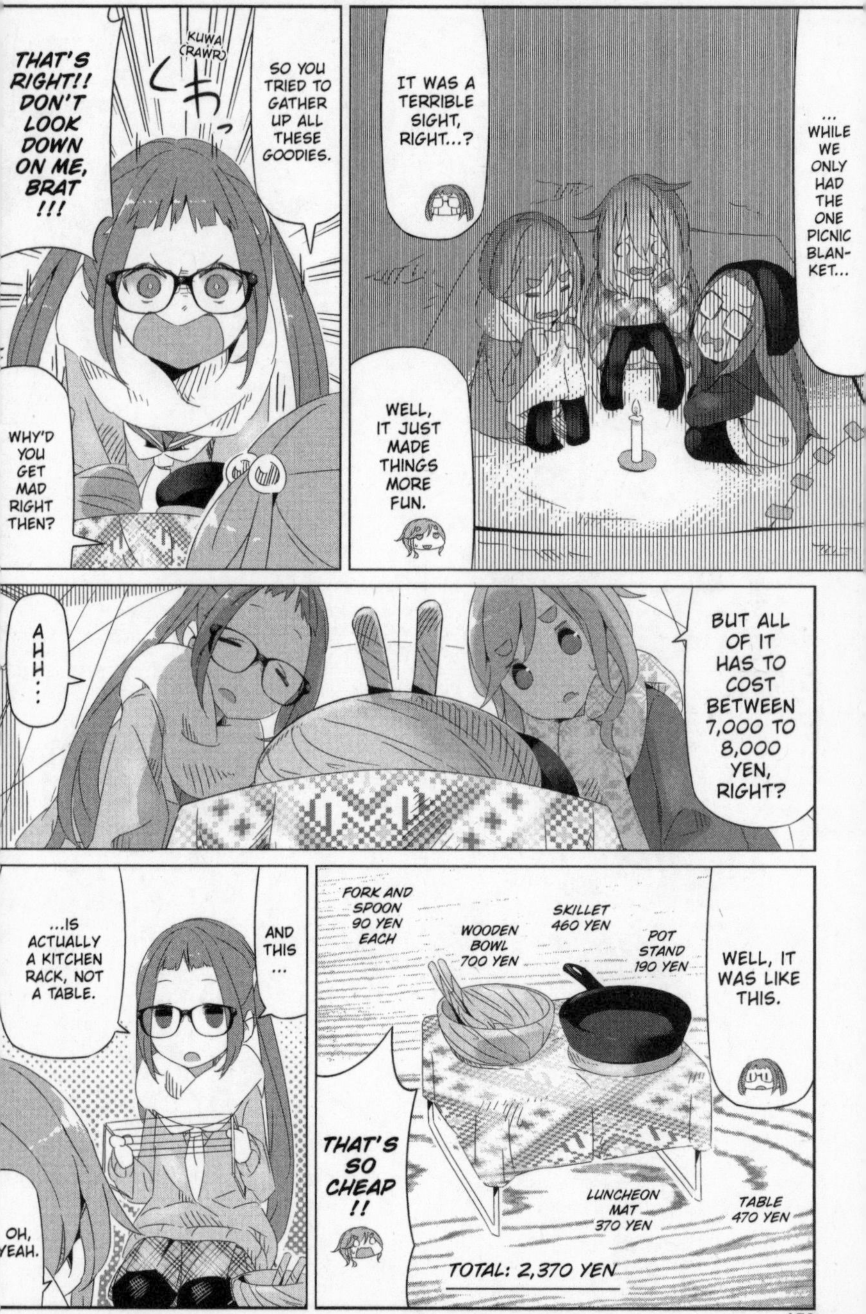

...WHILE WE ONLY HAD THE ONE PICNIC BLANKET...
IT WAS A TERRIBLE SIGHT, RIGHT...?
WELL, IT JUST MADE THINGS MORE FUN.
SO YOU TRIED TO GATHER UP ALL THESE GOODIES.
KUWA (RAWR)
THAT'S RIGHT!! DON'T LOOK DOWN ON ME, BRAT!!!
WHY'D YOU GET MAD RIGHT THEN?
BUT ALL OF IT HAS TO COST BETWEEN 7,000 TO 8,000 YEN, RIGHT?
AHH...
WELL, IT WAS LIKE THIS.
POT STAND 190 YEN
SKILLET 460 YEN
WOODEN BOWL 700 YEN
FORK AND SPOON 90 YEN EACH
TABLE 470 YEN
LUNCHEON MAT 370 YEN
THAT'S SO CHEAP!!
TOTAL: 2,370 YEN
AND THIS...
...IS ACTUALLY A KITCHEN RACK, NOT A TABLE.
OH, YEAH.

SIGNS : TSUKAMOTO / LIFESTYLE SUNDRIES

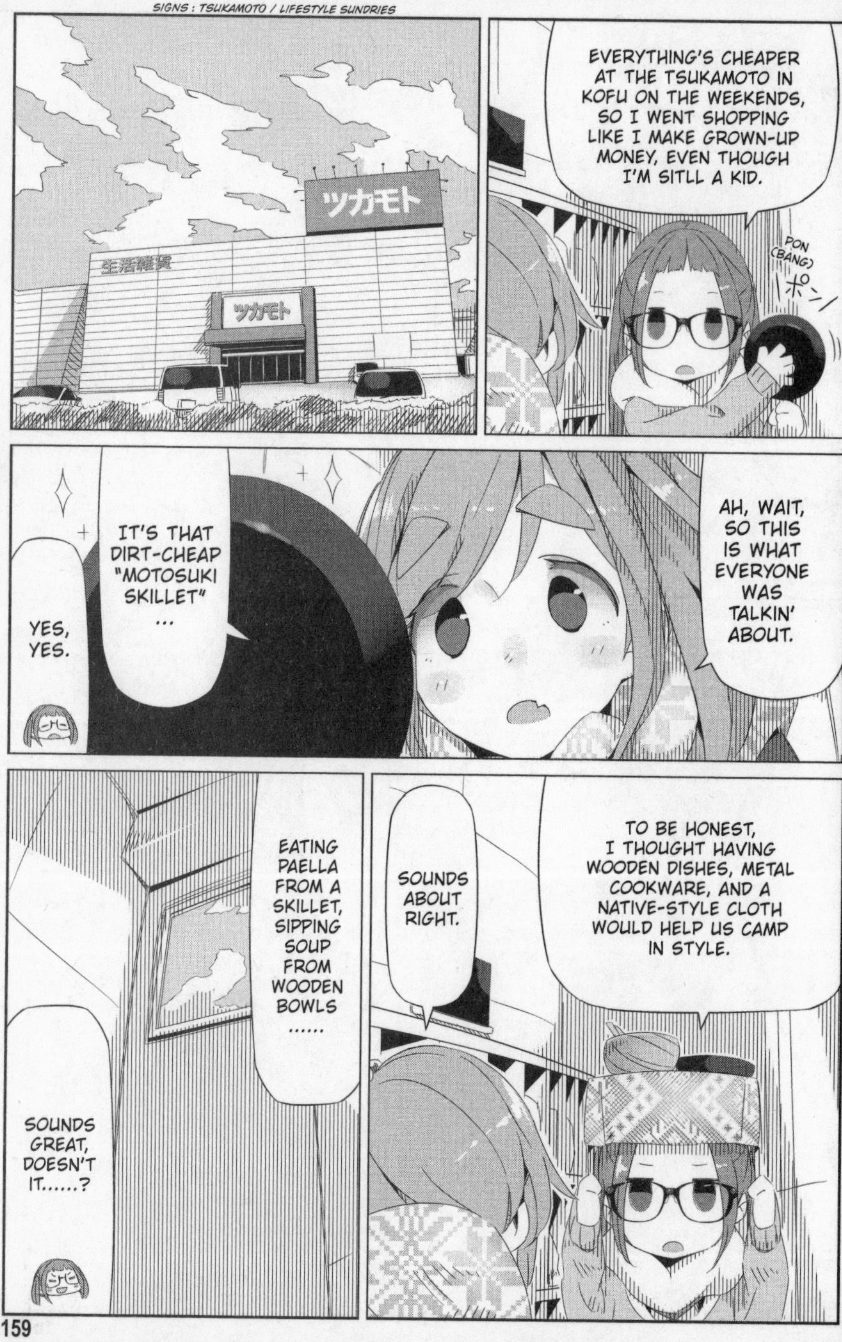
EVERYTHING'S CHEAPER AT THE TSUKAMOTO IN KOFU ON THE WEEKENDS, SO I WENT SHOPPING LIKE I MAKE GROWN-UP MONEY, EVEN THOUGH I'M SITLL A KID.
PON (BANG)
ポン
ツカモト
生活雑貨
ツカモト
AH, WAIT, SO THIS IS WHAT EVERYONE WAS TALKIN' ABOUT.
IT'S THAT DIRT-CHEAP "MOTOSUKI SKILLET" ...
YES, YES.
TO BE HONEST, I THOUGHT HAVING WOODEN DISHES, METAL COOKWARE, AND A NATIVE-STYLE CLOTH WOULD HELP US CAMP IN STYLE.
SOUNDS ABOUT RIGHT.
EATING PAELLA FROM A SKILLET, SIPPING SOUP FROM WOODEN BOWLS ......
SOUNDS GREAT, DOESN'T IT......?

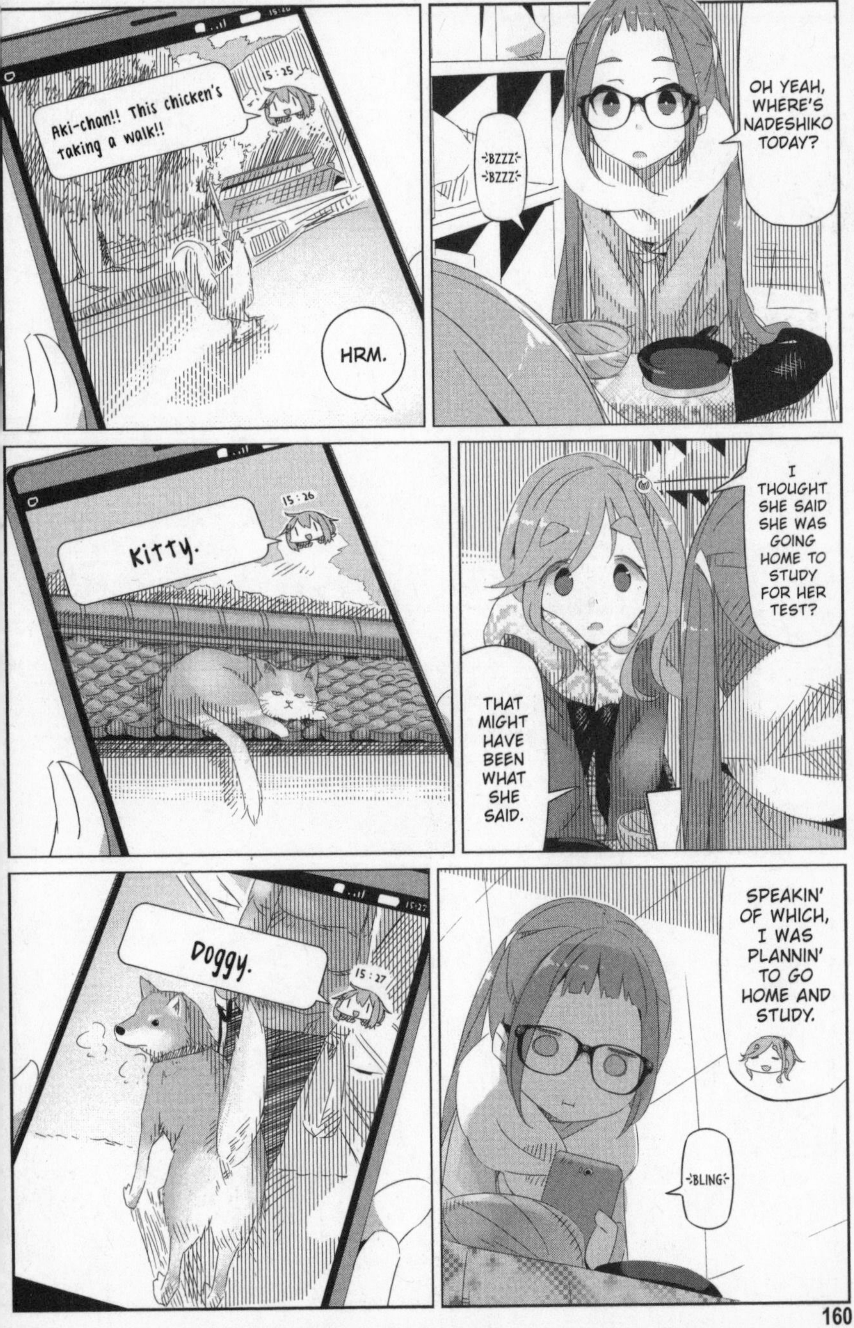
OH YEAH, WHERE'S NADESHIKO TODAY?
BZZZ BZZZ
15:25
Aki-chan!! This chicken's taking a walk!!
HRM.
I THOUGHT SHE SAID SHE WAS GOING HOME TO STUDY FOR HER TEST?
THAT MIGHT HAVE BEEN WHAT SHE SAID.
15:26
Kitty.
SPEAKIN' OF WHICH, I WAS PLANNIN' TO GO HOME AND STUDY.
BLING
Doggy.
15:27

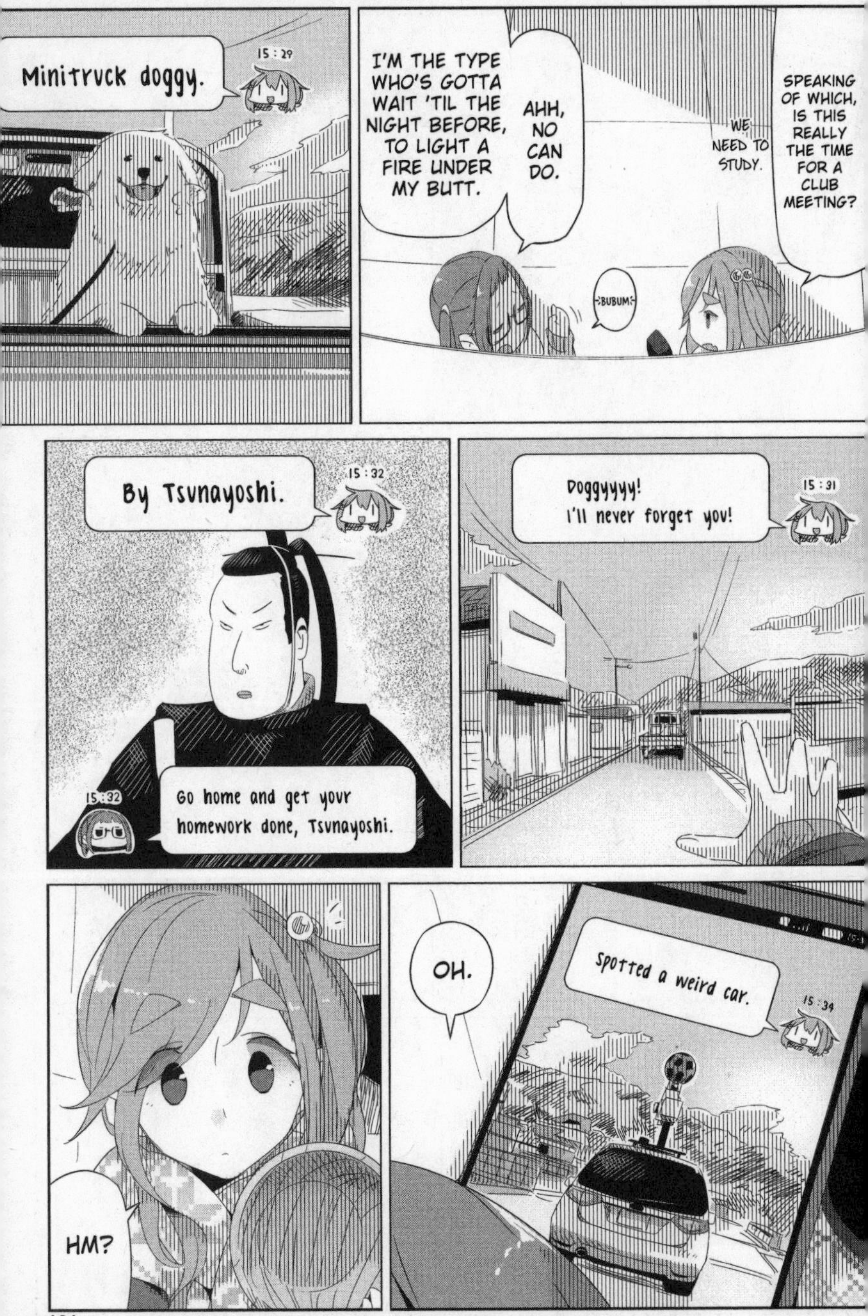
SPEAKING OF WHICH, IS THIS REALLY THE TIME FOR A CLUB MEETING?
WE NEED TO STUDY.
AHH, NO CAN DO.
I'M THE TYPE WHO'S GOTTA WAIT 'TIL THE NIGHT BEFORE, TO LIGHT A FIRE UNDER MY BUTT.
BUBUM
15:29
Minitruck doggy.
15:31
Doggyyyy! I'll never forget you!
15:32
By Tsunayoshi.
15:32
Go home and get your homework done, Tsunayoshi.
OH.
Spotted a weird car.
15:34
HM?

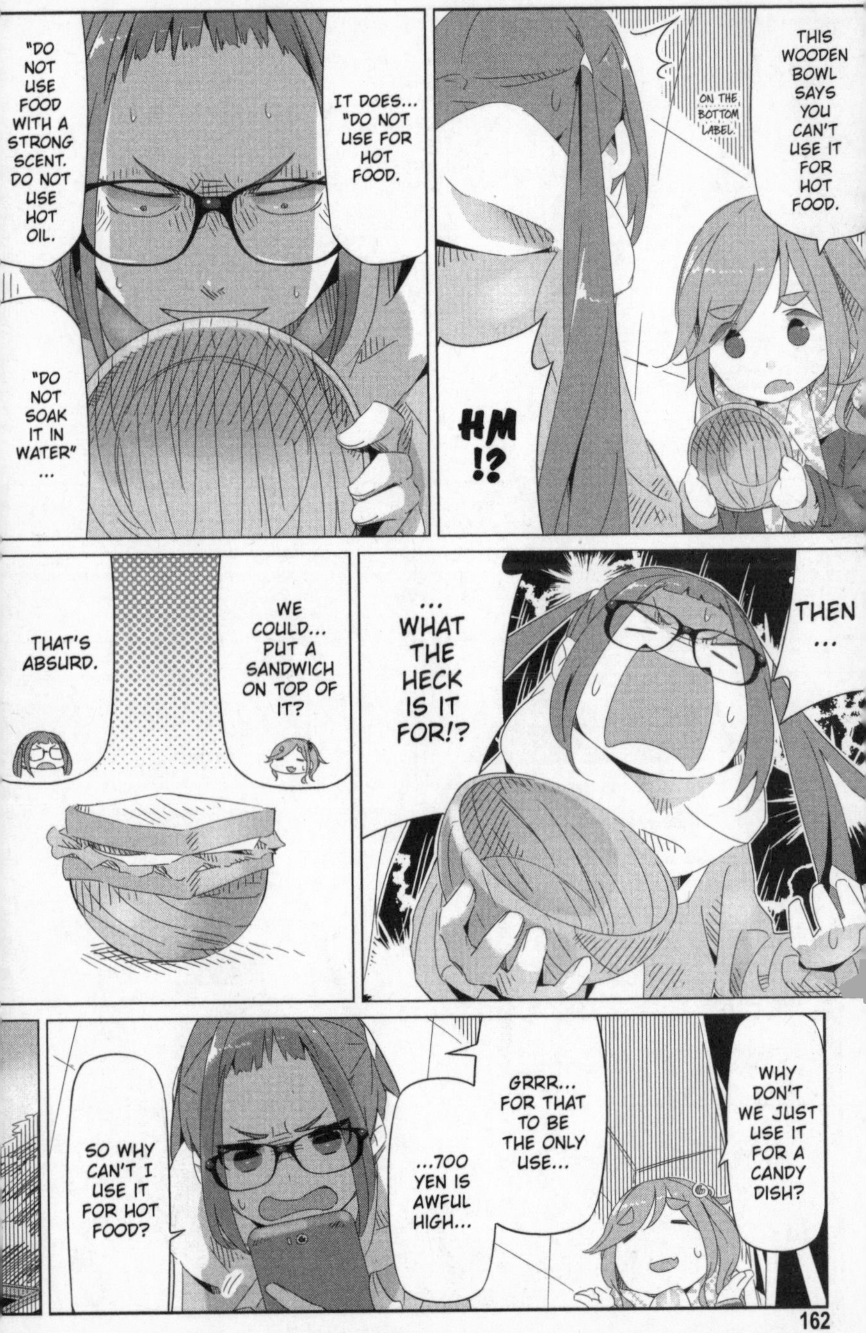
THIS WOODEN BOWL SAYS YOU CAN'T USE IT FOR HOT FOOD.
ON THE BOTTOM LABEL.
HM !?
IT DOES... "DO NOT USE FOR HOT FOOD.
"DO NOT USE FOOD WITH A STRONG SCENT. DO NOT USE HOT OIL.
"DO NOT SOAK IT IN WATER" ...
THEN ...
... WHAT THE HECK IS IT FOR!?
WE COULD... PUT A SANDWICH ON TOP OF IT?
THAT'S ABSURD.
WHY DON'T WE JUST USE IT FOR A CANDY DISH?
GRRR... FOR THAT TO BE THE ONLY USE...
...700 YEN IS AWFUL HIGH...
SO WHY CAN'T I USE IT FOR HOT FOOD?

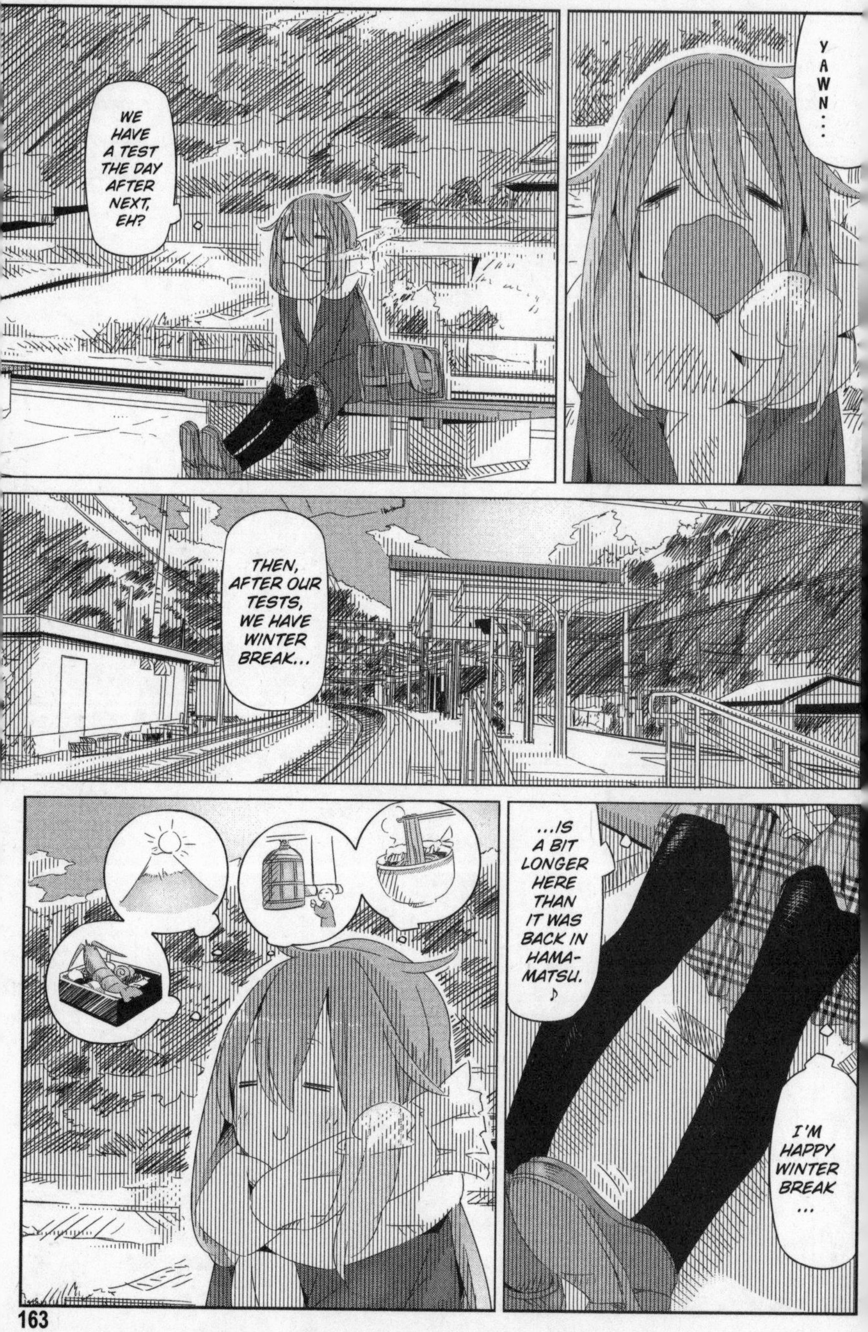
YAWN...
WE HAVE A TEST THE DAY AFTER NEXT, EH?
THEN, AFTER OUR TESTS, WE HAVE WINTER BREAK...
...IS A BIT LONGER HERE THAN IT WAS BACK IN HAMAMATSU. ♪
I'M HAPPY WINTER BREAK...

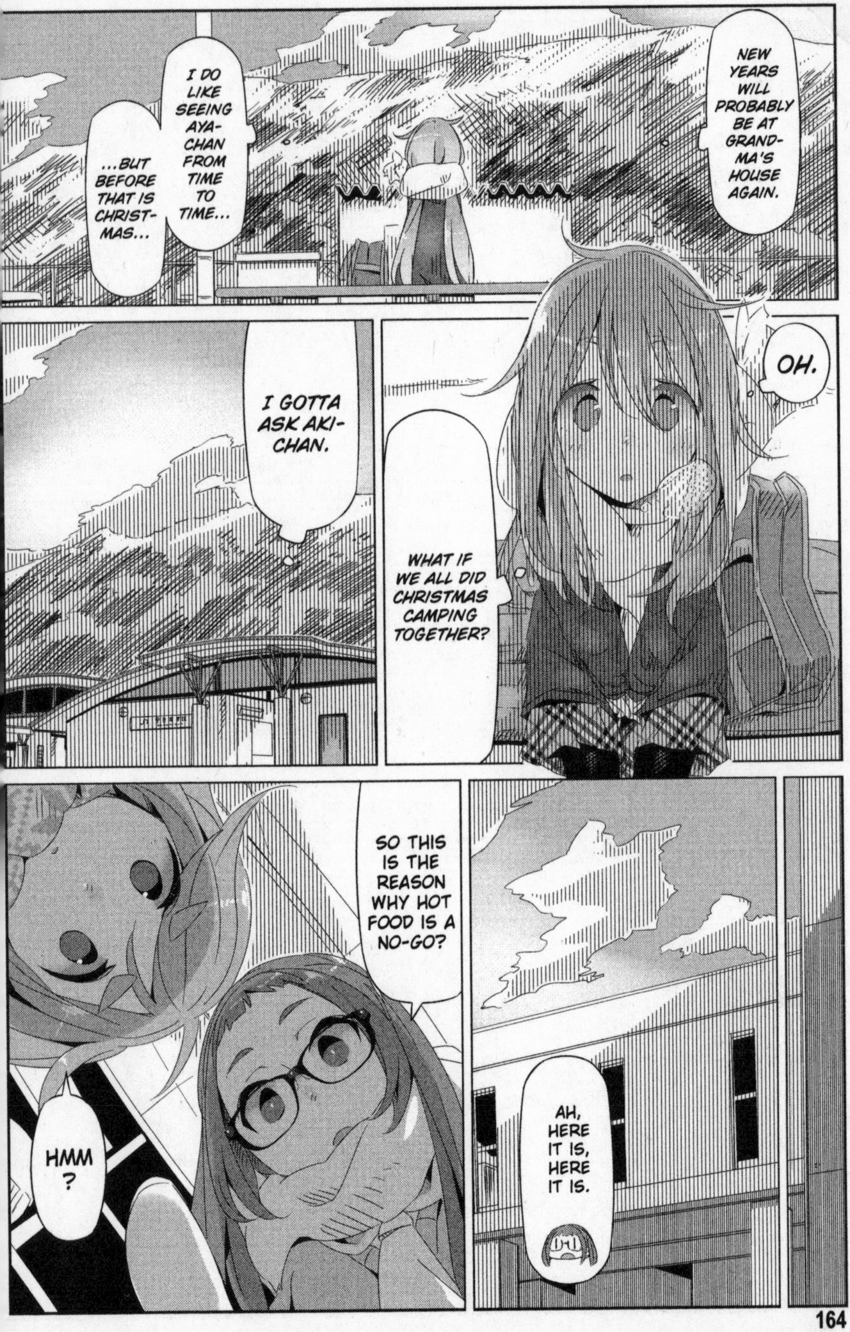
NEW YEARS WILL PROBABLY BE AT GRAND-MA'S HOUSE AGAIN.
I DO LIKE SEEING AYA-CHAN FROM TIME TO TIME...
...BUT BEFORE THAT IS CHRIST-MAS...
OH.
WHAT IF WE ALL DID CHRISTMAS CAMPING TOGETHER?
I GOTTA ASK AKI-CHAN.
AH, HERE IT IS, HERE IT IS.
SO THIS IS THE REASON WHY HOT FOOD IS A NO-GO?
HMM?

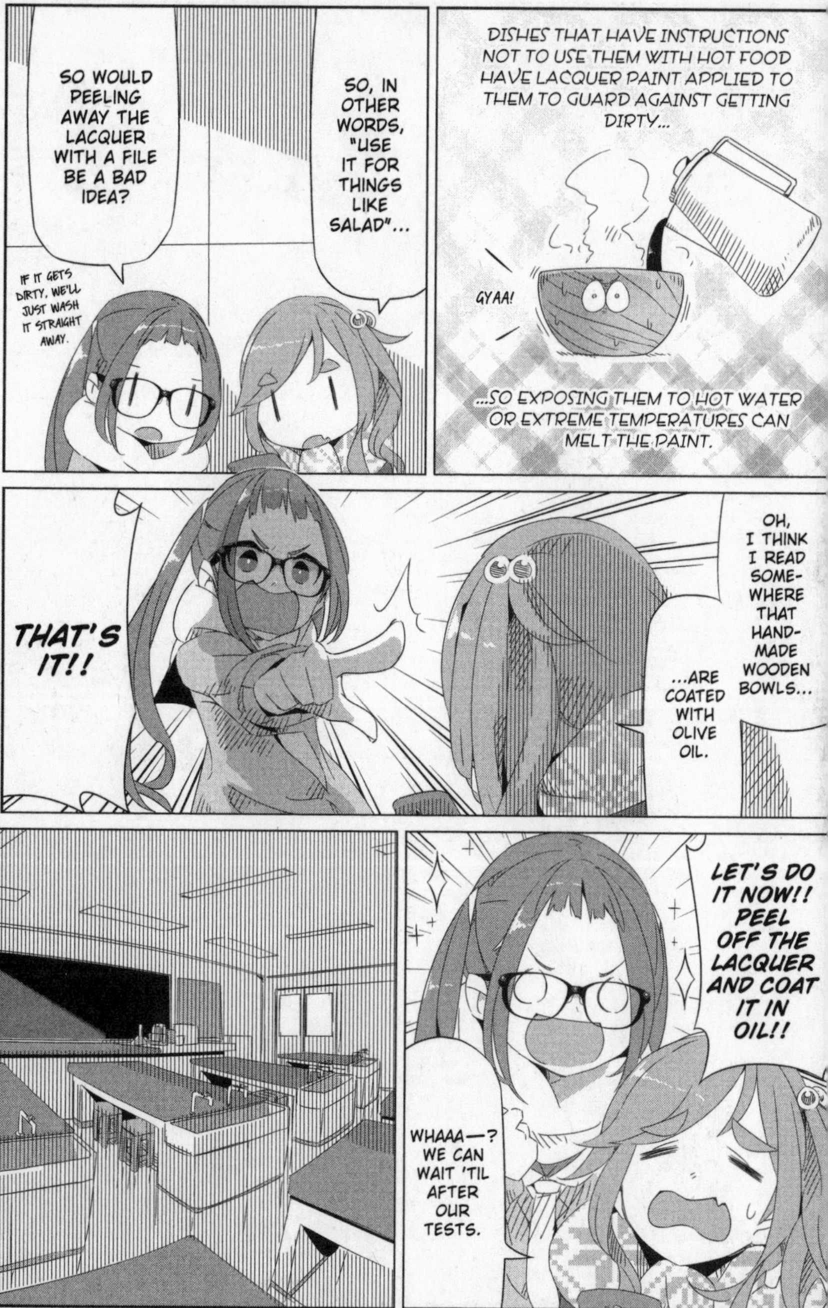
DISHES THAT HAVE INSTRUCTIONS NOT TO USE THEM WITH HOT FOOD HAVE LACQUER PAINT APPLIED TO THEM TO GUARD AGAINST GETTING DIRTY...
GYAA!
...SO EXPOSING THEM TO HOT WATER OR EXTREME TEMPERATURES CAN MELT THE PAINT.
SO, IN OTHER WORDS, "USE IT FOR THINGS LIKE SALAD"...
SO WOULD PEELING AWAY THE LACQUER WITH A FILE BE A BAD IDEA?
IF IT GETS DIRTY, WE'LL JUST WASH IT STRAIGHT AWAY.
OH, I THINK I READ SOME-WHERE THAT HAND-MADE WOODEN BOWLS...
...ARE COATED WITH OLIVE OIL.
THAT'S IT!!
LET'S DO IT NOW!! PEEL OFF THE LACQUER AND COAT IT IN OIL!!
WHAAA—? WE CAN WAIT 'TIL AFTER OUR TESTS.

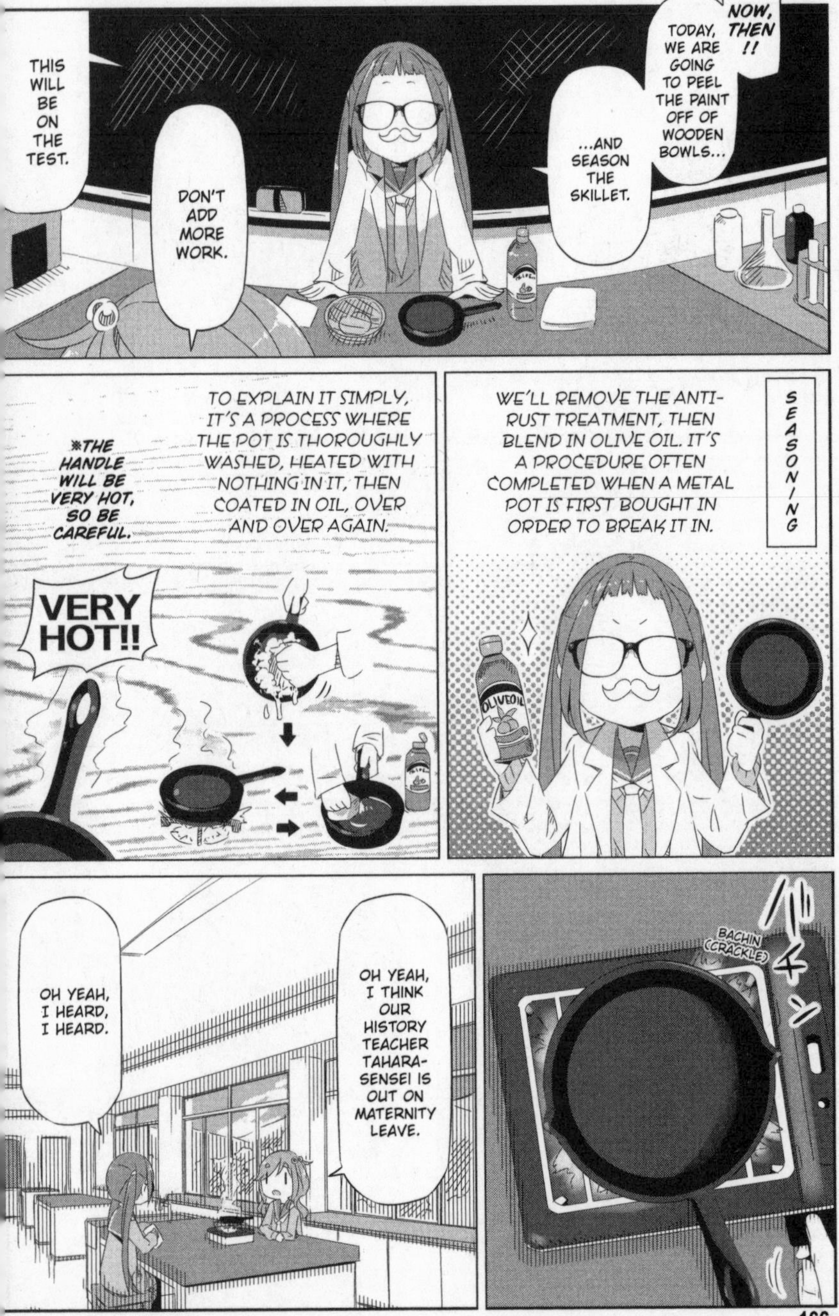
NOW, THEN!!
TODAY, WE ARE GOING TO PEEL THE PAINT OFF OF WOODEN BOWLS...
...AND SEASON THE SKILLET.
THIS WILL BE ON THE TEST.
DON'T ADD MORE WORK.
SEASONING
WE'LL REMOVE THE ANTI-RUST TREATMENT, THEN BLEND IN OLIVE OIL. IT'S A PROCEDURE OFTEN COMPLETED WHEN A METAL POT IS FIRST BOUGHT IN ORDER TO BREAK IT IN.
OLIVE OIL
TO EXPLAIN IT SIMPLY, IT'S A PROCESS WHERE THE POT IS THOROUGHLY WASHED, HEATED WITH NOTHING IN IT, THEN COATED IN OIL, OVER AND OVER AGAIN.
※THE HANDLE WILL BE VERY HOT, SO BE CAREFUL.
VERY HOT!!
BACHIN (CRACKLE)
OH YEAH, I THINK OUR HISTORY TEACHER TAHARA-SENSEI IS OUT ON MATERNITY LEAVE.
OH YEAH, I HEARD, I HEARD.

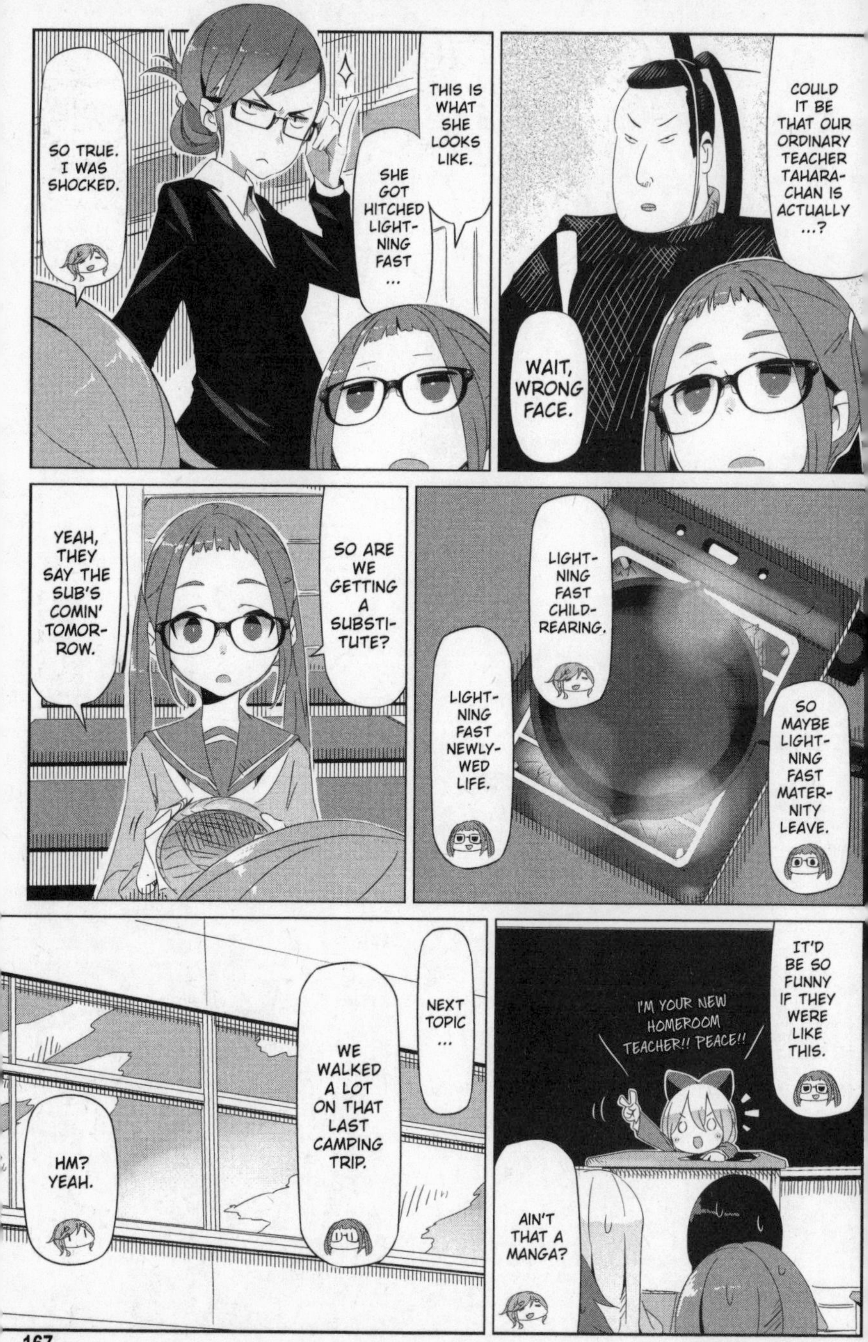
COULD IT BE THAT OUR ORDINARY TEACHER TAHARA-CHAN IS ACTUALLY ...?
WAIT, WRONG FACE.
THIS IS WHAT SHE LOOKS LIKE.
SHE GOT HITCHED LIGHTNING FAST ...
SO TRUE. I WAS SHOCKED.
LIGHTNING FAST NEWLYWED LIFE.
LIGHTNING FAST CHILD-REARING.
SO MAYBE LIGHTNING FAST MATERNITY LEAVE.
SO ARE WE GETTING A SUBSTITUTE?
YEAH, THEY SAY THE SUB'S COMIN' TOMORROW.
IT'D BE SO FUNNY IF THEY WERE LIKE THIS.
I'M YOUR NEW HOMEROOM TEACHER!! PEACE!!
AIN'T THAT A MANGA?
NEXT TOPIC ...
WE WALKED A LOT ON THAT LAST CAMPING TRIP.
HM? YEAH.

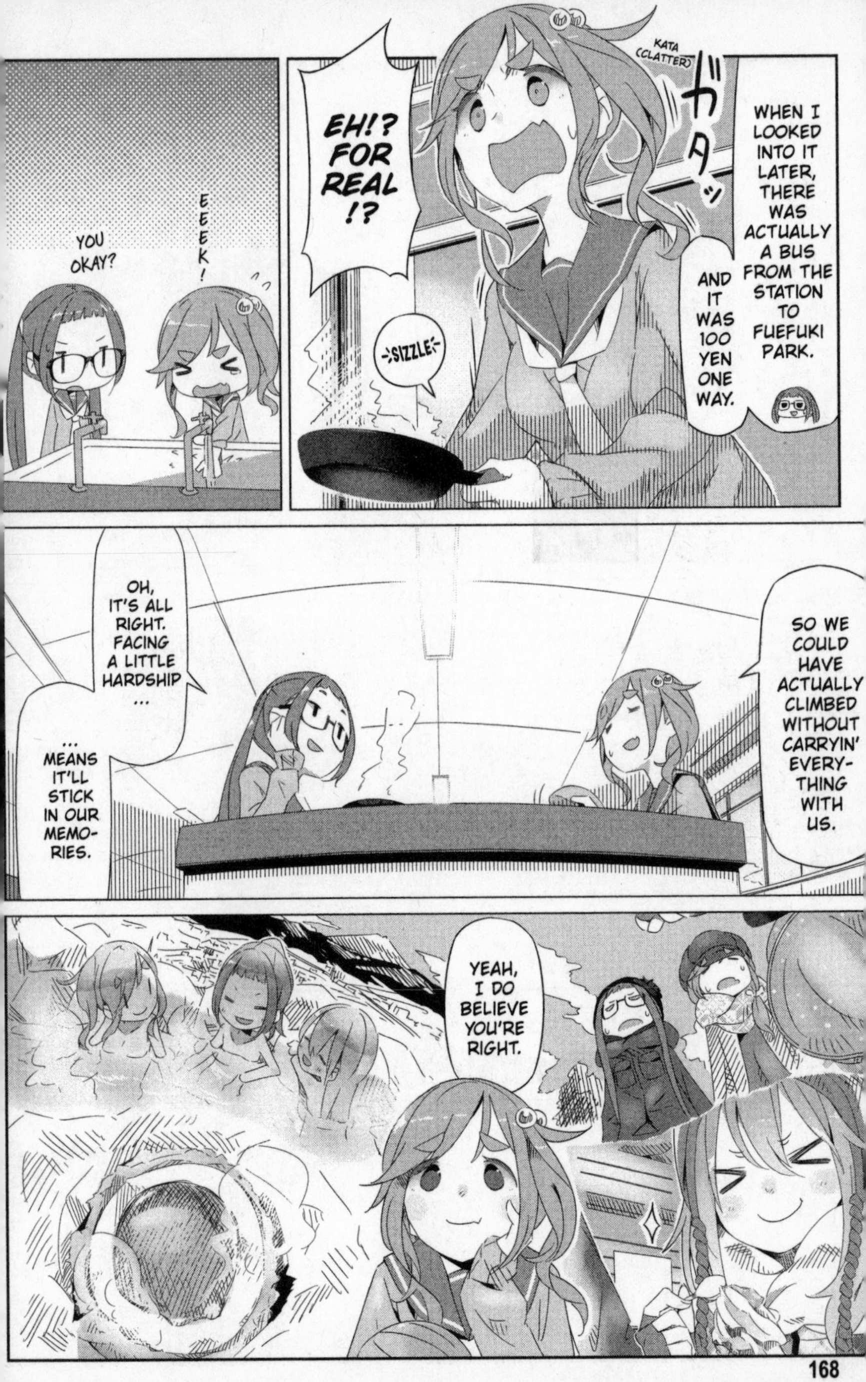
WHEN I LOOKED INTO IT LATER, THERE WAS ACTUALLY A BUS FROM THE STATION TO FUEFUKI PARK.
AND IT WAS 100 YEN ONE WAY.
KATA (CLATTER)
ガタッ
EH!? FOR REAL!?
SIZZLE
EEEEK!
YOU OKAY?
SO WE COULD HAVE ACTUALLY CLIMBED WITHOUT CARRYIN' EVERYTHING WITH US.
OH, IT'S ALL RIGHT. FACING A LITTLE HARDSHIP...
...MEANS IT'LL STICK IN OUR MEMORIES.
YEAH, I DO BELIEVE YOU'RE RIGHT.

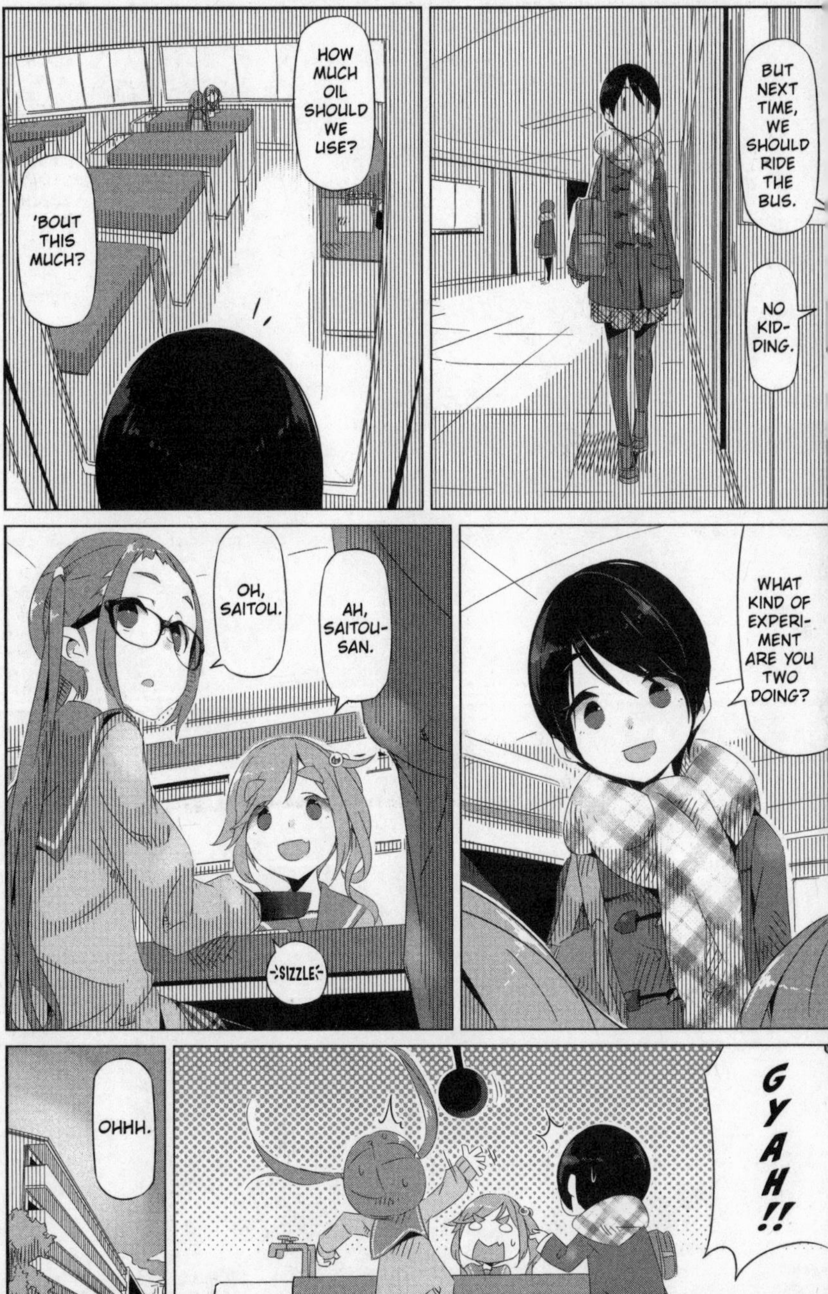
BUT NEXT TIME, WE SHOULD RIDE THE BUS.
NO KID-DING.
HOW MUCH OIL SHOULD WE USE?
'BOUT THIS MUCH?
WHAT KIND OF EXPERI-MENT ARE YOU TWO DOING?
OH, SAITOU.
AH, SAITOU-SAN.
SIZZLE
GYAH!!
OHHH.

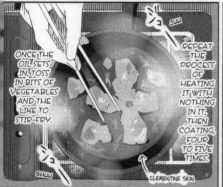

SO THIS IS WHAT YOU HAVE TO DO BEFORE USING A CAST-IRON PAN.
WOW.
JUU (SIZZLE)
JUU
JUU
REPEAT THE PROCESS OF HEATING IT WITH NOTHING IN IT, THEN COATING, FOUR TO FIVE TIMES.
ONCE THE OIL SETS IN, TOSS IN BITS OF VEGETABLES AND THE LIKE TO STIR-FRY.
CLEMENTINE SKIN
SHUU
BOKO (BUBBLE)
NEXT, BRING SOME WATER TO A BOIL.
BOKO
CLEAN IT THOROUGHLY WITH A SCRUBBING BRUSH.
HEAT IT WITH NOTHING IN IT ONCE MORE, COAT IT LIGHTLY WITH OIL ONCE AGAIN, AND IT'S DONE.
WHOA—
I'M DONE OVER HERE TOO.

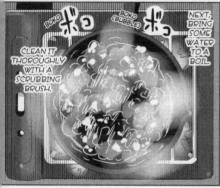

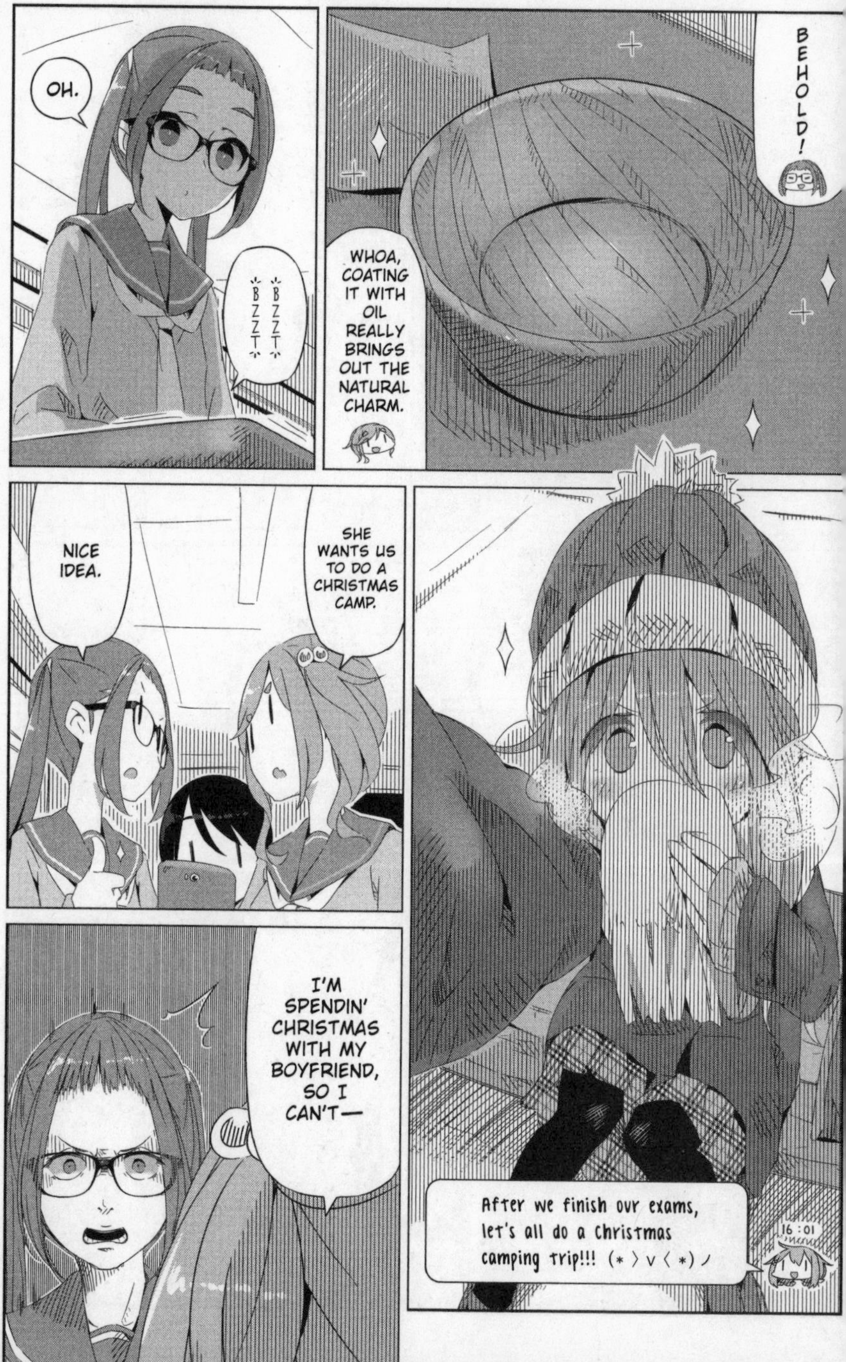
BEHOLD!
WHOA, COATING IT WITH OIL REALLY BRINGS OUT THE NATURAL CHARM.
OH.
BZZT BZZT
After we finish our exams, let's all do a Christmas camping trip!!! (*>v<*)ノ
16:01
SHE WANTS US TO DO A CHRISTMAS CAMP.
NICE IDEA.
I'M SPENDIN' CHRISTMAS WITH MY BOYFRIEND, SO I CAN'T—

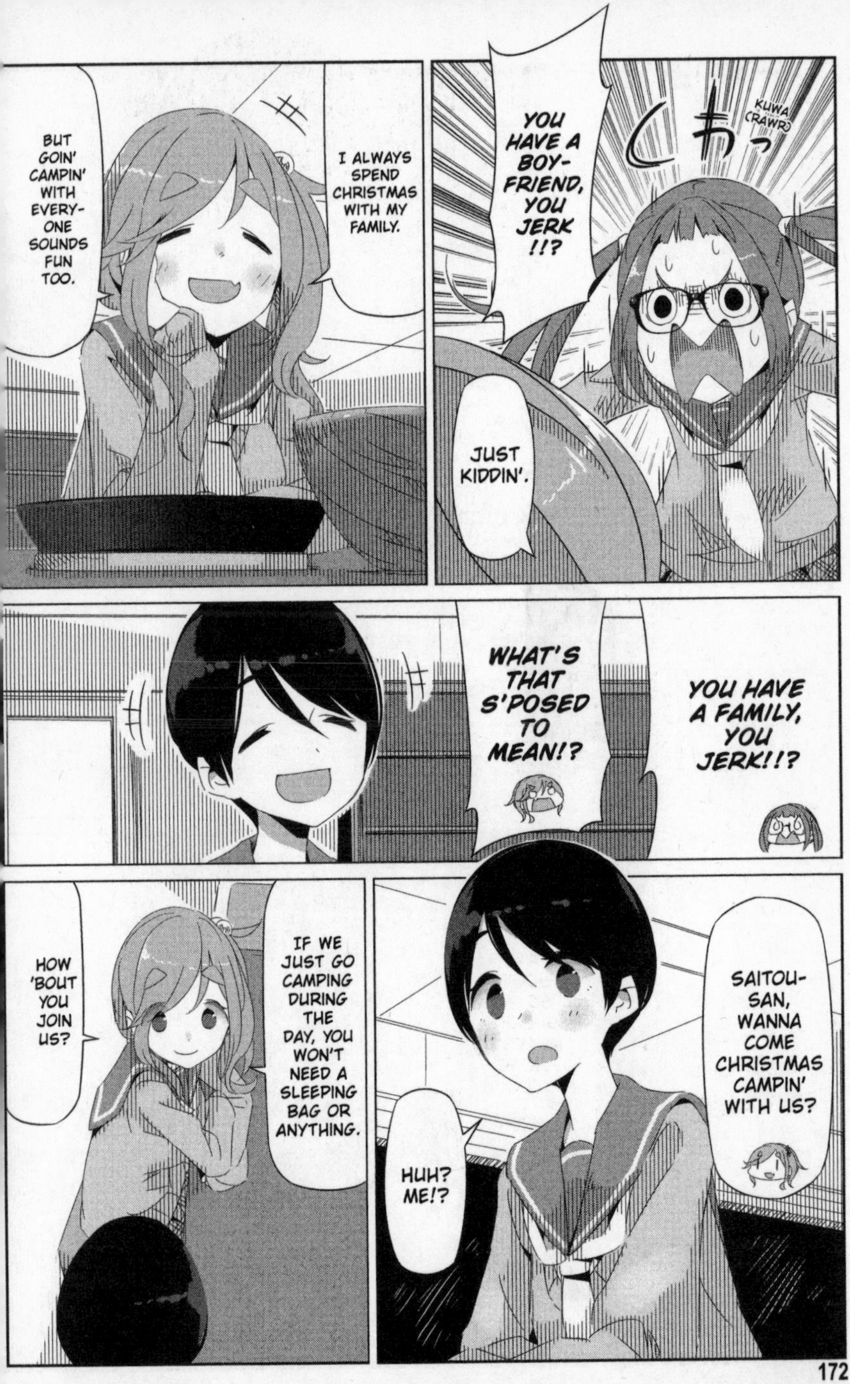
KUWA (RAWR)
YOU HAVE A BOY-FRIEND, YOU JERK!!?
JUST KIDDIN'.
I ALWAYS SPEND CHRISTMAS WITH MY FAMILY.
BUT GOIN' CAMPIN' WITH EVERY-ONE SOUNDS FUN TOO.
YOU HAVE A FAMILY, YOU JERK!!?
WHAT'S THAT S'POSED TO MEAN!?
SAITOU-SAN, WANNA COME CHRISTMAS CAMPIN' WITH US?
HUH? ME!?
IF WE JUST GO CAMPING DURING THE DAY, YOU WON'T NEED A SLEEPING BAG OR ANYTHING.
HOW 'BOUT YOU JOIN US?

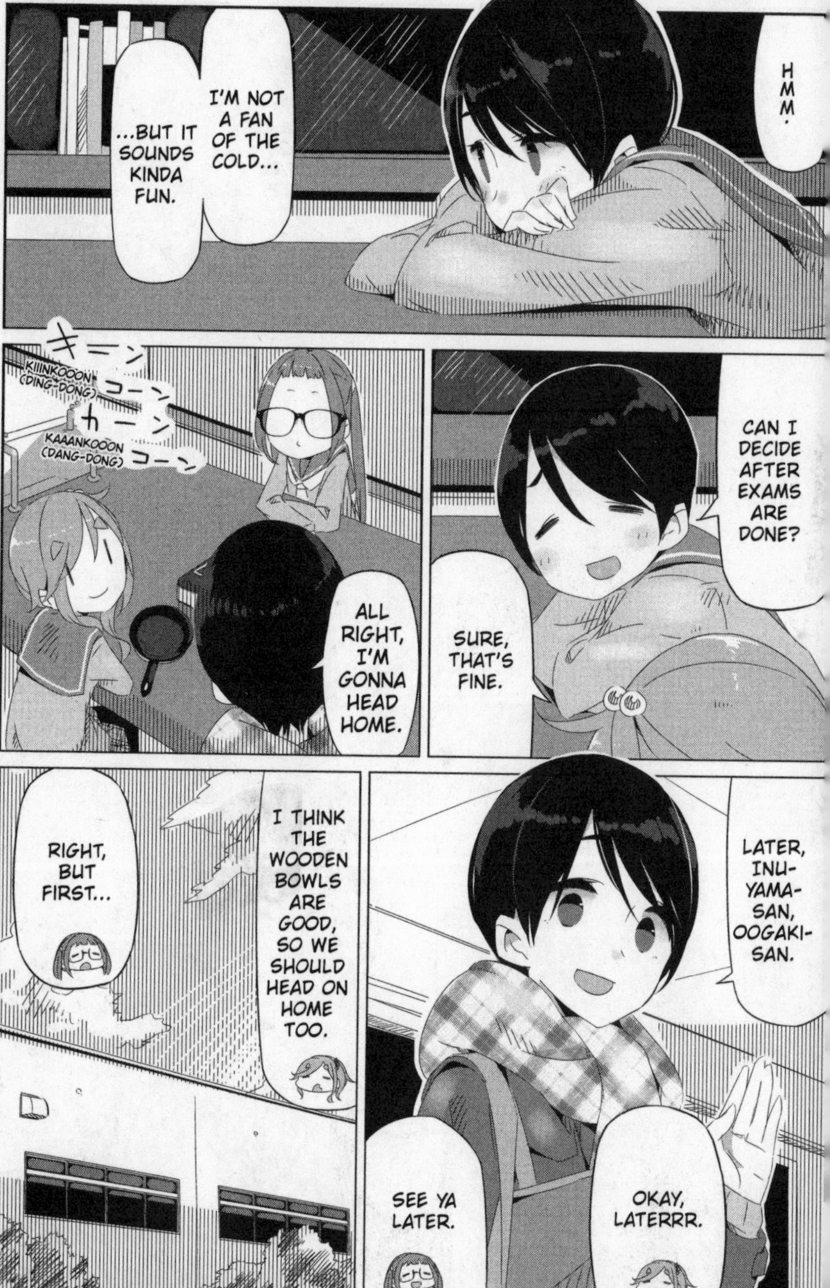
HMM.
I'M NOT A FAN OF THE COLD...
...BUT IT SOUNDS KINDA FUN.
CAN I DECIDE AFTER EXAMS ARE DONE?
SURE, THAT'S FINE.
キーン コーン
KIIINKOOON (DING-DONG)
カーン コーン
KAAANKOOON (DANG-DONG)
ALL RIGHT, I'M GONNA HEAD HOME.
LATER, INU-YAMA-SAN, OOGAKI-SAN.
OKAY, LATERRR.
SEE YA LATER.
I THINK THE WOODEN BOWLS ARE GOOD, SO WE SHOULD HEAD ON HOME TOO.
RIGHT, BUT FIRST...

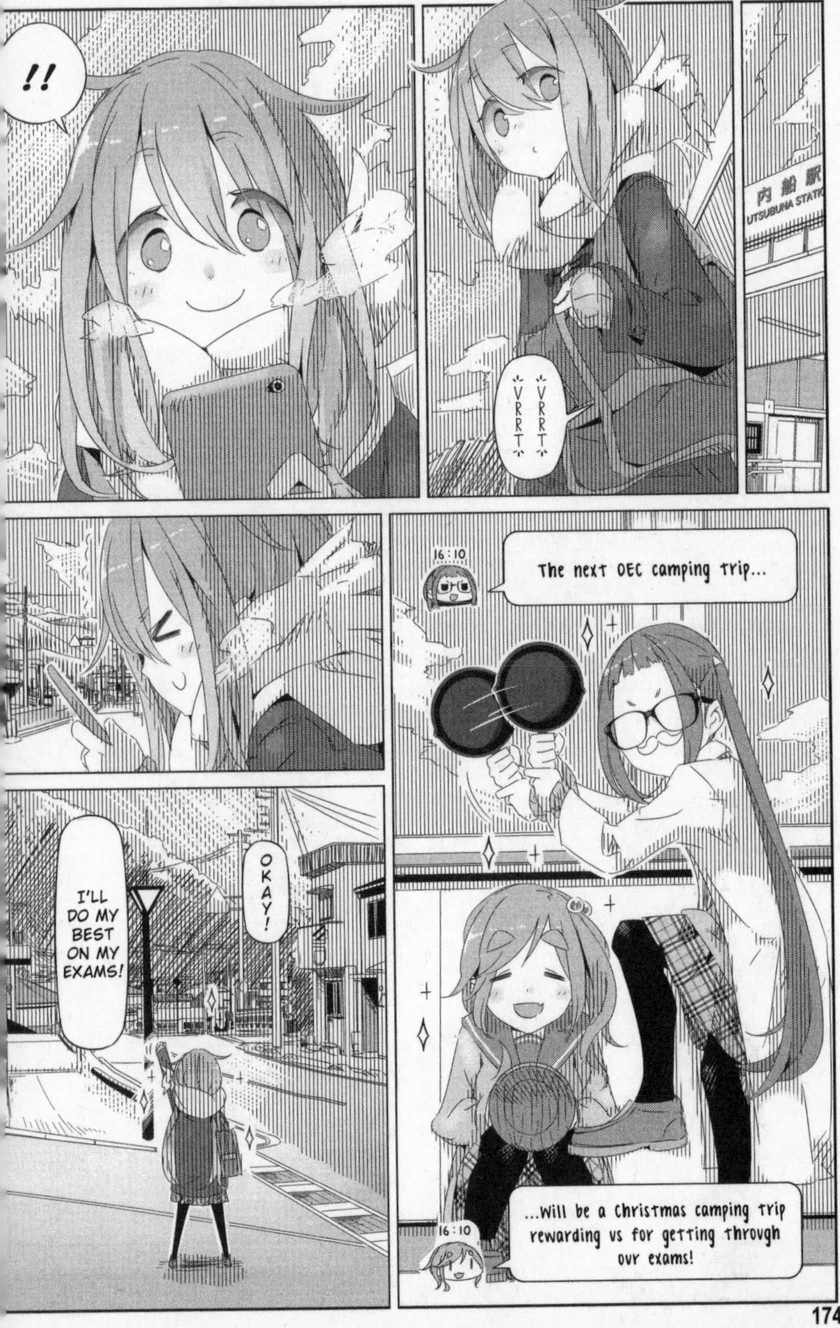

内船駅
UTSUBUNA STATIO
VRRT VRRT
!!
16:10
The next OEC camping trip...
16:10
...Will be a Christmas camping trip rewarding us for getting through our exams!
OKAY!
I'LL DO MY BEST ON MY EXAMS!

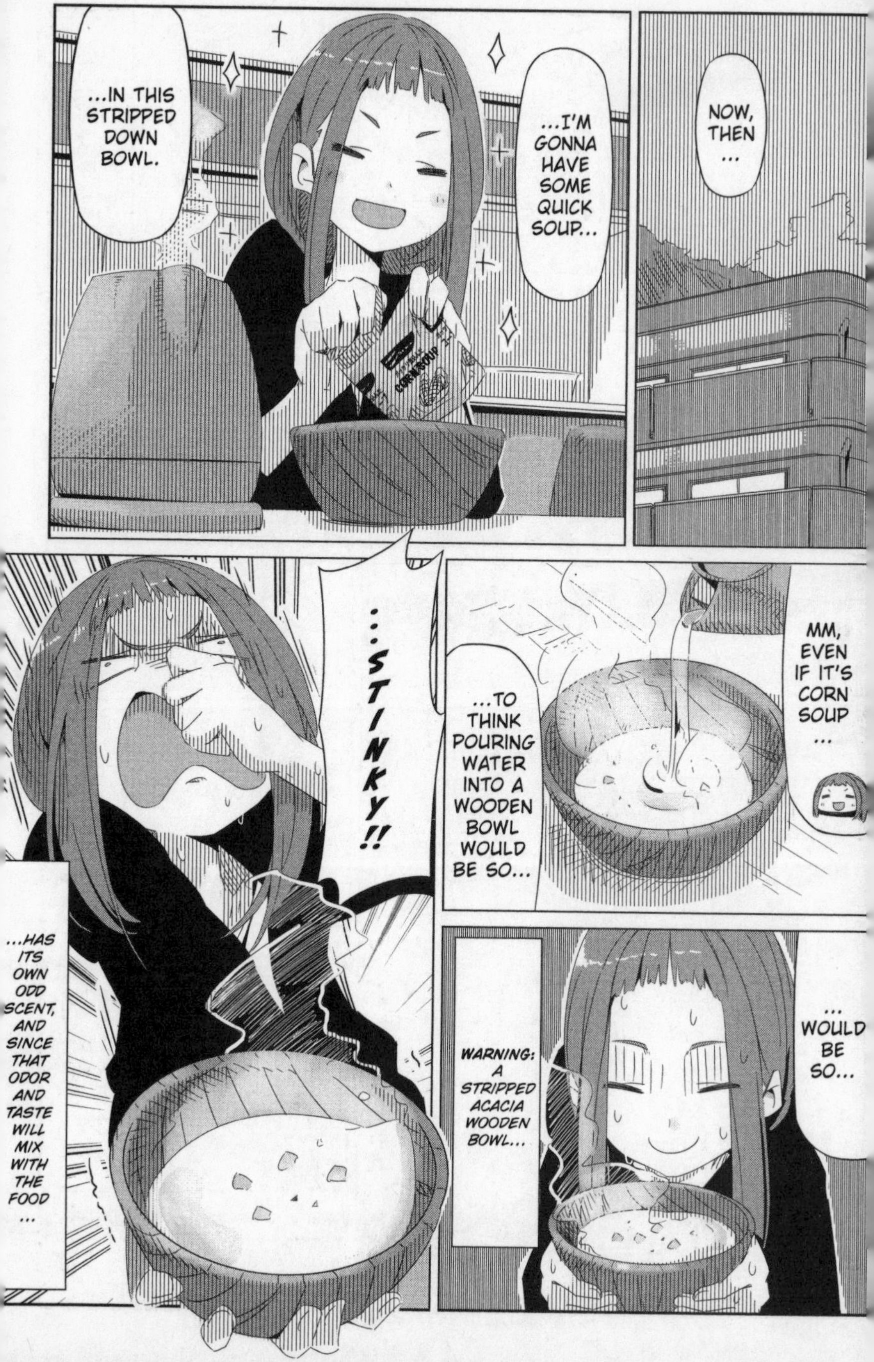
NOW, THEN ...
...I'M GONNA HAVE SOME QUICK SOUP...
...IN THIS STRIPPED DOWN BOWL.
CORN SOUP
MM, EVEN IF IT'S CORN SOUP ...
...TO THINK POURING WATER INTO A WOODEN BOWL WOULD BE SO...
... WOULD BE SO...
WARNING: A STRIPPED ACACIA WOODEN BOWL...
...HAS ITS OWN ODD SCENT, AND SINCE THAT ODOR AND TASTE WILL MIX WITH THE FOOD ...
...STINKY!!

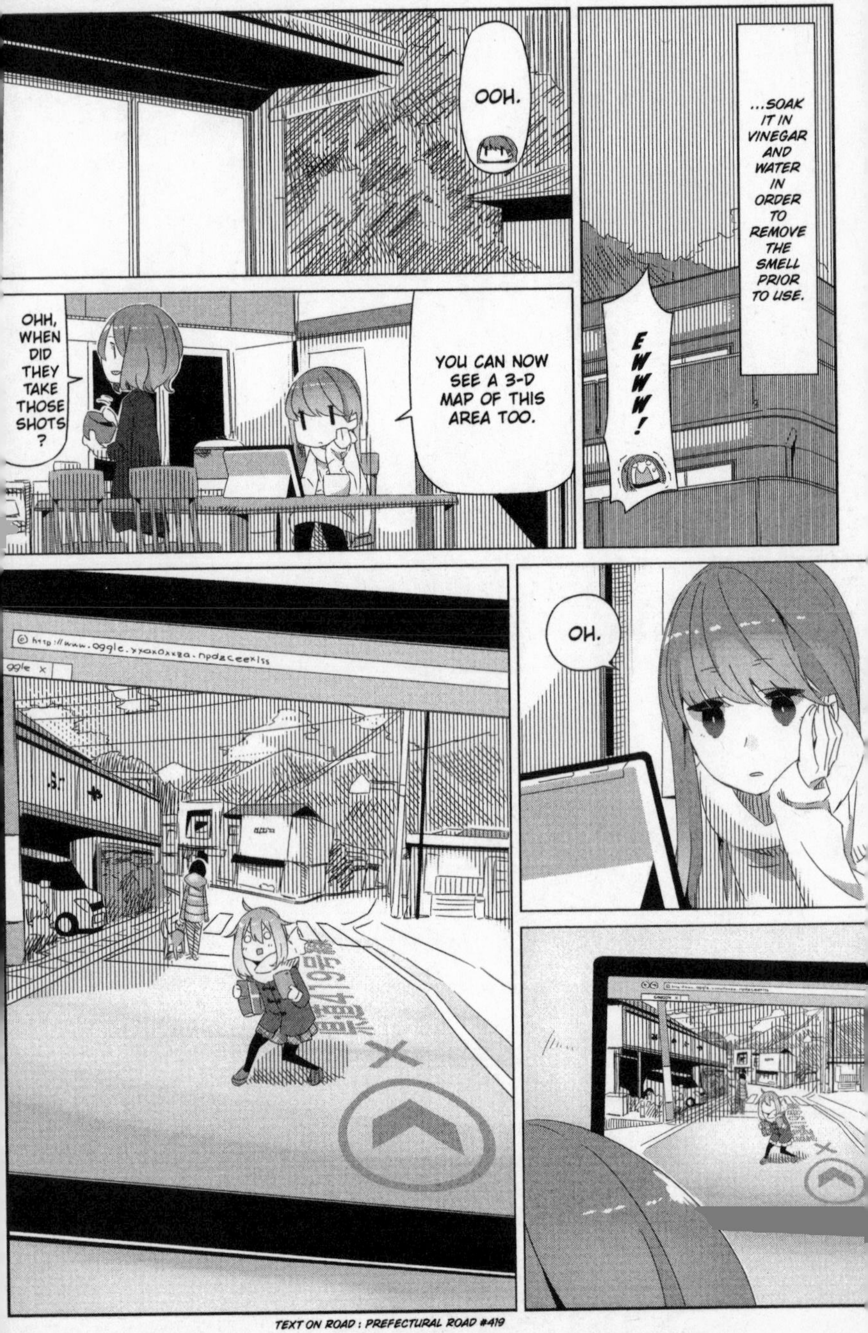
...SOAK IT IN VINEGAR AND WATER IN ORDER TO REMOVE THE SMELL PRIOR TO USE.
EWWW!
OOH.
YOU CAN NOW SEE A 3-D MAP OF THIS AREA TOO.
OHH, WHEN DID THEY TAKE THOSE SHOTS?
OH.

TEXT ON ROAD : PREFECTURAL ROAD #419

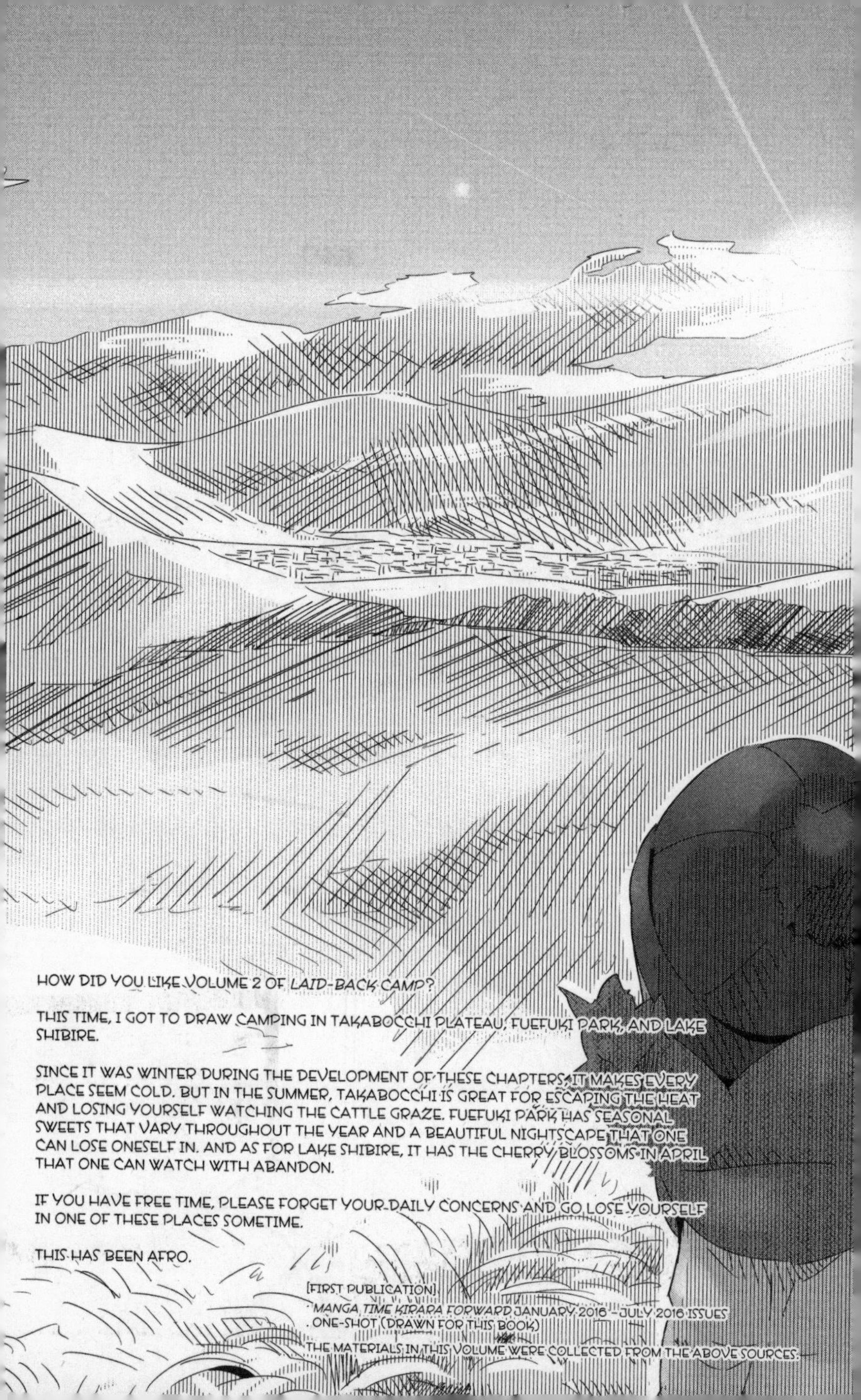

HOW DID YOU LIKE VOLUME 2 OF *LAID-BACK CAMP*?

THIS TIME, I GOT TO DRAW CAMPING IN TAKABOCCHI PLATEAU, FUEFUKI PARK, AND LAKE SHIBIRE.

SINCE IT WAS WINTER DURING THE DEVELOPMENT OF THESE CHAPTERS, IT MAKES EVERY PLACE SEEM COLD. BUT IN THE SUMMER, TAKABOCCHI IS GREAT FOR ESCAPING THE HEAT AND LOSING YOURSELF WATCHING THE CATTLE GRAZE. FUEFUKI PARK HAS SEASONAL SWEETS THAT VARY THROUGHOUT THE YEAR AND A BEAUTIFUL NIGHTSCAPE THAT ONE CAN LOSE ONESELF IN. AND AS FOR LAKE SHIBIRE, IT HAS THE CHERRY BLOSSOMS IN APRIL THAT ONE CAN WATCH WITH ABANDON.

IF YOU HAVE FREE TIME, PLEASE FORGET YOUR DAILY CONCERNS AND GO LOSE YOURSELF IN ONE OF THESE PLACES SOMETIME.

THIS HAS BEEN AFRO.

[FIRST PUBLICATION]

· *MANGA TIME KIRARA FORWARD* JANUARY 2016 – JULY 2016 ISSUES

· ONE-SHOT (DRAWN FOR THIS BOOK)

THE MATERIALS IN THIS VOLUME WERE COLLECTED FROM THE ABOVE SOURCES.

LAID ✦ BACK CAMP ②

Afro

Translation: **Amber Tamosaitis** ✳ Lettering: **DK**

YURUCAMP Vol. 2
© 2016 afro. All rights reserved. First published in Japan in 2016 by HOUBUNSHA CO., LTD., Tokyo. English translation rights in United States, Canada, and United Kingdom arranged with HOUBUNSHA CO., LTD. through Tuttle-Mori Agency, Inc., Tokyo.

English translation © 2018 by Yen Press, LLC

Yen Press
1290 Avenue of the Americas
New York, NY 10104

Visit us at yenpress.com
facebook.com/yenpress
twitter.com/yenpress
yenpress.tumblr.com
instagram.com/yenpress

First Yen Press Edition: May 2018

Yen Press is an imprint of Yen Press, LLC.
The Yen Press name and logo are trademarks of Yen Press, LLC.

The publisher is not responsible for websites (or their content) that are not owned by the publisher.

Library of Congress Control Number: 2017959206

ISBNs: 978-0-316-51782-9 (paperback)
       978-0-316-51783-6 (ebook)

10 9 8 7 6 5 4 3 2

WOR

Printed in the United States of America